Van Cliburn

Van Cliburn

Howard Reich

THOMAS NELSON PUBLISHERS
NASHVILLE

Published in Nashville, Tennessee, by Thomas Nelson, Inc., and distributed in Canada by Lawson Falle, Ltd., Cambridge, Ontario.

Library of Congress Cataloging-in-Publication Data
Reich, Howard.
　　Van Cliburn : a biography / Howard Reich.
　　　　p.　　cm.
　　Includes bibliographical references (p.　) and discography (p.　).
　　ISBN 0-8407-7681-0
　　1. Cliburn, Van, 1934-　. 2. Pianists–United States–Biography.
　　I. Title.
　　ML417.C67R44　1993
　　786.2′092–dc20　　　　　　　　　　　　　　　　92-41082
　　[B]　　　　　　　　　　　　　　　　　　　　　　CIP
　　　　　　　　　　　　　　　　　　　　　　　　　MN

Printed in the United States of America

1 2 3 4 5 6 7 - 97 96 95 94 93

For
my mother and the memory of my father,

For
Pam, my wife,
And, most of all,

For
Rildia Bee.

Contents

Acknowledgments

This book could not have been written without the generous support of many people, especially:

Susan Tilley and Jarrell McCracken, who believed in it from the beginning.

Bruce Barbour, Bob Zaloba, and Ken Stephens of Thomas Nelson, who championed this project for years.

Lonnie Hull and Jennifer Wells, my incredibly sensitive editors.

Barbara Reich-Abramovitz and Lou Abramovitz for their constant affection.

Mark Schubart, John Pfeiffer, Alan Kayes, Marilyn Egol, and Elizabeth Costello, all faithful Cliburn devotees.

Lisa Tilley and Mark Carter, my indefatigable researchers.

Charliss McMillan, who helped set up many interviews.

Jack Fuller and Colleen Dishon, who made so many things possible at the *Chicago Tribune*.

And, most of all, my dear friends Lynn Van Matre, Tom Popson, and Richard Christiansen.

Foreword

When the citizens of the former Soviet Union flooded the streets of Moscow in August 1991 to demand a measure of freedom and change, they may have been inspired by something more than just the bungled, right-wing coup attempt against Mikhail Gorbachev.

The series of events leading to that incredible month may have begun when the Soviets enjoyed their first, vicarious taste of Western-style freedom and openness, which had come in a decidedly unexpected form.

It was April of 1958, and a tall, skinny, extravagantly gifted Texas pianist named Van Cliburn had become the sensation of the first Tchaikovsky International Piano Competition. More than that, the generous spirit of Cliburn's playing and the easy charm of his words and gestures had symbolized to Soviets life on the other side of the Iron Curtain.

"Van looked and played like some kind of angel; he didn't fit the evil image of capitalists that had been painted for us by the Soviet government," recalls Andrei Gavrilov, the brilliant Russian pianist. "So Van was really the first person who changed for us this frightening image of the 'capitalist enemies.' It was a kind of beginning of melting the ice, of a new life for us. To the Soviet people, Van was something very deeply touching, something totally free and absolutely, wonderfully different.

"Everyone was talking about him. He reached all the people, the simple people, the intelligentsia—they all were enchanted with this young American. It is something that happens maybe once in a century."[1]

Exactly why it happened, why an unpretentious twenty-three-year-old from tiny Kilgore, Texas, so inspired the people of the Soviet Union and, later, music lovers around the world, is a question that inspired this book. Just as important, though, is what happened in the aftermath of Cliburn's monumental triumph.

The tremendous political and artistic pressures placed upon him, the ghastly turn of events that nearly cost him his right arm, the fickle critics who sometimes turned against him, the aspiring young pianists whose careers he effectively launched and nurtured—these chapters of Cliburn's extraordinary life are often forgotten alongside his unprecedented triumph of 1958.

Instead, multiple layers of myth have gathered on the story of Van Cliburn: His career fizzled a year or two after the Tchaikovsky competition, his repertoire consisted of only two or three major pieces, he was hounded from the stage by unrepentant reviewers and wearied audiences, he retired to the life of a recluse for nearly eleven years—these and other fictions still flourish in the minds of some musicians and fans alike.

Of course, they're about as true as the latest sighting of Elvis, another 1950s pop phenomenon to whom Cliburn, alas, repeatedly was compared. Unlike Elvis, however, Cliburn survived the frightening implications of global fame. Along the way, he gathered hard-learned lessons.

"Life in general has many terribly rough roads," says Cliburn. "That's really what life is—a succession of many instabilities, rocky roads, and the like. But you can transcend those inevitable difficulties by where you set your ideals.

"So if I can tell young people, if I can get them onto a path of realizing what is real and enduring, as opposed to what is transitory and unreal, that's worthwhile."

Inevitably, the story of Van Cliburn's life does exactly that.

Howard Reich
Chicago
December 1992

1

Texas Bound

*T*hough born in Shreveport, Louisiana, Van Cliburn was a Texan from the first day he drew breath. Maybe sooner.

Considering that his maternal great-grandfathers were early settlers of McLennan County, Texas,[1] and that one of them, Dr. Solomon G. O'Bryan, was pastor to Sam Houston (twice president of the Republic of Texas) how could it have been otherwise? Because Dr. O'Bryan also was a traveling evangelist, circuit rider, and a founder of two Waco, Texas, institutions— the First Baptist Church and Waco University, which merged with Baylor University in 1886 [2]–Van's roots run deep in both Texas history and religious tradition.

Similarly, Van's maternal grandfather, Judge William Carey O'Bryan, was a Texas state legislator who eventually became adviser to the likes of Texas Governor Pat Neff, U.S. Supreme Court Justice Tom Clark, and U.S. Congressman Sam Rayburn (longtime Speaker of the U.S. House of Representatives).[3] Judge O'Bryan graduated from Baylor, worked as a teacher, and married one of his students, Sirilda McClain, a semiprofessional actress who was the daughter of Jack McClain, owner of 12,000 acres of blacklands where the towns of Moody and McGregor are now.[4]

Most of that oil-rich earth didn't stay in the family, but the Southern roots did when the youngest of their six children,[5] Rildia Bee O'Bryan (born in McGregor on October 14, 1896), married Harvey Lavan Cliburn of Neshoba County, Mississippi,[6] on June 6, 1923.[7]

While the O'Bryan family came from Protestant Irish lineage,[8] the Cliburn side of the family had its origins in Britain, in the name Claiborne. In 1621, William Claiborne traveled to Virginia as a surveyor, eventually being appointed treasurer of the colony.[9] His descendant John Marshall Cliburn and his wife, Ella Strickland Cliburn, welcomed a son, Harvey Lavan, one of nine children,[10] on December 3, 1898.[11]

A generation later, with the birth of Harvey Lavan Cliburn, Jr.—whom everyone called Van, to avoid confusion with his father—the family proudly considered itself four generations deep into Texas culture.

"We Texans are very attached to the earth and the soil," says Van. "It's in our history. The land, the farms, the ranches—they're a part of every Texan. And Texas is so huge that even the different parts of the state have their own way of life and their own culture." [12]

Into these profoundly Texan ways of life Van was born on July 12, 1934. The place was Shreveport, Louisiana, simply because the Magnolia Oil Company, where Van's father had been a crude oil purchase and sales representative since 1926,[13] had stationed him there. By the time Van turned six, the family had moved back where it belonged, to an East Texas oil boom town called Kilgore.

Still, those first years set the tone for Van's life, at least as far as music was concerned. From his first days, he heard the piano played at all hours, his mother giving lessons from sunup to past sundown, then practicing her own repertoire after that.

By all rights, Rildia Bee should have been a concert pianist herself, for she had the gifts, the intelligence, the training, and the will. Because her mother and grandmothers had played the piano, and because she came from a tightly knit family, it probably was inevitable that she would play the piano too.[14]

But, in many ways, Rildia Bee was different from the other young women of her day in McGregor. She graduated from Richmond High School as valedictorian. "I think I got to be valedictorian because I was good at math," she once said. "Back then girls were good in English, but they were not so good at math." [15]

As a child, Rildia Bee had studied piano with Prebble Drake, a graduate of the Cincinnati Conservatory of Music,[16] where Rildia Bee herself later would study piano with Frederick Shailer Evans.[17] before venturing to New York in 1917 to attend the New York School of Musical Art (a precursor of the Juilliard School of Music).[18] There, at the school's Riverside Drive building, she studied with Arthur Friedheim, the celebrated, turn-of-the-century virtuoso who was an important student of and personal secretary to Franz Liszt himself.[19]

Of Friedheim's playing, the great pianist-composer Ferruccio Busoni once remarked, "He seizes the keys 'as the wild beast seizes his prey,' to quote [nineteenth-century critic Eduard] Hanslick." [20] What's more, Friedheim, whose Germanic surname masks the fact that he was born in St. Petersburg, also studied with Anton Rubinstein, the era's preeminent pianist after Liszt.[21] Rubinstein also founded the St. Petersburg Conservatory[22] and, with it, essentially the Russian school of pianism.[23]

In New York, Rildia Bee also studied voice with Ralph Leech Sterner, president of the New York School of Musical Art. She once recalled, "My voice teacher told me I was the best pupil in his class and that he wished I didn't play the piano. All my teachers were so sweet to me, and here I was, just a little girl from Texas." [24]

"Mother would have had a fabulous career," says Van,[25] who once told the *New York Times* that "Friedheim called her the most talented pupil he had, one with great strength at the piano, great facility.[26]

"She was a great pianist," he adds. "When she played, it seemed so effortless. She had such facility—really more facility than I ever had. I wish I had it.

"But she was somewhat incapacitated, in one way, because you have to remember that she came along at a period when it was a little bit risque, a little 'not nice,' for a woman to travel around as a performer. Her parents were, oh, so terribly proper and, I don't want to say rigid, but they were rather socially prominent in Texas," adds Van, referring especially to Rildia Bee's father, who served three terms in the Texas legislature.[27] "It just wasn't thought nice for a young lady to do certain things.

"Mother did get to do a few social things that were pleasant, but, always, either her mother or her sister went with her [as chaperon]. It was all very proper. One time even her brother [one of four] went with her." [28]

Or as Rildia Bee's longtime student Annette Davies Morgan says, "She used to tell me stories about her childhood. She was extremely close to her parents, and so proud of them. They wanted her to develop musically, but they were against her concertizing professionally. They were just afraid for her to do that as a career.

"Her family was really quite prominent in town; they were looked up to, and they were leaders. She was very close to all of them. When she dated, her brothers were so protective of her and were very interested in exactly who her dates were. She and Mr. Cliburn would come into the house—things were very different then, quite formal—and they scrutinized Mr. Cliburn. It was very rigid.

"I think she wanted very much for her parents' will to be met; I think she wanted, above all, for her parents to be pleased, and so she did their bidding because she did not want to oppose them." [29]

Predictably, then, on the verge of launching her first concert tour, Rildia Bee met up with the concerns of her parents. She probably wasn't too surprised, for in truth she had been a little amazed that they allowed her to venture to New York in the first place.[30] Still, living in Manhattan was heaven for Rildia Bee.

When she wasn't studying, she savored performances by Sergei Rachmaninoff, Ignace Paderewski, Enrico Caruso, Nellie Melba—practically all the musical legends of that era.

Devoted to her family and uninterested in distressing them, Rildia Bee simply abandoned her concert plans and returned quietly to Texas, where she became briefly engaged to a local dentist before meeting Harvey Lavan in church. Their courtship proceeded smoothly and steadily, inevitably leading to their marriage in June of 1923.

"Rildia Bee loves to say how times have changed so much since then," recalls Susan Tilley, a longtime family friend and chairman of the Van Cliburn Foundation, which runs the quadrennial Van Cliburn International Piano Competition. "When she watches a movie on television and they have all these explicit scenes, she'll say, 'I never kissed but two boys in my whole life, and I was engaged to both of them.' " [31]

The weight of Rildia Bee's parental influence was such that even her betrothed was persuaded to put aside his dreams and take up work at Magnolia Oil Company (which eventually became Mobil Oil).

"My father really wanted me to be a doctor because that was always one of his ambitions," says Van. "But my mother's parents used their influence in a way that steered him into the oil business because my grandfather always had great faith in oil. So Daddy didn't get to pursue some of the things that he wanted to." [32]

Long before Harvey Lavan could express the plans he had made for his son, however, music began to command Van's attention.

"All Mother had to do was play, and I'd come running into the house," says Van of his earliest childhood memories. "I'd just sit in the corner and listen—I can see myself there now.

"We had this small house. Mother and Daddy built it, and it was a cute little thing—I loved it—at 507 Stephenson Street in Shreveport. When I was little, the rooms seemed very long. I would sit off in the corner as Mother gave her lessons. I can still see that so well.

"There was a living room, and off that was the music room. We had a music room! And there was the music, in that special room. Everything happened there. I would just sit and listen to Mother practice and practice. It mesmerized me." [33]

More than that, it reached Van, and not simply in a superficial way. Evidently born with the appetite to absorb the sounds he heard and the ability to "focus in on the eye of the sound," as he puts it, Van dumbfounded his mother one day when he was barely three years old.

"This little boy, Sammy Talbot, had been studying with Mother, and I just sat around listening, as usual," recalls Van. "I kind of pretended [not to be paying attention] in one way; I just sat for hours and listened to Mother. I was just fascinated by it all. I was very self-contained in some ways. So on this particular occasion my mother said to Sammy, 'You've studied very well.' And when Sammy left the house, Mother went to the kitchen, and I went directly to the piano.

"I started playing this little waltz that Sammy had been working on ['Arpeggio Waltz' by Crawford]," [34] says Van. A deceptively complex little number for a child, it involved crossing the left hand over the right, as well as some tricky little rests and syncopations.

"Well, when Mother heard this going on, she said, 'I can still hear you, Sammy. You'd better go home because your mother will be worried.' Then she came into the music room and said, 'Hah! You! Well, if that isn't—you're not going to play by ear. You're going to really know what you're doing.' She said that matter-of-factly, and that was the law: No more playing by ear." [35]

In a way, though, Rildia Bee probably was not completely surprised by what she saw and heard. As she wrote in *Music Journal* years later:

> Practically every musician in history who achieved a career began as a "Wunderkind," and Van was no exception to the rule. Before he could walk, as a babe in arms, he would make rhythmic motions and gestures whenever he heard music. Actually, this basic

sense of rhythm is common to many children and
would not in itself be a sure sign of musical talent.

What really impressed me in Van's earliest years
was the way he would touch the keyboard, also before he could walk or talk. Most children, seeing the
keys of a piano for the first time, instinctively bang
upon them with all their might, expressing the universal human desire to make a noise.

But when I held little Van over the keyboard he
leaned down and touched one key at a time, very
gently. This gave me my first indication of his true mu-
sicality. Always thereafter I would say, "Gently,
gently," as he sounded the notes, and he seemed to
understand me and act accordingly.

It seemed only a short time before the boy began
picking out little tunes by ear, and he actually played
his first piece in public at the age of three. It was
called "See the Kite up in the Air," and he naturally
learned it by rote. He could soon imitate almost any
simple passage that I played for him, and when he
was four we started regular lessons.[36]

The challenge of having a mother doubling as private piano
teacher was not necessarily easy.

"It was a strange relationship because she was my mother,
but, then again, she wasn't," says Van. "She even said, 'When
I'm teaching you, I'm not your mother,' although, come to
think of it, I don't know what she expected me to call her! She
was a very stern teacher, and she was a very wonderful mother.
But she'd always remind me when I had my lessons, 'You
know, I'm not your mother now.' Somehow, I had no trouble
making that distinction.

"My mother was such a strong, dynamic person. She did not
coddle me. She never wanted to lead a person on. That was
never her way. Whether it was I or another student, she just
never coddled. She was always terribly realistic. She'd say, 'No,

I don't think that's possible. I don't think you should do it. You're not ready for this.' " [37]

Musically, Van reaped ample advantage from living with his piano teacher. As he once said in a *Vogue* magazine interview,

> From age three, she gave me a piano lesson every day of my life. Every single day. And she supervised my practice time, too. We'd sit down to the piano and she'd say, "Now just forget I'm your mother. I'm your piano teacher, and we must be very serious." Because of that strictness and closeness—and we continued that way until I was seventeen—I never developed any bad habits at the keyboard. She watched me like a hawk, even if she wasn't in the same room.[38]

The training took hold quickly, for by age four, Van made public appearances as a pianist, performing as accompanist for fellow Sunday school children at the First Baptist Church's Sunday Evening Story Hour in Shreveport. The performance generally regarded as his "official" debut was at Dodd College, an event recalled years later in the *Shreveport Times:* "In an incident that is now local history, he was lifted to the piano stool by Dr. M. E. Dodd, then pastor of the local church, for a program before the faculty and students of Dodd College." [39]

What did the music world's newest pianist play? The first Prelude in C Major from Bach's "Well-Tempered Clavier," Book 1.

Referring to that performance, Rildia Bee later recalled in her *Music Journal* article: "In one of our first public performances together, he played Bach's opening Prelude in C, while I added the Gounod 'Ave Maria' melody on a second piano. This might offend a purist, but the listeners seemed to enjoy it as much as the players." [40]

Before Van entered public school, before he could read words, he read music and played it at sight. Obviously, to achieve that feat took talent, labor, and patience. As Rildia Bee later noted in the *Music Journal* piece,

With the realization of Van's unusual gifts, our relationship while at work became that of teacher and pupil rather than mother and child.

Yet even outside of lessons and practice we communicated musically. I never had to call him from another room. Instead I would clap my hands rhythmically or play a few notes on the piano, and he invariably responded to the signal. I do not believe in forcing music lessons on a child, and it was only when the four-year-old Van showed both a capacity and a willingness to work that we began to take his music seriously.

Both lessons and practice periods were short at first, perhaps totaling an hour a day, but broken up into sections of not more than twenty minutes at a time. Later, of course, the working time gradually expanded, until Van was old and strong enough to stand considerable effort.[41]

Rildia Bee introduced a moral dimension to Van's earliest training as well. She continues,

From the outset, I cautioned young Van against "showing off" and tried to teach him humility, reminding him that his ability was a divine gift, for which he should be deeply grateful, without taking undue credit for himself. I also emphasized the importance of learning to read notes from the start. . . .

Before he had completed his fourth year, Van was able to read at sight whatever music was within the range of his finger-technique. Later I was amused to hear from one of his schoolteachers that when he was asked if he could read, he promptly answered: "I can read *music!*"[42]

So it wasn't long before Van had found a direction in life. The turning point probably was a Shreveport recital by Sergei

Rachmaninoff, whose records Van already revered and whose recital he eagerly awaited. Rildia Bee served on the committee that brought Rachmaninoff to Shreveport, and she had visited him backstage.

"Unfortunately, I never did get to hear that recital," says Van, "and I'm sick about it. I was supposed to hear him, but wouldn't you know I got a cold or flu or something and had to stay in bed. . . . Mother went, but I listened on the radio, and I just felt, *I'm going to be a pianist,* and I told my parents about it. My father said, 'Well, son, we'll see about that.' He wasn't too happy." [43]

Of course, Harvey Lavan and Rildia Bee had heard Van's other career plans, including his yearning to be a taxi driver.[44] Nonetheless, Van was all the more inspired when his mother returned from the Rachmaninoff concert, eager to share the details. "I can still remember that she told me how shy and kind Rachmaninoff was, and how benign," Van recalls. His mother described to him "how wonderful it was to talk to this truly great man, [going] over the whole evening again and again." [45]

Though they hadn't planned it that way, Van's parents only intensified his fascination with music in general, Russian music in particular, when, for Christmas of 1939, they bought Van a child's picture history book of the world. He recalls, "In it I saw this picture of the Church of St. Basil and the Kremlin in Moscow, and it practically sent me off into the ether. For some reason it just transported me. And I said, 'Mother and Daddy, please take me there, I want to see that.' And they said, 'Oh sure, son, we'll take you there. Sure.' " [46]

No one but Van could have sensed, at so intuitive a level, that St. Basil and the Kremlin could mean so much to him, that eighteen years later he would stand in front of those storied facades, on the eve of taking the Tchaikovsky International Piano Competition—and the rest of Moscow—by storm.

For the time being, Van had to content himself with a less exalted change of scenery: A few months later, in 1940, Magnolia Oil transferred Van's father to Kilgore, Texas. At first, Harvey Lavan commuted the seventy miles from Shreveport so that Van could finish out the semester. Then in January 1941, the family moved to 808 South Martin Street, a tiny, one-story, white frame house. They had chosen the place because its back yard led to the school from which Rildia Bee would draw her piano students. Van grew up in that house.

Kilgore would never be the same.

2

Boom Town

On October 10, 1930, the biggest oil gusher in the history of the United States erupted in East Texas.

A cantankerous, seventy-year-old wildcatter named Columbus Marion "Dad" Joiner—long ridiculed for drilling on the Daisy Bradford farm in Rusk County—found oil where others before him had not. As the black liquid began to spray, "A jubilant crowd of some 5,000 clogged the country roads leading to [Joiner's] well," in the words of one vivid account of East Texas history. "In the Woodbine stratum beneath the pine-covered hills and red dust of Rusk County, the sleeping giant was awakened." [1]

Within weeks, other wells in East Texas let loose with thousands of barrels a day. Yet for all the dreams of fortune they produced, "The early boom days were traumatic for the native population as lease hounds, oil promoters, roughnecks and drillers, camp followers, and finally the National Guard and Texas Rangers moved into the region. Boom town pictures changed but little, regardless of the location. The dirt streets turned into quagmires as overflowing traffic contended with ever present rains." [2]

At one point the oil field spewed more than 123 million gallons a day. By August 16, 1931, "1,300 armed National Guardsmen were ordered into the area, and the field was shut down until order could be restored." [3]

In the center of this glorious mayhem was Kilgore, Texas, a dusty little town instantly reborn and transformed. In the wake of the oil boon, "Kilgore's population skyrocketed from the 500s to an estimated 10,000, and the field gushed forth hundreds of wells," reported the *Kilgore News Herald,* [4] a newspaper whose front page still proudly carries the motto: "America's No. 1 small city—capital of the East Texas Oil Field."

Life in Kilgore in those early boom days, in the words of one history:

> . . . defies description and makes the rowdiest wild west movie seem tame. The area was wide open to everyone, large company and wildcatter alike. Every man was forced to . . . out-bid at the other man's speed.
>
> The "natives" saw their community revolutionized. Within seven months there were 92 restaurants, 32 supply houses, 5 welding shops, 5 boiler shops, 6 machine shops, 9 garages, 2 automobile agencies, 23 filling stations, 26 lumber companies, 8 building contractors, 15 real estate agencies, 20 dry goods stores, 9 general merchandise stores, 11 ladies' and men's specialty shops, 12 cleaning and pressing shops, 11 furniture stores, 35 grocery stores, 19 meat markets, 5 bakeries, 9 drug stores, 2 ice plants, 20 hotels, 25 barber shops, and 8 beauty salons.[5]

Steam-powered drilling rigs popped up everywhere, and, as any East Texan will proudly tell you, during World War II the wells of East Texas "produced more oil than Hitler had for his war machine. [The United States] literally floated to victory on a sea of oil, with East Texas being the big factor." [6]

On the eve of America's entry into World War II, January 1941, the Cliburn family moved to Kilgore. The Texas oil culture brought Van's father there, and in a way, the Texas oil culture afforded young Van a life much richer and more edifying than that in many like-sized cities across America.

Though only 10,000 to 11,000 people lived there, Kilgore was an unusually sophisticated place, its cultural life graced by a variety of concert series, plays, movies, and the like, plus similar attractions in towns in nearby Arkansas, Louisiana, and elsewhere in Texas (an area locals still call "Ark-La-Tex").

"I remember when *Song of Love,* with Katharine Hepburn and Paul Henreid came out," recalls Van of the 1947 film biography of Robert and Clara Schumann. "I rushed to see it at the Crim Theater. I remember that so well—as a matter of fact, I persuaded my parents to let me go the next afternoon to see it again. Because it was nice and very lovely, of course I was allowed—they were thrilled that I wanted to see it.

"We also had one of the best, well-run variety series you could ask for. A remarkable lady, Frances Gertz, was the chairman forever, for life, of the Community Concerts of Kilgore. She had such excellent artists. She was a dynamo.

"At church we had organists like you wouldn't believe. Roy Perry, who had played at Westminster Abbey in England, was organist at Kilgore's First Presbyterian Church. Marcel Dupré [the brilliant French composer and virtuoso] came to little old Kilgore. I remember one day, much later, I was somewhere in New York, and somebody—some very big snob type, started to say, 'Well, you know, the g*rrrr*eat organist Marcel Dupré—' And I immediately jumped in and said, 'Marcel Dupré? Why, he came to our town of Kilgore to play.' And this snob said, *'What?! What?!?'* It just knocked the wind right out of the sails of this character." [7]

By all indications, life in Kilgore was pleasant and culturally alive.

Visually, too, Kilgore was something to behold. "It was so gorgeous, it was the prettiest thing you've ever seen," recalls Gussie Nell Davis, an octogenarian who founded America's first marching drill team, the Kilgore Rangerettes, at Kilgore College in 1940.[8] "We had a thousand oil derricks downtown. . . . They had stars on top that were lighted during Christmas, and there was a great big sign that said 'Merry Christmas' and then 'Happy New Year,' the words strung from derrick to derrick! The people coming into town on trains couldn't believe what they were seeing. Oh, it was gorgeous. Everyone who lived here, before the boom and during, stayed and they had pretty homes. We always used to say, 'Kilgore is the town with the "Go" in it.' "[9]

For the people of Kilgore, Van's gifts announced themselves early and startlingly, as he arrived in the first-grade classroom of Oleta Gray, in January of 1941.[10]

"Van enrolled in our class at midterm, and we were rehearsing a program that included 'Tom Thumb Wedding,' " recalls Gray. "I had already given all the parts to the other members of the class. So when Van came in the first day, . . . I told him he could sit and watch us, and we would find a place for him. In a few minutes he tugged at my skirt, while the [school's] music teacher played the piano, . . . Van said, 'I can play that.'

"Well, of course, I didn't believe him. I didn't think too much about it, and then we went ahead and practiced the play, and when it came to the recessional, Van again said, 'I can play that.' So finally I just decided I'd see if he were telling me the truth, and I said, 'Why don't you just get on the piano stool and play it?' And he sat right down and he played the 'Bridal Chorus' from Wagner's *Lohengrin* to perfection, just as the little bride and groom made their procession to take the nuptial vows. I ran out into the hall and beckoned my principal and all my co-workers to come and hear this prodigy."[11]

For Van, too, that moment was a signal event in his young life, even if it contained a hint of disappointment. "I was so glad because Mrs. Gray had said she would find a little part for me to walk on and to be a member of the wedding in 'Tom

Thumb,'" he remembers. "I was all excited because I loved the stage, and I came home and told Mother. I think I was going to have all of two words to say, and that was it, but I was going to be in the play.

"I told my mother that she was going to have to come see it, and that she'd have to stop her teaching because she had to come over and see me in this play. But when I told Mrs. Gray I could play the piano, she got all excited and told my mother, 'I didn't realize how he could play!' Which was fun, except that, because I was playing the piano, I never did get to walk on the stage and say those lines after all." [12]

The new prodigy in town quickly acquired a degree of renown, his accomplishments witnessed and commented upon by the long list of youngsters who began taking lessons from Rildia Bee. Because the Cliburn house abutted Kilgore Heights Elementary School, and because of Rildia Bee's reputation as one of the most accomplished musicians in East Texas, several of Van's young friends at school began studying with her.

Like Van himself, they were allowed to leave the school grounds during recess, whereupon they would cut through the bushes separating the school from the Cliburn house and show up for their lessons.

"The rest of the kids were absolutely awed by Van's playing," recalls Oleta Gray. "A lot of them looked up to Van, and they thought he must be from outer space or something." [13]

Even as a child, Van apparently cut a rather imposing image at the piano. "He was a showman from the beginning," recalls Eloise Bean, another Kilgore resident since those days. "He just looked like he was destined for the stage. That's the impression almost everyone had from his earliest days in Kilgore." [14]

Or, as Mrs. Henry S. Miller, a longtime Dallas supporter of Van's, puts it, "I've known Van since he was a child, and I've always been interested in him. He's brilliant—he could sit down and play like a mad dog at age nine." [15]

Yet each of Van's friends regarded his musical prodigiousness a little differently.

Joyce Anne Goyne Stanley got to know Van "in the second-grade Glee Club, and we probably were together most every day when we were growing up. Van was the Glee Club pianist, and even in the first grade he could sit down and read all this music. It was amazing because the teachers had trouble playing these pieces, but Van could just sit down and read any piece of music and play it.

"When I was in fourth grade, I started taking music from Mrs. Cliburn, so I would come over to the house, and that's how Van and I became good friends. We had a wonderful time all those years. He was a remarkable person, even as a small child.

"Basically, he was the way he is now. He had a marvelous sense of humor, he was fun loving, rarely moody—serious though, very deep thoughts. He loved people, and he never seemed to get his feelings hurt or get mad. He was usually laughing, having fun. Now he surely did spend a lot of time practicing, and there were times when I'm sure he would have rather been out with the rest of us. But he had that dedication that his mother instilled in him. It seemed like he practiced about eight hours a day.

"I remember one time he tried out for the school play—*Mr. Belvidere*—and he got the lead. He was a wonderful actor. Mrs. Cliburn didn't know he was doing it, but she did know what it took to get where he wanted to go [musically], where he was destined.

"So when I went to my music lesson that afternoon, I said, 'Van, congratulations.' And he looked real funny. And Mrs. Cliburn said, 'For what?'

"Well, you can imagine, he dropped right out of that play, but he was never ugly about it. He accepted her good judgment, and at least he had the thrill of knowing he could have done it." [16]

Van's taste for the dramatic stage was whetted by another cultural lure that his parents provided—weekly, private drama lessons.

"I had studied speech and dramatics since I was seven. One of Daddy's colleagues in business married a woman who was a graduate of Northwestern University's School of Speech," remembers Van of Mrs. Leo Satterwhite Allen. "She lived around the corner from us. I think the arrangement was that her child studied piano with Mother, and I went to study speech and dramatics with Mrs. Allen. In those days you had to speak Oxfordian—you had to really know the *English* English. And it was not mumbling—you had to know how to breathe. Even to children she would say, 'You breathe from here, and you must project this and that.' You'd have to say, 'I have beeeeeen to town.' It was wonderful training. I studied with her for several years." [17]

Some of Van's friends at school, however, sometimes wished that Van could be liberated from his immersion in the arts, even if they admired the results of his efforts.

"I think the kids were proud of knowing him. They admired him for his ability, but they felt a little sorry for him too," recalls school friend Lottie Guttry. "I remember listening to Van and thinking, *How can someone my age play this well?* Van could play the Minuet in G, which I just thought was something else. And he could play with both hands and all the chords and all.

"He was incredible, a sweet child, friendly, and warm. Everybody liked him. But, then again, a lot of the kids thought, *Well, his mother makes him practice all the time. She won't let him play baseball because he might hurt his hands.* And we thought it wasn't fair that he never got to play with us and had to practice all the time.

"I remember one time he told me that he practiced three hours a day, that he would get up and practice an hour in the morning, and that he would practice two hours in the afternoon. And I thought, *Golly, three hours a day!* This was around fifth or sixth grade. I was astounded that he practiced that much.

"We felt like maybe he wasn't getting a fair shake. I guess those were some of the feelings, along with the admiration we had for him." [18]

Regardless, the work was paying off. When Van was nine, Rildia Bee placed him in the Dallas Section of the National

Piano Playing auditions in Ft. Worth,[19] where Dr. Irl Allison, founder of the National Guild of Piano Teachers, served as a judge and presciently wrote of Van, "An unusual talent. Your piano-playing proclivities will undoubtedly carry you far." [20]

Ultimately, though, Van approached the keyboard very much on his own terms. Those who recall his early years in Kilgore consistently note that the constant practice was driven not so much by obedience to his teacher-mother, but by a sense of self-determination.

"I don't think Van really had too much of a problem with what other people thought of him or his hard work at the piano, because of his 'independence,'" says John Shenaut, conductor emeritus of the Shreveport Symphony. "I think he was an independent thinker, and I'm sure he showed those qualities even when he was very young. He could make decisions. He really could. He had the ability of self-evaluation, and he knew what was important to him." [21]

Perhaps Shenaut has in mind an incident such as the notorious clash between Van and the administration of Kilgore Junior High School.

"Van was always asked to play programs in neighboring towns. On one occasion he was invited to be in a program in a very small neighboring community, where the local music club was putting on a concert," recalls Lottie Guttry. "The day before the performance the principal, Mr. [C. L.] Newsome, decided not to allow Van to be excused from school so he could go to play the program. Well, Van decided he was going to go anyway and said so. So the principal said to Van, 'If you go, all of your grades will be lowered.' Van was very upset about that because that got him down to a 'C' in one subject [algebra].

"So he wasn't at all happy about all this, and the teachers went to bat for him. They said to the principal, 'If this were a football player, what would you do?' And the principal said, 'Well, that's different,' which made the teachers really angry. Well, Van went ahead anyway and did the program, and the principal went ahead and took the points off the grades, the whole bit.

"The funny thing is that, years later, when the principal retired, one of Van's friends, Mrs. Gertz, was handing out some kind of a scholarship program in honor of this man. And she called and said, 'Van, we're putting together a scholarship fund for this person, and would you and your mother lead out with a generous contribution?' And Van said, 'You know, we really will, we'd be delighted. We're going to give fifty dollars.'

"And she said, 'Fifty dollars?! Only fifty dollars?!' Then he told her the whole story." [22]

Van's unswerving and somewhat precocious dedication to playing the piano owes equally to the grit of his personality and the way his parents had raised him. Early on they treated him less as a child than a grown-up.

"Yes, there were other things I would like to have done [besides practicing the piano]," says Van, "but I knew my mother was right about what I *should* do because she had a good track record with me as a youngster. I knew that she knew what she was talking about.

"I was not the kind of child who followed blindly. I questioned things. But my mother was also bright enough and had the ability to answer my questions. My parents didn't treat me as a child. They would never answer a question of mine by saying, 'Just because.'

"Even in other ways I was just like another grown-up in the family. My parents never, never treated me like a child or dressed me up like a little boy. It was always like I was a hundred-year-old man.

"There was nothing I ever wanted for, nothing that I ever needed, nothing I ever wished for that I didn't have. I didn't know that we didn't have a lot of money. Everything seemed to be there that I needed or wanted.

"We did all kinds of things because my parents and my grandparents were very culturally oriented. So I went to all kinds of nice places with my parents. Maybe we didn't have the money to do it but once a month, where others could do it every day or whatever, but my parents knew the best things to give me, and the best concerts, the best artists, the best operas—whatever.

"I had all these things that were very uplifting to me. I can remember going to Dallas, Ft. Worth, Shreveport, Houston, San Antonio—if anything happened in those cities that my parents heard about that was a great work, they'd get right in the car.

"And you know Texans—they're notorious about driving. They'll drive seventy-five miles to have lunch on a Saturday. I mean, we're great car riders here in this state.

"So they didn't look at me and think, *Oh, we must get little Van to bed because he has school tomorrow.* No—a pillow and a blanket in the back seat. And they'd say, 'Now, be quiet. Lie down. Go to sleep.' And I'd be right back in school the next day.

"I can remember the night we went over to Dallas to hear [violinist] Fritz Kreisler. And I was just on a cloud. They couldn't shut me up. I just chattered away. 'Now, be quiet, Van. Lie down. Go to sleep,' they said. And I said, 'But this was so wonderful!' 'Be quiet now. Go to sleep. You have to go to school in the morning.'

"So I was with young people my own age in the daytime and with older people at night." [23]

Or, as Van once told an interviewer, "Neither of my parents forced music on me. It was just there, always part of the atmosphere. On Saturday afternoon the radio was turned to the Metropolitan [Opera] broadcasts. Then on Sunday it was the New York Philharmonic. No one told me to like it. It was just taken for granted as a part of life.

"As I grew older and wanted live music, my family kept the highways busy between Shreveport, Kilgore, and Dallas. Someone once asked me where I lived, and I told them, 'On Highway 80.' " [24]

Today, Van remembers that "the first opera I saw was *Carmen*. Mother took me to a dress rehearsal at Shreveport Opera when I was four just to see if I could sit through a whole production. I was enchanted and asked her to take me again and again. So here's this four year old becoming a regular opera-goer!"

Clearly Van's life was, in some ways, distinctly different from that of his friends at school. "Later on, I realized that some of the kids I went to school with couldn't remember what they wanted to do yesterday," he says, "and I was having to think about what I had to do three months from now." [25]

Specifically, that meant continuously learning new repertoire, developing technique, preparing for performances and competitions. That routine has been a central part of Van's life since he was four, even if it wasn't quite so demanding in the earliest years of his training.

Virtually every facet of Van's education and development was personally directed by his parents. "I taught Van when he was in the fourth grade, the school year of 1944-45, and I can tell you his mother, Rildia Bee, was very supportive," recalls long-time Kilgore resident and teacher Alice Morton. "She came several times early in the morning, before school, to talk about him with me. I thought he was just a lovely child, and I told her so.

"That year, he came to my home and played the piano for my mother, who was an invalid in my home at that time. And Van played beautifully. He was only nine years old." [26]

Van's third-grade choir teacher, Velma Dickson, recalls writing a vignette about her first brush with the Cliburns:

> It was my very first day on my very first job. I had just signed in at the principal's office on that September morning and started down the hall at Kilgore Heights [Elementary School] when this tall, effervescent lady called me: "Please wait, I want my son to meet you," and then, gesturing to the bright young man at her side, said, "This is my son, Van. Van, this is your music teacher."
>
> He was tall and slender, dressed in a white linen suit, with short pants, blue shirt that exactly matched his blue, expressive eyes. How typical of both of

them: Rildia Bee had done her homework, she already had prepared Van to accept me, and Van was eager for a new friend and a new experience.

That year I had a third- and fourth-grade choral club, and he came early before school and played the accompaniment. He was a very accomplished pianist— I was amazed. I can't really remember whether he sight-read the music or not; I expect he could have.

Of course, he was far above what I was teaching, but he was a little gentleman. He acted like he was having as much fun as the rest of us.[27]

Though Rildia Bee is widely and justly credited with having shaped Van musically, people sometimes forget the role played by his father.

"I think he's the unsung hero in this whole thing," says John Shenaut, conductor emeritus of the Shreveport Symphony. "I really believe that. I think underneath it all, he is the one who had to keep everything together and get enough money together to keep Van going, which was a tremendous struggle [for the family] at one time. . . . He stayed home when Rildia Bee and Van went to Van's performances; he went through almost every moment of Van's life with him.

"I remember his bringing over clippings and little things about Van to the *Shreveport Times* and to the [Shreveport] *Journal,* so the local music editors and critics would put them in the paper.

"Van's father also had a very strong will, but it didn't surface. His mother has even more, but she can let it fly out. But his father, I think, frequently would control himself and his nervousness and all of that. He kept his emotions more under the surface."[28]

A longtime family friend, Louise Jeter, affirms that. "You know you don't hear a whole lot about his dad, but his dad was really the power behind the throne. He really supported both of them in all that they did; he was right there as a staunch backer.

"You hear so much about his mother, Rildia Bee, because she taught him so much music; but his father was a strong supporter and a wonderful man." [29]

Such was his devotion to Van's music that "I never had a summer job, like selling papers or anything," Van once said. "My father wouldn't even let me cut the grass." [30]

Together, Rildia Bee, Harvey Lavan, and Van formed a world of their own, into which others were welcome to visit, study, and linger. But the unique balance among the three gave young Van a sense of security and warmth.

"Obviously, Mr. Cliburn was very quiet, while Van and Mrs. Cliburn were very gregarious," says Joyce Anne Goyne Stanley. "Mr. Cliburn was a wonderful balance for the two of them. He was very quiet and very pleasant, a man of quiet integrity. But when he said something, it was important—you listened." [31]

Van agrees. To this day he says, "My shy side comes from my father."

Around Kilgore, Van's music and his dedication to it were well known, accepted, and sometimes even honored. Once, Rildia Bee gave Van permission to go to the record shop and buy a selection or two. Later, while she was teaching, she noticed Van struggling to get into the house, loaded down with records. "Van, whatever are you doing with all those records?" she said, recalling the incident for *American Music Teacher* magazine. "Well," he drawled casually, "he [the music store owner] said, 'Van, help yourself. Take all you want and pay for them any old time.' " [32]

Not surprisingly, there were moments of rebellion too, even if they were few and sporadic. One occurred "when Van was all of thirteen," recalls Kilgore friend Bill Hallman, "and he committed what I think was a little act of madness. He suddenly decided he wanted me to give him his first driving lesson—in my car. I was a couple of years older, and I already had a license.

"He jumped in the car, I jumped in after him, and he started driving, even though he didn't know how, and we started swerving and sliding like crazy! He had a kind of madcap determination to do this. It was almost a manic moment. I think it was the reflection of a kind of person who has intense powers of concentration for long periods of time but who has to transfer that attention to something else occasionally.

"It strikes me that it was a situation in which he thought, *Let's see, I've got forty-two free minutes now, so I'm just going to learn to do this.* It was as if he were thinking, *I've done the same thing with complicated arpeggios that I'm going to do with your Oldsmobile.*

"Let me tell you, it was scary; we almost clipped a couple of people out on the Gladewater Highway." [33]

School friend Lottie Guttry remembers being one of the first people Van kissed. "He got me after a piano lesson. We were in sixth grade, and he said, 'I just would love to kiss you.' It was really cute; it was kind of a little girlfriend-boyfriend stuff in about the sixth grade." [34]

Though Van's young life clearly was steeped in culture—how many other Kilgore kids, after all, were regularly reading *Opera News?* [35]—a few critical events inspired him to turn from talented young pianist to serious artist.

First, at age eleven, Van heard the glorious news that one of his favorite opera stars might be coming to Kilgore.

"Mother was on the board of the Kilgore Community Concerts," recalls Van. "She came home from one of the meetings and said—knowing full well that I was a great fan of Risë Stevens—'Oh, Van, guess what? There is a possibility, if we can raise the money, that we can have Risë Stevens perform here.'

"And after I picked myself up off the floor I said, 'Mother, I'll work, and I'll get out and raise that money myself if I have to.' I had first met Risë Stevens when she came to Dallas to do *Mignon,* and she was fabulous. She also was one of the great *Carmen*s of all time.

"Well, I sold about fifty memberships to the Kilgore Community Concerts. I went door to door, and I sold some people —on my enthusiasm—who had been trying to get by in life [on what little money they had].

"Not only did this one particular couple buy, but they bought for their grandchildren and their daughter and her husband.

I'm telling you, I was a hero. I wouldn't leave their door until they bought. And I almost started a crying scene. So that was one of my first important moments in music." [36]

As for Stevens' recital, "I remember it as if it were tonight, it was so thrilling," says Van. "I'm telling you, the people [in the audience] were hanging from the woodwork. The performance was in the Kilgore High School Auditorium, which was the best auditorium we had at that time. And I remember that night was so exciting, people were trembling. I had been enchanted with Risë's movies—*The Chocolate Soldier, Going My Way,* and *Carnegie Hall.*

"She was an excellent recitalist, very serious, so very beautiful, just ravishing, a movie-star kind of beauty. She moved well and she was a great actress. She just exuded charisma." [37]

Stevens, for her part, remembers the enthusiastic youngster who paid her a visit backstage that night: "He was just this sweet, very young boy, and he came backstage with his mother and talked with me at great length," she says. "And he told me how much he loved me. And all of a sudden I said, 'Well, what do you do?' And he said, 'I play the piano—I'm a pianist.' And I said to him, 'Well, I'm sure you're going to be a very famous pianist.' That's all I said to him—but I don't think he ever forgot it." [38]

Nor could Van ever forget the afternoon when he met and played for Jose Iturbi, a celebrated concert pianist and musical star of such MGM musicals as *Anchors Aweigh* and *Thousands Cheer.*

"When Van was eleven, Mr. Iturbi came to Dallas," Rildia Bee once recalled. "He was brought there by Colonel [D. Harold] Byrd, the big oil man, who was a good friend of ours. . . . Through the colonel, Van met Iturbi and played for him." [39]

For Van, a lifelong movie buff, it was a precious opportunity to meet "the most successful pianist in Hollywood," he recalls. "I'll never forget A Song to Remember with Merle Oberon and Cornel Wilde, the movie on the life of Chopin. Mr. Iturbi performed the soundtrack and became one of the first big-selling classical artists. He got a lot of people, a lot of children, excited about classical music. They saw those movies, and they wanted to play the piano.

"When I met Iturbi that first time, it was because Mother used to always take me to piano recitals in Kilgore and Dallas and all around Texas to see whatever great pianist was performing. We usually went backstage to meet the artist because Mother always wanted advice on who she should take me to study with. And I always told her, 'Mother, I don't need to study with anyone else—I can keep studying with you.'

"I met Arthur Rubinstein the first time that way too. Mother took me backstage to meet him, and he was so wonderful to me. He made such a fuss over me, which I guess was his way of encouraging me.

"On this occasion I played for Iturbi, and, of course, as always, Mother asked him who she should take me to. And he said, 'Who should you take him to? Take him to no one—he has the best teacher you could find already.' And I distinctly remember looking up and saying, 'See, Mother, I told you!' " [40]

Lest anyone think that Iturbi simply was trying to make the best of an awkward situation, Rildia Bee once recalled that, after Iturbi paid her the compliment, she quickly told him that "I was flattered to death and thanked him for being so nice. Mr. Iturbi said, 'I'm not being nice. I auditioned somebody else this morning, and I told him to *change* teachers.' " [41]

Inspired by his moments with Jose Iturbi, Risë Stevens, Arthur Rubinstein, and the like, Van began to emerge as a professional himself, in the genuine meaning of the term. By the start of 1947, when Van was twelve, he already had accrued a long resume of performances for local music clubs, school assemblies, church groups, hospitals, and virtually anyone else who would have him. Now, the local newspapers began to take note.

On the eve of a performance in his former hometown, for instance, the *Shreveport Times* devoted considerable space to the prodigy in chronicling his growing list of credits: "In a recent statewide contest sponsored by a Texas oil company [Texas Gulf Sulphur Company, in cooperation with the Texas

State Department of Education and the Houston Symphony Society [42]] Van played—and won a prize. . . . As a result of the contest he will play with the Houston Symphony in a short radio program April 12.

"When Van was eight years old he played for the Southwestern Bible and Evangelical Conference held in Shreveport and for the Baptist Sunday School Convention in Dallas. Four years later he was presented on a recital by the Musical Arts Society of Muskogee, Oklahoma, and was called a prodigy by critics. The same year, Van played for Jose Iturbi, who said he was 'extremely talented.' " [43]

The *Kilgore News Herald* went the *Shreveport Times* one better the following month, offering a two-column, rave review that said:

> The audience thrilled to his interpretation of Chopin's "Polonaise in A-flat Major," which drew a resounding applause. They expressed appreciation for Moszkowski's[44] "Valse in E," which Van played as a concluding number. The spirited "Ritual Fire Dance" by de Falla also proved a favorite. . . .
> [He also played] Sonata in C Major by Scarlatti; Gavotte in B Minor by Bach; Sonata ("Pathétique") Op. 13 by Beethoven; "Minuetto" by Schubert; "Liebestraume" No. 3 by Liszt; Valse in C-sharp Minor by Chopin; and . . . one of his own compositions, a delightful number entitled "Nocturne," Op. 1, No. 2, as an encore.[45]

In further coverage of Van, the *Kilgore News Herald* reminded readers that, at age six, Van made his first official Kilgore appearance in a concert sponsored by the Kilgore Music Club; at age seven he was invited to give a recital for the Dallas Conservatory of Music, though a bout of scarlet fever precluded the performance; at age eight he performed fifteen pieces at the National Piano Playing Audition in Ft. Worth, "receiving superior rating on all"; at age nine he was presented in recital by the Musical Arts Society of Muskogee, Oklahoma, where he was described as a musical prodigy by music critics and invited for a return concert.

Other appearances in 1946, the *News Herald* noted, "were with the Kilgore High School Band as guest soloist in concerts at Kilgore and North Texas State Teachers College, and at Mississippi College in Clinton, Mississippi. . . . The youth's last two public concert appearances were at Brookhaven, Mississippi, High School on Feb. 18 [1947] and the First Baptist Church in Shreveport on Feb. 23 [1947]. Reviews of the programs were highly complimentary of Van's musical ability." [46]

Considering his already substantial performing experience and sizable repertoire, perhaps it was no surprise that Van had won a $200 prize and a coveted appearance with the Houston Symphony Orchestra at the state convention of the Texas Federation of Music Clubs.[47]

Now, at age twelve, Van would perform with a major symphony orchestra in a concert broadcast on the Texas Radio Network.[48] The piece? The first movement of the Tchaikovsky Piano Concerto in B-flat Minor, the same work that eventually would help carry him to triumph in Moscow at the height of the Cold War. His mother said he could attempt the monumental piece as long as he was certain he was committed to the rigors of mastering it. Convinced that he was, reported the *Kilgore News Herald,*

> She chalked on the blackboard the number of days left until the preliminaries of the auditions.
> Each day she subtracted one, and at the end of 21 days Van had memorized the Tchaikovsky B-flat Minor Concerto.
> He won the finals and performed the work, at 12, with the orchestra.[49]

The quickness with which Van had learned the piece, however, apparently didn't diminish the musical results. "The speed and technical clearness exhibited by Van Cliburn, young

Kilgore pianist, was praised by Conductor Ernest Hoffman when the youth appeared as student guest artist with the Houston Symphony Orchestra," reported the *Kilgore News Herald.* "The conductor's words of praise were heard by Miss Katharine Crawford, Kilgore teacher who attended the performance." [50]

Specifically, Hoffman said he had "never seen greater talent in one so young." [51] That sentiment was widely shared, for, following his performance, Van received a standing ovation from the orchestra itself. [52]

Even to Van's fellow competitors, his performance was stunning. "The first time I ever heard Van he was twelve years old and rattling through the Tchaikovsky Concerto," remembers James Mathis, a contemporary of Van's who lived in Dallas. "He was already playing at least the first movement, with Rildia Bee at the second piano, and it was obvious he had enormous talent. Of course, his playing was kind of messy still, but he was so gifted.

"A great big boy, he was almost as tall as he is now [six feet four]. He grew big fast, and he had huge hands already. By age twelve they spanned the twelfth or thirteenth on the piano easily. Frankly, I don't think Rildia Bee ever spent a lot of time working on technique with Van—he just was a natural technician. And with those big hands, he could practically cover the keyboard, which was a great help for the kinds of music that Van was drawn to—the big, romantic pieces." [53]

Van, too, remembers the size of his hands at this point in his life: "Yes, I always had these big, gangly things. In fact, I have this picture of me as a kid of twelve with these huge hands hanging down. I always thought my hands were too big and not as facile as my mother's, but that's just it—everybody has their own hangup, something they wish they could have. The idea is: You work with what you've got.

"As I said, my father really had wanted me to be a doctor because that was one of his ambitions. Daddy didn't get to pursue some of the things that he wanted to, so he hoped they would happen for me.

"But when I made my debut in Houston, with the symphony on the big radio broadcast, he turned right around and said, 'Well, sonny boy, if that's what you want, believe me, I'll help you.' And he always did." [54]

Not long after, Van's father proved more than true to his word, building a studio onto the back of the house and furnishing it with a piano, in addition to the two grand pianos in the main portion of the house, on which Van and Rildia Bee could study and rehearse.

Now, as a teenager emerging as a professional concert pianist, Van bade farewell to his childhood—yet with few regrets. "There are so many people who say, 'Oh, I missed my childhood,' " says Van. "Well I had an absolutely fabulous childhood. I sometimes have such a nostalgia about it that I wish I could go back and be a child again because I had a marvelous time. I had devoted parents. I never felt unloved. And number two, I had such exciting times sitting up late with the adults, always being included in everything, seeing and hearing the greatest artists in the world. It was a fabulous time." [55]

But bigger thrills and more formidable challenges lay ahead. At an age when most youngsters are still thinking about frivolous matters, Van was heading inexorably to a Carnegie Hall debut—years before he dreamed it possible.

3

Carnegie Hall

*T*he flyer said it all: "Van Cliburn: Kilgore's Contribution to the World of Music, Carnegie Hall— March 12, 1948." [1]

Alongside those words, and tilted at a slight angle, was a sleek, black-and-white photograph of a young, tuxedoed man at the piano, eyes fixed on the keyboard, a portrait of concentration and poise. His inordinately thick, blond, unruly hair had been heroically combed down and back. His elegant image was softly reflected on the underside of the opened lid of the ebony grand piano.

Van's career was off and running, as the *Shreveport Times* duly noted in a piece proudly headlined, "Former Local Boy to Play at Carnegie": "A small, blond-haired boy of 13 years walked onto the stage at the Dallas YWCA Jan. 6 [1948]; sat down at the piano and played several selections. The boy, Van Cliburn of Kilgore, Texas, formerly of Shreveport, won a date in Carnegie Hall by his performance." [2]

Lest any *Times* reader wonder whether the prodigy had won by virtue of mere luck, the article hastened to add: "Concerts and contests do not create stage fright and an inferiority complex for Van. He is an old hand at beating the ivories with spectators present. . . . The young Kilgore musician competed with about 16 persons of all ages, including college graduates, in the recent Dallas audition." [3]

Though no coverage of Van's Carnegie Hall performance exists, it can be measured in at least one, slightly indirect way.

"When I was at Carnegie Hall, Mother was approached by a manager who wanted to give me some concerts and have me travel and all that," recalls Van, whose performance—on a bill with several other youngsters—apparently had impressed at least one listener.

"My mother thanked him very profusely and said she appreciated it and all, but said, 'No, I don't want to subject him to that because I don't want him to fade away—I want him to progress. And that will make him fade away.' She was very right." [4]

To her eternal credit, Rildia Bee would not have Van exploited. An occasional performance, yes; an important competition, absolutely; but not a concert tour at the expense of a life at home and in school, among friends, contemporaries, and others uninterested in making a dollar on a gifted, rising artist.

And yet Van's performing career, even from his relatively obscure base of Kilgore, was inexorably gaining momentum. Local concerts, choral rehearsals, church programs, competitions, lessons, practice—his musical life overflowed by the late 1940s. Even the summers were occupied, as Van ventured to the Juilliard School in New York with his mother, who attended master classes there in 1947 and 1948. Later, though, she acknowledged that she had gone to Juilliard and taken Van with her to examine the school and find the right teacher for him, should he be accepted. [5]

While his mother checked out Juilliard, Van attended classes in harmony, theory, sight reading, dictation, and the like and took a few lessons with the pedagogues Ernest Hutcheson and Carl Friedberg, at Rildia Bee's insistence.

Already, while a student at Kilgore High School, which he had entered in the fall of 1948, Van had made a name for himself at Juilliard.

"Van used to come to Juilliard to summer school—although he was just a boy and I didn't know him from a bar of soap in those days," recalls Josef Raeiff, who is still on the piano faculty at Juilliard. "The school had these Wednesday noon recitals, so that the students who had signed up for the six-week course not only got their lessons in chamber music and theory and whatever they signed up for, but they could go to recitals every day too.

"So I had booked one of my students on one of those recitals to play some Brahms pieces, and I figured my student was playing at around 12:30 or so. So I made sure to get there a little earlier, in order not to miss him.

"I walked into the hall, stood in back of it—this was in the old school, on Claremont Avenue [Juilliard is now located at New York's Lincoln Center], and I walked in there to make sure that my student was next. And this kid was playing [Liszt's] 'Liebestraume' [no.3], and I was about to walk out and wait in the hall until my student came on, but something grabbed me, and I didn't walk out.

"I just stood there listening. The piece is beautiful, and if it's beautifully played, it's a marvelous piece, and it just held me. By the time he finished, I wondered, *This is so exquisite! Who is that kid?*

"A day or two later, I was in the cafeteria, and Van and his mother rushed up to me to greet me, as they always did in the cafeteria. Then I recognized him. I said, 'Was that you who played the "Liebestraume" the other day? And he said, 'Yes, Mr. Raeiff,' so I put my arms around him and told him how beautiful and extraordinary it was." [6]

Others who heard Van at Juilliard during those summers in the late 1940s shared Raeiff's view. Mitchell Andrews, a pianist who now teaches at Ball State University in Muncie, Indiana, remembers that he "first heard Van in the summer of '48, and even then Van had an extraordinary equipment and flair. He was obviously extremely gifted." [7]

And pianist Ivan Davis, a fellow Texan, found Van's playing in his early and midteens to be "technically wonderful. He always had a wonderful sound—with those huge hands of his—and control. And there was a freedom about his playing that was absolutely fantastic.

"For instance, one of his main pieces, which he never commercially recorded, was the Twelfth Hungarian Rhapsody of Liszt [actually, Van did record the piece for RCA, but never approved its release [8]]. Van simply won every competition with that piece. It truly was extraordinary—it was free and had many colors and tremendous range." [9]

So Van was noticed, in high school and outside of it. In Kilgore, his physical stature, musical gifts, and ebullient personality were somewhat hard to miss.

"The basketball coaches would moan about Van," recalls Annette Davies Morgan, a friend since childhood. "They'd say, 'I only wish that I could have him because of those hands and that coordination, his size and agility and all.' " [10]

Indeed, as Van's junior high school physical education teacher, Q. L. Bradford, once told the *Dallas Morning News:* "At about 13, he was just about the height he is right now [6 feet, 4 inches]. His hands were incredible, the hands of a basketball player. He's got hands like Magic Johnson. He was also graceful and moved well. I wanted him for the basketball team." [11]

So Bradford decided to ask Rildia Bee's permission.

"Mrs. Cliburn was a lovely Southern lady," he recalled in the *Dallas Morning News* article. "We all thought so much of her. She couldn't have been more gracious. She appreciated my wanting Van for the team, but she told me he couldn't. He was already well known for his piano playing. . . . He needed his hands in good shape for the piano." [12]

The closest Van got to high school sports was playing clarinet in the marching band, "Terribly, I might add," Van once told an interviewer.[13]

In high school, though, his personality began to emerge vividly. Van enjoyed the full range of activities of high school in the 1950s, minus the gridiron, the basketball court, and the like.

"He certainly was more fun than ever before—he really was a blast in high school because he became a bit of a daredevil," recalls Lottie Guttry. "I think he had a crush on my car. . . . This was a Buick, a big old gas-eating thing. My parents had driven it for several years, and they couldn't get a good price for it, and I needed a car to drive to high school, so they let me drive this big old white Buick.

"Well, Van just thought that was the most wonderful car. We didn't ever have a closed campus, and being crazy like we both were, we would drive off-campus for lunch.

"Van and several of us kids would get in that car—he always liked to go with a bunch of us—and we'd drive around as fast as we could. I'd let him drive it, and he drove fast! I'm telling you, it was awful. It's a wonder we're not all dead.

"Van would laugh and tell jokes—he was so funny." [14] Once Van started laughing, there would be no end to it until he was good and ready.

"When Van got tickled, no matter where he was, there was no stopping him. He would start laughing, and it was really funny to watch," recalls Alice Whittlesey, a longtime family friend.

"Now, of course, Mrs. Cliburn would have none of that. She was very prim and very proper. One day in church, I was sitting by Van and Mrs. Cliburn, and there was an old, old gentleman sitting in front of us. He sneezed—and lost his upper dentures in the process. And those dentures fell out of the old gentleman's mouth and rolled a little way down the aisle.

"Well, I thought Van was going to die. He just came unglued. But his mother, she just didn't think he ought to laugh. And I could see—she had him. She had a piece of his shoulder between her fingers, and I thought she was going to pinch it off. But if she had killed him, he couldn't have quit laughing. And he laughed and laughed." [15]

Van remembers, "Daddy sat on the other side of me, pinching the other shoulder. My parents were such great pinchers." [16]

In class, Van often daydreamed—fantasized, really—about the future. At one point, "He started doodling a little program," says Van's longtime friend Susan Tilley. "And this imaginary program said, 'Sol Hurok presents Van Cliburn, Steinway piano, RCA Victor recording artist.' " Eventually this dream became a reality, down to the last detail. [17]

Van also applied his imagination to high school dramatics, taking the Clifton Webb role in *Sitting Pretty* and the Ralph Bellamy role in *Tomorrow the World.* [18]

"I auditioned and got the leads, and both times something happened that the plays did not come to finality," remembers Van, who had been elected president of the Thespians Society.

"And when these plays didn't get produced, we kids were just hurt and disappointed. And so Miss [Ann] Whatley [the high school drama instructor] said, 'Well, I know one person who will be delighted that these are not being produced this time, and that's Mrs. Cliburn. I know that Van has some concerts he has to play, and his practice time will not be interrupted inordinately.'

"I was only in one play [that was staged]. It was about Lazarus. I was Lazarus, and I thought we were never going to live through the giggle times when we had rehearsals. We'd just get to giggling, and it was awful. We would break down every time." [19]

Laughter notwithstanding, Van went headlong through high school, determined to finish in three years instead of the usual four. "I think partly I wanted to do that because my mother had graduated when she was sixteen," recalls Van, "and then there was a friend of the family's who also graduated early, and they would come over to the house and talk about how they had graduated at sixteen.

"And when I heard that, it was just like this magic number—I wanted to do it too. I'm sure that's where it came from. But I had it so well mapped out in my mind. I had my strategy. I was terribly ambitious, and in my strategy I saw this plan, and I was going to do it. And when I had a vision to do something, that was what I wanted to do and was going to do, no matter what." [20]

First, though, Van had a little persuasion to do at home. "When I told my parents, they said, 'Well, how are you going to do it, son?' I just told them my plan, and they believed in me." [21]

Indeed, Rildia Bee went right to the principal, Bob Waters, who recalls that she said, "'Will you help me try to get Van through high school as quickly as we can, so that he can move on to study piano with someone else?' And I said yes, that we could accept so many extra credits from Van—say, two credits in music—and summer school. So Van went over to Kilgore College and took an English course over there [as well as Psychology 101 and French], did well in it, and it was transferred back to a high school English subject. We thought it was important so that he could go on to take his advanced courses in music at Juilliard." [22]

As for his pianistic development, a program Van played for the Kilgore Music Club on March 13, 1951, indicates just how far he had come. The repertoire included the Bach-Liszt Organ Fantasia and Fugue in G Minor; an all-Chopin group including the Sonata no. 2 in B-flat Minor, Ballade in A-flat Major, three etudes, and a valse; a Debussy group including the "Etude for Octaves," "La Cathédrale engloutie," and "Jardins sous la pluie"; a Liszt group, with his Valse-Impromptu, Transcendental Etude no. IV ("Mazeppa"), and the Wagner-Liszt "Liebestod"; and "The Void: Tone Poem Suite," a three-movement work by one Van Cliburn. Not bad for an evening's work.

That the program also carried ads from Smith Lumber Company and Phillips Electric Company added a quaint touch to the proceedings, an indication of how strongly the local business community felt about their talented native son.[23]

Such was Van's intellectual reach that his composition, "The Void," shared its title with a poem he had written that had won him a certificate of acceptance from the National High School Poetry Association:

The years ahead, the years behind,
Ah, what's the use, you'll get there in time.
Just as the sun and moon fight, as do rivals,
For strength of state for revival,
So does the moon reign over the midnight,
And the sun o'er revenging dawn!
And the stars all seek to ignite
To survey the planets' brawn.
O, Life, full of pity and disgrace,
Look up to this beautiful place
To see through the degrading maze
Of the hatred, disgust and laze,
Only surfaced by that lovely living
And in service that is life-giving.

Little wonder that, after his whirlwind three years in high school, Van was elected "most ambitious" of his class. "Not the most talented," he quips, "just the most ambitious." [24]

On balance, it's worth noting that not everyone at Kilgore High was impressed with his industry and talent, even if he ranked twelfth in a graduating class of 103, with a 91 average out of a possible 95. For instance, Lottie Guttry remembers "going to see my counselor, who asked me, 'Well, what are you going to major in at college?' And I said, 'I'm going to major in music.' To which he said, 'Well, I'll tell you just like I told Van Cliburn—there's no future in music.' " [25]

4

Juilliard

*T*he great artist who held court in Room 412 of the Juilliard School on Claremont Avenue in New York had heard practically everyone there was to hear in the "golden age" of pianism. Born March 28, 1880, in Kiev, Rosina Lhevinne heard Anton Rubinstein when she was a child; the titanic pianism of Josef Hofmann in 1899; the hyper-romantic composer-pianist Alexander Scriabin; and the technical wizardry of Leopold Godowsky.[1]

In her own right, she graduated from the Moscow Conservatory in 1898 with the Gold Medal, just as Rachmaninoff had a few years before her (though his coveted award was for composition). But when she married the revered pianist Josef Lhevinne, Madame Rosina Lhevinne essentially put her performing career aside, contenting herself to aid him in his career and, meanwhile, becoming perhaps the most influential piano teacher of her generation. Through the doors of Room 412 would pass no less than John Browning, Garrick Ohlsson, Misha Dichter, David Bar-Illan, Ilana Vered, Adele Marcus, Ralph Votapek, and inevitably, Van Cliburn.

Not that Van automatically would turn up at the great teacher's studio; first there were hurdles—expected and unexpected—to finesse.

By 1951, "I had forgotten about Van," says Josef Raeiff, the longtime Juilliard piano faculty member who had been mesmerized by Van's performance of Liszt's "Liebestraume" no. 3 during the Juilliard summer session in 1948. "Two years later, the next thing I know, he's up for entrance exam. I'm on the jury, and this kid comes up to play. I don't remember specifically what he played for his entrance exam, except for one piece—he ended with the Twelfth Hungarian Rhapsody of Liszt. And except for Josef Hofmann, who used to play it a lot and was just nonpareil, nobody I have ever heard in my life played that piece as marvelously as Van did that day. He had studied it with his mother, who studied it with Arthur Friedheim, who, of course, studied with Liszt himself. Whether it was his mother who taught him to play like that or the kid was a natural or both. . . . It was so gorgeous." [2]

Mark Schubart, then the dean of Juilliard, also attended the entrance exam and found it "obvious that Van was enormously talented, an extraordinary talent, although [his music] seemed a little wild at the time, but that's normal in someone that young. He was a tall, gangly, very jovial, outgoing person. Right from the beginning [of the audition] there was no doubt that he was unusual, no doubt that he would be admitted." [3]

Naturally, Van planned to study with the revered Madame Lhevinne. That she represented the Russian school of pianism, with its emphasis on technically brilliant repertoire and oft-extravagant emotional expression suited both Van's temperament and the Russian tint of his mother's teaching.

"So Van came into the school," recalls Raeiff, "and in those days I helped Mrs. Lhevinne with some of her students. She was so crowded that she used to ask me to take two or three students every year, to help her out.

"That did not mean I was her assistant, but I used to do it because if I had room on my schedule I was always willing to take one of her students. She always got talented ones, so I didn't mind teaching them. Basically, I'd teach them for a year or two, and as soon as they made an A, she would take them, and so forth. Well, Van was going to go to her, but she was crowded, and the school asked me to take him." [4]

Though Van admired Raeiff both as teacher and pianist, he had made up his mind that he was going to study with Madame Lhevinne. In fact, he turned down a full scholarship to Columbia College for study with pianist Carl Friedberg, who had known Brahms and Schumann. "I simply wanted to be at the Juilliard School, and I wanted to study with Madame Lhevinne," says Van.

All manner of fiction and fable has been offered to explain how Van persuaded Madame Lhevinne to allow him into her studio, including one popular but apocryphal story about other Juilliard students' twisting her arm on his behalf.

What really happened, however, was that "even before the auditions, my mother had written in to Juilliard that the one we wanted was Mrs. Lhevinne," explains Van. "And so Mrs. Lhevinne had a meeting with me [before the jury examination] and said, in her thick Russian accent, 'Vell, I am so booooked, my class is all full. So you study vith another teacher, and then I can see you maybe vonce every two or three veeks.' " [5]

Madame Lhevinne, however, not knowing how determined and mature a teenager Van was, did not anticipate his response. Perhaps expecting the usual entreaties, she apparently was caught off guard by Van's answer: "I just said to her, 'Oh no, Madame. With whom I begin is with whom I end.' [6]

"I remember that scene very well," continues Van. "My mother was listening outside the room. In fact, my mother was a little shocked at what I had said, so that after we left she said to me, 'Shhhhh.' And I said, 'No, Mother. She's a very nice lady, but I want her to know—when I begin, I stay and I end.' I'm not the person to go here and switch around. I like stability, not instability." [7]

Shortly thereafter, Lhevinne attended the school's entrance examinations, and after hearing Van play, she suddenly found room for him in her crowded class.

When Van arrived in New York, he settled into the apartment of Hazel and Allen Spicer on Claremont Avenue, near Juilliard.[8] He soon joined the Calvary Baptist Church on West 57th Street, where he attended services regularly.

For the next three years, the time it took him to earn his Juilliard diploma—and several national piano competitions to boot—Van studied with one of the most colorful, enigmatic, brilliant, irascible, tempestuous, and devoted piano teachers to have graced music education in America.

At the heart of Lhevinne's "method"—if her informal and apparently intuitive style of teaching can be called that—was the Russian piano school.

"I think the thing that made her so important was that she was, in a sense, the last bridge not only to her husband, Josef Lhevinne, but particularly to the tradition of Anton Rubinstein, which had been so dominant," explains John Browning. "After all, he founded the conservatories in Russia, both in Leningrad [now St. Petersburg] and Moscow, and he gave those final recitals, covering practically the entire piano repertory, in Moscow.

"And those that heard them apparently have carried those memories for years. [Author] Abram Chasins would have told you that Hofmann told him all about those recitals. And when Abram and I talked together, our stories were exactly the same. What Abram got from Hofmann, and what I got from Rosina, was a portrait of this particular genius and the kind of interpretive approach that became the Russian tradition—and this stemmed from Anton Rubinstein.

"There was really nothing [of a Russian piano school] to my knowledge before him. He established the whole school of Russian piano playing, and the people who heard those concerts remember practically in detail everything that he did. The things that he did in those recitals were passed on through generations—wild pedalings and things of that nature that became almost a religion.

"Or I should say they were wild in the sense that they were just so right. Things like at the end of the G Minor Schumann

Sonata, where you hit the big diminished chord—you hold the pedal all the way through—and you clear [the pedal] only when you can't stand it any longer. It's an incredible sound and perfectly right.

"But it was not just that. It was evidently that he had such power. His hands were evidently very fat—the fingers were very fat. So the story I got from both Hofmann, through Chasins, and on my own from Lhevinne was that [Rubinstein's] fingers were so wide they usually hit two keys rather than one, if he wasn't careful.

"There was in his followers a kind of passion and discipline, which new converts to a religion have, and they were very aware that there was something special about this newly formed Russian school of piano playing, which turned out all those legendary people, from say 1900 to 1940—Rachmaninoff, Hofmann, Lhevinne, Levitzki, you can just go down the list. It was very different from what apparently was the so-called German school.

"So there was a feeling of discipline; you were trained with a lot of humor, yes. But you were also trained to regard your profession as a holy vocation." [9]

This tradition permeated Room 412 of the Juilliard School from 1951 to 1954 (the years of Van's study there) as well as years before and after.

For Juilliard in general, and for the piano department in particular, it was an unusually rich period. Pianists Van Cliburn, John Browning, Daniel Pollack, Jerome Lowenthal, Jeaneane Dowis; singers Leontyne Price, Evelyn Lear, Thomas Stewart; conductor Jorge Mester; violinist Michael Rabin—a whole new generation of American artists on the verge of making national and international names for themselves was taking shape in a single institution.

"A musical sociologist I am not, but I do know it was a miraculous thing," recalls pianist George Pappastavrou, who now teaches at Syracuse University. "It was just a remarkable bunch of people. Of course, it was right after the war, it was right at the end of the veterans education programs, where veterans could go to school.

"Juilliard was up to about 600 people at that point, and they were doing performances of monster pieces from the baroque period, with all the brass instruments, and Wallingford Riegger's music for forty-six brass instruments—things like that. It was an amazing time; there was an electric quality about it."[10]

New York, itself, was bursting with energy, noise, and excitement, the city "a magnificent place for music," recalls Alexis Weissenberg, who lived there at the time. He came to know Van in 1954.

"Today, for example, people go to hear a good musician or a good technician—amazingly, the two seem never to blend together, which is insane. People go to hear somebody who is literally a good musician or somebody who makes tremendous noise on the piano.

"At that time, though, neither of these things alone seemed to be important enough because they were naturally an integral part of performance. What you did have on stage was artistry and originality, and these two things are vanishing completely today.

"Of course, there are exceptions. Naturally, we have some great artists, but we also have this army of people who play extraordinarily well and bore you to death, or who are maybe good musicians but don't communicate it to an audience.

"But at that time, concertizing in New York was wonderful. You had that same feeling of genuine improvisation in the jazz of the day. You would go to Harlem or the Village, and you would hear people improvise with originality—people like [jazz pianist] Art Tatum, who was the greatest of them all, of course. But I also heard at that time [singer] Ella Fitzgerald and [pianist] Oscar Peterson, and all the people who were great artists and still are.

"I think this influenced all of us. I would go to Carnegie Hall every night, almost, and listen to all the great people we adored. And then I would take the subway and go to the Village

Vanguard, or someplace like that, and listen to people improvise.

"The musicianship of these people was so authentic, so important, that naturally it had an influence on all of us. At that time, there was actually a connection between improvising and performing the [classical] repertoire." [11]

In a very direct way, the excitement of music in New York in the 1950s could be felt in the practice rooms, studios, and concert spaces at Juilliard, "where all of these insanely talented people suddenly started turning up," recalls George Pappastavrou.

"It was this period, from about 1948 to 1954, about six or seven years that were really unusual. And we had a ball. There were wonderfully talented people like Michael Rabin, an incredibly gifted violinist [who died at age thirty-five in 1972]. He would just walk down the hall with his violin under his chin and play double-stops and triple-stops and the most amazing things, and everybody just fell on the ground with awe. [Pianist] David Garvey, who already had an early association with Leontyne Price and is still her accompanist, was there too." [12]

Even in this remarkable setting, Van's playing apparently stood out. "He was an exciting, electric pianist, even in his youngest days at Juilliard," recalls Kay Kraber Lund,[13] who studied with Juilliard's Sascha Gorodnitzki at the time.

To Daniel Pollack, who also studied with Madame Lhevinne and ultimately competed against Van at the Tchaikovsky International Piano Competition in Moscow, Van's playing "was absolutely monumental. Whenever Lhevinne had a master class, which was frequently, Van always played. And, anyhow, sitting in class with Lhevinne at that time was like sitting in Carnegie Hall: one more spectacular student after another.

"But Van had a very special aura; the playing had a tremendous outgoing temperament, sensitivity, with great conviction. He made quite an impact every time he performed in class.

"I heard him play the Tchaikovsky Concerto [no. 1], the Rachmaninoff Third, Liszt etudes, Prokofiev Sixth Sonata,

Brahms Intermezzi, Beethoven 'Appassionata' Sonata—much of the repertoire that he has since recorded.

"His technique was phenomenal—no obstacles whatsoever. He just traversed the keyboard amazingly, not just with speed, but with a lot of phrasing, musicianship, beautiful coloring. Whenever he played it was really something special." [14]

Yet Van was hardly the only gifted pianist at Juilliard. With so many great talents under one roof, many of them in Madame Lhevinne's single studio, there were bound to be tensions.

"You don't know what it's like to play [in a master class] when there's Van Cliburn and John Browning and all these other people listening," recalls Jeaneane Dowis, a pianist who was among the best at Juilliard at the time. "You go out and play your piece, and you're only as good as your last performance. And though everybody was perfectly willing for you to do well, if you didn't do well, then they got slimy about it.

"It was an extremely stimulating time, I must say. And with all of the—you might call it 'sibling rivalry'—that we felt for each other, we were also very much behind each other, if you know what I mean." [15]

For a variety of reasons, many of these young virtuosos were from Texas. Cliburn, Mathis, Dowis, the late Herbert Rogers, and others were products of an unusual burst of talent from a single region of the country. In part, it likely had to do with the cluster of first-rate piano teachers in Texas, among them Silvio Scionti, Dalies Frantz, and Adele Marcus. [16]

"We just thought Texas was a big state, so big talents come out of big states," says Browning, only half joking. [17] And surely Jeaneane Dowis was not the only Juilliard pianist who noticed that, "at one point in Rosina's class, she had about fifteen or sixteen students, and they were mainly Texan or Israeli." [18]

Even beyond such ancillary matters as regional and ethnic origin, "I think we had a feeling that Rosina's class, particularly, had about four or five pianists that were really hot," says Browning. "And she would say herself, 'You know, dearrr, they come in clusters. Sometimes I have five big ones, and then ten years pass and I have nothing.'

"We also were a wild group. That was that Texas contingent, and they were wild. We all worked very hard, but we also partied very hard.

"And, yeah, we paid very little attention to anyone else. Juilliard in those days—it's probably still the same—the singers paid no attention to anybody else, the violinists paid no attention to anybody else, the pianists paid no attention to anybody else.

"And within the piano department, you paid attention only to the people in your class. If you were a Lhevinne student, you only associated with the Lhevinne contingent. So it was a very cliquish atmosphere, . . . filled with backbiting. We probably were just as insufferably cliquish and mean . . . but we had an awful lot of fun. We palled around together a good deal.

"Jeaneane and I were going together very steadily, so [we went to] a lot of big parties together. Jimmy Mathis had a fifteen-room apartment with friends on West 72nd, right on Riverside Drive, and we would go to parties, semester-ending parties, semester-opening parties, and finals parties—with about 200 or 250 people—and they became notorious. Notorious.

"In a funny way, we knew we were the clique that ran the school in terms of the piano department, and we were probably just horrible about it. We paid no attention to the singers. I mean, people like Leontyne Price were there, and we knew that there were some good singers, but they paid no attention to us and we did the same for them.

"Then there were the dance people, the Jose Limon people, the Doris Humphrey people—we just remembered that they always smelled a lot, that was it. It was a crazy place." [19]

It seemed obvious to most Juilliard pianists that the competitive center of this most competitive environment focused on the two most imposing pianists at the school, Van Cliburn and John Browning.

If there was an unspoken rivalry between them, it may have been because "they each had something the other didn't have," says Dowis. "Browning has a hyper-intellectual mind, and he's a wonderful musician and a wonderful pianist, but the things that made him so wonderful were the very things that Van was not.

"In other words, Van had—and has—this sort of huge flair and love of life all over him. And John had a different kind of flair, and heaven knows John plays with flair, but it's not the same joyous kind of thing that Van had, although the difference was probably more obvious back then than it would be now.

"And as far as rivalry goes, I think with men it's even worse than with women because they're out there, they're the bulls, sort of pawing over their little piece of turf, and each one wants it all." [20]

Dowis was hardly the only one to note that Van and Browning were virtual opposites in every way.

"Van was so much fun," recalls Mathis, "because he always had a breezy sense of humor, and he was a big talent, so he didn't overpractice. John Browning was so grim about practicing ten hours a day." [21]

Joan Brown, also a Juilliard pianist at the time, recalls that "Van was always such an easy-to-get-along-with fellow, and John had another kind of temperament—he was a driver. He was a beautiful pianist—I never heard anything like that kid at eighteen. And yet their paths were so different. I don't think they really ever got in each other's way, but they weren't at all the same kind of pianist. In other words, John worked extremely hard, was compulsive about his perfectionism. But Van didn't obsess so much about the notes that he didn't get—it was a whole different approach.

"They were friends, they were in the same class with Rosina, and they were always full of jokes and stories about her, but there was always that little edge. You always felt that they never could be close friends, and they never were. They were together at parties occasionally, but as far as palling around, they didn't." [22]

Not surprisingly, the most intriguing analysis of Van and Browning comes from Rosina Lhevinne herself, via the conversations she had with then Juilliard dean Mark Schubart. "Very often we'd talk about Van, and she would tell me how extraordinary she thought he was, and that at the time her two leading pianists were Van and John Browning," recalls Schubart. "And she always said that Van was 'red' and John was 'blue-green,' in comparing their talents." No doubt, Lhevinne symbolized the boldly emotional qualities of Van's playing with the color "red," the coolly intellectual facet of Browning's pianism with "blue-green."

"She felt both were extraordinary—she admired them both enormously—but they were different, and that was that," Schubart adds. "John, you see, was an excellent student, a brilliant academic student, and he was in the 'degree' course [meaning academic and music courses].

"Van was in the 'diploma' course—the complete music program without the academics. I would say Van was always a bit of an *enfant terrible*—it was always his natural talent that came out, which is what was so fascinating and alluring about him.

"Regarding any rivalry between them, all I can say is that Juilliard was and is made up of rivalries—that's part of the psyche of the place." [23]

To Browning, the situation with Van was as apparent as it was uncomfortable. "I suppose we were both aware that, in Rosina's class, we were probably the two who would be the most likely to have a career," he says. "To some extent, people started comparing us in the beginning—and more than we compared ourselves. Many times that happens—people will say, 'Well, I prefer John's playing,' or 'I prefer Van's playing.' People made the comparison, and we were forced to accept it.

"We were very good friends, but I think we knew we were terribly different. And we were less competitive than people made us out to be. I think that's the most honest answer that I can give—that if there was a sense of competition, it was pushed on us by other people, and it was other people who felt it much more than we did. Some people sort of pitted us against each other as if the question were: Do you prefer Browning, or do you prefer Cliburn?" [24]

That situation is not unique. The history of music is filled with chapters in which hostile camps formed around the likes of Chopin vs. Liszt, Debussy vs. Ravel, Horowitz vs. Rubinstein, and on and on.

"Or Brahms and Wagner," adds Browning. "[Eduard] Hanslick and the coteries kept that one going. Or Sam Barber and Aaron Copland—you were either a Barberite or a Copland-ite, and the respective circles wouldn't talk to each other. . . . Leonard Bernstein wouldn't conduct anything of Sam's.

"Those divisions of the camps were so incredibly stupid. But it happened, and a lot of those things were forced on compos-ers or performers by the people around them.

"I really don't think it had anything to do with Van and me specifically. I think we were aware of our differences." [25]

Van says that he considered Browning "a wonderful pianist and a brilliant mind." In fact, years later, RCA had taken an option for Van to record the Barber Piano Concerto, which Browning premiered at Lincoln Center in 1962. "I heard that performance," says Van, "and right away I went to RCA and said, 'Please release this option. I can think of no one who can do that piece more wonderfully than John Browning.' " [26]

As for Van, his personality and his presence could not be missed. "When Van arrived at Juilliard, we all took him in different ways, so to speak," says Jeaneane Dowis. "I was a little annoyed by the Baptist thing of his because that is not my thing at all, and I distrusted it slightly. So, at first, I held back from him.

"But Van was extremely generous, I must say. He was always taking people out to dinner, and we would do just about anything for a free dinner. None of us had any money—we weren't dirt poor, but our allowance was out by the tenth of the month and then we started thinking, *Well, who's got some money?* Van had a little more money than we did, though not much. So we would all get together, and gradually Van and I got to be quite good friends, and we had some really amusing experiences.

"We had classes together, and we telephoned each other at night, and that's when I realized that Van had a tremendous sweetness that finally won me over, although he did take us to a few Billy Graham meetings, and that was quite an experience." [27]

It was hard for even the more skeptical Juilliard students to resist the outsized affection of the man. "If Van saw you eating in a restaurant, and if he cared for you, he'd run right across the room to you," recalls Joan Brown. "That happened to me several times. He leaped over all the tables, and he was so big it didn't take him long to get over there. But you were aware he was coming, I can tell you that.

"He was a warm, natural person—it's a real gift, and you could hear that in his playing: the naturalness of his playing, no impediment of the flow. He obviously had a very large gift." [28]

Those who surmised that Van was entirely a natural pianist, rather than an intellectually sophisticated one, probably misunderstood the nature of his talents. It takes elements of both to achieve the kind of interpretations Van eventually refined, and at least one famous episode at Juilliard confirmed, for many students, just how sophisticated a musician Van was.

"The one thing that Van and I could both do that none of the others could do is improvise," recalls Jeaneane Dowis. "So one day we sat down, and just for fun we started fooling around, and we started to improvise this sonata for two pianos. We had a marvelous time. And I told Van, 'Why don't we have a little fun with this?'

"So we went to see our 'L & M' teacher [Literature and Materials], who was [composer] Norman Lloyd. And I said to him, 'Listen, we have something to play for you.' And Van and I had decided what we were going to do [musically], and then we played a little bit of it. And it was a real sonata, a four-movement sonata.

"So there we were, playing around at the keyboards, and when we told Norman Lloyd we had improvised this thing, he was tickled to death. He said, 'I want you to play this in class.'And I said, 'Oh, come on. We're just fooling around.' And he said, 'Well, you can call it a planned improvisation.'

"Well, I had never heard of anything like that, but we said, 'Okay.' So Van and I went tearing down to Rosina's studio and said, 'We just learned this new piece, and we're going to play it for you, and you get to guess who wrote it.' And she couldn't guess. She just had a fit when she found out that we had improvised the thing.

"Then we played it in class, and everybody was very serious, and they wrote down who they thought it was, whether it was Russian or this, that, and the other.

"My point is that this showed how much Van knows about music because in this [improvised] 'piece' we planned out what key we would move to for the second theme, and in the second movement we had a scherzo-trio form, and all these complex things that Van could handle so beautifully while simply improvising. He knew the structures of music, and he knew how to improvise upon them.

"The only problem, in fact, was getting Van to end the piece. He got so carried away in the last movement, he was just careening up and down the keyboard and wouldn't quit!" [29]

Attending that class, and somewhat awestruck at what he heard, was Jorge Mester, who eventually went on to become an important conductor in his own right. "For this particular class, all of Norman Lloyd's students—first year, second year, third year, and fourth year—got together every Wednesday to do experimental stuff or just group-type things," remembers Mester.

"So there was Van, whom I knew, and Jeaneane at the pianos, and we were asked to try to identify the composer whose sonata was going to be performed, and they were going to play it by memory.

"So they sat down and played this thing, and I don't know how long it was—for all I know it was fifteen minutes, I can't remember, really. So we tried to guess. . . . And then we were astonished to be told that they had improvised the whole thing.

"Well, I had come out of military school, and at that time, I wasn't too secure in my knowledge of my own talent. And I knew that I was at Juilliard, and I knew I wasn't even a hotshot conducting student. I was not getting along that first year very well with my teacher, or so I thought.

"So after this performance with Van and Jeaneane, I thought, *This is incredible. It's great to be in a school where they have these kind of people, but maybe I don't belong here. If all these people can sit down and improvise a four-movement sonata like that, they must be geniuses. What am I doing in this company? I could never do that.*" [30]

Of course, there were aspects of Van's personality and approach to life that did not always endear themselves to his colleagues. For instance, Van had consistent and inordinate difficulty in getting himself to classes on time—or something remotely close to it.

"He'd never make his nine o'clock class—he was always late," recalls Kay Kraber Lund. "So we all pitched in fifty cents or a dollar one day and bought him a Big Ben alarm clock.

"The thing is, a lot of people didn't realize it, but Van was really driven too. He practiced a lot. I know that we'd all be at the practice rooms in school till ten o'clock at night, and then we'd walk down to 110th Street, to the subway or something. And some of us would go and have a beer, but Van never would. He'd always just get on the subway and go on downtown, and I think he had a practice room somewhere [Steinway Hall on 57th Street], so that he could go practice some more until two or three in the morning, and then he'd go to bed. The thing about Van is that when he's working [at the piano], he goes off in another world, and . . . time doesn't really mean that much to him." [31]

By the time Van had reached Juilliard, he already was a nocturnal creature who "never could go to bed at night," recalls Joan Brown. "But then he never could make it to class on time, either, and he was the bane of everybody's existence, which is why we all bought him an alarm clock." [32]

Not that this quaint, symbolic gesture really could change Van's ways. Browning remembers "one time when we were to do the Liszt E-flat [Piano Concerto] in Rosina's class, and Van was late. We couldn't figure out where he was, and somebody finally called him in his room and found out he had simply fallen asleep.

"So he quickly dressed and came flying into the studio, and I was asked to do the second-piano part [for Van's reading of the concerto]. And, somehow, Van gave a dazzling performance of the Liszt E-flat. It was really breathtaking. I mean, he had no right to play that well, considering the circumstances, but it was just—wow!" [33]

In another instance, "Probably in the early spring of 1952, Van made an appearance on what was called 'The Pianist's Forum,' at Juilliard," recalls George Katz, who was studying with Josef Raeiff. "Van was listed on the second half of the program—I don't remember who played on the first half. Van was supposed to play after the intermission, and we waited and we waited and we waited and he didn't show up. There were about forty or fifty pianists there [in the audience] waiting for him.

"And finally, we all started to make for the exit, and just as we were going down the stairway to leave the building, Van walked in and excused himself prolifically. He said, 'I'm terribly sorry. I was relaxing and I fell asleep, and that's why I'm so terribly late.'

"So we all begrudgingly went back to the hall, and I'll never forget Van's performance. He played the 'Paysage,' which is one of Liszt's lyrical Transcendental Etudes [no. 3], then he played 'Mazeppa' [Liszt's Transcendental Etude no. 4] and of course he played Liszt's Twelfth Hungarian Rhapsody. Everybody was bowled over, absolutely. We were amazed. Not only from the technical level—the technical aspect, of course, was amazing. But his playing was absolutely a knockout; it was so musical, sensitive.

"And then, of course, there was this rare ability to communicate that catapulted him to tremendous fame. There are pianists, for example, who make gestures [while performing] that one finds disturbing. But Van's gestures seemed totally appropriate, and they seemed to indicate a complete involvement with the music.

"So even though Lhevinne at one point told him that if he was going to be a 'no-no' pianist [meaning that he shakes his head back and forth during performance, as if saying 'no no'] that at least he should turn his head away from the audience a little bit, it didn't matter. He had this exceptional ability to get it across from the stage to the listener." [34]

For Van, music, above all else, was more about personal communication than exhibitionistic virtuosity. That philosophy had been all but driven into him by Rildia Bee. Thus, even in a theory or aural skills class, Van approached the routine exercises just as he would a piano concerto or a solo piece—all music had an expressive purpose.

"I remember that one of the things we used to do in class was sing the music we were studying," recalls pianist Jerome Lowenthal, another of Van's contemporaries at Juilliard. "When Van was involved in one of these exercises, there was an air of total commitment or total hamming or whatever you wanted to call it. But in any case, he looked quite different from everyone else who was singing, or what you might very loosely term *singing*.

"Van raised his eyebrows and projected a great deal of emotion—and these were just silly little exercises. It stood out, and I've never forgotten it." [35]

Pappastavrou remembers a Beethoven seminar class when Van played the "Appassionata" Sonata: "Your mouth just fell open, and you thought, *Well, I can't envy anybody who played as incredibly well as that because it's just too moving.*" [36]

Surely no one could have expected that a garrulous, six-foot-four pianist from an East Texas boomtown who had studied with only one teacher—his mother—would hit it off so famously with a petite, heavily accented, cosmopolitan Russian woman who had heard the greatest legends of the keyboard. And yet Van and Rosina proved to be an exquisite match. Most observers believed that not long after he first sauntered into her studio, Van became the dearest student Rosina had ever had.

"I think that Van touched something quite special in Mrs. Lhevinne, although she never capitalized on it by trying to make each student jealous of the other," says Jeaneane Dowis, who studied with Lhevinne and worked as her assistant in the late 1950s and '60s. "Quite to the contrary, I would say that she tried very hard to minimize that as much as she could because she knew it was trouble.

"I know that what she felt about Van was very special. She recognized that incredible flair he has, and it spoke to something in her. She loved the rest of us too, and she appreciated what the rest of us could do, but there was some kind of quite Russian-Texan thing in Van that spoke like crazy to her." [37]

Or, in the words of Josef Raeiff, who worked closely with Lhevinne for several decades, "She felt Van was a kind of genius." [38]

Not that working with Lhevinne was easy. Browning recalls that "she brooked no nonsense. She was not artificial in the way she wanted things, but you had to wear a coat and tie for lessons, and you had to be ready with at least twenty minutes of memorized music each week. And if you couldn't—if you got a little stuck, she would dictate from the couch [where she sat listening], and if you couldn't get it after that, the lesson was over. That was that. A lot of teachers today do not train to memorize every week, but that training stood all of us in tremendously good stead later on when we had to learn things very quickly." [39]

Pianist Jeffrey Siegel recalls, "James Levine, who was a piano pupil of hers, once said something that I think is dead-on. He said, 'You could play something for her, of any composer, any piece, and you'd look over at her when you would finish, and you could tell by the expression on her face if, instinctively, it got to her or not.'

"She was very broadminded in accepting interpretations that were other than what she wished, but as Jimmy would say, 'If you looked over at her and you sensed that it didn't go down with her, you were on the wrong track with that piece.' He trusted her musical instincts that highly because she was so broad. It didn't have to be just one way. But if it went outside a certain parameter, even before she verbalized it, those of us who knew her well could tell just from looking at her that this simply is not too convincing." [40]

Still, she had distinct musical priorities. Siegel recalls, "If there's one general appraisal of her better pupils, it would be that they strive to make the piano a singing instrument, and that there is a certain facility in their approach to the instrument. A tightness of pianism, and a percussive sound was very much against what she strove for. She was for flexibility and a limpid sound." [41]

Violinist Robert Mann, founding member of the Juilliard String Quartet, says that "some of the best chamber music we've ever done with a pianist has been with her because she played as if her instrument was a string instrument—it was that sensitive." [42]

And John Browning remembers that "she wasn't very good at talking about structure, but she could tell you if your performance didn't hold together. She taught more by her nose, by her intuition. It either smelled right or it didn't. And very often, a student would bring in something to her that was very individual, and was just not the way she preferred it, but it was convincing enough, and she'd say, 'You know, dearrrr, I'd leave eet alone. It vorks. I move een only ven you sound like you don't know vat you'rrr doing.'

"But that doesn't mean she didn't care," continues Browning. "Rosina took a very active interest in her students and their personal lives. If she thought you slept late, and she thought I did—she thought I stayed out too late and got up too late in the morning—she'd call me every morning at eight o'clock: 'You know, dearrr, get up. And beforrre you even have cup of coffee, you get to piano immediately. Prrractice.'

"Maybe what made her a great teacher was that she wasn't like other teachers. There were others who would say, in effect, 'You're stupid. You don't know anything. You don't know how to play the piano, I will teach you from the beginning.' Mrs. Lhevinne never corrected what didn't need to be fixed. If you came in with a big technique, she said, 'Fine, I'll leave it alone.' If you came in with a good sound: 'I'll leave it alone.' If you came in knowing how to pedal, she didn't interfere.

"She corrected only what was wrong, so that her students were not damaged psychologically. There were a lot of other teachers who caused their students to be nervous or terrified or tore down their egos. She didn't do that. She built you up so that you played your best and you were stable as a performer.

"And I think maybe that might be the greatest single thing, because other people tend to turn out students who all sound alike, but at the same time they lose their personality, and they lose their confidence in themselves.

"And if someone really good came to Rosina, she would leave alone 90 percent and change the 10 percent that needed change.

"So I think she was very good for Van because he did come [to Juilliard] as a real individual. The technique was all there." [43]

In Van, Rosina found an ideal match, a highly individual student with considerable technical and interpretive accomplishment already behind him, but a student in need of more repertoire, more performing experience, and a bit of direction.

The chemistry apparently was right because not long after Van had entered Juilliard he launched one of the most remarkable winning streaks in the history of American musical competitions. From April of 1952 to April of 1958 he won every piano competition he entered.

Van opened his series of triumphs with the G. B. Dealey Memorial Award, a Dallas competition that attracted a national field and offered as first prize $250 and, more important, a performance with the Dallas Symphony Orchestra and a solo recital date. Van became the eighth winner of the competition, selected by a panel of judges that included then Dallas Symphony Orchestra conductor Walter Hendl; Dallas Morning News amusements editor and nationally respected music critic John Rosenfield; and Ft. Worth Star-Telegram music critic E. Clyde Whitlock.[44]

Two months later, Van competed against two hundred pianists for the Kosciuszko Foundation's Chopin Scholarship Award of $1,000, selected by a panel of judges, including the esteemed teacher Madame Isabelle Vengerova, pianist Constance Keene, Ft. Wayne [Indiana] Symphony conductor Igor Buketoff, and author Abram Chasins, who was music director of New York radio station WQXR.[45]

When Van sat down at the piano and announced his first selection, Liszt's Twelfth Hungarian Rhapsody, Chasin's jaw

> just about fell to the floor. And as I looked around I
> saw that the other judges were reacting identically.
> *He* knew, *we* knew, and we knew he knew that this
> was a daring choice. Ordinarily, a contestant tries to
> make a serious impression by first playing some seri-
> ous classical work of Bach or Mozart or Beethoven.
> No one—well, almost no one—deliberately sets out to
> bowl over a jury with flashy gymnastics, for that is
> like impugning its musicianship or exposing one's
> own to doubt. . . .
>
> Fully expecting the Liszt to sound like a glass chan-
> delier, I waved an arm and said, "If you wish." Van
> began. It took little more than a few seconds for us to
> realize what we were hearing and that actually we
> had been paid the highest of compliments. This
> young artist—for his artistry was evident the instant
> his huge hands touched the keys—had trusted us to
> recognize the musical purpose of his virtuosity, to un-
> derstand his wish to endow this gaudy old war horse
> with nobility and expressive power. He came
> through handsomely. Only then did he turn to Bach,
> Mozart, Beethoven, Chopin, in a demonstration of pia-
> nism, sensitivity, and showmanship I have never
> known equaled in a competition. How well he suc-
> ceeded was reflected later in Madame Vengerova's be-

wildered question: "What for he wants the money to study? He is already an artist. All he needs now is more experience and repertoire." [46]

Together, the board of judges called Van "a remarkably gifted pianist already very well developed" and "on the way to an important career." [47]

Van's first "test" alongside his high-powered Juilliard peers came in the beginning of his second year, during the school's annual concerto competition.

"I remember I had entered my star pupil, George Katz, in the contest," says Josef Raeiff. "And I not only hoped he would win it—because George was first class, a real heavyweight, on the Van Cliburn level—I expected at the very least for George to be a finalist. Usually there were three finalists.

"And, to my dismay, I remember that one of the jury members said, 'Well, we don't really need to have any finals—Van won the competition.' That was one of the rare times when there simply were no finalists." [48]

No sooner did Van pick up that prize than he was off to Texas to play his debut with the Dallas Symphony Orchestra, the prize for having won the Dealey earlier in the year. No doubt he was aware that if this performance went well, it could win him a measure of national recognition.

In chronicling Van's December 21 performance of Edward MacDowell's Piano Concerto no. 2 in D Minor in McFarlin Auditorium, Rosenfield's review in the *Dallas Morning News* sums up what happened:

> Young Cliburn's reception was so acclamatory that he was not mentally prepared for it. Standing alone while the hall thundered applause he shook hands twice with Leonard Posner, the concertmaster, and begged the orchestra to share the bows. . . .
>
> The work tested both the performer's romantic sensibilities and his fingers. While it was too much to ask a teenager to plumb its mellow and brooding quali-

ties, one could demand and in this case did get a prevailing lyrical feeling, a notable sense of form, a fine
talent for making simple expressiveness with a liquid,
songlike tone.[49]

Van was launched. The Shreveport Symphony inquired about
his availability;[50] the folks back in Kilgore laid plans for Van
Cliburn Day later in 1953. Lavish and critically generous cover
profiles of him turned up in Texas magazines, among them
Southwestern Musician[51] and *Magnolia News,* the house
publication of the Magnolia Oil Company where Van's father
worked.[52]

Later in 1953, Van made his debut with the Shreveport
Symphony. Its conductor, John Shenaut, remembers: "He
played the Mozart D Minor [Piano Concerto, K. 466] and the
Liszt E-flat. Everybody then called it talent, but I would call it a
gift. It was obvious right then. And he had a strong will, which
was evident even then.

"His Mozart was—well some people think he's sentimental,
you know? But it isn't that at all. I thought then that he had a
certain innocence, an essential kind of innocence. I remember
the second movement of the Mozart was just unbelievably
beautiful, the innocence with which he played it." [53]

Such was Kilgore's pride in Van, even at this relatively early
point in his career, that Mayor E. C. Elder officially proclaimed
April 9, 1953, "Van Cliburn Day," the occasion drawing together an audience of nearly 1,500 to hear Van play a recital at
the Kilgore College Auditorium, sponsored by the Kilgore
Music Club.

During the intermission of Van's leonine recital program,[54]
reported the *Kilgore News Herald:*

> Mrs. Raymond Whittlesey, president of the Kilgore
> Music Club, called Van's parents, Mr. and Mrs. H. L.
> Cliburn to the stage, and presented their son with a
> check for $600 as a "gift from the people of your
> hometown, Kilgore, Texas." The gift, she said, "is in

appreciation of your work and the acclaim you have brought to Kilgore," and added that "we are very proud of you."

Van replied that he was "deeply grateful" and said he would always remember the help of "the people I know, if I ever do anything really big." [55]

Already Van had become enamored of opening his recital on an unexpected note, bringing "the audience to its feet with the surprise playing of the National Anthem," as the *Kilgore News Herald* reported.[56]

Three days later, Van was back in Dallas to play the recital portion of his Dealey prize, his performance prompting *Dallas Morning News* critic Frank Gagnard to write: "Chopin's F Minor Fantasie [sic] was given a memorable performance of dramatic contrasts, building to a stunning climax. Cliburn played with an assurance belying the formidable demands of this great work. The Mozart Sonata in C Major (K. 330) was neatly organized and cleanly played, adding to the effectiveness of Prokofiev's Sonata [no. 6] which followed." [57]

So Van pressed on, entering the prestigious (but long-since defunct) Michaels Memorial Music Award in Chicago in June of 1953. This was not a piano competition but a contest for all instrumentalists and vocalists. From a field of thirty-three musicians playing a variety of instruments, the $1,000 first prize went to twenty-seven-year-old cellist Paul Olefsky; second prize to Van; third prize to violinist Joyce Flissler, who later ventured to Moscow to win a degree of acclaim as a finalist in the 1958 Tchaikovsky International Violin Competition.[58]

The results of the fourth biennial competition, which had featured public concerto performances accompanied by the Chicago Philharmonic Orchestra led by Izler Solomon, caused a minor *scandale.*

During the spring semi-finals, judge Solomon had written of Van, "technique excellent . . . fine natural talent"; judge Felix Borowski, then dean of Chicago critics, had noted Van's "excellent projection" and considered him a "highly gifted pianist." But during the finals, something odd happened behind closed doors. Recalling the incident five years later in a *New York Times* article, then-Chicago critic Roger Dettmer wrote:

> Later that year the finalists, including Mr. Cliburn, faced eight judges. Mr. Cliburn played music, during the decisive closed session [meaning not open to the public], by Chopin, Liszt, Beethoven ("Les Adieux" Sonata) and Prokofiev (Sonata no. 6). It was unanimously decided, however, before the evening concert [which would be held in public] that Mr. Olefsky would be winner because of his greater age, maturity and professional attainments.
>
> That evening fellow-judges were jolted from their unanimity when Dr. Borowski shifted his vote from Mr. Olefsky to Mr. Cliburn, explaining later to his wife, "I could not vote against that great talent." [59]

So Olefsky had been selected for his age and experience, and not necessarily because he played better in either portion of the competition. What's more, Van—who always was at his best before a live audience—managed to win over at least one of the judges based on musical performance rather than perceived credentials.

But there's more.

Dettmer, who attended the 1953 Michaels competition, today remembers the performances vividly. "Actually, I remember Olefsky's playing because he played quite poorly," says Dettmer. "So I was pretty surprised by the final results. In fact, I wrote the *Times* piece because I was outraged" by the track record of the Michaels Award, which "had not had much luck picking winners." [60]

Continues Dettmer, "I had come from New York, and I knew Ross Parmenter [a *New York Times* music editor], and I said, 'Would you like a piece on this?' He said, 'Sure,' so I wrote it.

"Also, the Michaels Awards were always a sort of family affair, and they weren't always run in a kosher fashion, I'm sorry to say," adds Dettmer, referring to an award that had been created in the memory of Mr. and Mrs. Joseph E. Michaels, Chicago-area arts patrons who died in a plane crash in 1949.

"They loved the publicity, but how they reached their conclusions frequently was based on recitals that were given in advance of the [public] concerts.

"Of course, they wanted to give the concerts in Grant Park, which they did, with the orchestra. And what the family felt, and whatever conclusions the judges arrived at, were something quite different." [61]

Another observer who remembers the contretemps in Chicago is Tom Porter, the veteran piano technician for the Chicago Symphony Orchestra. "It seems like the fellow who played cello, Mr. Olefsky, was the fair-haired boy all the way from square one," says Porter. "I also remember that Van Cliburn played a pretty outstanding performance. Even in those days, he was quite a glamorous pianist. He had a lot of fire and excitement, and I don't know what the grounds were that they didn't choose him as a winner. I'm sure they were pretty embarrassed [in retrospect]. But, then on the other hand, the Michaels Awards have gone by the wayside while Van Cliburn is still one of the great pianists." [62]

Perhaps Rildia Bee put the matter into the most telling perspective. She told the judges she was "just as happy Van was not a winner all the time—one has to learn to lose too." [63]

Undaunted, Van continued forth, performing everywhere he could before the next competition. In August, he played in Chautauqua, New York, the local paper saying, in rather unbridled fashion:

> Sunday decorum was thrown to the winds at the conclusion of the Chautauqua Symphony Orchestra's concert as a packed Amphitheater called Van Cliburn back to the stage six times with a prolonged ovation. . . .
>
> From the very beginning it was evident that the Tchaikovsky concerto was Van Cliburn's meat. Tall-torsoed and broad-palmed, he could put his back

> powerfully into the volume of tone this work de-
> mands and encompass with ease its crashing chords
> and octave passages. . . .
>   This is a wonderful equipment. But in addition he
> exhibited a tonal control which built broadly con-
> ceived climaxes and gradually released their ten-
> sions.[64]

So Van's nascent career soared, that year darkened only by the news of October 30, 1953, when a British Commonwealth Pacific Airlines plane crashed near San Francisco, killing the nineteen passengers on board, including the brilliant American pianist William Kapell.[65]

In retrospect, it seems evident that Kapell, at thirty-one, was the leading young American pianist of the day. His premature death robbed modern-day pianism of one of its most probing minds and imposing techniques. The tragedy seemed exacerbated by the circumstances preceding the death of Kapell, who was returning from a tour of Australia and left behind a wife, two toddlers, and his parents.

"Australian music lovers were deeply shocked today to learn of the death of Mr. Kapell," read one story. "They were disturbed because he had ended his tour on a bitter note, charging he had been treated unfairly by the critics. His strangely prophetic parting remark was: 'I shall never return. I mean what I say.' "[66]

In March of 1954, Van entered the biggest competition of his life and, arguably, the most demanding in America at the time. Since 1951, in fact, no winner had been chosen for the Edgar M. Leventritt Award.[67] No candidate was deemed worthy of the honor.

In 1954, the remarkable Leventritt jury included pianists Rudolf Serkin, Nadia Reisenberg, Leopold Mannes, and Eugene Istomin (who had won the Leventritt in 1943); conductors George Szell and Leonard Bernstein; violinist Alexander Schneider; violinist-violist Lillian Fuchs; New York Philharmonic manager Arthur Judson; and the omnipresent author and WQXR broadcaster Abram Chasins.[68]

Even before Van played his first note, however, he had made an impression. "I remember that before the competition, we were going over the applications—the kids had to send in the documents that indicated that they had professional experience," recalls Naomi Graffman, who worked for the Leventritt Competition at the time. "So the pianists usually sent in little eight-by-ten envelopes with a few sheets in them. And I'll never forget this thing from Van that looked like the Manhattan telephone directory. It had a baby picture of him on the cover. It had been lovingly made by his father, and I remember it said that he had won the G. B. Dealey Award, but it was the first time I had ever heard of that.

"So Rosalie Berner [Mrs. Leventritt's daughter] and I were very amused [by Van's application]. Rosalie and I actually had our own private competition—we would pick the winners, or the losers, by looking at the applications.

"So of course, when we looked at that application of Van's we actually doubled over with laughter, but I remember thinking, *He's gonna win; he's gonna win.*"[69]

By all accounts, once Van began playing, he virtually had the contest sewn up.

"There wasn't a specific imposed repertoire, but there were general types of things that people had to play to give a general idea of how they played," continues Graffman. "When Van started to play the Liszt Twelfth Hungarian Rhapsody, everybody sat there with jaws hanging down because nobody could believe it.

"And he was so striking. The size of him—and he was so very thin at that time—and he seemed eleven feet tall. And he wasn't even Jewish! It's so funny, but back then you just hardly saw a great pianist who wasn't Jewish. Van was incredible. We were just enchanted by this magical creature."[70]

On Van's repertoire list for the competition were Bach's E Minor Partita; Mozart's Sonata in C Major, K. 330; Beethoven's "Les Adieux" Sonata; Ravel's Toccata and "Jeux d'Eau";

Hindemith's Third Sonata; Prokofiev's Sixth Sonata; Chopin's
F Minor Fantaisie and B Major Nocturne op. 62; Liszt's
Twelfth Hungarian Rhapsody; Mozart's D Minor Piano Con-
certo, K. 466; Brahms's B-flat Piano Concerto no. 2; and
Tchaikovsky's Piano Concerto no. 1 in B-flat Minor.[71]

Certainly the judges were impressed. Leopold Mannes said,
"This boy's the real thing, and he has one of the most eloquent
left hands in the business." [72] Nadia Reisenberg called Van's
reading of the Mozart "exquisite. . . . So much serenity and
classic poise, yet it always sings." [73]

As Istomin remembers today, "Van's performance was extraordinary, and I voted for him as winner. It was not quite a
unanimous vote—it was all but one, probably because the
Leventritt was the sort of award that did not have the particular
sort of bias that Van would have been able to take advantage
of. The Leventritt Competition leaned toward the classical
repertoire.

"The finalists were all of such extraordinary gifts and abilities.
But [pianist Claude] Frank didn't really play up to his potential.

"On the other hand, the second finalist was John Browning,
who was magnificent and perfect and, actually, he was so
perfect that in a sense he rather alienated the jury. There was
a feeling that his playing was slick.

"But Van projected a kind of charm and electricity. He was
adorable, charming, and projected that image to everybody,
and he played the Twelfth Liszt Rhapsody most magnificently.

"In the Tchaikovsky Concerto he had the kind of a touch in
the hands—we [judges] all scratched our heads and said, 'Well,
we're really not for this particular kind of repertoire, but you
can't *not* give it to somebody who has that extraordinary power
of projection and communication, which Van had then and
always has had." [74]

Istomin was so excited about what he heard, in fact, that
between stages of the competition "he called me up to tell me
that there's this incredible talent he just heard," remembers
pianist Gary Graffman (Naomi Graffman's husband).

"He said, 'It's something really incredible. You have to hear this.' And this was a competition with talents like John Browning and Claude Frank. Sometimes, you know, people win competitions when there's no one to compete against. But here there were some really strong, terrific players.

"Claude Frank's playing would appeal much more to Rudolf Serkin and George Szell and Alexander Schneider and Eugene Istomin than Van's would.

"So I went to the finals, and it really was incredible. Van sounded like the old-fashioned Russian kind of players, where everything was technically under control, and yet it sounded like he was improvising. It was a gorgeous, wonderful sound, and not overdone, either." [75]

The finals, in particular, lit up the jury, as Abram Chasins wrote later:

> As our long, cool drink of water threaded his way to the piano, I scribbled a note to George Szell, who had just joined us. "Wait till you hear *this* boy. Remarkable."
>
> I must explain that we judges usually sat with several empty seats between us so we could listen more "alone" and with a sense of detachment. Notes were therefore often passed in lieu of whispered comments which might distract the contestants.
>
> Van opened with the Tchaikovsky. After a time Szell slipped me the answer to my note: "He *is* remarkable," he had written. "No philosopher, in spite of the soulful facial expressions, but he makes beautiful sounds. Extraordinary skill and projection." In the last movement fire leaped from the instrument, and it was evident to us then—as it was later to become evident to spellbound audiences—that Van had a special flair for the Russian school. Leonard Bernstein said, "He really loves music, loves to play it, and loves the way *he* plays it. It's so honest and refreshing." [76]

Before Van had left the spotlight, the jury asked if he would play the last movement of Brahms's Second Concerto.

"I shall never forget his reply, for it was my first experience with the Van Cliburn tact and method of address, which have since become so famous," wrote Chasins later.

> "May I explain," he said quietly, "that I have been ill much of this past week. I feel it would be an injustice not only to myself but, far more important, to this great work and to the patience and integrity of this jury if I attempted to play the Brahms. Would you permit me to play something else?" It was all stated so gracefully yet firmly, with such implied confidence in our understanding and fairness—What could we say?
>
> I'll tell you what I said, I asked him to play the Liszt Twelfth Rhapsody. . . .
>
> It was Mrs. Cliburn who enlightened me later that she had advised Van to open contest performances with the Rhapsody. Judges usually allow contestants to choose their own first piece. After that they call the shots. Mrs. Cliburn feared that if Van didn't play the Liszt immediately he might never get the chance to play it.[77]

The judges weren't the only ones impressed. Evidently, Van's colleague-competitors realized that the string of orchestral dates the Leventritt prize included—New York, Cleveland, Pittsburgh, Buffalo, Denver—probably would be Van's.

"Of course, the Leventritt was the kind of competition where people usually played Mozart and Beethoven, but then along came Van with a Tchaikovsky concerto," recalls Claude Frank. "As soon as he played that, I think everybody felt that he would most likely be the winner.

"And he played the Liszt Twelfth Hungarian Rhapsody, which, again, was not the kind of piece the Leventritt judges usually preferred. But the way it was played, they had no choice but to go for it because it was that outstanding.

"Not only was it tremendously virtuoso, and with a huge and virtuoso sound, but it was extremely communicative." [78]

And Browning, who won the Leventritt the following year, says, "I expected that Van would probably win. He had a roller-coaster quality to the playing, and it was spellbinding." [79]

So Van, still nineteen, won the Leventritt, his father telling the local newspaper that "this has been Van's goal for many years." [80]

Now Van's career took on a breathtaking clip. In May, he graduated from Juilliard with two honors, the Frank Damrosch Scholarship and the Carl M. Roeder Award. These complemented the $600 Olga Samaroff Grant he had won in 1953. And he was listed as a Juilliard scholarship student, an honor that did not include cash because "we were just a shade on the wrong side of the poorhouse to qualify for a grant," in Rildia Bee's words.[81]

In June, the news was made public that Van had signed with Columbia Artists Management, "to be administered under the personal direction of the Judson, O'Neill and Judd Division," [82] though "I had signed my contract with Arthur Judson in November of 1953," recalls Van. "Even before I won the Leventritt I was already with Columbia Artists Management, and that was thanks to [Juilliard Dean] Mark Schubart. He believed in me very much." [83]

And in November, Van would make his debut with the New York Philharmonic.

How much effect Rosina Lhevinne had on Van's playing is an open question, though most observers of the time insist that Van had arrived at Juilliard an almost-finished pianist in need of minimal guidance.

"I heard all his juries and his graduation recital, and I would say there was no big leap from when he arrived to when he graduated Juilliard," says Josef Raeiff. "Because, even from the beginning, his playing always was so natural and so musical. The man's technique was tremendous, it was comprehensive, and he had such a beautiful tone. And he never had the problem that most kids have of playing too fast. As a matter of fact, if anything, he plays a little on the slow side, so sometimes there's a lack of momentum. That would be the only criticism that I would make." [84]

Ivan Davis, Van's longtime friend from Texas, also recalls, "His playing was refined from the beginning [of his tenure at Juilliard]. He was not a raw pianist, like some people that age. It always was refined, even back in Texas days, and that's why it was amazing." [85]

To Schubart, though, "Van seemed more controlled and more disciplined," as a result of his Juilliard years. "His playing was a little wild, really all over the place, when he came here. And by the time he left he was more accomplished, and that was Rosina's impact on him." [86]

To Van, Rosina was nothing less than a pianistic inspiration. "As a teacher, she would demonstrate some, though not as much as my mother," says Van. "But I remember one day I got there a little late for a lesson, and she was playing the 'Aeolian Harp' [etude of Chopin] op. 25, no. 1, and I listened in, and it was extraordinarily beautiful. She really was a marvelous pianist.

"I also was there when she turned eighty and played the Chopin E Minor [Piano Concerto] with the Juilliard Orchestra, another absolutely beautiful performance." [87]

Perhaps it's safest to say that it took all three components—Van's innate gifts and determination, Rildia Bee's long years of tutoring and care, and Rosina's finishing touches to create the splendid artist who graduated in 1954.

James Mathis, Van's longtime Texas friend, will never forget the moment when that graduating class met for its final photo. "The photographer and everybody had gathered for the picture, but Van wasn't there—he was running late," says Mathis, who could not have been surprised by this development. "So, somewhat brashly, I told the photographer and the people running the session that they'd be pretty sorry if they didn't have Van in the picture. And since he lived down the block on Claremont, I just said, 'He's probably asleep—I'll go get him.'

"So I made everyone wait half an hour on the steps of the old Juilliard building on Claremont Avenue. I just felt that someday they would want to know that Van Cliburn had belonged to that class. I was sure he was going to make it; he was so talented.

"And I think even he sort of knew he was going to be a star. I think people know that; I don't think it comes as such a bolt out of the blue. But, for sure, *I* knew he would." [88]

5

Rising Star

*B*y any measure, Van was flying
high. In August of 1954 he returned to Chautauqua, New York,
to appear with conductor Walter Hendl and to play
Rachmaninoff's Third Piano Concerto. The *Chautauquan
Daily* reported, "Van Cliburn's transcendental pianism last
Saturday evening brought cheers at the close of the program
and the 19-year-old Texan [actually, he had just turned 20] was
returned to the platform six times by the ovation from a
well-filled Amphitheater." [1]

By fall, Van wrote to Juilliard dean Mark Schubart:

My dear Dean—
This is just advance warning that I will soon be
around the old institution to hound you a little more!
I am looking forward to seeing you next week and
hearing about your interesting summers.
Believe it or not, I have really worked this summer.
Hope it brings the desired results on November 14th
[the date of Van's scheduled debut with the New

York Philharmonic]. Please have one of your inspiring and inimitable lectures ready for my moral support!

Mother and Daddy join me in the very best of wishes.

As ever, Van[2]

Van's performance with the New York Philharmonic had the potential to heighten an already notable career. Naturally, before the performance Van visited New York Philharmonic conductor Dimitri Mitropoulos to go over tempos, interpretation, and various other details before the orchestral rehearsal.

"He was one of those marvelous, saintly people whom you feel it's just God's blessing that you're in the presence of," recalls Van of his first meeting with the great conductor. "You know, he was a priest, a very saintly man. I went for my chat with him before November 14 of 1954. He lived in one of the penthouses at the Great Northern Hotel [in New York].

"I walked in, and it looked like a monastery. There was a piano—a seven-foot Steinway, and on it was a lectern with the Bible open. There was a long table, a lamp, three chairs, very spartan.

"And all three walls of another room, floor to ceiling, were lined with books and scores. He had a day bed with just a little lamp—he lived like a monk. He was so deeply spiritual and I cannot forget what beautiful eyes, so big and inspiring." [3]

Mitropoulos took a liking to Van, as well, and would prove to be a loyal and devoted colleague/mentor in coming years.

Meanwhile, though, November 14 arrived. Van strode onto the stage of Carnegie Hall and played the magnificent, granite chords that open the Tchaikovsky Piano Concerto.

"He got this rich, deep tone out of the instrument that nobody else really got," recalls Naomi Graffman of that performance. "It was such a singing sound that, immediately, when you heard those first chords, you knew something spectacular was going to happen.

"He did not exaggerate too much. He didn't have too many of those 'magic moments,' where he'd linger over something. He played pretty straightforwardly.

"There was a little slurpiness, but it wasn't overdone. It was just beautiful and it was convincing—that was what was important. But it was an exceptional performance because it wasn't the routine kind of thing where somebody just sat there and played all the notes.

"Van put his heart into it, and he cared, and it came out. The audience went bonkers when he finished playing. The enthusiasm for him was so sincere because he spoke to people." [4]

The critics universally concurred with the audience, which gave Van seven curtain calls.[5] Louis Biancolli of the *New York World-Telegram & Sun* wrote, "This is one of the most genuine and refreshing keyboard talents to come out of the West—or anywhere else—in a long time. Van Cliburn is obviously going places, except that he plays like he had already been there." [6]

Harold C. Schonberg, in the *New York Times:* "Spirit and enthusiasm were present, plus a commanding technique, a good degree of musical excitement and a certain degree of musical rawness. Mr. Cliburn's immaturities, however, were secondary to his natural facility for playing the piano and his instinctively big style. His career will be watched with interest." [7]

Harriet Johnson in the *New York Post:* "Cliburn played with the spontaneity of a veteran and in addition demonstrated a masterly, brilliant technique. He obviously has a tremendous musical instinct which has been guided in the proper direction, so that already he plays with maturity and poetic sensitivity, extraordinary in one so young." [8]

Francis Perkins in the *New York Herald Tribune:* "The work's outspoken measures were proclaimed with brilliance and climactic impact. Auspiciously, he did not display his pianistic energy in the wrong places; his dynamic shading and interpretive treatment were also appropriate in the more intimate and romantic episodes of the concerto." [9]

Miles Mastendieck in the New York Journal-American: "He ranks as the finest potential talent introduced through this means [the Leventritt Award]. . . . A clarity of note, fullness of tone and a roundness of phrase that mark him as outstanding." [10]

Even the more restrained, scholarly music journals hardly could contain their enthusiasm. Robert Sabin in Musical America: "It was a performance in the grand manner, yet in no way artificial. The natural exuberance and hearty feelings of the young pianist found a place in it for all its discipline and skill." [11]

And Henry W. Levinger in *Musical Courier:* "He has technique which is as rich as it is reliable. His octave passages thunder, his lyric episodes sing, and though he gives the minor phrases great importance, he never loses sight of the overall monumental conception." [12]

It was a remarkable day in music in America: Following Van's afternoon performance in Carnegie Hall, a rising young soprano named Leontyne Price would make her New York recital debut that night in Town Hall. Van went to her recital and remembers, "It was a wonderfully full house. Samuel Barber accompanied her in the 'Hermit Songs,' and there were tremendous ovations. You just knew something big was going to happen for Leontyne." Like Van, Price was warmly received by the critics. [13]

Even before the reviews were out, however, the celebration was on. More than three hundred friends, fans, out-of-towners and the like swamped the Carnegie Hall backstage area in pursuit of Van. [14]

"Mrs. Leventritt had arranged a party for Van afterward, and she told him to invite about thirty or forty people," recalls Naomi Graffman. "I'll never forget this crush of people going backstage at Carnegie Hall because, apparently, planeloads of friends of his had come up from Texas, and they all trampled up the stairs. I remember thinking, *They're so much larger than New Yorkers.* They were huge, they occupied so much space, and they all had red faces. They were all just ho-ho-hoing, as they clomped up the stairs.

"Well, Mrs. Leventritt was rather small and very fragile, and she climbed up the stairs, and Van grabbed her in this bear hug, and he pulled her up off her feet and twirled her around. She laughed and laughed.

"'Honey,' he said, 'You see all these people? Well, they're all coming to your party!' And so we got there, and she was panic-stricken. It was the first time in my life I ever saw her look nervous because she was such an experienced partygoer.

"She ran around the room telling us, 'Don't eat anything. Don't drink anything. We're not going to have enough food.'

"Van had sent her his usual dozen roses, and somebody had unthinkingly put them in this big Ming vase on her piano, which wasn't supposed to have anything in it. And somebody put water in it and put the roses in it, and the vase started to leak. It was one of those scenes where it was absolute crisis after crisis, but everybody got through it." [15]

Amid all the fanfare, only one publication noted that Van had made another musical offering on that day. "One of the latest important contributions to church music repertory is a setting of Psalm 123 ('Unto Thee Lift I Up Mine Eyes') by Van Cliburn," reported the *Musical Courier* of a premiere on the same night as his Leventritt appearance. "The work is dedicated to Clifford Tucker, organist and choirmaster at Calvary Baptist Church, and the choir, and was performed for the first time on Nov. 14, the service being broadcast over station WMGM." [16]

So Van was launched in New York and making his name across the country, as well. The life of the concert pianist—concerts, rehearsals, celebrations, reunions, old friends, new friends—appealed to the bon vivant in Van. Each town, whether major city or tiny village, offered its own adventure and diversion, such as the turn of events surrounding his appearance in Baraboo, Wisconsin.

"After my recital they were going to have a dinner for me at the local restaurant, and it was snowing like crazy," recalls Van. "But these very gracious people took me anyway, and they introduced me to the president of the organization that presented me, a Mrs. Moorehead. And during dinner, all of a sudden she said, 'Oh, I just enjoyed your recital so much. I know your parents are proud.' And I said, 'Well, I hope they are.' And she said, 'Oh, I just think it's so wonderful that you're artistic. I have a daughter, and she's artistic too.' So I said, 'That's nice.' She asked, 'Are you an only child?' I said, 'Yes, I am.' And she said, 'Oh, I only had one child too.'

"Now she was an older lady, very lovely, very stately, refined and all, and when she said her daughter was artistic, I thought, *Maybe she's a painter.* And the lady said, 'No, she went more into speech and dramatics.' And I said, 'Oh, does she live here?' And she said, 'No, she lives now in Los Angeles.' And I'm thinking, *Moorehead, Moorehead, lives in Los Angeles. Hmmm. Name sounds familiar.* So I said, 'Is she in the movies?' And she said, 'Well, she has been before the camera.' Can you imagine? 'She has been before the camera!' What a way to put it. And then I said, 'Your daughter isn't Agnes Moorehead?!' And she said, 'Yes, she is. Have you heard of her?' Well, I thought that was the dearest thing, and it was no put-on.

"Later on, I got to meet Agnes Moorehead, and we became good, good friends. Agnes was such a sweet, dear person. And I said to myself, *I can see why she's so wonderful because her mother was so special, just the essence of culture.* And then Aggie later told me that her father was a Scottish Presbyterian minister, and he thought going out to Hollywood was not very lovely at all." [17]

For the most part, Van's performances drew warm reviews, as he made his debut in one city after another. In 1954, Allen Young wrote in the *Denver Post:* "Tear out this name, write it somewhere, get to know it: Van Cliburn. This is one to reckon with, one musician whose prodigious talent marks him as the most important young pianist of his generation." [18]

When Van played with the Pittsburgh Symphony Orchestra, conducted by William Steinberg, Donald Steinfirst wrote in the *Pittsburgh Post-Gazette,*

> Young Mr. Cliburn, a rangy 6-foot 4-inch Texan
> from the oil country, has the build of a basketball

player, but I am sure more than one listener must have been inevitably drawn toward his resemblance to the legendary Franz Liszt as the latter burst upon a fashionable Parisian music world at the age of 20.

We are told that the leonine handsome Liszt literally towered over his piano. No less does the blond, equally handsome young Mr. Cliburn. The word "towered" is used musically. He literally enveloped the keyboard.[19]

And the *Pittsburgh Press* noted, "He proved he is the most exciting young pianist of our era." [20]

Similarly, the *Houston Post* reported that "Mr. Cliburn added some real heat to the evening and brought the greatest ovation any guest has caused all winter." [21] The *Detroit News* added, "If a truly great pianist is to come out of this generation, it may well be this tall, talented Texan." [22]

Along the way, Van came to know artists and music devotees who helped him in both concrete and intangible ways. Pianist Alexis Weissenberg befriended Van at the time of his New York Philharmonic debut. "He was my hero," recalls Van, "and I never missed one of his recitals. He's one of the loveliest people I've ever known. He constantly encouraged me, and I've never forgotten it." [23]

Recalls Weissenberg, "Mrs. Leventritt actually talked to me about Van, just after the Leventritt [performance], and she said, 'That's somebody you must hear.'

"Actually, I called him, and we met in a coffee shop and talked for three hours—before I heard him play. It was wonderful to be with him because he was hungry to learn things, to find out about Europe, to learn about concertizing in Europe. He had this quality—which he has kept even now—this fantastic childlike quality of wanting to know about things in a completely crystal way." [24]

Among Van's supporters, two took special interest in him: Schuyler Chapin (who then worked for Bill Judd at Columbia Artists and later would become general manager of the Metropolitan Opera in New York) and Skitch Henderson (musical director of "The Tonight Show" when its host was Steve Allen).

"I had first heard Van in my mother-in-law's living room," recalls Chapin, who is married to the former Betty Steinway, of the famed piano-making family. "And Betty's mother had heard from the Concerts and Artists head at Steinway, Alexander Greiner, that this extraordinary youngster was on the New York scene. And she met him and liked him a lot, so she did something quite unusual for her, which was to have a little musicale in her living room, a very intimate setting.

"He had played some Chopin, which is when I came in—I was a little bit late—and it was an extraordinary experience. I just had this visceral, gut feeling. The poetry and the romantic communication that came out of the keyboard from that great big skinny frame were incredible. It was as if he were saying to the audience, 'I love you all. I love this music. You must love the music with me.' Not, 'You must love me,' but, 'You must love the music with me.'

"It reminded me of Leonard Bernstein's definition of music, which is one of the greatest definitions. He said, 'It's the only art that does not require the censorship of the brain before reaching the heart.' And Van, it seemed to me, was the perfect example of a musical message going right to the listener's heart." [25]

Chapin shrewdly told Skitch Henderson about Van, realizing that a pianist of Van's musical gifts and obvious good looks might be perfect for TV. "I thought he had skill and was a comer," recalls Henderson. "He had great charm, and I use the word in the best sense." [26]

So Henderson booked Van for an appearance on "The Tonight Show," a feat not so easily accomplished. "Booking anybody classical was considered death," says Henderson. "I mean, classical music was three minutes and off. You just didn't book so-called highbrow." [27]

Still, Henderson persevered, and Van made his "Tonight Show" debut on January 19, 1955, playing Ravel's Toccata and a Chopin etude.[28] As Henderson later recalled, "In the whole history of 'The Tonight Show,' that was one of the four or five peak nights that stand out in memory. Vaniel [as Henderson always has called Van] was terrific. In the language of show business, 'He broke it up.' " [29]

Of course, there were mishaps alongside the triumphs. Playing in Buffalo in March of 1955, Van made all the wire services, thanks to a remarkable turn of events in mid-performance.

Reported Associated Press,

> Van Cliburn was left musically stranded today during his guest appearance with the Buffalo Philharmonic Orchestra.
> The pedals dropped off the piano in the middle of Schumann's Concerto in A Minor.
> Anthony Gilio, clarinetist with the orchestra and a piano repair man in his spare time, fixed the pedal unit as Cliburn and the audience cooled their heels in good humor.[30]

Of course, what else could one do but laugh?

"Now this was the first time I played the Schumann Concerto in public," remembers Van, whose performance was conducted by Josef Krips. "And in the middle of the first movement the whole pedalboard broke, collapsed right on the floor. And I said, 'Dr. Krips, the pedals just collapsed.' And you know, here I was, this little kid—it was like a train wreck! How could this be happening to me? And I thought, *Well, if I have to, I will go through the whole thing without any assistance from the damper pedals.*

"Meanwhile, the orchestra saw what was happening, and one by one they stopped playing. Then Dr. Krips gave them this big cut-off sign, as if it were necessary. Dr. Krips turned around and said, in his Prussian accent, 'Laties and gentlement, ze pedals have collapsed,' and he stormed off the stage." [31]

Krips went backstage to look for the piano technician. To his dismay, the gentleman had left as soon as the concerto began, and Krips was furious. But once the pedals were restored,

"Cliburn started over again and completed the concerto to thunderous applause," reported the AP story.[32]

Fortunately for Van, such incidents remained the exception, his live appearances still drawing mostly glowing reviews. More important, he was invited back for engagements with the orchestras of Cleveland, Denver, Dallas, Buffalo, and South Bend, Indiana.

Denver Post music columnist Allen Young noted his return, in November 1955: "Justifying the fine impression he made last year with the Rachmaninoff Third Piano Concerto, he proceeded to leap into the fray with two concerti, the dazzling 3d Prokofiev and the wondrous Mozart K. 503." In the Mozart, "he played with expressive, fine tone, engaging appreciation of the rapturous measures, and very cleanly, directly and musically made it something to listen to." And in Prokofiev's Piano Concerto no. 3, "Van Cliburn followed [Prokofiev's] course with avid interest, throwing off exhilarating splashes of tunes, catching them up in striking variations, with flashing pianism up and down the keyboard." [33]

Now earning about $19,000 in his first year after the Leventritt, Van picked out an apartment, a three-room place at 205 West 57th Street[34] that comfortably held his grand piano, a daybed, and not much else.

By the summer of 1956, he received the distinct honor of an invitation to attend Rudolf Serkin's Marlboro Music Festival in Vermont, for which Van was given a scholarship. Here he played four-hands with a precocious, up-and-coming pianist named James Levine (who went on to become music director of the Metropolitan Opera in New York) and worked on the Dvorak Quintet.

"The whole idea at Marlboro," recalls violinist-conductor Alexander Schneider, who taught at the festival that summer, "was to learn how to play music, not just to play the instruments. It was and still is the best school in the world. I remember Van there—it was obvious he was extremely gifted." [35]

Van's summer at Marlboro was shortened, however, for in mid-July he was invited to play the Rachmaninoff Second Piano

Concerto in Cleveland on August 4. He rather boldly accepted the invitation, though he didn't know the concerto.

So he rushed back to New York to buy the score, then devour it. After nearly two weeks of intense study, it was time to try it out with another pianist playing the orchestral part.

"On a sweltering summer day we went down into the basement of Steinway Hall [on West 57th Street], where they have around eighty concert grands. And we picked two of them side by side, and we started to work on it," recalls pianist Joseph Esposito.

"First we thought, *Let's do it straight through,* because we just wanted to have the entrances [of orchestra and soloist] cleared up, and we did.

"And then Van said, 'Would you mind doing it again for me straight through?' And so we did it straight through the second time. And then he would say, 'Well, let's do page 11, let's do page 25, let's do this, let's do that.'

"It was eleven o'clock by now, and in the meantime the custodian wanted to go home—he had to close the place up. Finally he came and said, 'Well, I'm sorry, but I have to go. You fellows can stay—and make sure that these lights are turned off when you leave, and shut the door. But I'm afraid I have to turn off the air conditioning.'

"This was August, and now without air-conditioning it became an oven. So we started to disrobe because it was sweltering, we were just covered with perspiration.

"First we took off our jackets, then our ties, then our shirts, and soon we were just down to our pants at a little after twelve, playing the Rachmaninoff Second. It must have been some sight." [36]

Apparently Van learned the piece well enough, judging by the *Cleveland Plain Dealer* review of August 5: "Last night, for an audience of 3,500, he played the most popular and expansive of all Rachmaninoff's big works (the Second Piano Concerto in C minor). Cliburn's playing has always been highly musical and forceful, and this was no exception," wrote the *Plain Dealer* critic, adding that Van's performance was "warmly received," prompting an encore performance of Ravel's Toccata.[37]

There was a dark side to that summer, however, when a carefree vacation nearly turned tragic. "You see, I never had learned to swim. I never had quite gotten the hang of it," recalls Van. "So one weekend I was visiting Schuyler Chapin and his family at their country home. And their kids always liked me and called me Uncle Moving Van. So I was sitting on the edge of this landing, right near the water, and they jumped on me from behind.

"It took me completely by surprise. I fell right into this deep water, with them right on top of me. They could swim like fish, so off they swam to the shore. But I went straight down, which was the most frightening feeling in my life. I was just frantic. At first, I think Schuyler and everyone thought I was just clowning around. I always told them I couldn't swim, but I don't think they believed me. Then Schuyler, I think, got a funny feeling that something was really wrong, and he jumped right in and saved me." [38]

Chapin never has forgotten the incident. "The water there is deceptive because it's beautiful fresh water and sand, so it's actually easy to walk," says Chapin. "But there was a dropoff after a while. It's not abrupt, but you have to be careful. I wasn't thinking anything about it, and then the next thing I knew, Van disappeared. Then one of the kids said something was wrong with Uncle Van, so I went up on the dock, and as I was looking down I could see him. My wife came down at about that point. And when we looked down, we knew something was very wrong.

"We didn't know what he was doing, so we both jumped in and got him and dragged him out and made him lean down on the dock and sort of gave him artificial respiration, just to bang that water out of him. We were just horror struck. Then he got up.

"So we didn't say anything more about it, and it wasn't mentioned again until about three years later. We saw Van at a concert, and as we were going back into the auditorium, he turned around and said, 'By the way, I can swim now—I took swimming lessons.' " [39]

Obviously, it was traumatic for all involved, including Van, who says, "That man saved my life, saved me from drowning. From then on I became obsessed with learning how to swim—it was like an *idée fixe*. I took lessons, but I couldn't get the hang of it.

"Then I found someone who said the thing to do was take lessons at this pool where they had salt water, and since the water would help you float, you could get enough confidence that you could relax and really begin to swim. So we tried that—nothing. I mean nothing worked.

"Finally, I was desperate, and I went into a pool—there was no one else there, no lifeguards, no one—and I thought, *I'm doing this now, and I don't care if I drown trying.* So I jumped into the pool, and then, it just happened. I couldn't believe it—I just swam.

"But, you know, even now, sometimes I'll be in a pool, and I'll think, 'Hmmm, this water is deep, isn't it?' And then I feel tense again." [40]

❖   ❖   ❖

Some myths are repeated so often as to become accepted fact, such as the notion that Van's career had come to a halt a season or so after he won the Leventritt. After enjoying a flurry of dates following that victory, this line of thinking goes, interest in him waned, so, in 1957, he packed up his bags and headed back to Kilgore to take over his mother's studio.

The truth, however, is much stranger than that fiction. Though it's true that Van returned to Kilgore in 1957 to help teach his mother's students, the circumstances leading to that move were as incredible as they were unpredictable and had almost nothing to do with his career as a pianist.

Van's career was going exceptionally well for a young musician. Honors from Juilliard, competition wins across the country, a New York Philharmonic debut, management by one of the most important firms in the world—all this he had achieved by age twenty, solely on his gifts as an artist.

No one, not Van, not even the sage Rildia Bee, could have anticipated what happened next.

After two seasons of a brisk concert career, Van was called up to the service in 1957. Knowing that meant he would not be able to concertize, he told his managers not to book dates for him.

Then something amazing happened. "One of the most promising careers in American concert life will not have to take time out for the Army, although willing," reported the *Dallas Morning News* in April of 1957.

> In fact, pianist Van Cliburn was standing with hand raised taking the oath at the induction center here Friday afternoon when an orderly interrupted. He asked the noted young artist to return to the medical office.
>
> It had been discovered that Cliburn's medical record showed chronic nasal hemorrhages since youth and nasal allergies. The Army then rejected Van Cliburn emphatically. He left town by plane in the afternoon for his home in Kilgore, "to readjust my thinking to the virtuoso life." . . .
>
> A big 1957-58 season loomed for the 22-year-old pianist, student of his mother and of Rosina Lhevinne in New York.
>
> Then the draft board at Longview came up with his name. Cliburn claimed no exemptions or deferments, although military service at this time would seriously break his professional stride.
>
> Cliburn simply called off $30,000 or more early engagements, played a "farewell" concert at Longview last Friday night for the Civic Music Association and told everybody goodbye. Now he is notifying New York that he is ready to resume his career work." [41]

Actually, Van had looked forward to his military stint, since he would be joining the Army Band in a tour of Africa. "It was a shock when I found I wasn't going," he says. "I was disappointed."

Classical concert engagements are booked years in advance, so he was essentially out of luck for the 1957-58 season that had looked so hopeful not long before. Worse still, in July, Van's parents drove up to Cleveland to attend a performance of his, but in the hotel room Rildia Bee slipped and broke a vertebra in her back. She didn't realize the severity of the injury, so after Van's performance, the family drove up to New York, whereupon Rildia Bee was admitted to a hospital.[42]

Still in pain when she was released five and a half weeks later, she and Harvey Lavan headed back home.[43] For Van, there was little question about what to do. He closed up his New York apartment and headed back to Kilgore to keep his mother's studio afloat.

On one rare occasion, Van discussed this grim period with the press, speaking with John Rosenfield of the *Dallas Morning News*. Reflecting on the events of April 1957, Van remembered having dropped by Rosenfield's office, where

> "I used your [Rosenfield's] telephone to notify my parents in Kilgore that I was out of the Army. And I called Bill Judd, my New York manager, to complain that I had no concert dates for 1957-58."
>
> Cliburn called the summer of 1957 the lowest and most disheartening period in his life.
>
> "[Rilda Bee] fell in her hotel room and broke her back. Seven weeks later my father was injured in an auto-bus collision. I had to give over some time to take care of both." [44]

Those who knew Van were not surprised that he dropped everything to help out at home.

"There's just about nothing Van wouldn't do for his mother or his father," says Annette Davies Morgan, who remembers

Van's sad Kilgore homecoming. "Her teaching meant a lot to her. She wanted very much for the teaching to continue, so he did it for her." [45]

Says Van, "I actually wasn't teaching that much for her. She would lie down on the sofa because she tired easily. She would call me in to demonstrate something on the piano. I just made sure everything ran smoothly." [46]

As for Van's career simply petering out, nothing could have been further from reality. "You have to put Van's career in the context of the other artists," says Naomi Graffman. "What was typical in those days was that, first of all, even our young artists were older than Van. We did not have any other nineteen-year-old artists. Usually they were in their middle twenties. And a young artist like that would go on what they called the 'community circuit.' He would play community concerts for a fee—the artist's 'sell fee' was usually $300. The artist took home considerably less than that.

"And for these community concerts, sometimes the pianist would play eighty or ninety concerts in a season in towns that nobody ever even heard of, towns where you would never go back to play again because they never reengaged people.

"They were very lucky if they had one or two orchestra engagements—that was considered just absolutely manna from heaven. But Van was always different because from the very beginning there was interest in him from conductors, from major managers, from everyone because they knew that he had a certain [ticket] sales potential. So he played what we called 'straight sales' engagements, which meant that he had really decent bookings. He played with major orchestras, he played with minor orchestras, he even gave recitals. For a low fee, it's true. But the point is that if you compare that against the workhorse pianists who went around giving a concert every other day, no, Van didn't do a lot of concerts. He had fewer but better dates.

"The other thing that people forget is that a first season for an artist was usually a terrific season. The first season an artist came under management was always good because then the managers were gung-ho, and they would do what they could, whether it was community concerts or straight sales or whatever. Then there was something called the 'second-season syndrome'—although I guess they didn't use the word *syndrome* in those days. There was always a drop after the first exciting season. But in Van's case, it was much less of a drop than people say.

"Van had very good seasons—as did Leon Fleisher, who was another unusual case because he had won the Queen Elisabeth Competition in 1952. Leon [Fleisher] was the first American to win it. So suddenly he had a terrific situation—one year he played with twenty-two orchestras, which was an amazing thing in those days.

"But aside from Leon Fleisher, the most successful pianist at that point, at least since Willi Kappel had died, Van was doing the best. In his last year [before going to Moscow], it was considered inevitable that Van would be drafted. And there was a definite understanding [at Bill Judd's office] that he would not be booked. Then when he wasn't drafted after all, his season didn't have any concerts.

"Again, that wasn't the fault of his career. It was just a strange accident. Unfortunately, people don't seem to accept that, they all go through this whole thing about: 'Only Moscow gave Van a career,' which is so ridiculous." [47]

Says Van, "In retrospect, that period was a blessing in disguise. If I had been in the Army, I never would have gone to Moscow. I was able to spend some time at home, and I needed that. By October, I felt pretty happy; Mother was recovered, and Daddy was on the mend." [48]

Still, after all his efforts, all the contest triumphs, all the brilliant reviews, Van wondered what to do for an encore when he'd already won all the biggest prizes in America.

How could he have guessed that the answer was to be found on the other side of the world?

6

Moscow Nights

Out of the Army even before he was in it, Van now found himself in the odd position of being one of the most acclaimed young pianists in America—yet with a virtually blank season ahead.

His friends at Columbia Management wasted no time, however, in booking a European debut tour for him. Because Van had been out of the country only for brief visits to Canada, and because major dates in the U.S. seemed unlikely for the next season, his managers apparently determined that Van might as well use the time breaking into Europe, if the recital halls could be booked.

They quickly found that it was indeed possible. "They lined up for me this recital debut tour of Europe," recalls Van. "I'll never forget, William Judd and Arthur Judson planned all this out. I remember saying to Mother, 'I don't think I'm going.' She said, 'Oh, of course you are. Now you just practice. This is absolutely going to be it.' But I just couldn't see it." [1]

Fortunately for Van, some remarkable events were taking place in New York, Moscow, and Brazil that would change everything. Olegna Fuschi, a colleague of Van's during Juilliard days, recalls, "I was in Brazil, and Pavel Seribriakov said to me, 'I hope you will come to Moscow—we're having our first competition there,' and he was going to be on the jury. We talked for a long time, and he gave me a whole packet of things [about the new competition].

"When I got back to New York [in the fall of 1957], I showed it to Rosina, and right away, I could see immediately that she thought of Van. He was the one she thought should go, not me." [2]

At about the same time, Alexander Greiner of Steinway leaped into the act. "He knew Rosina very well, and they would yakety-yak at each other in Russian all the time," recalls Fritz Steinway, of the great piano-manufacturing family. "Between the two of them, they felt that Van would be a most appropriate representative from the United States and that he had a good chance of coming in near the top, if not being the winner." [3]

Though Van still wasn't aware of the forces at work, the campaign gathered momentum. Mark Schubart, who had stuck out his neck on Van's behalf since Van's Juilliard entrance exam, also took up the cause. "It so happened that by this time, in late 1957, and even before that, there had been a lot of concern about American representation at competitions abroad," recalls Schubart. "The problem was that international competitions were not very well known here, and everybody thought these competitions were for students and not for professionals or near-professionals.

"Consequently, the Americans who entered the competitions were basically students, not nearly ready, so they rarely won anything. In fact, when I ultimately went to Moscow to observe the [Tchaikovsky] competition, the American ambassador said to me, 'So are we going to place second or third again?' That was the prevailing attitude about American talent.

"When the Moscow competition came up, Rosina and I and others had talked about the need to get an American in there. And of course Rosina had a strong feeling about the Moscow Competition, since she herself was a graduate of the Moscow

Conservatory. And she was very concerned that the United States would be poorly represented, so we worked together to line up some people. We thought Van would be perfect." [4]

Obviously finding wide support for the idea, Rosina sent a letter to Van suggesting he enter the competition, and others began working on him as well.

"When I was home teaching classes for my mother," Van later recalled, "actually just helping her get back into the general swing of teaching after her broken back, I got a letter from Madame Lhevinne. It seems that Sascha [Alexander] Greiner had received the brochures from Moscow telling about this first International Competition for Piano and Violin to be held in the Soviet Union. . . . He did call Mrs. Lhevinne after receiving these brochures and said, 'You know, I hope you will encourage Van to go because I think he should.'

"So she wrote me a letter. When I got back to New York [in November], Sascha took me to lunch three times and, in his inimitable fashion, he said, 'Dear Van, I beg of you, *please* go. You should.' " [5]

Greiner's persuasion proved effective. "He seemed so confident I would win that he had a great deal to do with making up my mind," Van later recalled.[6]

Eugene Istomin, who had been on the Leventritt jury, also talked to Van about the Moscow prospects, taking him to lunch at Reuben's restaurant in New York. "I told him that I thought he would win the prize hands down if he entered," says Istomin. "I felt so sure about it because he was obviously a tremendous talent, and that he could play the Tchaikovsky Concerto more beautifully than anybody that I knew the Russians had, except, perhaps, [Emil] Gilels and [Sviatoslav] Richter, who were going to be on the jury." [7]

For her part, Lhevinne felt that Van's treatment of the Rachmaninoff Third, which had earned superlative reviews across the country, "was getting better and better," as she said at the time. "Not even Rachmaninoff ever played it better. It couldn't be done." [8]

But even if Van decided to go, there was the matter of paying for an expensive trip to Moscow. Schubart turned to the Institute of International Education, which set up a committee to explore the possibilities. "The purpose of that committee," says Schubart, "was to encourage and to provide travel grants for young Americans to go to competitions abroad and to screen [the candidates] beforehand." [9]

The search was wide and exhaustive with Van and Juilliard violinist Joyce Flissler ultimately invited to compete in Moscow. Because the Soviet government was paying for the contestants' stay in the U.S.S.R. and their flights home, money had to be found for the trip to the competition. It came from the Martha Baird Rockefeller Aid to Music Program, which agreed to pay $1,000 each for Van and Flissler's venture. [10]

Uninterested in pursuing the European tour planned for him, wooed by a variety of persuasive figures in New York music, and offered a grant to cover expenses, Van decided to take the plunge. "Actually, I told Mark [Schubart] that I didn't need the money," says Van, "but he said, 'Take it. You're crazy if you don't.' "

But there were other, more personal reasons he decided to go. "First of all, I always had to envision something before I did it, and I never really saw this European tour for me," says Van. "And I looked at the competition as an opportunity to finally see Russia, which I wanted so badly to visit.

"Ever since I was a child and got that picture book, I wanted so to see the Church of St. Basil and the Kremlin. That was a dream I had had for years, and this was a chance to fulfill it." [11]

Meanwhile, Schubart rounded up other first-rate Juilliard students to compete. Among them, Daniel Pollack, Jerome Lowenthal, and Norman Shetler were studying in Europe but planned to venture to Moscow for the competition.

All the contestants would have a tremendous amount of preparatory work to do. Though Van already had brought the Rachmaninoff and Tchaikovsky concertos to a high finish, the repertoire demands for the competition were immense. The thirty-two-page application/information brochure detailed the required repertoire:

First preliminary auditions:
a. Johann Sebastian Bach—Prelude and Fugue for four or five parts [meaning a fugue written in at least four "voices" or contrapuntal "lines"].
b. Mozart—One of the Sonatas.
c. Four etudes demanding great virtuosity, one by each of the following composers: Chopin; Liszt; Scriabin (Op. 8, Op. 42, Op. 65); Rachmaninoff (Op. 33, Op. 39).
d. Tchaikovsky—Theme with Variations, Op. 19 in F major.[12]

Those who made it through that round would be required to play repertoire for the "Second Preliminary Audition" [generally referred to in the United States as semifinals]:

a. Any one of the following compositions: Taneyev—Prelude and Fugue in G-sharp minor; Tchaikovsky-Katuar—Prelude and Fugue in D minor; Tchaikovsky—Prelude and Fugue in G-sharp minor; Shostakovich—Prelude and Fugue.
b. Four long compositions of great difficulty, including one by a Russian classical composer or Soviet composer, from the following list: Glazunov—Sonatas in B-flat minor and E minor; Mussorgsky—"Pictures at an Exhibition"; Balakirev—"Islamei"; Rachmaninoff—Sonata No. 2 in B-flat minor (2nd version); Scriabin—Sonatas; Medtner—Sonata in G minor; Prokofiev—Sonatas; Myaskovsky—Sonatas; Shostakovich—Sonata No. 2; A. Alexandrov—Sonata No. 2; Kabalevsky—Sonatas Nos. 2 and 3.
c. Tchaikovsky—One movement from the Sonata in G major, or one movement from the Sonata in C-sharp minor.

d. A composition by a contemporary composer, prefera-
bly of the country represented by the Contestant (not
more than 10 min. in length).[13]

And those who passed this portion would move on to the
"Final Audition":

a. Tchaikovsky—Concerto No. 1 or 2 (1st version).
b. A work by a Soviet composer, written specially for
the Contest and announced two months before the
opening date (up to 15 min. in length).
c. Concerto chosen by the Contestant (Concertos are accompanied by orchestra).

Note: Long compositions (concertos or sonatas) are to
be played in their entirety or partially, at the discretion
of the Jury.[14]

In addition, the brochure noted, "The Entrants shall receive
an answer to their application and the announcement of the
[exact] date of the Contest not later than January 25, 1958." [15]

The winners would receive, respectively, 25,000 rubles and
a gold medal; 20,000 rubles and a silver medal; 15,000 rubles
and a bronze medal; 12,000 rubles and a badge of honor; 10,000
rubles and a badge of honor; 8,000 rubles and a badge of honor;
6,000 rubles and a badge of honor; 5,000 rubles and a badge of
honor.[16]

By the end of 1957, the race already was on, with potential
contestants around the world preparing their repertoire.

Meanwhile, Schubart—who had been integrally involved in
the competition since news of it reached the U.S.—was summoned by governmental powers in Washington, D.C. "I was
told to come down to the State Department for some kind of
briefing," recalls Schubart. "Now you remember, here were
some Juilliard people and myself who were going to the big
bad Soviet Union. So I was told to report to Mr. So-and-So's
office, which I did.

"I sat down and I expected to be grilled, and a guy walked into the room, and started saying these strange things: 'Now, Mr. Schubart, the day is divided into three eight-hour periods: 12-8, 8-4, and 4-12, and activities that take place in the first eight-hour period that go over into the second eight-hour period must be reported to the second period.'

"I couldn't even figure out what this guy was talking about," says Schubart, who finally determined that the State Department wanted him to file a report on his observations of the competition and the U.S.S.R., and that, therefore, he would be allowed to file for expenses in the previously stated manner. "So I suddenly realized this State Department guy was talking about my expense account, and he was telling me how to fill it out, where to list the taxi receipts and everything." [17]

Of course, paranoia in the United States had run high since the early 1950s, when reports of the Soviet space program began to reach the popular media. In 1955, Associated Press noted, "Moscow radio said today Russia is considering a plan to explore the moon with a tank remotely controlled by radio. It predicted lunar trips by human beings would follow in a year or two." [18]

On October 4, 1957, the Soviet Union launched its first *Sputnik* rocket into space and on November 3 fired its second, with newspaper headlines asserting that the scientific triumph "Catches U.S. Teams Napping." And though the U.S. government hastened to stress that "Russian sputniks do not by themselves prove the Russians have an intercontinental ballistics missile," that was the overriding fear of the day. [19]

"I remember being in Switzerland for a competition in Geneva in 1957 and picking up a paper in Switzerland with a headline about *Sputnik,*" recalls pianist George Katz. "Well, you cannot imagine how much animosity existed in the relationship between the United States and the U.S.S.R. The competition and the military posturing and the threat of communism—at that point some people believed that it would take over the world, so we Americans were very fearful of it.

"And then *Sputnik* suggested that the Russians had this tremendous technological lead, and we [Americans] felt tremendously inferior and at risk. It seemed to say that they could send intercontinental ballistic missiles to destroy us, and we would not be able to respond." [20]

This, then, was the backdrop against which the State Department had enlisted Mark Schubart's services in reporting on what he observed in Moscow.

"What was very interesting to me and sort of ironic," recalled William Schuman, the former Juilliard president who died in 1992, "is that we wanted Van to go on tour with the Juilliard Orchestra to the World's Fair in Brussels in '58. We asked the State Department for some [financial] help to make that possible, but they wouldn't give us the extra $500 or $1,000 that we needed to pay Van. They said, 'Just take any student, or any pianist in the orchestra can play the solo—you don't need a big name alum.' " [21]

Despite the grim political circumstances between the superpowers in the waning days of 1957, many individuals held faith that Van at least had a shot at winning the Tchaikovsky Competition and did what they could to help and encourage him.

Lhevinne began giving him long lessons every Sunday. And Dimitri Mitropoulos, who had conducted Van's New York Philharmonic debut in 1954, began to counsel him.

"It was Mitropoulos who helped me plan my repertoire [for the competition]," says Van. "He told me what he thought I should play. And particularly in the second round, it was a choice between a Shostakovich Prelude and Fugue, Tchaikovsky Prelude and Fugue, or the Taneyev Prelude and Fugue in G-sharp minor. Mitropoulos said to me, 'You play G-sharp Minor Prelude and Fugue of Taneyev. Taneyev is the director of the Moscow Conservatory and a very respected man in Russia. I have played the Prelude and Fugue—it's very difficult, but you can do it.'

"So Mitropoulos got me the music, and he was right. It's a wonderful piece but very, very difficult, so difficult, so exploitative of the piano. Mitropoulos also had gotten me the music for the G Major Grand Sonata [of Tchaikovsky]." [22]

Thus Van set to work, his intense practice sessions—combined with a few concert dates—possibly contributing to a bad flu he caught in December. Later he would refer to this period as "a physical collapse . . . from overwork and worry." [23]

Following an intense vitamin regimen, however, Van was back at the keyboard by mid-January, rehearsing heatedly until his March departure for Moscow.

Those who heard Van's work at the time cannot forget it.

"I had gotten back to New York from a concert tour a week or two before Van left for Moscow," remembers Jeaneane Dowis. "So I happened to be at Rosina's class—she had a class in which people could try out their repertoire—and that's where I heard Van play the Rachmaninoff Third [Piano Concerto] and all kinds of Russian pieces and so on. And I'm telling you, it was glorious. I was not always a great fan of Van's playing. I mean, there was no gainsaying that he was talented, but I sometimes like a different approach.

"But I tell you, he played like a god, and I was just completely won over. I thought, *Barring some extraordinary performances I had heard of Horowitz with Toscanini, this is some of the best playing I ever heard in my life.* It was totally satisfying, and I remember thinking, *If there's a minute's justice in this whole world, he ought to carry that competition in Moscow.* Not only did the playing have that tremendous sweep of his, but also every detail had been polished. It had everything.

"And there was another thing. All of us who were playing at that time wanted to be famous. But Van really was rushing forward with open arms to embrace it. He was ready." [24]

Martin Canin, who also had been one of Lhevinne's assistants at Juilliard, heard Van's pre-Tchaikovsky repertoire too. "I just felt in my heart that Van would win," he says, "and I don't think I was alone in that. A lot of people knew how terrific Van was. I can imagine there was some skepticism about an American doing well in a Russian competition that stressed Russian music at the height of the Cold War. But Van's playing was so poetic and beautiful and free and with an exceptionally beautiful touch and a wonderful technique." [25]

And yet, Van was far from certain he was going to win or particularly optimistic about what might happen. Just going to Russia apparently was the payoff for him.

"I can't remember that he was rushing off with bells on, or anything like that," says Lucy Mann, violinist Robert Mann's wife, who worked in the Juilliard office at the time. "He didn't seem wildly enthusiastic. He came into my office beforehand, and he said, 'Lucy, they're sending me to Moscow, I'm going to Moscow,' and then he sort of shrugged. He was wearing an overcoat with some buttons missing, and it seemed like a slightly forlorn scene. A couple of days later he was on his way." [26]

On March 22, the night before Van boarded the plane to Moscow, Lhevinne invited a few close friends to the Leventritt apartment, where Van spent several hours performing his entire Moscow repertoire. It must have been an incredible night.

"There were half a dozen friends and colleagues there, including me and my wife," recalls Juilliard's Josef Raciff. "And we sat and listened to Van play it all, including the [Beethoven] 'Appassionata,' the Rachmaninoff Etude Tableau—the big one in E-flat minor, the Liszt Twelfth Hungarian Rhapsody, lots of Rachmaninoff, Chopin F Minor Fantaisie, the works. We sat and listened and knew that it was one of the most fabulous things you could ever hear." [27]

His suitcase liberally packed with bottles of vitamins, Van boarded an Air France plane to Paris on March 23. During the two-hour layover there, he dashed off a letter to his parents, then caught another plane to Prague, and then a third to the Soviet Union.

When he arrived in Moscow roughly forty hours later, one familiar and one unfamiliar face awaited him: Harriet Wingreen, another Juilliard pianist, had arrived in Moscow a couple of weeks before as accompanist for Joyce Flissler, who had entered the Tchaikovsky International Violin Competition. Wingreen, eager to see another American, had decided to come to the airport, as did Henrietta Belayaeva, the interpreter who had been assigned to him.

"When I came to the airport," recalls Belayaeva, "I didn't know how he looked, and I hadn't even seen his photograph. But people said, 'The tallest boy to get off the airplane will be Van Cliburn,' because when he sent his papers [application], he had to write down how tall he was. So they said, 'You will definitely find him.'

"That was true. When I saw people coming down the stairs from the plane, I found the tallest boy, and I came up to him and said, 'Is this Van Klee-burn?' because in the competition material they had misspelled, or misinterpreted his name when they put it into Russian.

"When I said this to him, he looked at me and said, 'What?' I said, 'Mr. Van Klee-burn, welcome to Moscow.'

"He was a very open person; very open, and it was striking because it seemed like he was not walking on the ground but floating above—one could feel it right away. He was so happy. You could see that he was an extremely open person, very generous to other people. Right away he was taking care of everybody." [28]

Yet there may have been a certain wariness in Van's manner as well.

"Since I had known Van in Juilliard," recalls Wingreen, "I went to meet him at the airport. And this big, tall, gangly thing gets off the plane. And, of course, nobody knew anything about the Soviet Union at that time—everybody thought it was this big black monster. So Van's first words to me, he looked a little scared, and he said, 'Is everything all right?' And I said, 'Everything is just fine.' " [29]

Nevertheless, Van knew precisely what he wanted to do first in Moscow, and it wasn't to begin practicing or go to sleep.

"These people were so nice to me when I arrived," he recalls, "but they were somewhat shocked that I wanted to go immediately to the Church of St. Basil. But they said, 'Oh yes, sure, we can drive you there.'

"And there I was, eighteen years after I got that picture book as a child, standing there looking at the Church of St. Basil. For me, it was one of the great experiences of my life. It was so wonderful, so beautiful.

"Then someone asked me, 'Aren't you thinking about the competition?' I really never gave it another thought that night. I knew I shouldn't say that, but suddenly I felt as if I were living in the last century. I could see the czar coming with his white horse outside the gate, and as I saw this, I could feel myself living in the past.

"This night when we arrived, on the 25th of March, they had up strings of light bulbs, not sophisticated lighting like every city in the entire world has today. It was like a string of diamonds. It was the most beautiful sight I had ever seen, and it was sophisticated in such a way as to give me a completely sleepless night, even though I had been on that airplane—or three different plancs, for so many hours.

"This was thrilling. I still have a thrill when I see it today, but it was so different to me then. There was snow as I had never seen in my entire life. Before I went to Russia I had played a concert in Minot, North Dakota, and the night I played the recital, I had never seen snow like that, either.

"I had seen snow before, but this night in Moscow, to see that snow and the diamond-lights strung above it, it was a sight that I shall never forget." [30]

That was but the first inspiration that lifted Van in Moscow. After checking into the Peking Hotel, dashing off a cable to his parents in Kilgore and catching a few hours' sleep, he found himself being escorted into the Great Hall of the Moscow Conservatory. "The first night that I set foot in Moscow the violin competition was still going on," recalls Van. "But after the violin competition was over they had rehearsal times for the entrants of the piano competition [in the Great Hall].

"The next morning they told me that my practice time would be at midnight. The person [rehearsing] before me was Nadia Gedda-Nova, and when we got to the conservatory, I was thrilled beyond words to arrive there. To get into the hall, you ascend this staircase, and as I did, the music I heard was the E-flat Minor op. 33 of [Rachmaninoff's] Etude Tableaux, swirling above me.

"When you get to the top of the stairs, there's an open area before you go directly into the hall, and this pinlight was on the statue of Mussorgsky, and this music still swirled around me—it was the most magical, overwhelming thing I had ever experienced, and that was my first look at that hall." [31]

Thereafter, Van spent his waking hours toiling in a practice room at the Moscow Conservatory, and "it seemed that whenever he touched the keys, he immediately dissolved into the music," remembers Balayaeva, his interpreter. "If I came up behind him and touched him, he would get scared, you see, because he didn't realize I was there. It's amazing.

"People used to tell me that, in America, there are many musicians like Van Cliburn. I traveled with many, many musicians [as translator], but it wasn't the same, not at all.

"When he came to Moscow, he worked very hard. He practiced all the time. And I don't think he expected to win or that he was aiming at first prize. He was just working hard and trying to play well and never satisfied with his playing." [32]

When Mark Schubart arrived in Moscow, a few days after Van, he was struck by what he saw. "It was quite extraordinary because at that time there were no tourists at all to speak of," says Schubart. "You have to remember what the world was like at that time; it was very different. Russia was a remote, distant, strange country that was sort of shut off from the rest of the world." [33]

Daniel Pollack, who had arrived from Vienna, had a different kind of shock in store. "Of course, I wasn't surprised to see Van there because I very much thought I would run into him," says Pollack. "The shock was finding out that I had learned most of the wrong repertoire. When I was in Vienna, I had been ill-advised on what I was supposed to play. Someone had read me the repertoire list in German, and they had gotten it wrong.

"When I found out, of course, I was terribly upset, after all the work and effort—I had practiced ten hours a day since December, when I first found out about the competition.

"So I made an appeal to Dmitri Shostakovich [chairman of the organizing committee of the competition], who took it up with the jury. And they decided that I should stay [in the competition] with the incorrect repertoire, and they allowed me to participate.

"Naturally, I was surprised by that decision. Here's everybody playing Mozart, Chopin, whatever, and here I am with all kinds of works that I didn't even need.

"I don't know why they let me stay. Maybe they felt I was honest in coming to tell them the error and offering to withdraw. And maybe they felt that if I already had made the trip and I was there and I had come clean and told them everything, then they would let me stay.

"Still, it was totally awesome to be in that place—having seen the Kremlin, the Red Square in all the picture books, and the things we know about Russia—it was an exciting time to be in the Soviet Union." [34]

Not that exploring the city was easy.

"The political atmosphere at that time and place was absolutely ironclad," recalls Pollack. "It was the Khrushchev era. We couldn't roam around and go where we wanted, like you can do today. It was a very supervised, regimented place, not an open society. Although, interestingly enough, Russian people tried to be in contact with us in the hotel and so forth. We were a rarity because we were from the West, and many had never seen an American before.

"The people who worked in the hotel or the conservatory or wherever were absolutely, wonderfully warm and extremely excited at our presence there. I'm not just talking about Americans but French or Japanese or whatever; this was a unique breakthrough." [35]

All the more because Khrushchev, in particular, remained a figure of mystery to the West, having assumed office only weeks before.[36]

Now, as the piano competition was about to begin, the violin contest had ended, with Joyce Flissler having placed seventh. Immediately, she and her accompanist were rushed into a recording studio, then booked for a Soviet tour including stops in Leningrad, Kiev, Riga, and Odessa.[37]

As for the piano competition, a case can be made that there never has been a piano jury of this stature gathered together before or since. The chairman was Emil Gilels, a revered Soviet pianist whose reputation was equalled or bested only by Sviatoslav Richter, another juror who, to this day, is considered the greatest living Russian pianist. Also on the jury were the distinguished Russian pianists Lev Oborin and Heinrich Neuhaus, the latter having taught both Gilels and Richter.

Among composers, the jury was represented by the British master Sir Arthur Bliss and Soviet composer Dmitri Kabalevsky, who had composed a rondo for the finals. The rest of the jurors were Armand de Gontaut Biron (from France), George Georgescu (Romania), Camargo Guarniere (Brazil), Lajos Hernadi (Hungary), Boris Lyatoshinski (U.S.S.R.), Frantisek Maxian (Czechoslovakia), Fernand Quinet (Belgium), Sequeira Costa (Portugal), Pavel Seribriakov (U.S.S.R.), Henryk Sztompka (Poland), and Pantcho Vladigerov (Bulgaria).[38]

The organizing committee for the competition included pianist Alexander Goldenweiser, who had been a friend of Rachmaninoff, Scriabin, and Tolstoy and teacher of at least two generations of Russian pianists, including composer Dmitri Kabalevsky and virtuoso Lazar Berman.[39]

The contestants drew lots for order of play. Van drew number 15; he would play on April 2. Before then he had some personal business to attend to. First he sent off a telegram to Rosina Lhevinne, who planned to play a concert at Juilliard for the Josef Lhevinne Scholarship Fund on March 28. The cable read: "My love and thoughts are with you. Tremendous excitement and joy." [40]

The night before his performance, he phoned home to Kilgore, asking for his parents' prayers. Rildia Bee later recalled that "I didn't pray that he would win, but that he could take either success or failure, that he would do and say the right things and remain true to his convictions." [41]

Van took the stage at 9:30 A.M., "an impossible time," he says, for a nocturnal person such as he. Still, by most accounts, Van acquitted himself well from the first notes he played, his preliminary-round repertoire comprising Bach's Prelude and Fugue in B-flat Minor from Book 1 of "The Well-Tempered Clavier"; Mozart's Sonata in C Major, K. 330; Chopin's Etude in A Minor, "Winter Wind," op. 25, no. 11; Scriabin's Etude in D-sharp Minor; Rachmaninoff's Etude Tableau in E-flat Minor op. 39; Liszt's "Mazeppa"; and Tchaikovsky's Theme with Variations op. 19. [42]

"His Bach was magnificent," recalls violinist Igor Oistrakh, [43] whose father, violinist David Oistrakh, was chairman of the Tchaikovsky Violin Competition that had just ended.

"When he played the Mozart Sonata," says pianist Sergei Dorensky, who also was in attendance at the preliminaries, "it was like he was speaking. He spoke with our auditorium, with our public. It was so expressive in every phrase, in every detail." [44]

From Van's vantage point, the first critical moment came with his performance of the Mozart Sonata in the preliminary round—that's when he felt he had established contact with his audience. "That was really the first reception for me, after I finished the Mozart," he recalls. "In fact, I was always a little amused when, after the competition, certain people in the United States would say, 'Well, we've got to wait and hear his Mozart and his Beethoven,' because that was the turning point in Moscow.

"And, in this competition, you weren't just playing parts of pieces. You weren't stopped; you played everything. And if you were playing a [classical] piece, you played it with all the repeats.

"After I finished the Mozart, they kept clapping and clapping. Then I went into the four etudes of Rachmaninoff, Scriabin, Chopin, and Liszt, and that was another thing the audience responded to.

"The required piece for the first round was the F Major Variations of Tchaikovsky, which went very well, and they seemed to like that. They clapped after that. Even after I had left the stage, they clapped quite a lot." [45]

Already Van was creating a bit of a stir. Members of the audience began shouting, "Vanya!" and "Vanyusha!"

As soon as the jury convened in private session, however, matters became tense. "There was some debate about Van's interpretation of the classics [meaning Mozart] because Cliburn's approach was extremely personal," recalls Sequeira Costa, who was on the jury. "He did not take the traditional approach, and some members of the jury were not happy about this." [46]

What's more, some members of the jury may have decided, in this Cold War era, that a Russian should be steered toward the first prize.

"Before I say what I am going to say, I must explain that I spent an enormous amount of time with Slava," says pianist Andrei Gavrilov, referring to his mentor, Sviatoslav Richter, who was one of the foremost names on the jury. "Slava and I had spent enormous amount of time playing together. We were almost living under one roof for seven or eight years. He described me as his 'spiritual son,' so we had discussions about everything.

"I asked him many times why he never attended a jury [after the Tchaikovsky Competition in 1958]. He said, 'First of all, it's pretty boring. Second, it's a terrible lot of time. And then, it's very few chances that you'll really catch something outstanding.' Then he said, 'It's absolutely disgusting because they [other judges] were trying to boycott Van Cliburn.'

"The scale [for judging], as you know, was from 0 to 25 points. And Slava said to me, 'They started to do with Van little tricks, giving him 15s, 16s, and 19s, and giving one or two points more—not too much—to the other contestants, just to make it seem that nothing [illegal] was happening. And to [Soviet contestant] Lev Vlasenko, they give just one or three points extra because he is supposed to be new Soviet hero.

"Slava found out about it, and he was sitting together with Heinrich Neuhaus. They were, of course, very free-minded people. So they discovered a very powerful weapon. They gave to others complete zeros, and to Van 25 points. So they destroyed completely this whole plan of the jury.

"Now this is unknown—I doubt Slava told anybody except me, but I think now is the time when it can be said openly what they were doing. It caused a mess in the second round. So in the second round Slava did the same." [47] Richter, who does not grant interviews, declined to comment on this subject.

Sequeira Costa, also on the jury, confirms most of the facts of Gavrilov's story but offers a different interpretation of them. "I would say that Vlasenko was really the chosen one. He was supposed to win," says Costa. "Nobody expected that someone from Western world would show up and would really do it.

"But about the 0 and 25 marks, it's very simple—I was on the jury and attended all the jury conferences, and it went like this: We all sat down at a big table and gave our marks and our remarks about the playing. And Richter stood alone—you know, this was a huge room—very far away from the jury table. They had a piano in the corner of the room, and he stood there. And from there, he sent his written marks.

"Gilels, the president of the jury, read the marks, and when it came to Richter's marks—there were just a couple of marks to all contestants. Either 0 or 25. This distorted completely the system of voting.

"Gilels asked Richter in front of everybody, 'Why do you do this? Because this is not good for the general results.' Richter answered, 'For me, people either make music or not music.' He gave twelve contestants zeros, and some were quite good pianists." [48]

Was Richter so aloof from the rest of the jury because of his belief a voting conspiracy was underway? "No," says Costa, "he is very shy man. He's a very cultivated man, extremely intelligent too.

"And he doesn't like crowds. He doesn't like people too much, you know? He's very nice, but when he gives a concert, for instance, he only receives one or two people at the end, no crowd—the closest friends, and that's all. He doesn't like to be among people." [49]

At the very least, then, there was considerable jockeying among the jurors regarding Van's position. At worst, there was a concerted attempt among some jurors to keep the popular American out and maintain a clear path for the anointed Soviet, Lev Vlasenko.

In either event, Van passed to the second round, and tickets for his upcoming performance, April 7, were impossible to come by. The box office fielded more requests than there were seats available.[50] The early connection that Van had made in the first round apparently was enduring, even thriving.

Daniel Pollack and Jerome Lowenthal, too, would be in the second round, but for a different reason: The rules specified that competitors who had won awards in previous international competitions would skip the preliminaries and automatically move right along to the next step. The other American pianist, Norman Shetler, was not so fortunate.

Despite the obvious pressure and politicking of this first Tchaikovsky Competition, the feeling among the competitors was surprisingly warm, even if only fourteen pianists had survived to the semifinals round.[51]

"When we weren't onstage competing, we played for each other in the practice rooms," recalls Naum Shtarkman, a Soviet competitor whose son, in a sweet twist of fate, competed in the Van Cliburn International Piano Competition in Ft. Worth in 1989.

"After we played for each other, we talked to each other. And Van Cliburn told me that I would get the first prize, and I told Van that he would get the first prize. I very much liked his sincerity and his charm," adds Shtarkman,[52] who, along with fellow Soviet contestant Eduard Miansarov, became Van's closest friend during the trials ahead.

Another contestant, Thorunn Tryggvason of Iceland (who later married the brilliant pianist-conductor Vladimir Ashkenazy), remembers, "Van was just very friendly and very, very kind and loved caviar. Since he was the sweetest possible person, and since I hated caviar at the time, I gave him mine." [53]

Van's prospects for the second round looked quite good, for the required repertoire—mostly Russian, monumental, and demanding of both technique and gesture—was perfectly suited to Van's pianism. More important, Van would be playing Russian music in a way that would visibly inspire his Russian listeners. (Specifically, he offered Taneyev's Prelude and Fugue in G-sharp Minor; the first movement of Tchaikovsky's Sonata in G Major; Chopin Fantaisie in F Minor; Liszt Twelfth Hungarian Rhapsody; and the fugue finale of Samuel Barber's Piano Sonata.)[54]

"He had almost a soulmate-like connection with the Soviet audience," recalls Soviet pianist Lev Naumov, who was in the audience. "Somehow, Cliburn gave the people what they thirsted for. Not just musicians, but also the simple people. He opened all kinds of musical relationships to people, and it was open to nonmusicians." [55]

Says Lev Vlasenko, "You cannot imagine how well Van played. I can only say that his playing sounded the most Russian of everyone. I mean, he was more Russian than we were. And after all these dismal years [in postwar, Stalinist Russia], Van was like a ray of sun penetrating the clouds.

"But the most important thing was how well he played, and not only the Russian music. The Twelfth Rhapsody of Liszt and F Minor Fantaisie of Chopin and Sixth Prokofiev Sonata—the audience reaction was not just hysteria, because such people as Richter and Gilels and Neuhaus are not easily taken." [56]

Now, on April 10, came time to announce the finalists.

"They called us together, to tell us who passed from second round to third," remembers Pollack. "You can imagine all of the excitement, with everybody waiting to find out who survived. Someone stood up and read the names, and it was incredibly tense because you had this extraordinarily distinguished jury. Queen Elizabeth of Belgium was just arriving to hear the finals, so there was an excitement that practically crackled anywhere you went in Moscow. Plus all the business of America versus Russia and all of that.

"Performing in this situation had been very difficult because of the excruciatingly tense circumstances. I was thrilled, of course, when I heard them call my name. But, really, the only thing in my head at the time was that in a couple of days I had to play the Tchaikovsky Concerto for the first time in my life," says Pollack,[57] who had prepared the piece but never had performed it with orchestra.

When the list of finalists had been read, only nine remained of the original fifty-plus contestants. Van and Daniel Pollack were among them, as were Naum Shtarkman, Lev Vlasenko, a Chinese pianist named Liu Shih Kun, the Soviet pianist Eduard Miansarov, Bulgarian Milena Mollova, France's Nadia Gedda-Nova, and Japan's Toyoaki Matsuura.

Lowenthal probably had erred in his choice of repertoire, or, to put it another way, perhaps he wasn't the right kind of pianist for this particular competition. Either way, "He was playing Bartok and Schoenberg," recalls Juilliard dean Mark Schubart, referring to two fiercely modern composers (at least for the time). "Playing that in Moscow in 1958—forget it." [58]

Now, by April 11, news of Van's success was beginning to make its way back to the United States. Associated Press reported that

> Van Cliburn of Kilgore, Tex., and Daniel Pollack of Los Angeles advanced Wednesday night to the final round of the piano competition in the Tchaikovsky International piano competition.
>
> The two are the only Americans among the nine finalists picked by a panel of judges headed by Emil Gilels, Soviet pianist. . . .

Gilels said the excellence of the contestants caused
the panel to raise the finalist total from 8 to 9. The
winner gets 25,000 rubles (officially $6,230).[59]

Back in the U.S.S.R., the Tchaikovsky International Piano
Competition—and Van Cliburn particularly—had become the
most pressing subject of conversation. Because some of the
proceedings were broadcast on radio and television (though
the latter was still relatively new to the U.S.S.R.), everyone
knew what was happening.

"I wasn't there in the hall, but I was watching it on TV," recalls
Vladimir Feltsman, the Soviet emigré pianist. "It was one of the
first live musical shows in the history of Russia. Not only was
Van good, unbelievably good, definitely the best, but this was
the Khrushchev era of Cold War. And for many Russians, Van
was the first live American that they could really touch and feel
and see. And he had a very beautiful image, a beautiful big smile.
It was one of the happiest occasions for Russian people." [60]

Another young pianist watching on TV, Alexander Toradze,
couldn't believe his eyes or ears. "The people in the hall gave
him, threw to him on stage their most dear pieces of memora-
bilia, the dearest mementos of their life," he recalls. "Not only
pictures, not only old program notes, not only that type of
thing, but old diamond jewelry. And just on stage, unknown
people gave him all these dear things.

"And the flowers, it was again a one-of-a-kind experience.
They showered the stage with flowers. He couldn't walk onstage, there were so many flowers. The piano had flowers
outside and inside. He caught the flowers they threw at him.

"It was just one of those things that, if it happened in the
United States, you would think that someone spent billions of
dollars on publicity, plus another billion dollars on flowers. You
wouldn't believe that can happen in that Soviet society. But the
more the government suppressed the people, the more excitement the people had to express.

"It was like a pop concert, except better, because at pop concerts they don't really care who is on stage. Next week, they'll do the same thing for the next pop concert.

"But this was different because, first of all, it was an entirely different audience, a very sophisticated audience [in the hall]." [61]

Even on TV, the sight, sound, and spectacle of Van's performance "hypnotized" the whole country, says Van's interpreter during the competition, Henrietta Balayaeva.[62]

By the time Van walked out on stage to play, in the final round, the Tchaikovsky Piano Concerto no. 1 in B-flat Minor, on April 11, with Kiril Kondrashin conducting the Moscow State Symphony, the crowd had become nearly hysterical. Roughly 1,500 people had jammed the Great Hall of the Moscow Conservatory; thousands more waited outside.

When the throng finally calmed down, Van settled himself at the piano, looked out into the audience and saw Queen Elizabeth of Belgium sitting in a box, "which was a thrill because she was one of the world's great ladies," says Van. "She and her daughter and various others were sitting there, and it was an honor to play for her." [63] All the more because the queen was widely considered Europe's foremost patron of the arts.

Few in the hall seemed to notice, or at least express any concern, that Van had walked onto the stage with "a bandaged right index finger," as the *Kilgore News Herald* later reported to readers back home.[64] (Van had cut the finger during a rehearsal,[65] and now "it was split down the side," Van later recalled.[66])

By all accounts, Van's reading of the Tchaikovsky offered not mere spectacle but profoundly expressive music-making, an unusual merging of solo part with orchestral accompaniment.

"Kondrashin was one of the best accompanists in the Soviet Union at the time," recalls pianist Oxana Yablonskaya, who was in the audience. "The orchestra was excellent, and Van Cliburn seemed inspired to be there. Just being in the great old beautiful hall of Moscow Conservatory, he seemed touched to be there. And he really played differently from everyone else.

"In the Russian system, before you can be in competition, you have to play so many auditions. You have to go through so much to be able to go to a competition. So finally, of course, you're a fighter; you have to be a fighter; you have to try to play perfectly.

"But Cliburn, I think, was the one person who really performed. He loved this music, and he enjoyed every minute of it, and this is what you heard. He didn't play like he was trying to win." [67]

After the Tchaikovsky and the instantaneous ovations, Van performed the newly composed solo piece required of all finalists, a rondo by Kabalevsky. Like the other contestants, he had received the piece in February; he then had memorized it in a couple of days and, again like the other finalists, played it publicly for the first time during the competition. His performance won a standing ovation.[68]

Then came a brief pause—due to a broken string on Van's piano[69]—and, finally, Rachmaninoff's Third Piano Concerto in D Minor, one of the most technically difficult and musically elusive pieces in the piano concerto repertoire.

When Van and Kondrashin finished this monumental piece of music, the Great Hall went wild. The ovations would not stop, even after Van had left the stage.

"Backstage it was absolutely crazy. Everything was going on," remembers Van. "And there was a rule [at the Tchaikovsky] that you could not take another bow after you had left the stage. You could never return to the stage." [70]

At this point, even the judges broke down. "The whole jury stood up—I had never seen anything like that before," recalls Costa. "We stood up, and there was an ovation, and Slava Richter was crying." [71]

Elsewhere at the judges' table, "Neuhaus and Goldenweiser, who were always against each other, jumped up and hugged each other," recalls Oxana Yablonskaya, "because this was really something special." [72]

Finally, apparently overcome by what was happening, "Suddenly Gilels came backstage," remembers Van. "This was interesting, since there was still one more night to go in the finals. He took me by the hand and took me out onto the stage and kissed me.

"Magic. It gave me an assurance that maybe I had really won. Then later in the night some people had written my name on the big poster outside. It was really sort of embarrassing." [73]

In the audience that remarkable night was Max Frankel, then Moscow correspondent of the *New York Times*. He had been tipped off by Schubart that something unusual might happen on this night, and indeed it did. Frankel wrote his story, which, to everyone's surprise—including Frankel's—wound up on the bottom of page 1 of the *Times* the next day, April 12:

"A boyish-looking, curly-haired young man from Kilgore, Tex., took musical Moscow by storm tonight," began Frankel's piece, which was headlined: "Russians Cheer U.S. Pianist, 23: Texan Wins Ovation for His Brilliance at Moscow Fete."

The story continued:

> Van Cliburn, a 23-year-old pianist, played in the finals of the Tchaikovsky International Piano and Violin Festival. He dazzled the audience with a display of technical skill that Russians have long considered their special forte. He added to it a majestic romantic style that his 1,500 listeners could not resist.
>
> Mr. Cliburn had emerged from the first two rounds of the competition as the rage of the town. Nothing has been so scarce here in a long time as a ticket to his performance.
>
> Militiamen were ranged in front of the Tchaikovsky Conservatory to keep order among the enthusiastic crowds. Members of the well-dressed audience greeted each other as influential persons for having managed to get to the concert. Standees filled the aisles into deep balconies. The conservatory's office was telling hundreds of callers: "Cliburn is playing tonight. Call back for tickets tomorrow."

When the young pianist finished his final piece, Rachmaninoff's Third Piano Concerto in D minor, he received a standing ovation. Even some of the jurors applauded. Shouts of "Bravo" rang out for eight and a half minutes until the judges permitted a violation of the contest rules and sent Mr. Cliburn out for a second bow.

Backstage, Emil Gilels, one of the leading Soviet pianists and chairman of the international jury in the contest, embraced the young American. So did other jurors, and Kiril P. Kondrashin, who had conducted. Members of the orchestra stood on stage to join in the applause.

Although six other young pianists were still to perform in the finals, including three highly rated Russians, conservatory students were shouting "First prize" throughout the ovation for Mr. Cliburn. Alexander M. Goldenweiser, white-haired octogenarian who is dean of Soviet pianists and a contemporary of Rachmaninoff, said he had never heard the concerto played better since Rachmaninoff last performed. He walked down the center aisle mumbling "genius."

It is far from certain that Mr. Cliburn will win first prize in the competition. The nine finalists are all first rate and include another American, Daniel Pollack of Los Angeles. But Mr. Cliburn is clearly the popular favorite and all Moscow is wondering whether an American will walk off with top honors.[74]

That indeed was the question, and despite the hysteria, it crossed the minds particularly of the Soviet and Soviet bloc judges who had to cast the deciding votes.

"Yes, the jury was nervous about possibly picking an American as the winner," says Sequeira Costa, referring to the retribution that might be wrought on those who denied a Soviet the first prize. "We were nervous because the Cold War was still going on, and because Khrushchev was at that time the new chairman." [75]

In a society in which "all decisions went through the Politburo," in the words of Maxim Shostakovich,[76] the son of composer Dmitri Shostakovich, there was only one way to be safe: Get permission from Khrushchev himself.

"It was really the Cold War then," says Sergei Dorensky, today chairman of the piano faculty at the Moscow Conservatory. "So the minister of culture asked Khrushchev what to do—Gilels himself told me this. The minister was very afraid of an American pianist who was so wonderful, the best pianist in the competition, and this was the first Tchaikovsky Competition.

"So the minister went to Khrushchev and said, 'We don't know what to do.' And Khrushchev said, 'What? What do you mean?' And the minister of culture said, 'We now have a Tchaikovsky Competition and an American pianist who plays very well, and we don't know what to do.' And Khruschev asked, 'What do the professionals say about him? Is he the best?' And the minister of culture said, 'Yes, he is the best.' So Khrushchev said, 'In this case, give him the first prize.' " [77]

Why would Khrushchev and the Soviet government allow such a stunning public defeat? "You must remember that Khrushchev was very, very simple folk but with a very long nose," says Russian pianist Andrei Gavrilov, referring to Khrushchev's "nose" for which way the political winds were blowing. "He actually survived during Stalin's terror and made his career in the most difficult time. And actually he was the one who eventually started to melt Stalin's image.

"So I think all of this mixed together with the appearance of Van, whom everyone in Soviet Union fell in love with, including Khrushchev—everything happened at just the right time. I believe this is the same sentiment that began *perestroika,* if you want, the same sentiment that touched Gorbachev thirty years later. It's like defying the rules a little bit, a leader making a wise decision to help relieve a little of his people's suffering." [78]

Even before Khrushchev's permission was officially granted, however, many in the audience were convinced that Van could not be denied the prize.

"Many of us had no doubt Van would win," remembers Vladimir Ashkenazy, "because the gap [between Van and his competitors] was too great. You see, we were afraid that, in spite of even such an obvious gap, some political hacks might reverse the tide, if they were ordered by the Central Committee of the party. So we were afraid. At the same time, we thought, *Oh no, with a gap like this, even they won't be able to do anything.*

"The whole thing had to go to Khrushchev because it was the first Tchaikovsky Competition, and national pride was involved." [79]

Or as interpreter Henrietta Belayaeva says, "It was impossible to give it to anybody else because Van stood so much higher than the others. I believe if Van hadn't been given the prize, the people would have pulled down the conservatory. They would have destroyed the building brick by brick." [80]

As it was, they nearly did as much. At one point, "The police military cordons fell down," says pianist Alexander Slobodyanik, who witnessed the spectacle, "and the public climbed to the roofs [near the hall] by fire escapes. I also went up the fire escape; it was very high and dangerous to go up there. Outside the building there were riots. It was just crazy." [81]

Once news of this phenomenon reached the United States, tremendous chains of events began to occur.

"I could sense what was happening [back home]," recalls Frankel, "because the minute my first story landed, [impresario] Sol Hurok sent a cable asking if I could put him in touch with Van." [82]

Hurok evidently was keeping busy because he also sent Schubart a telegram reading: "Congratulations on your work re Tchaikowsky [sic] contest a great service to American culture —Hurok." [83]

And RCA Victor, the premier classical label in the United States at the time, also went into action, though "since Van had won the Leventritt we knew about him," recalls veteran RCA Victor producer John Pfeiffer. "We had thought, *This is someone to watch and see how his career develops.* But it wasn't really until the Tchaikovsky that the tumblers fell into place and the lock opened." [84]

Specifically, RCA executive Alan Kayes fired off a telegram to Schubart, requesting "that he use his good offices to explain to Van Cliburn that I had made a formal contract proposal for his services as a recording artist to Bill Judd," recalls Kayes. The cable also asked Schubart "to ask [Van] in our behalf that he hold off making a contractual commitment to any other record company until he returned to the States and had an opportunity to review our proposed contract in detail and discuss it with us." [85]

At this point, though, it was all Van could do to stand up straight.

Associated Press reported,

> Van Cliburn started out on another task today: Gaining back the 10 pounds he lost playing the piano.
>
> "All I want to do is relax for the next few days, . . . I've never known so much joy," Cliburn said. But he admitted he was tired.
>
> "It's like a ton of bricks being lifted off my back."
>
> Cliburn, who has played the piano since he was 3, is finished playing for a few days at least. He had played through the preliminary rounds and practiced in between. But Soviet recording agencies are besieging him with offers.[86]

The winner was to be named on Monday, April 14, but Frankel shrewdly figured it out earlier, making it possible for the *New York Times* to carry the news on Monday.

"We got a scoop on that—well, we had it a few hours earlier than we normally would have gotten it," says Frankel. "The judges were going to announce their decision the next day [Monday, April 14] after the finals were played [Sunday, April

13]. But when the finals were concluded, I hung around the concert hall and I realized that Van and Kondrashin, the conductor, were being filmed. That was the tip-off, that he had won, and so I wrote the story." [87] But not before checking with Schubart for a reaction and insight.

"I got a telephone call—Max Frankel called me at four o'clock in the morning and said that Van had won," remembers Schubart. "And he told me that his stories were on the front page of the *New York Times,* and I couldn't believe it. It was incredible. He sounded like he was a little bit surprised too. He said, 'I can't believe this—why is anyone paying attention to this?' And then he wrote his piece," says Schubart.[88]

Schubart immediately sent a telegram to Juilliard president William Schuman reading: "We Are In Orbit." [89]

This time, Frankel's story was on the top of page 1, stretching across four columns, with a three-column picture of Van shaking hands with juror Lev Oborin.

> Mr. Cliburn, a Southerner who lives in New York, triumphed in what had been regarded as a contest of extremely high standards over three young Soviet pianists and one from communist China.
>
> The awards were voted late last night by a panel of sixteen jurors, including six leading Soviet musicians. Their choice clearly coincided with that of the Moscow public. Muscovites wildly cheered Mr. Cliburn's performance in the finals Friday night.[90]

After noting the placement of the finalists (Liu Shih Kun and Lev Vlasenko shared second place; Naum Shtarkman, third; Eduard Miansarov fourth; Milena Mollova, fifth; Nadia Gedda-Nova, sixth; Toyoaki Matsuura, seventh; Daniel Pollack, eighth), Frankel offered a parting quote from Pollack. " 'Thank God it's over!' he said backstage. 'I feel like sleeping for twenty years.' " [91]

As if this weren't enough, the *New York Times* ran an editorial the same day headlined, "The Arts as Bridges":

It has long been all too evident that bridges of friendship and understanding need to be built between the Soviet and American peoples. So far as politics are concerned, we seem unfortunately to be still far from such bridge building. But events such as Mr. Cliburn's appearance in Moscow and the Moiseyev dancers' performances here remind us that the arts give us alternative means of promoting such understanding.[92]

With the early leak of the news, word of Van's still "unofficial" win raced back to the United States via the airwaves.

"The very first word that Mr. and Mrs. Cliburn received," recalls family friend Annie Lou Ballard, "was when one of the networks called them and told them he had won. But they said, 'We won't believe it till we hear from Van.' " [93]

In a matter of hours, they would.

❖   ❖   ❖

Why did it happen? Why did one musician's performance set off international interest and passions?

At the eye of the storm, of course, was the music, the way Van interpreted a long list of works, many of them revered Russian masterpieces.

"He played incredibly the Third Concerto by Rachmaninoff," remembers Naum Shtarkman, the competitor who placed third. "After this, there was not any question that Van must win. It was as if he played the piece in one long, deep breath. And he had incredible ensemble with the conductor, Kondrashin. It was not conductor and soloist. They had the same approach; they were both in one music. It was something unbelievable." [94]

To Russian audiences, the romance and unabashed warmth of Van's playing were "like discovering parts of our own culture that were lost during the hard Stalin period," says Slobodyanik. "It was returning to old Russian culture through Rachmaninoff, Rosina Lhevinne, Josef Lhevinne—this is what people like Goldenweiser and Neuhaus noticed, and this is what the Russian people responded to." [95]

And something extraordinary happened to Van himself when he sat down to play in the most famous conservatory of the continent he had dreamed of seeing since childhood.

"It was as if a dam burst," surmises veteran critic Claudia Cassidy, who reviewed many Cliburn performances through the years. "In Russia, on his own, inspired, free—it all came pouring out." [96]

Imagine the shock of hearing this music from a Westerner, about whom the Soviet people knew so little. Though violinist Yehudi Menuhin had performed in the Soviet Union in 1945, and violinist Isaac Stern had toured there in 1955, that was about the extent of American soloists that post-War Russia knew.

"His playing was warm, open-souled, with big climaxes, a scale that was huge—it was not what we expected from a Western pianist," says Vladimir Viardo, who later went on to win the gold medal in the Van Cliburn International Piano Competition in Ft. Worth, Texas. "It was a fine mixture of openness, warmth, implicit structuring, which was great, and strangeness in the best sense—he was tall, he was specifically Texan, he was very naturally charming to the public; not only during the playing but also the way he behaved. There was an aura." [97]

To Vladimir Ashkenazy, who would go on to win the next Tchaikovsky International Piano Competition, in 1962 (in a tie with British pianist John Ogdon), "the best would be to say: generosity of the spirit. That's what we all felt at that time. His playing was open, it was reaching for everybody, reaching out for everyone.

"It was very generous and he played with obvious enjoyment. That is what so captivated everybody." [98]

Put another way, "His playing was not only emotional, it was also very spiritual," says Viktoria Postnikova, a concert pianist who was in the audience and is married to the Russian conductor Gennady Rozhdestvensky.[99]

Then there was the matter of Van's personality, which was unmistakably warm, openly affectionate, and vastly expressive.

"He enchanted everybody," says Ashchen Mikoyan, whose grandfather was Soviet First Deputy Premier Anastas I. Mikoyan. "I think, apart from showing great talent, he also enchanted everybody by his sincerity, his youth, his charm. He also seemed a little inexperienced, and everybody was really taken by his sincerity. He wasn't one of those who come prepared to win; that added to his charm." [100]

Of course, tremendous extramusical factors redefined a piano competition into an event of global and political interest.

"All these young Russian girls were swooning, and I was very surprised by that," recalls Frankel. "But of course, in the first instance, that was due to his wonderfully Russian, romantic style of play. Two, he was a young, sort of bobby-sox idol, very handsome. And three, he was American. There was no question that, to be able to lavish that kind of affection and to sort of reach out, sympathetically, to an American—in a safe political context—appealed to the Russians. I mean everything in the Soviet Union in those days was political." [101]

So why did the Soviets, at the height of the Cold War, give this prestigious award, and all their affection, to an American pianist?

Frankel says, "I think the arts establishment, and the people running the competition, were so eager to gain a reputation for the competition itself, by way of putting the Soviet Union on the cultural map internationally, and causing people to believe that they get a fair shake in Moscow, that that was more important than the narrow parochial interest of making sure some Russian won.

"And in fact a Chinese fellow came in second [Liu Shih Kun]. So it was for the same reason that the Russians wanted the Olympics—they were looking for acceptance in the world. Therefore their political interest in acceptance overrode their chauvinism." [102]

Incredibly for Van, his Soviet fans, and his American supporters, the most thrilling moments were yet to come.

7

Whirlwind

Several hours after word leaked that Van had won the Tchaikovsky, the official announcement came on Monday afternoon, April 14.[1] The scene was pure chaos.

"All the cameras and photographs and flashbulbs were going off and reporters were everywhere. It was incredible," recalls Pollack. "Everybody was jammed into this tiny room, and because it was so small, it created a psychologically bigger impact. It was as if the room had been stuffed with ten times the number of people that could fit into it. There was a lot of screaming that Van was first, and we were interviewed by correspondents. There was a lot of commotion going on." [2]

Gilels made the formal announcement, saying first prize went to "the merited of the merited," [3] a phrase that also had been translated as "the most deserved of the deserving." [4]

After reciting the order of the winners, "Mr. Gilels kissed Van on both cheeks as other contestants and fans jamming the Moscow Conservatory applauded wildly and chanted Van's name over and over," reported the *Kilgore News Herald*. "He responded by blowing a kiss in their direction." [5]

Now came Van's first lesson in dealing with loaded questions. "A reporter from Trud asked, 'What is your father? Is he a worker?'" recalls Van. "He collared me, so I said, 'He is a worker.' And then the reporter asked, 'What is your mother?' And I said, 'She teaches piano.' 'Ah, yes, good,' he said. I guess that meant the answers were acceptable. It was only after we got home that they found out my father worked for an oil company." [6]

There was no telling what they might have thought of Van's trip having been financed by a wing of the Rockefeller fortune.

Since stepping off that plane less than three weeks before, Van had become a figure of adoration in the Soviet Union. No more would his time, his space, his privacy be his own.

"None of us was really prepared for what happened, including Van," says Harriet Wingreen, who had greeted a slightly wary Van at the airport a few weeks earlier, before most anyone in the Soviet Union had heard of him.

Now, however, "When I went around to Van's hotel room and knocked on the door, he wouldn't open it," adds Wingreen. "I knocked again and again, and the door opened very slowly. And [fellow American competitor] Norman Shetler, who was in the room with Van, sort of peeked his head out and said, 'Oh, it's you—come in fast.'

"They apparently had been stormed by all the Russians, and Van hadn't expected this. Nobody did.

"When I got inside the room, Van told me that he had gotten all kinds of calls all day long from recording companies and managers, and all the Russian people who were trying to see him and touch him and get into his room. It was really something." [7]

While recovering from the emotional and physical strain of the past weeks—plus the months of preparation beforehand—Van managed to sneak in a couple of phone calls.

First he phoned home. "I never expected to get as much attention in my life as I did by winning that competition," Van later told an interviewer. "The funny thing was, I was sitting in Moscow and calling my parents back home to ask if they had told our friends across town that I had won, and my mother said, 'Yes, dear, they know all about it.' I didn't know what she meant by that until I got back to New York and realized what had gone on." [8]

Back home, however, the *Kilgore News Herald* reported:

> His parents are besieged by telephone calls, wires, flowers and other congratulatory messages. . . . At their residence on South Martin Street this morning they would hang up their telephone from talking to one person and the bell would immediately ring again.
> The Cliburns' first inkling of their son's success in the contest came Sunday when a friend called from Shreveport to say she had heard the news. Next, Columbia Broadcasting System called from New York and arranged a telephone call to Van for them. [9]

Specifically, Van asked his parents if they had heard the news, reported the United Press wire service. "They said they had, and he told them, 'It's official.' " [10]

Rildia Bee felt that "he sounded very calm and so pleased and overjoyed. He was as happy as could be. He said they have been wonderful to him over there." [11]

As for Rildia Bee's reaction, "We're thrilled to death," she told the *Shreveport Times*. "I am so overwhelmed with joy and gratitude I hardly know what to say." [12]

When UP reminded him that, due to Soviet law, he probably would not be allowed to take his rubles outside the country, he told the wire service, "Money doesn't mean anything to me. There are so many things you cannot buy with it. Winning just means a great deal to me as an American. I would not take a million for this trip." [13]

(Shortly thereafter, however, the Soviet government waived that rule, announcing that the American winners would be allowed to export half their cash winnings.)[14]

Regarding his energy level, Van said, "I would really like to go back to Texas. I'm just about to break down." [15]

Yet for all the strain, Van seemed to be the right person at the center of international attention.

"He just basked in it," recalls Frankel. "He seemed to love every minute of it." [16]

He wasn't the only one.

"It was a tremendous satisfaction to the Russian people," says pianist Alexander Toradze. "It gave them a satisfaction that something they wanted could happen. It was like the first democratic moment for Russian people." [17]

Such was their glee that a joke about the Tchaikovsky Violin and Piano competitions quickly began to circulate in Moscow. Because a Soviet musician had won the violin contest, and because the winner—Valery Klimov (pronounced KLEE-mov)—was not particularly popular, someone came up with a devilish quip.

"It was popular joke at the time," recalls pianist Alexander Slobodyanik. "It went like this: 'What three things do the Tchaikovsky winners have in common? Both of their last names begin with "Kli" (because Russians pronounced Van's name Klee-burn), both won first prize, and both don't play violin very well.' " [18]

❖   ❖   ❖

Reaction to Van's victory was swift and sweeping back home in Texas, in New York, and across Europe.

Once word was out, "It took about six hours before the newspeople from across the state were all over the Cliburns' little house on Martin Street," recalls Annette Davies Morgan. "Reporters flew in from everywhere. People were standing around the newspaper [honor] boxes to see if they could find something. Mrs. Cliburn just went ahead with what she already had planned—a prayer meeting at church.

"I think that mostly people around town were amazed, stunned, and very proud. A lot of people around here had watched Van grow and develop all his life. He had won some contests as he came along through Kilgore High School, and he had played in recitals. Van played and sang at funerals, played weddings, anything. So there were a lot of local memories. It was as if people felt, 'We have seen this boy grow up, and now the world knows what we've known all along.' But I don't think anybody here—not even Van's greatest fans—was prepared for such a tremendous ovation." [19]

Least prepared of all were Van's parents, who found at their doorstep "three *Life* Magazine representatives [who] were gathering material for a possible 'spread,'" reported the *Kilgore News Herald.* "A *Life* photographer also is trailing Van in Russia." [20]

Meanwhile, "Congratulatory messages keep pouring into the Cliburn home," added the *News Herald.* "Their mail box hasn't been able to hold the mail. The letters and cards to Mr. and Mrs. Cliburn are being tied in bundles at the post office." [21]

In a burst of civic pride that the occasion probably justified, the local paper offered a glowing editorial, congratulating Van. If its metaphors are a bit exalted, its unabashed affection for its subject comes through nonetheless:

> There may be those who, hearing or seeing Van's name in its current sparkling prominence, may regard him as a "Johnny-come-lately." They could not be more in error.
>
> From childhood days when he had trouble sitting on the piano stool, Van has made himself a slave to the keyboard. No one (except his parents) knows the countless hours of practice which developed his skill to the point that he is today numbered among the world's foremost pianists. . . .

In some circles, Van has been termed "the best ambassador since Lindbergh" and the appellation is entirely fitting.[22]

In Dallas, "everybody was pretty well bowled over," recalls Van's old friend, Bill Hallman. "It was kind of like winning the sweepstakes. Not that anyone doubted Van's gifts. But it was tinged with the air of the concerns of the day, the political concerns of those years, and the incredible fact that our Van could be such a darling to those strange, exotic, wonderful people who gave us Chekhov and Stalin. It astonished people that Van managed to gain entrance to what was then still a very closed and mysterious world." [23]

Musically, "The victory of the young man from East Texas," wrote *Dallas Times-Herald* music critic Dr. Jack Kilpatrick, "could be compared to that of a Russian lad who succeeded in persuading a panel of the most discriminating ears in America that his interpretation of Gershwin had more style, tradition and technical know-how than the best that our own country had to offer, not to mention the competitors from other countries." [24]

In New York, Madame Lhevinne summed up the situation adroitly, telling friends that Van had become "the American answer to Russia's *Sputnik.*" [25] (Later, Radio Moscow came to a similar conclusion, asserting, "He is the American *Sputnik*— developed in secret." [26])

Elsewhere in the halls of Juilliard, "All the students were awed," recalls Juilliard's Josef Raieff. "They were in awe that one of their classmates, one of their buddies, this kid who was going to all the student parties with them, had become a kind of hero. The excitement was tremendous." [27]

Gary Graffman remembers "sitting with Naomi [Graffman] in our apartment on 55th Street, along with Bill Judd, right by the radio and television in our apartment, waiting for something to happen because Bill was getting daily reports from Moscow that Van was the favorite.

"We knew there was a good chance he was going to win. And yet, he could have gotten second prize, or the first prize might have been [shared] with a Russian or who knows what might happen.

"So we waited, sitting on the floor. We had had a big dinner, and we were just waiting and hoping. Every now and then Bill Judd would phone wherever he was phoning, and then he found out that Van won, and we all got up, cheered, screamed, and started sending telegrams to Van." [28]

Then "Bill Judd called his brother George, who was the manager of the New York Philharmonic," recalls Naomi Graffman. "We were all laughing because Van already had been engaged [before he went to Moscow] to play with the New York Philharmonic the following season. It was going to be for one night, for $500 for the performance, which was a perfectly normal fee for a young artist.

"But Bill called George and said, 'I know it isn't considered good cricket to renegotiate a contract, dear brother, but under the circumstances, don't you think you could make it $1,000 for Van?' or something like that. And then George bargained him down to $750.

"This is something else that people forget. Van was already booked to play with the New York Philharmonic for his second engagement in three or four years, which was an amazing thing for a young person in those days. It was most unusual. After he won the Tchaikovsky, they merely extended the number of appearances." [29]

Officially, the New York Philharmonic released this statement: "In view of the outstanding record of Van Cliburn in the Tchaikovsky Competition in Moscow, the New York Philharmonic is pleased to announce that his engagement as soloist next season with Leonard Bernstein conducting has been extended from the one performance originally scheduled to four performances December 11, 12, 13 and 14." [30]

Violinist Yehudi Menuhin, who had been America's first internationally revered soloist and had toured the Soviet Union in 1945, remembers thinking "what a great feather this was in

America's cap. I felt that it came particularly during a period when we needed to measure up to certain Russian achievements in space and who knows what else.

"And when an American won over the Russians, in the Russian competition, it gave the country something we needed. The U.S. had triumphed because of him." [31]

Outside the United States and the Soviet Union, the reactions were equally vivid, if not always so warm.

"When I got back to Paris," recalls pianist Jerome Lowenthal, "I told my landlord about it, and he said to me that he had heard all about this person who had won the competition. And he added, 'It seems it was a Mexican who won.' I snapped, 'Not at all,' my bad temper sort of flaring. I said, 'He is from Texas, in the United States.' And he said, 'Really? From Texas, not Mexico?' So I said, 'Texas, you know, has been part of the United States for 150 years.' Apparently he and his friends felt that Texas was really a part of Mexico. But I thought that was a very French attitude, to think that it couldn't be possible that an American could have won such a thing." [32]

And in Italy, Ivan Davis, Van's longtime Texas friend, found that "I had a fight with several pianists who said, 'Look, if this had happened to any of us, it would have been the same.' And I insisted, 'It would *not* have been the same because we all look more ordinary. Because Van is so tall and glamorous and with his charisma, it makes all the difference in the world. It's the whole combination that's important, and I don't think it would be equalled any other time by any other person.'

"As an analogy, I said, 'No matter how well Joan Sutherland sang, she would never be the same as Maria Callas. Callas was just so extraordinary, and so extraordinary-looking. There are no comparisons.' It's exactly the same thing with Van." [33]

Or, as James Mathis likes to point out, "Van's triumph was not only because he was American. You have to remember there were other Americans competing too—Danny Pollack, Norman Shetler, and Jerry Lowenthal. But Van was the clear favorite. It was Van the Russians adored." [34]

❖   ❖   ❖

Monday, April 14, was to be Van's most spectacular day of all in Moscow.

Frankel reported in the *New York Times,*

> After a few hours' sleep, he was whisked off to the conservatory to hear the prizes announced by Emil Gilels. . . .
>
> It took more than an hour to get Mr. Cliburn away from the hall for a snack and an hour's practice. . . . Recording and concert offers poured in as a veritable East-West tug-of-war developed for his talent.
>
> At five P.M. Mr. Cliburn became the center of attention at a Kremlin reception . . . given by the visiting Belgian Queen.[35]

The dowager Queen Elizabeth of Belgium had become an ardent fan of Van's, and she, along with high-ranking Soviet officialdom, was eager to meet him. The guest list included Soviet chief of state Marshal Kliment Y. Voroshilov and First Deputy Premier Anastas I. Mikoyan.[36]

"While Van had his audience with the Queen and Voroshilov, he was approached with an unusual invitation," wrote Abram Chasins later. "Although there was, of course, to be another Kremlin reception the next afternoon for the contest winners, would he, as a most highly esteemed guest, now care to be presented to Mr. Khrushchev?"

" 'So I was taken to him,' says Van, 'and he was very cordial and gracious.' "[37]

What was said?

"Cliburn told newsmen later," reported Associated Press, "Khrushchev greeted him with a hug and asked, 'Why are you so tall?'

" 'Because I'm from Texas,' Cliburn replied.

" 'You must have lots of yeast in Texas,' said Khrushchev. And Cliburn replied, 'No, it's vitamin pills.' "[38]

Later, though, Van realized he had missed a chance for an even more adroit comeback. Reported the *Kilgore News Herald*, Van "still wished he'd said, 'Yes, we do, and I come from Yeast-Texas.' " [39]

This remarkable, impromptu meeting yielded a photo quickly beamed around the world: Khrushchev, the leader of the United States' Cold War foe, stood smiling broadly, reaching out to Van, who warmly took Khrushchev's hands to his heart. Here was a historic image and the predominant one to emerge from Van's heady weeks in Moscow: East touching West, a moment of openness that would not fully bloom until three decades later with Mikhail Gorbachev's *perestroika.*

Khrushchev, a cannier politician than his sometimes blunt gestures might have suggested, must have known well the significance of the moment. "You have to remember that, particularly at that time, Khrushchev was angling toward the United States," says Irwin Weil, professor in the Slavic Department of Northwestern University in Evanston, Illinois. "People don't always remember that he was making up with Eisenhower. Detente was in the wind. That's why it is also no surprise that he gave his permission for the jury to choose Van as winner." [40]

But what of the popular image of Khrushchev as a bully, pounding his shoe on the table as he addressed the United Nations? "That's by no means Khrushchev's major thrust as a politician," adds Weil. "Of course, that was stupid to do, but you have to remember, that wasn't done entirely in malice. Khrushchev was being expansive, as he always was.

"He'd say something like, 'Ah, you guys all think you're so good, but we'll show you we're better,' and he slammed [his shoe on the table] and said, 'We'll bury you,' thereby burying himself. And remember, he said things like, 'Everything in America is terrible, but, oh boy, the sausages—I love them.'

"It's clear that at that time Khrushchev wanted to make gestures toward the States and was looking toward a better arrangement, so he could balance at home the Stalinism he was trying to get rid of." [41]

To Van, the embrace of Khrushchev was as stunning as it was unexpected, not least because it revealed a side of Khrushchev that Van never suspected was there. As Van later recalled, "He told me, 'I'm so sorry I didn't get to hear you in the semifinals. My daughter was there, and she told me what a beautiful performance you played of the Fantaisie in F Minor of Chopin. It's one of my favorite pieces.'

"I thought, *My gracious!* He couldn't have been coached because I heard him say it, and though I'm very fond of Viktor Sukhodrev, who was translating [for Khrushchev], he doesn't know very much about classical music and couldn't have been making it up." [42]

As Van later told an interviewer, "I shall never forget that and will always appreciate it from him." [43]

Having allowed the embrace with Van to be photographed and released, Khrushchev had delivered a message to the United States more vivid and personal than any speech could have done.

"It's critical to remember that at that time there was this monolithic structure known as Stalinist Russia," says American conductor Lorin Maazel. "And the idea that an American could come out of the cold and walk away with their most prized of prizes—there was a very deep psychological factor working there.

"Because Van had found the first chink in that armor, and he became a symbol, at the time, of the possibility that everyone had ignored: that there might be a people-to-people contact between the United States and Russia, and that that contact might prove strong enough to pull down the wall, which it eventually did—literally and figuratively. Van just happened to be the right person at the right time." [44]

The photograph taken, the reception ended, Khrushchev, Van, the Queen, and entourage then headed to the concert hall.[45] There, "With Premier Khrushchev looking on from a box, a capacity audience to Tchaikovsky Hall went wild . . . when composer Dmitri Shostakovich presented the blond young Texan with the gold medal symbolizing his victory," reported the *New York Herald Tribune.* [46]

Van responded "with three Russian sentences expressing his gratitude," noted the *New York Times,* "and the audience laughed and cheered." [47]

According to the *Herald Tribune,*

> All three [of the top prize winners] played at Tchai-kovsky Hall tonight. Mr. Vlasenko was well received. Mr. Liu was called back for one encore. After Mr. Cliburn played the first movement of Tchaikovsky's Piano Concerto, the audience refused to let him leave and demanded three encores.
>
> By the final encore Mr. Khrushchev and half the audience had left the hall. The lights had to be turned out to get the hard core Cliburn fans out. They were still demanding more at this point.[48]

The house finally cleared an hour later, and Van and the orchestra were ordered back onstage for another filming session, according to the *Times.*

The festivities went on until the wee hours, "But since tomorrow is still two days from Mr. Cliburn's next scheduled public recital [as part of his obligation as prize winner] there was no telling what else would be planned for him by dawn." [49]

If there were any doubt that Khrushchev had been charmed by Van, it was erased the next day, Tuesday, April 15. Just as the competition had seduced audiences in Moscow and far-flung parts of the Soviet Union, so had it won Khrushchev's interest.

"This city just would not let go of Van Cliburn's coattails today," reported the *New York Times* of the April 15 events.

The giants of contemporary Soviet music took up columns in all papers to lavish superlatives on the young man from Texas. The giants of Soviet politics gave a party at the Kremlin to philosophize about peaceful competition, in music and in general.

Premier Nikita S. Khrushchev devoted his second straight evening to the music competition. At the reception he pointed to Mr. Cliburn and to the Chinese and Soviet pianists who came in second, third and fourth in the contest and said,

"Here we are without a roundtable, having an ideal example of peaceful coexistence." [50]

Back home in the States, each day brought more news of Van's comings and goings in the Soviet Union and his plans for his return home. Speculation about possible concerts in New York, Dallas, and Kilgore; questions about which TV show would snare the first post-Moscow Cliburn performance (though Van and Skitch Henderson knew the answer to that one); and, of course, endless documentation on Van's fees then and now—these matters now ranked with international affairs as the burning questions of the day.

"Cliburn's fee has been around $1,000 a concert," reported Associated Press. "Now Columbia [Artists] reports it at $2,500 to $3,000 for 1958-59. One millionaire in South Texas is said to have offered $30,000 for 10 dates. Another impresario from the Old South has taken 30 dates at $2,500 each. The New York Philharmonic, which had him booked for one engagement, has extended his appearances to four." [51]

For Van, far more meaningful was "an invitation from Tchaikovsky's nephew in Russia to play the great musician's personal piano, an honor accorded only one pianist each year," reported the *Dallas Morning News*. "And he has been invited by the Queen of Belgium, who termed Van a 'genius,' to play in Brussels during the World's Fair opening Thursday." [52]

The latter must have seemed an ironic twist to Juilliard president William Schuman, who had been unable to secure $500 from the U.S. State Department to send Van to the World's Fair with the Juilliard Orchestra.

As for the former, Van eagerly accepted the invitation to play Tchaikovsky's piano in the composer's home at Klin, which had been turned into a museum.[53] While there, as a sentimental gesture he took some earth to bring back to the United States.

Just before he set out, he honored the Moscow Conservatory's request "to have a life mask made for its collection."[54]

Besieged with requests for interviews, Van wrote a reflective piece about his experiences at the request of the United Press. Newspapers around the world picked it up. It summed up his thoughts about the remarkable political, social, and musical events at which he was the center, a remarkable document to come from the hand of a twenty-three year old:

> There are no political barriers to music. The same blood running through Americans also runs through the Soviet people and compels us to create and enjoy the same art.
>
> I've become even more aware of this since I have been in Russia. What has thrilled me so much is the great spirit of musical unity achieved here at the Tchaikovsky Competition by the different peoples of the world whose governments are at political logger-heads. . . .
>
> They are so pleased to learn that America loves their music . . . as much as they do.[55]

During a few precious spare moments, Van fielded phone calls from around the world, one from his loyal supporter in less-celebrated days, Skitch Henderson.

"Van said something quite touching to me that made him forever a part of my life," remembers Henderson, then musical director of "The Tonight Show." "With that boyish charm and that Texas accent, he said, 'Well, it looks like I've won this thing.' Then he said, 'Skitch, you have helped me immeasurably [by booking him for "The Tonight Show" in pre-Moscow days]. Are you doing anything on the telly that I could be of any aid with? Because now all of those people are calling me for these TV engagements.' " [56]

Weeks later, when Van returned to the United States, television offers multiplied, but he stuck to his promise to Henderson.

On Friday, April 18, Van played his award recital. The result, of course, was "a wildly pushing crowd [that] jammed the Moscow Conservatory," reported Associated Press. "The young Kilgore, Texas, pianist drew another big ovation and played seven encores, including a piece he wrote called 'Nostalgia.' " [57] In the audience were Dmitri Shostakovich and Sviatoslav Richter.

By this day, plans were announced for Van's return home to the States. Already dates had been set for his performances in Carnegie Hall (May 19), Philadelphia (May 21), Washington, D.C. (May 23), and "The Tonight Show" with Steve Allen (May 25). Bill Judd, Van's manager, "said a ticker tape parade would greet Van on his return to New York City." [58]

Now too, "President Eisenhower sent his congratulations to Van Cliburn," reported the *Dallas Morning News.* "The President forwarded his message to Cliburn through Llewellyn E. Thompson, U.S. Ambassador to Russia.

" 'When he returns to the United States,' the president said, 'I hope he can come to the White House so that I can congratulate him personally on his triumph.

" 'It is good to see artistic talent recognized, and I believe such contests are good for a better understanding between peoples of all nations.' " [59]

For reasons perhaps no one can explain, fame in American culture often is used both to reward and to punish its recipients, particularly performing artists. Given generously at one moment, it can be turned to cynicism or contempt almost overnight.

Thus, less than one week after Van had won the greatest recognition accorded any American classical musician before and, arguably, since, the naysayers were doing their corrosive work.

Skepticism and cynicism about Van's art, which the *Kilgore News Herald* shrewdly had anticipated when it warned against those who would view Van as a "Johnny-come-lately," set in quickly in the United States. Or at least it was prevalent enough for the *New York Times'* Howard Taubman to try to dispel it, only six days after Van had triumphed in a fiercely demanding musical competition judged by one of the most august juries ever assembled for such an event. Taubman's commentary had been defiantly headlined: "A Winner On His Merits":

> Over and over again the question last week has been: "Is this Van Cliburn really that good?"
>
> It was asked by people who were delighted with his triumph in Moscow and were eager to believe the best. It was asked by a skeptical few who cannot rid themselves of the prejudice that a foreigner is somehow automatically superior as a virtuoso to a tall young man from Texas. It was asked rhetorically by some who were convinced that this was just another example of Russian duplicity.
>
> This column assumed that Van Cliburn won the Tchaikovsky piano contest on his merits.[60]

That Taubman felt the need to defend Van, as if his newfound fame and American origins made him artistically suspect, seems incredible today and says a great deal about the way American audiences regarded American artists.

"I began my career in the early 1950s, in an area of music [conducting] which, at that time, had been thought of as the happy hunting grounds of gentlemen over forty, and certainly not Americans," recalls Lorin Maazel, the distinguished American conductor who was raised in the United States since infancy, though born in France. "I noted that right from the beginning. There was at that time a feeling in the United States that an American product, so to speak, was somewhat suspicious.

"Whereas in Europe I continued to enjoy the good fortune of being an accepted artist and respected and well known and so forth, let's say the reaction to my work in the United States was always somewhat colored by the fact that I was making most of my career in Europe. And the Americans felt that they were being asked to accept something at an evaluation made by others. You know, in short: 'Run the mile here too,' which I was always happy to do." [61]

That point of view was deeply ingrained in American culture long before Van had entered the picture.

"When I grew up, in the 1920s and '30s, it was still necessary to have the approval of Berlin and London and Paris. That meant a great deal," says Yehudi Menuhin, probably the first American soloist to earn a major international reputation. "The great American conservatories, the great achievements in American music and chamber music and even baroque music had not yet happened.

"And most of the conductors [of American orchestras] were still foreigners. They were Germans, like Alfred Hertz; French, like [Pierre] Monteux; Italian, like [Arturo] Toscanini. I don't think there were even any English at the time. So one had to go to Europe at the time, not only to complete one's understanding of European style, but also to get a certain stamp of approval." [62]

Van never had followed that route. Yet, the long and comprehensive list of awards he had won in the United States, even the award he had won in Moscow, apparently did not render him less suspect.

Still, there were a few more welcoming voices being heard in the United States, as a radio broadcast by Washington, D.C., impresario Patrick Hayes suggested: "A few years ago he [Van] would not have been allowed to go to Russia, such was the climate of opinion and the general relationship of the two countries," said Hayes. "If someone else had won this time, and Van Cliburn should in a year or two from now, it would not be quite the same in dramatic impact. Just now, early in 1958, only several weeks after the signing of the American-Soviet Exchange Program, Van Cliburn got there first, with the most—the most talent and experience and training, the most hair, the most height." [63]

In the Soviet Union, meanwhile, Van's celebrity only continued to grow, his Moscow recital of April 18 followed by a quick concert tour of Leningrad, Riga, Kiev, and Minsk. In each city, his concerts were broadcast on TV and radio.[64] When it became obvious that ticket demand was too great, Van opened up his rehearsals for those who wanted to hear them.[65] Little wonder he was near exhaustion by the time the tour ended with his Minsk concert of May 9.

Arriving in Moscow the next day, "The Kilgore artist said he was tired but happy and headed straight for bed," reported Associated Press.

> Of his last few days in Russia, he said, "They've been rough and tough but lots of fun. I am so exhausted that sometimes on the trip I thought I would die—but it's a good way to die." . . .
> Asked how much rest he expected to get when he comes back at the end of summer, he hugged one of the girl musicians and said, "None at all. But when you have only one life you may as well burn it up." [66]

By now, several of the Soviet Union's most prominent artists had published critical evaluations of Van.

Among them, Sviatoslav Richter had written: "Van Cliburn is a phenomenal player. Even in the first part of the contest, when he played the B-flat Minor Prelude of the first volume of 'The Well-Tempered Clavichord' by J.S. Bach and then the C Major Sonata of Mozart, it grew increasingly evident that the piano was in the hands of a true artist. His consecutive performance of four etudes by Chopin, Liszt, Scriabin and Rachmaninoff only strengthened this view." [67]

In conversation, Richter had called Van a genius, adding that was "a word I do not use lightly about performers." [68]

On the other hand, an apparently propagandistic article credited to Shostakovich in *Pravda* said, "Musical circles in the United States can rightly be proud of the bright success of their young countryman, especially since until now the musical successes of that country resulted not from efforts of Americans but of famous performers of European countries. We, for our part, are extremely happy that this outstanding young American artist earned his first wide and entirely deserved recognition among us here in Moscow." [69]

The Soviets, however, weren't the only ones looking for propaganda advantages. In Washington, D.C., the U.S. government began jockeying to sign Van for a performance at the World's Fair in Brussels. The *New York Times* noted:

> The United States is hoping that it will be able to capture the spotlight of the music, ballet and arts festival at the World's Fair here with a spectacular new entry—Van Cliburn, 23-year-old pianist. . . .
>
> A good many Americans associated with the performing arts have felt that the United States offering, even though it will include some famous artists and organizations, has suffered by comparison with that of the Soviet Union as the result of a limitation on funds.[70]

Of course, the United States could have signed Van for the World's Fair for $500, when William Schuman asked the State Department to cover Van's fee. He had been turned down.

On a more personal level, in New York, Rosina Lhevinne found that Van's triumph had changed the course of her life too. She wrote to Schubart on April 24, 1958:

Your warm letter gave me tremendous pleasure,
and I can hardly wait for your arrival in order to
know all the details of this most exciting event.
When I look back at our first conversation about Van
going to Moscow, I think that in our wildest dreams
we could not have anticipated the outcome of this
competition.

I am besieged with interviews, telephone calls, photographers and congratulatory letters—letters from
United States Sen. Ives and Congressman Zelenko.

Bill Schuman and I tried to reach Van ahead of time
to prevent his playing in New York so soon, but he
had already consented via telephone conversation
with Bill Judd. Let us hope that it will not affect the
high standard that he has achieved in Moscow. . . .

With best wishes and affectionate friendship,
Rosina.[71]

Lest anyone wonder who was making decisions in Van's life
and career, the Lhevinne letter suggests it was Van deciding for
himself when and where he would play.

Back in Moscow on Sunday, May 11, he "crawled into bed
and tried to get a little sleep," Van later told an interviewer,
"because at eleven Sunday night I was to begin a long recording
session. Leonard Warren, of the Met, was singing at the Bolshoi
that evening, and I went backstage to say hello. After Warren
had left and the stage had been cleared, the orchestra came on,
the piano was tuned, and we started to record. That session
lasted till half past five Monday morning." [72]

On Monday, May 12, Van called a number of people in
Moscow, trying to obtain permission for conductor Kiril
Kondrashin to accompany him to New York for his scheduled
Carnegie Hall concert of May 19. The okay came through the
office of First Deputy Premier Anastas I. Mikoyan.

"I had gotten to be friends with Mr. Khrushchev's daughter
and son-in-law," recalls Van, "so, through them, I requested
from Mr. Khrushchev to allow Kondrashin to come to the

United States. Now, I did this on my own, I had no money whatsoever, and I didn't know how anything was going to get paid. But I was determined to play with Kondrashin, so I called Bill Judd and said, 'I want Kondrashin.' He said, 'Oh, fine, fine, sure.'

"I thought, *Oh my, but Mr. Khrushchev signed the paper to let him go, I hope they [Judd's office] realize I'm serious and that Kondrashin is really, truly coming to America [and someone was going to have to pay him]*.

"He had never been to America, nor had we ever had a Soviet conductor on U.S. soil. Kondrashin was the first, and he was the great Russian conductor. Of course, Mravinsky was in Leningrad, and he was unbelievable. But Kondrashin was the conductor that [violinist David] Oistrakh, [violinist Leonid] Kogan, [pianist Emil] Gilels, [pianist Sviatoslav] Richter always wanted—and got for their concertos.

"It was my good fortune that he was assigned the piano competition because he was a pianist himself. Well, from the moment I struck the first note with this man—it was so thrilling, the sound he got from the orchestra. But what was even more thrilling was hearing the comments from the men of the Symphony of the Air [after Van returned to New York]. That was a fabulous orchestra, and those men had every right to be hard [in judging conductors] because they were marvelous. And the things they said about Kondrashin—ha! He made sounds that were so incredible. It was as if he revealed something of this music to men who had played it for years. He never used a score, he knew these pieces backward and forward. I still can't believe he's gone." [73]

Kondrashin died March 7, 1981.

After sleeping through the night, Van headed for another four-and-a-half hour recording session at the Bolshoi. "The orchestra members were all sitting around," Van later recalled. "I was feeling very sad, for we had been onstage together for a total of forty-five hours since I came to Moscow.

" 'We have something for you,' they said, and the personnel manager came forward and presented me with a beautiful album containing a complete picture-history of my stay in Russia, with photographs of all the places I had been. And on top of that, they gave me a box of exquisite Russian artwork enamel illustrating scenes from Pushkin's fairy tales. It was filled with wonderful Russian chocolates. There was an enamel cigarette case and also a poster of our last concert together, autographed by every member of the orchestra." [74]

The night of Wednesday, May 14, Van was to play his Moscow farewell concert, and students "had been in line for three nights. They waited all night for tickets," Van later remembered. "One woman came to me and said that she and all these students had stood in line and had not gotten tickets. But they had heard I wanted to plant a lilac tree at the grave of Rachmaninoff, so they all went in together and bought me this tree." [75]

No doubt the students watched the concert on TV, as did an estimated seventeen million Soviets.

"He closed his Soviet tour to another thundering ovation here last night," reported the *New York Times,* [76] which already had noted that, since his win, Van was being called "Malchik [little boy] from the South." [77]

Shreveport magazine ran a first-person account of the concert by two local residents who happened to be visiting Moscow at the time:

> At its conclusion the applause was thunderous. Armload after armload of flowers were presented, and the procedure was repeated after each encore. Even a balalaika was presented over the footlights.
> After three encores Cliburn stepped to the front of the stage and read in Russian (quite well, we were told later) a prepared message expressing his appreciation. Then he went to the piano and began the strains which brought shouts of "Bravo!"
> The next morning through our interpreter we learned that the concluding number, which had obvi-

ously been a tribute to his audience, was "Moscow Nights." [78]

Later, *Variety* printed the impressions of an everyday Russian citizen named Sara Shaikevich, who had been a secretary to then-*New York Times* Moscow correspondent Clifton Daniel:

> This last concert was something one could never imagine. He was full of emotion and this emotion gained the public and from the public it returned to him and there was such a tension that it seemed that hearts stopped to beat. And what he produced was not just music—it was poetry and love and inspiration. It was something up to the summit, something almost unbearable. And the public in the conservatory cried and the public sitting at televisors cried and yesterday there was not other talk than everybody's emotion and tears.[79]

The next day, Van was taken to the airport, where he said a few words that he had memorized in Russian to the throng that waved farewell. Then he climbed the steps of an SAS plane bound for the United States, via Copenhagen, waved again, and stepped inside.

From the Soviet point of view, perhaps critic Z. Vartanyan summed it up most eloquently: "The majority of our musicians participating in the [Tchaikovsky] competition turned out to resemble each other very much in their creative character. . . . The mass shortcoming of our musicians is their leveling." [80]

In roughly two days, the young musician responsible for this remarkable triumph would be welcomed home as no other American artist had been before him.

8

Homecoming

*T*he flight to New York, via Copenhagen, should have been quiet and restful, and it would have been, had *Time* magazine not made Van its cover subject for the May 19 issue.

That alone would be cause for celebration, of course, but the story—marked by inaccuracies and considerable condescension—probably caused as much anguish as anything else.

"The reporter came [to Moscow] and said he was going to write an article for *Time* magazine," recalls Van. "And I thought, *Oh well, no big deal.* And he said it may—he didn't say it was going to be—but he said it may even get to be the cover story. So I thought, *Oh sure.* It wasn't that I was a cynical young man, but he just said, 'may.'

"One of my mother's favorite lines is: 'He that expecteth nothing is never disappointed,' and she would always quote that to me. Whenever I would say, 'Oh, it may be,' she'd say, 'Now wait, darling: He that expecteth nothing is never disappointed.' Great line. So I just took it that way.

"I was playing concerts [in the Soviet Union], and all I knew was that Bill Judd called me from time to time and said that he was working on a Carnegie Hall concert when I got back. I got on an SAS plane on the fifteenth of May, and we landed in Copenhagen," says Van,[1] who clearly had not yet accurately gauged the scope of his celebrity. Looking back on this period, for instance, he later told an interviewer, "I'm really basically shy, and when I came back [to the United States], I was thinking, *Oh my, what in the world will my school friends think of me? I was just hoping I could get on* [in the music business]."[2]

On that SAS plane ride, however, Van learned a great deal about the nature of his celebrity. "On the plane this hostess [in Copenhagen]—who didn't know me from Adam—had been loading people on the plane [for New York].

"And then she came back to me and said, 'Oh, you're the one on the magazine!' I said, 'What magazine?' She said, '*Time* magazine. Your picture is on the cover.' . . .

"And then she brought out this *Time* magazine with me on the front picture, and that was when I was able to read it. And I was able to see the errors of fact in that story. I was just horrified. There were a few quotes that were not accurate on some things, and I thought, *Oh my, why did he say that? I didn't say it like that.* The inferences and the nuances were all wrong."[3]

At first glance, all had appeared well. The cover was a sensitive, slightly idealized painting of Van at the keyboard, with the headline: "Texan Who Conquered Russia." At the bottom of the simple, elegant cover were three words: "Pianist Van Cliburn."

When readers opened to page 58, however, they found a story, beneath the headline "The All-American Virtuoso," that all but dripped with condescension. The piece opened with a quote from Van, cast in a thick regional accent more befitting Li'l Abner: "Ah swear to goodness, ah just can't believe all this is happenin' to li'l ole Van Cliburn from the piney woods of East Texas!"[4]

The idea, of course, was to instantly emphasize the alleged backwoods folksiness of the world's latest cultural star, hence the dialect (though it's worth noting that *Time* magazine wasn't in the habit of framing Eastern accents in that manner).

The absurdity of this quote went unchallenged in most quarters, with the exception of critic Frank Gagnard in the *New Orleans Item*, who wrote: "In view of his startling transformation from promising young talent to musical sensation, the *Time* biographers may be forgiven for putting too much mush in his mouth and endowing him with unlikely regional idiom. . . . We were in frequent contact with Van at a listening post in Dallas during the course of six years and heard him utter nothing more hominy-tinged than 'you all.' " [5]

A few paragraphs later, *Time* continued its rather exaggerated portrait: "Van Cliburn is a gangling . . . snub-nosed, mop-haired boy out of Kilgore, as Texan as pecan pie." [6]

As for his other features, "His pale baby face, with its cornflower-blue eyes beneath a tangle of yellow hair, might suggest a choir boy—which he has been. He is exuberantly gregarious, unsophisticated and, on the surface at least, totally untemperamental." [7]

The piece went on: "Irreverent sophisticates of the concert halls may laugh at Van—but not when he sits down to play." [8]

Thus, to *Time,* and to readers who believed its portrait, the world's newest culture star may be a "baby face," "unsophisticated," and the source of endless humor for "irreverent sophisticates," but he sure can play. In other words, he knew little of the world except how to push the keys of a piano. If only making music were that simple.

Later, the article made the incredible assertion that Van called his childhood a living hell.[9]

There was some resistance to various facets of the *Time* article. The *Dallas Morning News* pointed out that

> . . . the article states that the Cliburn fee for his [upcoming] November 29 concert in Dallas could be $9,000 and quotes Mrs. Samuel Shelburne, president

of the Symphony Society, as saying: "We want to be the first to pay him his biggest fee."

Mrs. Shelburne said Wednesday [May 14] she had not talked with a representative of *Time* about Cliburn, and that the concert contract calls for the pianist to receive 60 percent of the receipts; 40 percent going to the Symphony. She also said she understood the 60-40 contract is now being set up as the general arrangement for Cliburn concerts.[10]

If Van felt uneasy about the way *Time* had portrayed him, his qualms were justified shortly after the plane landed at 9:45 A.M. on Friday, May 16, in New York.[11]

Recalls Van, "They let me off the plane first—they had told me in advance that I'd be the first one out—and even before customs, I was immediately taken into this room where there were press people.

"I was able to see my mother and father sitting there, and I was so dying to go over there and hug them. But they had been put in the back row of this little press conference room, and the reporters were talking to me.

"I had enough insight to know the direction of these questions because fortunately I had read this *Time* magazine article. Immediately they questioned me: 'Why does this [*Time* article] say, "These are my people"?' I responded, 'I actually said, "These all remind me of Texas people." '

"Then a reporter retorted: 'You said Khrushchev was a nice man.' So I answered, 'He was to me. I only saw him socially. He was nice to me, and I was nice to him.'

"So the next one asked, 'You must think you're a big success.' And I said, 'Oh no, I'm not a success. I'm just a sensation.' I could see how their minds were going and that was a mild disappointment. These people were thinking I was just a Russian communist convert.

"But the [Russians'] sentiment was so very Texan, you know. We [Texans] are very emotional; we love passionately. But also, if we don't love something, we'll let you know." [12]

Van's perceptions about the tone of the press conference were confirmed by the *Dallas Morning News*:

> Newspapermen who had expected to find a cocky, boastful Texan Cliburn were disappointed. He was poised, modest and pleasant.
>
> But he took exception to some of the quotations attributed to him by a national magazine in which he reportedly gave high praise to Soviet Russia.
>
> "Who put those words in my mouth?" he demanded.
>
> He made it plain that his praise of Russia was solely on the artistic and not the political level.[13]

Thus far, Van had demonstrated that his virtuosity was not confined to the keyboard. Affirming as much, *Musical Courier* magazine noted: "Mr. Cliburn showed great ability in parrying questions from the press." [14]

The *New York Times* apparently had come closer in capturing Van's thoughts on Texans and Russians: "With a small group of home-towners in the crowd that welcomed him, he allowed that on the basis of his reception overseas there 'must be a bit of Texan in the Russians. And I told them so,' he said." [15]

Inevitably, with the passage of time, the sting of the *Time* magazine article has dulled.

"I don't blame the media," says Van. "This is humanity. It's like history—there is no such thing. History is a myth; all of humanity has a different view of something that happened. We are not even sure of what happened because I cannot be in your body and you cannot be in mine. So we don't know if everyone sees the same colors, hears the same things. I don't blame the media, and I don't blame *Time* magazine. It was a real human being who wrote that article. We are all fallible." [16]

After the impromptu press conference, family and friends headed to a twenty-second-floor suite at the Pierre Hotel, followed by Van's seventeen suitcases filled with gifts from his Russian admirers: silver cups, handmade miniatures, porcelain plates, historic photographs, a leather-bound volume of Shakespeare's sonnets, recordings, scores, tea sets, and much more.[17] Van had arrived in Moscow with all of three suitcases.

To follow later was the lilac bush that Russian piano students had given him, which he planned to plant at the grave of Rachmaninoff in New York, along with the scoops of Russian earth he had brought back. For now, though, the lilac bush was detained by plant quarantine authorities.[18]

Roughly twenty-four hours after arriving from the most grueling and thrilling experience of his life, Van headed back to the airport to meet conductor Kondrashin.

Van's parents, however, were "concerned that Van had not been getting any rest," noted the *New York Times*. "But he seemed not to need any. His presence at the airport created considerably more of a stir than that of Austrian Chancellor Julius Rabb, who arrived at about the same time as Mr. Kondrashin."[19]

After he stepped off the plane, Kondrashin made a quick comment to Associated Press about Van: "He had a very great triumph in Russia. People who know music there acclaimed him as a great musician." [20]

Then Van and Kondrashin headed directly to Carnegie Hall, "where the Symphony of the Air was waiting," reported the *New York Times*.

> A crowd rapidly built up and sought entry. Many persons argued that since they could not get tickets for tomorrow, they ought to have a chance to see the pianist rehearse.
>
> They were for the most part gently discouraged. . . .
>
> Although the pianist had had a much-needed haircut overnight, his height, his hatlessness, his thick, dusty-blond hair and his outgoing manner made him as conspicuous as the Statue of Liberty.[21]

One fellow in the passing crowd, noticing the fuss surrounding Van, extended a hand and said, "Are you Harvey Kilgore?" [22]

Back "at the Pierre Hotel, the young Texan was finally corralled in his suite," noted the *Kilgore News Herald.* "His parents and his manager hoped to keep him there all day." [23]

The following night, on Monday, May 19, Van played what would be one of the most critical concerts in his career—his post-Moscow performance in Carnegie Hall. Critics from around the country would be there, measuring their perceptions against the Russian acclaim Van had won.

Speaking to Associated Press, Van's old friend Skitch Henderson noted, "He faces the grimmest test any man can face. He faces the New York critics. He must have good reviews in New York." [24]

Perhaps it was no surprise, then, that before the concert, Van remarked that he felt a bit "unsure. . . . In general, I wish I didn't have to do it." [25]

Van was not the only one aware of what hinged on this performance. As Ed Wallace wrote in the *New York World-Telegram,* in a story that later was entered into the Congressional Record by Representative Eugene J. Keogh of New York,

> A great crowd had gathered at the place where the young man was to go on trial. It was an orderly crowd which made no move to liberate the boy.
>
> A woman said, "I'd give anything if I could go in there."
>
> Her companion played down the excitement. "Two months ago these people never heard of this kid. Now they're all worked up because he plays the piano. So what's a piano player?"
>
> Inside, where the trial was to take place, every seat in Carnegie Hall was filled.[26]

Onstage sat the Symphony of the Air, one of the supreme orchestras in the United States, its members predominantly representing players from Arturo Toscanini's virtuoso NBC Symphony, which had been disbanded after the maestro's death the previous year. In the audience were actress Mary

Martin, a Texas compatriot from Weatherford;[27] Mikhail
Menshikov, Russian ambassador to the United States;[28] Princess
Irina Volkonsky, daughter of Sergei Rachmaninoff;[29] and pia-
nist Jorge Bolet, who had postponed a trip to Cuba to attend.[30]

After the Symphony of the Air performed Prokofiev's "Classical" Symphony no. 1, "Van Cliburn, the piano's wonder boy,
came dangling out on stage," noted the *New York World-Telegram.* "The boy is so tall and thin, he had the appearance of a
rope hanging from the ceiling, until he bowed and smiled." [31]

Appearances notwithstanding, Van was a bit preoccupied,
slightly bumping his head on the doorway of the stage entrance. The sole of his shoe, meanwhile, had been so heavily
worn in recent weeks that it was loose, and backstage he had
whimsically fastened it with a rubber band.[32]

Despite these distractions, "the pianist smiled, strode confi-
dently to the piano—and let nothing mar his obvious confidence in himself and in the conductor [Kiril P. Kondrashin],"
reported the *New York Times.* [33]

"There was a polite ovation," reported the *New York World-
Telegram,* "but nothing wild. Van Cliburn came back from
Moscow this week where he won the Tchaikovsky International Contest. The Russians said he was the greatest player in
the contest—but who's going to believe the Russians?

Van and Kondrashin "sicked the band on Tchaikovsky's B-flat
Minor Concerto," [34] before 2,760 seated and 80 standing listeners,[35] with scalped tickets going for $150.[36]

The first half of the program, for which Van played the
Tchaikovsky First Piano Concerto, inspired numerous ovations. In fact, only two people in the house were not applauding, reported the *New York Times.*

> The exceptions were tremendously moving. Every
> time waves of applause swept the house, a man and a
> woman, seated in the center of the first-tier boxes,
> sat stiffly, with folded hands.
>   They were Harvey Lavan Cliburn, Sr., and his wife,
> the former Rildia Bee O'Bryan. They seemed not so

much bursting with pride—and perhaps disbelief—as transfixed by it.[37]

Instantly after the Tchaikovsky, Van stood up and embraced Kondrashin.

During the intermission, noted the *Kilgore News Herald,* Van "was able to report backstage as he changed his sweat-soaked shirt. 'I'm so happy to be home again,' he said." [38]

For the second half of the program, it was the Rachmaninoff Third Concerto, and this time Van took pains to clear the stage-door entrance.

Considering that the audience called Van back for six bows and three encores (a Rachmaninoff Etude Tableau, the fugue finale of the Barber Sonata and the Schumann-Liszt "Widmung"), the concert seemed to be at least a popular success.

Backstage, so many fans and friends flooded in that for "the first time in Carnegie Hall's history the artists' room backstage proved so utterly inadequate that the orchestra's enormous instrument room had to be thrown open to accommodate the mob," wrote Abram Chasins.[39]

Now the question was what the critics thought.

> Both those who have backed him in this country and the Russians were right. He is a major talent. Something else emerged too. Although the Texas pianist is only 23, he is already impressive both as a human being and as an artist. And surely the two things are not unrelated. Listening to him play the Rachmaninoff last night, one felt that it has been his devotion to his art that has held him steady through the enormous adulation that has been heaped on him since his victory in Moscow on April 13.[40]

Other reviews reflected similar enthusiasm. Paul Henry Lang in the *New York Herald-Tribune:* "To his everlasting credit, this young man proved himself far above the drumbeaters and entrepreneurs. . . . Mr. Cliburn can safely turn around his statement: he was not a sensation but a success." [41]

W. G. Rogers of Associated Press: "Cliburn went through both works with a fine fiery sweep, from the crashing chords which open the Tchaikovsky to the ripple and rush of the Rachmaninoff. They were his kind of pianism, in the grand manner." [42]

Douglas Watt of the *New York Daily News:* "He has arrived. He is now on the scene and last night's concert made it clear that his career holds great promise." [43]

The next morning, after the reviews had come in, Van was preparing for his New York ticker tape parade. Mayor Robert F. Wagner had declared May 20, 1958, as "American Music Day" with a grandiose proclamation.[44]

An estimated 100,000 New Yorkers—a population roughly ten times the size of Van's hometown—lined the parade route. Not bad considering that President Eisenhower was in New York the same day with "an impromptu motorcade parade that drew thousands of onlookers," reported Associated Press.[45]

"As usual, such estimates tend to be generous," noted the *New York Times.* "But men, women and children did stand three and four deep along the curbs between which another smiling youth, Charles A. Lindbergh, had passed on the back of an open car thirty-one years ago next month." [46]

Abram Chasins wrote that this time, there were

> troupes of marching youngsters, bands, choruses, majorettes, cheerleaders, baton twirlers, fife-and-drum corps, and all the pageantry and mummery that go into the making of a gala parade. Teenagers with hands outstretched ran up to the car. One very pretty, starry-eyed girl raised up on tiptoe and de-manded a kiss. Van nearly fell out of the car fulfilling the order—smack on the lips.[47]

Or, as the Associated Press reported, "As far as you could see both ways, there were people. People crowded a dozen deep on the sidewalks. People on tops of cars. People hanging out of windows 30 to 40 stories high, tossing out coils and scraps of paper." [48]

Van regarded this amazing scenario with disbelief.

"Just above Trinity Church," reported the *New York Times*, "someone made his way to the side of the paper-strewn car and asked the 23-year-old pianist, 'How does it feel?' 'How does it feel?' repeated the tall Texan who conquered Moscow at the keyboard. 'I wonder who it's for.' " [49]

Through most of the ride, Van blew kisses toward his fans, many of them "waving banners saying 'Music Students Hail Van Cliburn.' " [50]

"I was incredulous," Van says. "It was so overwhelming, more than I could ever have imagined. It was just mind-boggling. I was going through this, and I said, 'Oh, this is not real, this is not real.'

"The night before I played at Carnegie with two concertos and all of that. Then the next morning we had to get up early to go to the parade, and then I had to think about what I was going to say for a little speech at City Hall." [51]

When the caravan arrived there, five thousand more spectators watched[52] as Mayor Robert F. Wagner presented the city's scroll and medal to Van. Words did not fail him. The Associated Press reported Van's "little speech" this way:

> I shall always remember this day, and know that it wasn't to me that this happened, but to the fact that music is a language and a message we can all have at our disposal and that we can all enjoy.
>
> It was a wonderful thing to go to the Soviet Union, and I wish you could have been with me and seen the wonderful, heart-warming love and affection given. I only hope I shall always be worthy of the wonderful memory.[53]

The luncheon in the Waldorf Astoria Hotel's Empire Room was a glittering event, opened with an invocation by the

Reverend Richard R. Hamilton of Calvary Baptist Church, followed by speeches from composer Richard Rodgers, who honored "this young, this very old diplomat," [54] and Juilliard president William Schuman.[55]

Mayor Wagner toasted Van's parents with a glass of cabernet, and Van reciprocated with Vichy water.[56] Kondrashin did likewise, telling the crowd, through his interpreter, "You must be happy to have in this country such a great piano player." [57]

Between the speeches, Van presented a vase to Rosina Lhevinne[58] and again surveyed the proceedings with incredulity.

He remembers, "Robert Dowling [president of a firm called City Investing], was leaving that afternoon to go to Russia on a goodwill trip. So during the luncheon I was busy writing notes to Mr. Khrushchev and Mr. Bulganin and all these people who were so nice to me so that Mr. Dowling could take them to Moscow."

In addition, Van was urged to play the piano, which he did, offering the Schumann/Liszt "Widmung" and Liszt's Twelfth Hungarian Rhapsody.[59]

Noting that ticker tape parades were not exactly the norm for classical musicians in America, the *Ft. Worth Star-Telegram* ran an editorial, hoping against hope that perhaps some things finally were changing in American society:

> If this is the sort of thing our best musicians may expect in the future, we are indeed changing our attitude about who merits the Street's [Broadway's] plaudits. A few years ago Cliburn would have had to pitch a no-hit game in Yankee Stadium to receive the like of what he got.[60]

As for the New York papers, they all but tripped over each other covering the event.

The *Times,* the *Herald-Tribune,* the *World-Telegram,* the *Sun,* and the *Mirror* all came up with the same headline: "The Texan Who Conquered Russia." [61]

The *Sunday Daily News,* on the other hand, ran a story dubiously headlined: "He's the Eggheads' Elvis Presley!" [62] Under one photo, the paper ran the caption: "He Ain't Nothin' But a Genius." [63]

Of the other Americans who also had gone to Moscow, two shared distinctly different points of view on the day's extraordinary events.

Joyce Flissler, who had placed seventh in the Tchaikovsky International Violin Competition and now is an associate concertmaster with the New York City Ballet, says, "I remember thinking that all of this was sort of a hard pill to swallow because I felt excluded. But I didn't say so at the time because it would have sounded like sour grapes." [64]

Her accompanist Harriet Wingreen, however, says, "I thought it was great. I thought it was wonderful that this country was acknowledging culture here rather than baseball. Joyce did sort of pale [by comparison], but this was a big thing at that time, the first time an American had won anything like this, and in such a way that he really swept the whole country." [65]

Van's powers of endurance, as well as his pianism, were still to be fully tested. On Wednesday, May 21, family and friends drove to Philadelphia for Van's concert that night with the Symphony of the Air and Kondrashin in the historic Academy of Music. The *Philadelphia Inquirer* noted that "there can be no doubt on either side of the Atlantic that this is a magnificent new talent." [66]

The *Philadelphia Evening Bulletin* claimed Van possessed "the kind of technique which is generally labeled 'big.' " [67]

The crowd's reaction persuaded Van to play the second and third movements of the Tchaikovsky as an encore,[68] and when Van and his family finally pulled away from the Academy of Music, fans tore one of the handles off the car as it escaped.[69]

The next day, Van decided he needed to buy a few new clothes. "His appearance at Wanamaker's department store nearly incited a riot," wrote Abram Chasins. "People ran around like the denizens of an ant hill suddenly kicked open. 'Van Cliburn is here!' they shrilled to each other." [70]

On Friday, May 23, Van met President Eisenhower in Washington, D.C., with his parents and Kondrashin at his side. The president assured Van that all would go well during his concert that night in Constitution Hall.

"Well, it will be a big night," said Eisenhower, who noted that he wouldn't be able to make the concert himself. "After an ordeal like that up there [in New York] you'll be all right." [71]

During a Washington press conference, however, the loaded questions turned up again: Had he seen ordinary people in Russia or merely artists and intellectuals? "Of course, I was mostly with ordinary people—I found Russians very much like native Texans—they had humor and curiosity."

Asked if he had formed any opinion of Soviet government, Van replied, "That is not my business, I am happy to say." [72]

During the day, Van's parents visited with Speaker of the House Sam Rayburn of Bonham, Texas, who had been a protege of Rildia Bee's father, Judge William Carey O'Bryan, in the Texas legislature.

Then it was on to the concert in Constitution Hall. *Washington Post* critic Paul Hume wrote, "Cliburn has a brilliant technique and a control that is practically faultless. He shows no sign of strain, though he is playing under circumstances no American has played under before in our history. Indeed his Tchaikovsky was understated most of the way. We have rarely heard it more sensitively given, with finer singing sound or better restraint." [73]

After the concert there was a supper reception at the Soviet Embassy, at which Russian Ambassador Mikhail Menshikov toasted Van's parents, then Kondrashin, whom he referred to as the "number two papa of Van Cliburn. . . . and his papas don't compete, they co-exist." [74]

Later, Van went to the piano and played into the night.[75]

It did not go unnoticed, however, that even after all the hurrahs Van had won in Moscow and New York, official Washington still didn't welcome him all that warmly.

"In New York, there was a delicious concert at Carnegie Hall; a ticker tape parade up Broadway," noted Mary V. R. Thayer in the *Washington Post.* She went on:

> But what happened in Washington? There was no Texas fanfare. Senators Johnson and Yarborough were weekending out of town. There was no recognition from the lavish-spending Texas State Society.
>
> President Eisenhower chatted with Cliburn for fifteen minutes but skipped the concert for Gettysburg. (Wild horses couldn't have kept Harry Truman away!) The White House was represented by the Sherman Adamses and the Gabriel Hauges.
>
> No top drawer "hostess" gave him an after concert party. But the Soviet Embassy did.[76]

On Saturday, May 24, Van played another Washington concert, this time for the White House Correspondents Association, then returned to New York on Sunday for his much-anticipated appearance on Steve Allen's show on Sunday.

Now, at last, after the most demanding two months any American musician had seen, the pressure began to show on Van.

"Every television program in the country wanted him as a guest," recalls Schuyler Chapin, "and he refused everything except the Sunday night 'Tonight Show,' where he was going to play the last movement of the Tchaikovsky.

"I was in the theater when he rehearsed, and it was fine. And then he went over to do a little bit with Steve Allen, who held up a record jacket and said, 'The Tchaikovsky and Cliburn will be out shortly.'

"And Van asked, 'What is that you're holding?' And he saw what it was and started with a burst of temper: 'This is unauthorized. I never authorized this,' and built himself up to a head of steam, ripping the cover into shreds and running off and upstairs into his dressing room and slamming the door. That was very uncharacteristic of Van as far as I was concerned." [77]

Apparently, a specific aspect of that record jacket had incensed Van, recalls retired RCA Victor executive Alan Kayes. "The problem with the Tchaikovsky album was that in anticipation of its fast release, we used a color photograph that had been provided by a photographer who was in the Soviet Union at the time of the competition," recalls Kayes. "And Van blew up at the thought of a color photograph of himself, so we had to scrap it and settle for a black-and-white. The color photo, back then in the '50s, felt too much like show business for Van." [78]

As Van cooled down in his dressing room, Schuyler Chapin remembers, "Steve Allen went on with the rest of the rehearsal with Louis Armstrong, who also was on the program that night.

"And then, maybe a half-hour or forty minutes later, Van came down from the dressing room just as sweet and kind and thoughtful as he'd always been, and they'd gotten another record album as I recall." [79]

All went smoothly on the program. Henderson remembers, "That was one of the first times I ever saw any attempt at doing a classical concerto on a variety show, though Oscar Levant had played the [Gershwin] Concerto in F on TV. But we felt it was an unbelievable coup, at that time, to have Vaniel playing the Tchaikovsky on TV." [80]

The reviews suggest Henderson is right. Van's work was called "an illustration of television's role in contemporary culture" by Jack Gould in the *New York Times*. "The gangling youth with the thatch of blond hair is not only a virtuoso but a personality. His rapt absorption in the music was fascinating to watch in TV's close-up. His meticulous good manners as he congratulated the conductor, Skitch Henderson, and the concertmaster of the Symphony of the Air were a winning touch. His tolerance of the little jokes peculiar to video variety shows was also most disarming." [81]

Clearly Van was generating unprecedented interest in classical music in America. *Billboard,* normally chronicler of the pop music business, came in with a page-one story headlined: "Accent on Youth In Longhair Boom: Cliburn Impact Can Pave Way to Fat Era for Young, U.S. Talent."

The story, which years later proved correct in its thesis, opened:

> Watch for a boom in young classical talent, music magnates are saying this week. The emergence of Van Cliburn has provided an impact which the long-hair field hasn't experienced since Yehudi Menuhin's short pants were hailed by press and public. The re-discovery of the popular appeal and exploitation val-ues of youthful concert artists, together with the new and powerful strength of television as a starmaker, will result, many believe, in America's biggest and fat-test era for native under-25 performers.[82]

Actually, it would take many years until America would fully regard its own artists as equals, but *Billboard's* survey of artists who could benefit from Van's success proved largely prescient: Beverly Sills, Betheny Beardslee, Byron Janis, Stanley Babin, Claude Frank, Jacob Lateiner, Michael Rabin, and Thomas Schippers.[83]

On Monday, May 26, the day after the "Tonight Show" appearance, Van headed into the recording studio with Kondrashin. RCA was in such a rush to get this recording into the stores that "when we first began work on the recording . . . at Manhattan Center, we had no contract at all yet," recalls Alan Kayes, who had cabled Van in Moscow in hopes of luring him to the label. "All the negotiations were going on [while the tapes rolled] to produce a long-term contract." [84]

But it was well known that "Van had always wanted to be on RCA Red Seal—he told me so," says RCA producer John Pfeiffer, who had worked with harpsichordist Wanda Landowska, vio-linist Jascha Heifetz, pianists Vladimir Horowitz and Arthur Rubinstein, and other legends. "So as soon as he had the opportunity, he just signed on the dotted line, no question about it.

"Originally, the plan was to use the recording of the Tchai-kovsky from the Carnegie Hall performance, but Van found some things in the tape that he didn't especially like, so we decided to have this special recording session.

"When we said we'd do the recording at Manhattan Center—which was where we were in the habit of recording at the time—he said, 'Okay, but I'd like to have an audience.'

"Well, Manhattan Center is an enormous ballroom, basically, so there are no seats. But above the center there's a balcony that runs three-quarters of the way around it, where people used to sit at tables during the dances that they had there.

"So I arranged to seat the audience in that balcony up above, and Van wanted students from the High School of Music and Art there, so they were all invited. Of course, they were delighted to come. We brought them all in an hour beforehand and got them all settled.

"I had to make an announcement beforehand that we were doing a recording session, and they had to be quiet. Then Van came in, and we started recording.

"And he listened to the tape and said, 'I feel like I'm in a fishbowl, with all those people looking down at me.' Of course, it was so completely different from any regular performing situation, with the audience staring from right on top of you, so he just couldn't do it. We had to call it off." [85]

Van wasn't the only one who had been somewhat unnerved by the scenario. "It was a rather tough session," wrote producer John M. Conly afterward. "RCA Victor had followed its recent and laudable custom of inviting eighty students from New York's High School of Music and Art to come and watch. They were quiet as mice, but their chairs squeaked, which made the engineers nervous. Cliburn was nervous too, probably because of a month of activity that would have laid a lesser man prostrate. Some of the orchestra people were nervous also, maybe because they hadn't practiced enough." [86]

That night, Monday, May 26, Van and Kondrashin repeated their Carnegie Hall concert of a few days earlier, this time with the music broadcast live over WQXR, "and it was the week's event, television or no television," wrote Jack Gould in the *New York Times.* [87]

Now a new wave of critics attended, with the response about the same as before.[88]

Somewhere in this blur of activity, Naomi Graffman remembers "Van's playing with the Symphony of the Air the Rachmaninoff Third and the Tchaikovsky, and after that, he played his famous encore, the 'Dedication' ['Widmung'] of Schumann, in the Liszt arrangement.

"We sat backstage, and I remember saying to Van's mother, 'I really don't know where he gets all the energy, after doing all that.' And she said, 'Honey, that's where God comes in,' and that was my most beautiful and poetic memory of that time." [89]

The Tchaikovsky recording, however, was yet to be finished, "so we set up another recording session, this time at Carnegie [Hall]," recalls Pfeiffer. "Of course, the only time we could reserve at Carnegie was after a concert, and so we had to set it up at midnight [on May 30]. But Van liked working after dark, no question about it, so that was no problem.

"This time we didn't have an audience again. I think Van decided, 'It's midnight, and you can't get people to come out at that time, so let's forget about the whole thing.' I think he felt that as long as he was in Carnegie Hall that the atmosphere was proper for him. All he wanted an audience for was so that he would be playing to somebody. And by then we'd had a chance, also, to get more familiar with one another, and I think he wasn't so frightened by the idea of recording. He knew I was in there batting for him all the time and would watch over anything that came up. He was more at ease and therefore wasn't looking at the whole thing as being a totally new experience.

"The session went on until about five in the morning, which, for a full concerto recording, was not bad. We'd stop, of course, for periods of time. But all through that session I really had a feeling that this was something that would go down in history, and not simply because it came after winning the competition and all of the brouhaha that went on about that, but simply because here was a young musician really fulfilling every part of himself." [90]

Part of that process, of course, owed to the unique chemistry between Van and Kondrashin. "There was never any question that they saw eye to eye—they didn't have to communicate with words," says Pfeiffer. "They would do something, and they'd both know what the other one wanted to do. It was just one musical mind at work there, just one mind that controlled both of them. And there was the added excitement of the occasion, that a Russian could come out of Russia and conduct for him." [91]

How did Van work in a recording session? "Well, he would come in [to the recording booth] to listen to the tape and scowl and make a face about something or other that he had heard," says Pfeiffer, "and then he would look at Kondrashin. And Kondrashin would shrug his shoulders, as if to say, 'Don't worry about that.'

"It reminds me of what I used to tell Heifetz when a little [clinker] got into a tape: 'Oh, go ahead, leave it in. It will make all the other violinists happy.' And I wanted to say the same thing to Van, but I didn't dare." [92]

Though Van had been up through the night recording, Friday evening was Van's first major, national television interview, on Edward R. Murrow's "Person to Person." Murrow and crew flooded Van's suite at the Pierre Hotel. Then the show began.

Today, a videotape of the program seems a bit jarring—something about the sight of Edward R. Murrow, the veteran war correspondent, opening the program with a brief soliloquy about piano competitions.

Nevertheless, there he sat, talking piano, drawing on his trademark cigarette, then swiveling his chair toward a huge screen on which Van and his parents could be seen sitting in their hotel suite.

In describing the whirlwind pace of his life, Van told Murrow of the midnight recording session, which inspired Murrow to ask if this kind of thing is "customary" for performing artists.

"Well, it isn't customary," said Van, "but I must say that when you're involved in trying to find that type of perfection that is so elusive and never can be achieved in music, you will search and search to try to find the acoustics in the hall and recording [conditions] that will give you the best advantage for sound and inspiration.

"And I must say that probably the Hollywood glamour type of sensational publicity that has been created about this prize certainly doesn't hold true because music is really quite nerve-wracking, tedious, and quite demanding." [93]

From that moment on, it was more the Van Cliburn show than the Edward R. Murrow show. Clearly at ease in front of a TV camera, Van spoke casually and comfortably at the slightest provocation, walking nonchalantly around the suite to give Murrow and his viewers a tour.

When Rildia Bee recounted Van's first days in school, Van jumped in to add, "Well, of course, Mother, I always was famous for the fact that I loved to play, but if it interfered with any of my outside activities or my friends, I never quite enjoyed it."

When Harvey Lavan explained to Murrow that he wasn't a pianist but "a great music lover" who "always has done everything possible to encourage Van," the young Cliburn leaped in again.

"Mr. Murrow," said Van, "I would like to interrupt Daddy to say that he certainly has been a very great inspiration to Mother and me, and I think that Daddy's really great love and ambition was medicine. I know that if . . . thirty-two years ago Socony-Mobil Oil hadn't enticed him into the oil industry, I think he would have been a most fantastic doctor."

Asked about how he protected the gold medal he had won in Moscow, Van quipped, "Well . . . I practically slept with it."

And when Murrow inquired how Van had thanked the Russians for the prize, Van rattled off his acceptance speech—in Russian. He acknowledged that the sudden turn of events had forced him to learn the speech phonetically.

Then he offered Murrow a guided tour of the gifts he had received from his Russian fans, everything from dolls and collectors' plates to paintings, photographs, a photo album, icons, even "a balalaika given to me across the footlights."

The tour over, Van eased over to the piano to play a few bars of his composition "Nostalgia," which he explained to Murrow was "a mood picture after a short story I had read when I was fifteen, by Jack London." [94]

The next day, Van and Kondrashin went to the grave of Sergei Rachmaninoff at Kensico Cemetery in Valhalla, New York, where Van planted the earth and the white lilac bush he had brought from Russia. Princess Irina Volkonsky, Rachmaninoff's daughter, was there and gave Van a Czar Nicholas five-ruble gold coin that her father had carried as a kind of good luck piece.[95]

Then on Monday, June 9, Van and his family left for his first European tour, with Kondrashin conducting several of the dates.[96] Almost predictably by now, the reviews were consistently enthusiastic in London, Paris, The Hague.[97]

That Kondrashin was given so much time to tour with Van was owed specifically to Khrushchev, who had answered Van's request for Kondrashin in a telegram: "The conductor K. P. Kondrashin has been granted leave of absence from his duties. . . . I wish you the greatest success in your remarkable creative work." [98]

After Van's performance in London's Royal Albert Hall, the crush of visitors prevented even his parents from getting through the crowd to his dressing room. "Well, it doesn't matter," said Rildia Bee at the time. "He has a lot of people to talk to. We'll just wait until we get back to the hotel and tell him how he was." [99]

So it went, with Van making news everywhere he performed. In The Hague, he played an impromptu command performance for Prince Bernhard of the Netherlands.[100] And in Paris he won a standing ovation from four thousand listeners at Chaillot Palace Hall.[101]

At the Brussels World's Fair, the U.S. government had persuaded the visiting Philadelphia Orchestra to add a concert to its series to accommodate Van's jet-speed schedule. Howard Taubman wrote in the *New York Times,* "The most impressive thing about Mr. Cliburn's performance . . . to this listener, who had not heard the tall young Texan before, was the fact that acclaim and adulation have not tarnished his fine musical instincts. His playing had an unspoiled naturalness of feeling. Success has not tempted Mr. Cliburn to take on airs as a musician." [102]

With a European triumph behind him, Van deserved a much-postponed vacation, but the rest of the United States demanded to hear him, and he obliged. So much, in fact, that he agreed to fulfill the contract he had made before his Moscow victory to perform at Grant Park in Chicago—at the prearranged fee of $800 for two concerts, a fraction of what he now was commanding. [103]

"Personally I was a little bit nervous about it," recalls Edward Gordon, who was instrumental in signing Van in January[104] for Grant Park, before Moscow. "But then I thought he probably would honor the commitment, unless some crazies got to him and said, 'Look, you don't have to honor anything; we don't care what the paper [contract] says; this is now an international phenomenon and you don't have to do it.'

"So in my heart of hearts, I thought, *No, Van isn't going to do this to us.* I remember one of the park commissioners, Jake Arvey, calling me and saying, 'Is he going to show?' I said, 'Your guess is as good as mine, but I'm putting money on the fact that he will.'

"He did honor that contract. He could have said, 'My career is international,' but he didn't do that. That wasn't Van. It was ridiculous that Van Cliburn was playing for us under this old contract. And he didn't ask for anything. I mean, we laid out as much as we could to make him as comfortable as possible. I made a fuss about the piano they chose, made sure to have the technicians there, but he was relaxed about it all."

Gordon, a pianist who went on to become executive director of the Ravinia Festival near Chicago, had heard Van over the years and thought it a good idea to catch him on the way up. In trying to arrange the Grant Park performance, "I said to [Grant Park concert manager] Walter Larsen, 'I hear via the grapevine that Cliburn, whom I have been interested in over many years, and who's a great artist, is going to the Tchaikovsky in Moscow—why don't we engage him?'

"I really felt that if the jury was sensible, and no big nationalistic thing came into play, which does sometimes happen at competitions, then Van surely deserved to win. Because let's face it: He took all of the best that Lhevinne had to offer, internalized it, but never gave up Van." [105]

When Van arrived on Tuesday, July 15, Chicago was ready for him. At the airport, he was met by half a dozen Kilgore Rangerettes, who surrounded, smothered, and embraced him before news photographers.[106]

From the airport, Van was rushed to the Blackstone Hotel with a police escort, sirens screaming.[107] As he walked into the hotel, he was "greeted by 'The Eyes of Texas Are Upon You' and Tchaikovsky's Piano Concerto No. 1, as interpreted by the brass dance band of the Moolah Temple, St. Louis," reported the *Chicago Tribune*.

> "I'm honored," said the somewhat stunned pianist, who appears Wednesday and Friday nights at Grant Park.
> But about his fee for the concert performances, arranged last January before his triumph in winning the Soviet Union's International Tchaikovsky piano competition, in April, the extroverted Cliburn was as mum as the park district. . . .
> Cliburn put it this way: "I was thrilled to be asked to play here." [108]

On Wednesday, Van went through the Rachmaninoff during rehearsal, his performance making a profound impression on at least one listener's life. "I was at the rehearsals of the Rachmaninoff Third and the Tchaikovsky, and the rehearsal of the Third was, in many ways, the performance that put in focus my future direction," says pianist Jeffrey Siegel, who grew up in Chicago. "I loved particularly his approach to the piano as a singing medium, and he approached the Third Rachmaninoff in a very grand manner. It was very different from the [Vladimir] Horowitz and Byron Janis way of playing the piece. And in those days, it was very unusual to hear the piece this way. It was broad. It was majestic. It was singing. It was full of fire, as well. But it was a very different conception of the piece than anyone else.

"And when I heard this, I felt something inside me say, 'This is the kind of musicmaking, this is the kind of approach that I want to pursue.' Van does not know this—I've never said this to him—but that rehearsal of that piece had such a tremendous influence on me. With me it wasn't so much that he had won a competition or anything of that nature. It was the beauty of his playing that got me. I wouldn't have cared if he was last place in the competition. That would have been meaningless.

"And it made me feel I'd like to study with the woman who taught this man at Juilliard," adds Siegel, who, as a prodigy, had studied with Chicago's foremost piano teacher of the era, Rudolph Ganz. "And so the next year I went to Aspen to study with Rosina Lhevinne, and the following year I started with her at Juilliard—all of this with Rudolph Ganz's blessing, by the way. So Van was the catalyst for me.

"Also, I believe this performance was important to Van because it was one of the only engagements he had on the book before he went to Russia. And I believe he felt very honored to come to Grant Park to play because they had engaged him before the whole world knew about him." [109]

For now, Van had to keep in mind that anywhere from 55,000 to 80,000 fans (depending on who was counting) had flocked to Grant Park on Wednesday night. The throng spilled from the band shell to the steps of the Field Museum of Natural History, several blocks away. Chicago had not seen anything like it since Lily Pons had sung in Grant Park in 1939.[110]

The *Chicago Tribune* reported,

> In the crowd that spilled to Roosevelt Road were teenage worshippers of Presley. "Just curious," they grinned. There were others who admitted they couldn't tell a fugue from a march or a Callas from a boy tenor.
>
> But they drove in from Michigan and Indiana, they sat thru a broiling afternoon sun to assure good seats, and they dined on sandwiches and fried chicken partly, perhaps, as one matron put it, "because that was quite a thing he did in Moscow." [111]

Among the listeners, only 12,000 got seats, the rest would have to be content with blankets tossed onto the ground, of which there wasn't much. Roughly 150 police tried to maintain order.

"I was a little worried about what would happen if it began to rain—would we have a crush of people," says Edward Gordon. "In those days, of course, we hadn't yet reached the period where kids were taking hallucinogenic drugs, so we didn't think in terms of drugs or people boozing it up because that just wasn't allowed on park property. But the crowd control was quite phenomenal. Van's car even had to have an escort—two cars in front just to get through all those people." [112]

At 8:05 P.M., guest conductor Howard Mitchell walked onstage to begin the program, and at 8:50 P.M. Van was led to the stage to play the Rachmaninoff Third.

"I just couldn't get over it," says Van, remembering his thoughts on seeing an audience that stretched as far along Lake Shore Drive as the eye could see. "I said to myself, *Oh no, this isn't happening to me, no way.*" [113]

Claudia Cassidy, the formidable critic for the *Chicago Tribune,* embraced the performance in a language so poetic it bears quoting today:

This was big, brilliant, beautiful playing. Playing in the grand manner, with sweep and fire and style. Playing with bravura and the bite of the highly charged phrase turned at the point of impact. Playing rich in the liquid embroideries of the score, glittering in its love of spectacle. And something more, too. Even now, the imprint of something personal. Something of which you can say with conviction, "That's Cliburn." [114]

Not bad for a pianist who had just turned twenty-four.

Today, Cassidy remembers the event vividly. "It was a historic occasion, a historic place," she says. "Back then, when [Jascha] Heifetz said it was too noisy [in an outdoor performance], they stopped the trains; they really did, you know. So Van's playing at Grant Park was a story. He really was most extraordinary. I thought there was a certain shyness about him, and I thought he had a true and unusual talent, if you understand my use of the word. There was something very sweet about him.

"It wasn't the biggest crowd I had seen at Grant Park. The biggest was Lily Pons, of course, though they exaggerated the size of her crowd, saying it was 350,000. Of course, she was the darling of the world at that time, and she came on in full regalia, bouquet and all. She might have been at the Court of Versailles. Next to that, Van's nights were the only ones that compared." [115]

Donal Henahan, then music critic for the *Chicago Daily News*, shrewdly noted in his review that,

After discussing his dubious qualities, such as tendencies toward stretching phrases and a free use of rubato, one fact keeps coming back like a theme: he makes contact with his audience.

All shades of listeners, from musical gourmets to mere curiosity seekers, were able to marvel at him for their own reasons. . . .

This is no hothouse plant of an artist, either. After putting in a day that would lay a circus strongman low, he topped off one of the most trying of concertos with encores.[116]

But, once again, the exertion of the past few months showed signs of catching up with Van.

"After the first night at Grant Park," he recalls, "I came down with something awful. It was very strange. I had a 103-degree fever. I felt just absolutely horrible, and the thought of playing the Tchaikovsky First with a 103-degree fever was too terrible. Actually, the doctor said I had to cancel the second [Grant Park] concert because I was so sick, but I knew I absolutely couldn't, with all those people who were coming out. So the doctor gave me some medication, and then he had somebody go out and buy me some long-handled underwear. It started all this perspiration. And would you believe it? By the time I finally got to that performance, I felt okay. After that, whenever somebody asked me for advice on a fever, I told them to put on some long-handled underwear and play the Rachmaninoff Third." [117]

By Friday, July 18, Van was back on stage rehearsing the Tchaikovsky First with Howard Mitchell and the Grant Park Symphony, "and there was very little discussion between them," recalls Jeffrey Siegel, who listened in.

For this night's performance, Van followed the Tchaikovsky with more encores: the Schumann-Liszt "Widmung," Liszt's Twelfth Rhapsody, Chopin's Etude in E Major, and the Ravel Toccata.[118]

Only now, with his impending performances at the Hollywood Bowl in California and Lewisohn Stadium in New York, was there a chance that Van might be able to get off the treadmill.

The *Dallas Morning News* reported in July:

Van Cliburn will be pulled out of circulation for two months, early August through September, to pull himself together, to freshen his repertoire, to prepare for a busy 1958-59 season and to relax from the dizzy pace that has been his since he won the Tchaikovsky Memorial Award in Moscow last April.

His vacation will begin shortly after August 4 when he plays with the New [York] Philharmonic in the Lewishon [sic] Stadium. . . . More than 20 European dates and some in the Middle East were cancelled to make the holiday possible.[119]

So Van was off to California for his debut at the Hollywood Bowl, an important event for him for a variety of reasons. "When I had gotten back to New York after Russia, and after we had had some concerts," recalls Van, "Arthur Judson had said, 'Now Van, what would you like to do? What do you see for yourself?' And I said, 'I want to study with [conductor] Bruno Walter.' Judson replied, 'Easy—we'll call him.' And the next thing you know, he was on the line." [120]

Walter, who now lived in Beverly Hills, was born in Berlin in 1876, worked under composer-conductor Gustav Mahler at the Hamburg Stadttheatre, and conducted the premieres of Mahler's posthumous Symphony no. 9 and "Das Lied von der Erde." [121]

That Van felt compelled to study with the great musician, noted for the classical dimensions of his work, says something about Van's approach to music in general, romantic repertoire in particular.

"But my regular visits with Dr. Walter did not begin until September because he was in Europe at this time, when I first played at the Hollywood Bowl," remembers Van. "I had never played in Los Angeles, and here I was at the Hollywood Bowl—a legendary place." [122]

Again, the reviews were predictably enthusiastic.[123]

After the second Bowl concert, "Mr. [Cecil B.] DeMille invited me to his home," Van later recalled. "He and his daughter gave me a huge party and literally gave me the run of the house. I never have encountered his like." [124]

Beyond the glamour and glitter of the Hollywood performances, there was another, more important reason that this engagement meant so much to the family. Before Rildia Bee studied at the Cincinnati Conservatory of Music with Frederick Shailer Evans, she had studied as a child with Prebble Drake, herself a former student of the Cincinnati Conservatory of Music.[125]

"We found out she was still living when I won the Tchaikovsky in 1958," remembers Van. "She had heard about it, and she found my mother and called her. Miss Prebble was living in California with her niece. So when we went to the Hollywood Bowl, my mother was able to see her teacher, Prebble Drake, who was ninety-six years old.

"And I was sick about it, for two reasons. Number one, I didn't get to go. Number two, I guess we still didn't own a camera, so I don't have a picture of that reunion. Miss Prebble really felt a part of all this, and she certainly was." [126]

In the few days before Van's return to the East Coast for his Lewisohn Stadium date of Monday, August 4, the Soviet Union invited him to give two concerts at the Brussels World's Fair, August 16 and 17, "But the young Texan does not know whether he will be able to accept," reported the *New York Times.*

> Mr. Cliburn said yesterday [August 1] in Beverly Hills, Calif., that he had been waiting some time for the invitation, that its arrival yesterday constituted very short notice. . . . His season, he had thought, would come to an end with his appearance at Lewisohn Stadium in New York Monday evening. Mr. Cliburn has had a very taxing schedule since he won the competition, and his doctors, he said, had ordered him to take a rest.[127]

Meanwhile, though, it was on to New York, where, "One of the largest crowds in the history of Stadium concerts assembled at Lewisohn Stadium . . . to hear Van Cliburn," wrote Ross Parmenter in the *New York Times*. "An estimated 22,500 people attended. But these were only those who succeeded in gaining admission." [128]

As a coda to Parmenter's warm review,[129] he added, "One of the touching aspects of the evening was the sort of enormous hunger for beauty that one sensed in so large a crowd. Going toward the back for the slow movement of the Rachmaninoff, one heard the romantic strains which were being gratefully received by thousands of upturned faces." [130]

By concert's end, the applause was intense enough to yield seven encores: Schumann-Liszt "Widmung," Chopin's A-flat Polonaise and E Major Nocturne, Ravel's Toccata, Liszt's Twelfth Hungarian Rhapsody, a Brahms waltz, and Van's own "Nostalgia." [131]

The evening, a special post-season performance designed to cut the stadium's deficit, brought Lewisohn's highest box office revenues yet.[132] And the stadium wasn't the only beneficiary. At the surrounding buildings, roof space reportedly was sold to those who couldn't get into the concert.[133]

Even with this triumph in hand, there would be no rest. On Sunday, August 10, the *New York Times* reported that Van's long-awaited rest would be postponed again, for he would play at the Brussels World's Fair again, this time with a Russian orchestra.[134] Thus he would be the only artist to have appeared in the performing arts programs of both the United States and the Soviet Union at the fair.[135]

This feat caused some rumblings in a Cold War society. Howard Taubman of the *New York Times* wrote,

> There have been intimations in certain quarters that it was wrong of Mr. Cliburn, an American, to appear with a Soviet orchestra in the World's Fair forum, where competition in the performing arts between the two major powers is keen.
>
> But the pianist's willingness to appear and the Russians' to have him is a credit to both.

By inviting Mr. Cliburn the Russians were not only
honoring a Moscow prizewinner but also showing
that narrow nationalism has no place in music. They
were indeed paying Mr. Cliburn a high compliment.[136]

Even the political analysts noted the significance of these
performances.

"Cliburn's recent appearances with the Russian Philharmonic
in Brussels and Ostend were endorsed by our State Department," wrote syndicated columnist H. I. Phillips. "The Russians
invited him. This mutual accord suggests that the United Nations might be overlooking a bet in not insisting that he come
and tinkle the keys during the current emergency session. . . .
Maybe what the U.N. needs most is a piano player." [137]

After playing in Belgium, Van "flew to Heidelberg to play
before the U.S. Army servicemen and their families at a free
performance," reported *Variety,* pointing out that he was

> . . . theoretically on his vacation. . . . The concert,
> announced only the day previously, was an astound-
> ing success with the military men, not generally
> noted for much interest in classical music. Despite a
> drenching rain, fans started to line up at noon with
> chairs, lunches and umbrellas, to wait for the 8 p.m.
> performance.
>
> Only 500 were permitted inside the Patrick Henry
> Village Theatre, but hundreds more jammed the
> grounds outside and heard the Chopin and Beetho-
> ven concert via loudspeakers.[138]

By now, Van's recording of the Tchaikovsky Piano Concerto
No. 1, which had been released in July, was selling like mad.

In fact, *Billboard,* which was becoming a regular chronicler
of Van's activities, reported in August:

Chances of Van Cliburn's waxing of the Tchaikovsky Piano Concerto No. 1 becoming the first classical
LP to hit the million-seller mark appear to grow
stronger every day, with the Cliburn sales now close
to the 300,000 figure . . . a solid figure even for a hot
single record [as opposed to a full-length classical
album]. The Van Cliburn disk this week [August 18]
is in the number one slot on The *Billboard* Best Selling LP Chart. At Victor these days they mention the
names of Presley and Cliburn in one breath.[139]

RCA had taken pains to turn the record around quickly
because of the incredible demand for it.

"Van wouldn't approve things unless he was satisfied, although he probably felt a certain pressure to get the Tchaikovsky approved and get it out because everyone in the country
seemed to want a copy, and I guess everyone in the country
bought one, too," says RCA's John Pfeiffer. "So there wasn't a
big period of changing of his mind in any way. No, once he'd
heard it and decided on the best parts [of the recording sessions
to use for the final release], there was no question about it.

"Later, we set up listening sessions down at the 24th Street
offices. He came down and listened to the tapes and indicated
those takes that he liked, and then I edited them. It was
probably a process of at least two weeks. There wasn't that
much editing, actually, because he liked to do things in the full
sweep, you know. He always has.

"I never really thought of how popular it would or wouldn't
be. . . . I didn't know what would happen.

"I had been in the record business nine years, and I had seen
what happened to so many of what I considered really first-class
records by Heifetz and Rubinstein and Horowitz and [harpsi-
chordist Wanda] Landowska. Because I worked with them, I
realized the real solid musicianship that went into their records.
And they'd go out into the market, and that's it. If they sold five
thousand copies clear across the country, why, everyone was
happy.

"Of course, I knew that Van's recording would be very popular, but I had no idea it would be as popular as it was. I didn't lose sight of the fact that the publicity he got had a lot to do with it. But I was glad that some people had in their collection a popular record that was also a musically fine recording." [140]

Finally, on Thursday, August 21, Van returned to the United States for a long-deserved, much-postponed, but very brief rest. [141]

Still, he remained the media darling, pursued by interviewers, broadcasters, and even Hollywood.

"The 23-year-old [sic] pianist, who's done more to push piano popularity than anyone since Liberace lighted up the keyboard with candles, has just turned down two scripts from major Hollywood companies—both on the life of Liszt—because they were not the right plots for him," reported *Variety*. The article then quoted Van:

> "I would only do a very serious film. . . .
> "Playing music is one emotion that no matter how talented an actor or an actress is, cannot be emulated successfully. Whenever an actor tries to play a pianist or violinist, he doesn't look right in the musical scenes." [142]

With major concerts still to come through the rest of 1958, Van soon was back to practicing all hours of the day and night.

"'Right now I live on a court and I've gotten complaints from the neighbors,' he explained in a *New York Times* story. 'After all, I practice between six and eight hours a day.'

"The pianist said he solved his problem yesterday by practicing between midnight and 6 a.m. in the basement of Steinway Hall." [143]

As October arrived, the most momentous year in Van's life seemed only to gather speed. He was scheduled to be soloist for the annual pension concert of the Boston Symphony on October 5, but ticket demand required a second performance on October 6.[144] The *Boston Globe* was generous in its review of the opening concert,[145] conducted by Charles Munch, but also went beyond the realm of music to note: "I could perceive no showmanship (which is a display for effect) whatever; I recognized only the natural and sincere bearing of an artist with strong feelings. You would decide that all the honors and publicity since Mr. Cliburn won the Tchaikovsky competition in Soviet Russia last Winter [sic], has not influenced his ego whatever." [146]

The performance of the Rachmaninoff Third and Schumann concertos went so well, in fact, that Van, [conductor Charles] Munch, and RCA decided to run through it again for a recording. Van played the Schumann and the Third Rachmaninoff. As usual, the only available time slot was midnight. Unfortunately, the orchestra players had all left the hall by the time the final decision to record had been made.

"After the concert, I went into the conductor's room, and a lot of people had gathered there," recalls Rosario Mazzeo, who was personnel manager of the Boston Symphony at the time. "Van Cliburn was there—he had come upstairs to share in the handshaking and visits from the many people who came in. So the conductor's room was crowded. And at some point Munch said, 'It's so good, I'm delighted.' Then Van Cliburn said, 'Well, let's record it.' He was so excited about it, he said, 'Let's just record it—right now.'

"The recording people already were there from New York with all their instruments and everything [on the chance that Van would want to tape the performance], and Munch came to me and said, 'Can you get the orchestra together?' And I said, 'They've all gone home. And Saturday night is no time to try to gather men who have gone out to after-concert suppers and who knows what else.'

"But both Van and Munch insisted, so I said I would try, but I just could not guarantee that we could get the entire orchestra together. I never had quite that same thing ever happen before or, for that matter, after, and I was personnel manager of the Boston Symphony for over a quarter of a century. Gathering an orchestra is one thing, but gathering a full symphony orchestra for a midnight recording—that may be a first for anybody.

"So I pulled two secretaries out of their private lives and put them on the phone, and we called everybody. We had a terrible time tracking down some of the people.

"Finally we reached everybody except one—if I remember correctly, it was a horn player. Everybody else we did reach, and we had the session. It took us a good part of the night to get everybody.

"We recorded the piece, and when it was through, everybody thought it went on quite well. Everybody thought it was fine. And then later we learned that Van rejected it when he heard it." [147]

There are various reasons that the recording wasn't released. For one, "Munch was funny," remembers RCA producer John Pfeiffer. "He really didn't care, in a way. He could be a wonderful conductor, he liked working with artists, but when it came to recording with them, he thought, *Well, that's their business.*

"So he would record [a concerto], and then he would say, 'Oh well, you decide. You do it.' And he'd go off and leave you.

"Munch was that way with artists. He would do that with Rubinstein too. We'd record, and he would say, 'Oh, here, you listen, and I'll see you tomorrow.'

"Munch was that way with his performances too. He just wasn't a rehearsal conductor. He'd go through things, and then he would say, 'Well, theees ees okay. We'll do eet in performance.'

"And the musicians didn't have the faintest idea what he was going to do, so they were constantly just right on that point where they were just about to fall apart.

"But they were watching him constantly, and he would do little things, and they would respond. And sometimes it was a total disaster, but very often it was a real sensation, real musicmaking, and he was famous for that.

"But he couldn't do that with Van, somehow, it just didn't work, the chemistry wasn't there, which was too bad because I know Van liked him so much, and he loved Van.

"So this night with Van was difficult because we'd started at midnight after the concert and we went on until about six o'clock in the morning. They recorded this whole Schumann and the Rachmaninoff Third, and they did a Liszt A Major [Piano Concerto no. 2] at one point, but it never came off." [148]

By now, Van's fees had skyrocketed along with his reputation, reportedly $3,500 for a concert, and as much as $15,000 for a pair of concerts, such as the Hollywood Bowl dates. [149]

Still, he apparently did not lose perspective. When Rildia Bee came down with a nerve problem in her face, caused by an infected tooth, Van postponed his performance in Englewood, New Jersey, and flew home to Texas to find out what was going on. [150]

Reported the *Kilgore News Herald,* "His father said Mrs. Cliburn had previously planned to fly to New York today [October 9] to be with her son for a series of [New York] Philharmonic Orchestra concerts and the presentation of his new Anthem composition [an organ work].

"'When Mother didn't feel like coming, I thought I'd better come see about her,' Van told Associated Press." [151]

Better still, Van told the paper the next day, "'I brought a special prescription for her from New York. It seems to have been effective, and I shall take her back to New York with me when I go." [152]

Back in New York, Van played the Rachmaninoff Third for his Philharmonic dates in Carnegie Hall, with Ross Parmenter and Howard Taubman complimenting his work in the *New York Times.* [153]

The performances were notable for drawing one of the few negative reviews Van had yet received in his life, from Irving Kolodin in the *Saturday Review,* who complained of "a lack of tonal mass to override the orchestra at crucial points in the first and final movements . . . plus an inclination to indulge the weaker aspects of the composer's creation at cost to the stronger." [154]

Later, when Van and Rildia Bee attended the opening of the 75th Metropolitan Opera season, there was as much excitement in the audience as on the stage, as fans thrust their programs at him in hopes of an autograph.[155]

Van spent that Thanksgiving in Kilgore, then played critically applauded performances of the Tchaikovsky First in Newark, New Jersey,[156] and the Schumann and Rachmaninoff Third in Pittsburgh[157] before heading back for a run of Texas and Louisiana performances.

When Van landed at Dallas's Love Field, a *Dallas Morning News* reporter asked him about "a recent magazine article by a New York music critic, Winthrop Sargeant, in which the author stated that, 'the sputnik-like career of Mr. Van Cliburn . . . may fizzle out unless it is based on a somewhat larger repertory than he is playing at present.' " [158]

Van wasted no time in setting the record straight.

" 'I think the writer is ill-informed,' the unruffled Cliburn replied. 'At present we are carrying six concertos on tour, as well as three complete recital programs. I think Mr. Sargeant was just writing a conversation piece.' " [159]

In Waco, he played the Tchaikovsky with the Baylor Symphony Orchestra on November 6,[160] and after the performance it was announced that Van's father had donated $10,000 to the school, while Van had donated his $4,000 fee to establish four scholarships.[161]

On the following day, Baylor University presented him with an honorary degree of doctor of humanities. In conferring the degree, Baylor President Dr. W. R. White said, "We love you, Van Cliburn. You mean more to us and the world than you know." [162]

After playing in New Orleans,[163] Van picked up an honorary admiralship in the Texas Navy. Advised the *Kilgore News Herald,* "Now, for all of the Kilgore folks who won't know whether to address him as Admiral-Doctor Cliburn or Doctor-Admiral Cliburn when he returns here [to Kilgore] for Van Cliburn Day, we suggest this modest, unpretentious young man be addressed simply as 'Van.' " [164]

For his Dallas homecoming, Van was presented by no less than Speaker of the House and longtime family friend Sam

Rayburn. Because of the close family friendship, the O'Bryans and Cliburns always referred to him as "Brother Sam."

"I had known Brother Sam since we were back in Shreveport," says Van. "When I was four years old, he would come and have dinner with us. And then, every time we would go to Washington, from the time I was twelve, we'd go visit him in his office. He wanted to be the one to come down to introduce me to the Texas press. And he said, 'If anybody knows that little boy, I surely do. I know where he comes from. I know where he's going.' " [165]

At the gathering, Rayburn offered his own point of view on music, saying, "I like piano—and that old-time fiddling is good music, too." [166]

Then, on November 29, Van played the Schumann and Rachmaninoff Third concertos. John Rosenfield noted that Van was not the pianist some of his new fans anticipated him to be. "If patrons expected the leonine temperament and touch in Cliburn, they were victims of their own misinformation," wrote Rosenfield. "The deeply sincere Kilgore lad acts his age and also remains in tune with his nature. This is basically singing, lyrical and tender." [167]

Such was Van's rising popularity that he even turned up in the "Peanuts" comic strip, the *Kilgore News Herald* running a sequence in which Lucy ignores a piano-bound Linus, then tells him, "You're not the only fish in the sea." He looks shocked until she yells at him, "Van Cliburn!" [168]

The most valued homecoming of all, though, was Van's return to Kilgore, which had declared Tuesday, December 2, "Van Cliburn Day in Texas."

The *Dallas Morning News* reported,

> The community nestling in a thicket of 11,000 oil derricks sported a new and distinctive decoration. On the main thoroughfare [Main Street] was a hand-painted sign about the size of a 24-sheet poster. The left third was a good likeness of Van Cliburn in white tie. "Kilgore, the proud home of Van Cliburn" was

the lettering. It just went up at 11 a.m. Monday; it is expected to stand for decades. . . .

"I'll bet this is the only community in the United States that makes a concert pianist its proudest boast," said Kilgore Mayor L. N. Crim.[169]

Actually, the new billboard was ten feet by thirty feet, with a fourteen-foot cutout likeness of Van in color. When Van first laid eyes on it, "He was tempted to tell his driver to go around the block about thirty times," noted the Kilgore News Herald. [170]

The Van Cliburn Day festivities began at 11:00 A.M. December 2, as Van regaled the press from across the state that had converged on tiny Kilgore. " 'I don't know what I have done to measure up to this reception by these wonderful people,' he said," reported the *Kilgore News Herald.* " 'For perhaps the first time in my life, I am speechless.' . . .

"He admitted that he is a little apprehensive about tonight's concert. 'It is one thing to play before Eastern or Western critics; you can do that with impersonality,' he said.

" 'But when I know there are the Charles Devalls and John Rosenfield and others like them in my audience, it is a different thing.' " [171]

Next came a luncheon for Van at the National Guard Armory, with five hundred admirers seated at fifteen tables, flags from around the world hanging from the ceiling, Kilgore Rangerettes as far as the eye could see, copies of the special twenty-two-page edition of the *Kilgore News Herald* strewn about. Among the guests was Texas Governor Price Daniel, who had passed up an invitation to the inauguration of the new President of Mexico in order to be in Kilgore.[172]

After visiting with friends and family through the early afternoon, Van played a 3:00 P.M. matinee for schoolchildren. According to the *Kilgore News Herald,*

Kilgore's teenage set forgot all about bobby sox, blue jeans and rock 'n' roll music Tuesday afternoon, sat through 85 minutes of symphonic score and gave

Van one of the noisiest acclamations ever heard in the Kilgore College Auditorium. . . .

A 12-year-old girl, stars in her eyes, said, "It was gorgeous." . . .

"He's better than Elvis by far," declared another in the crowd that mysteriously appeared onstage a few seconds after Van left the keyboard and literally backed him into a corner seeking his autograph.[173]

Then came an 8:00 P.M. concert that, like the first, was assisted by the Dallas Symphony Orchestra.

Because Governor Daniel attended both performances, *Dallas Morning News* critic John Rosenfield wrote the next day:

This was probably the first time any governor of any state had heard the Rachmaninoff D Minor Concerto played twice within six hours. . . .

The evening concert with [Dallas Symphony] conductor [Paul] Kletzki was a far-ranging capstone to Kilgore's greatest day of jubilation. For Cliburn had exhibited the qualities of, not a musical sensation or prodigy, but of an important artist.[174]

After the performance and the obligatory encores, Van's parents rescued him, "bustling him into a topcoat," reported the *Kilgore News Herald,* and whisking him away to a reception.[175]

A few days later Van was back in Dallas, though close to the end of his rope. "All the long hours, travel and appearances coupled with my recording dates has put me in one of my dark states, and I am badly in need of a mental refresher," Van told the *Dallas Morning News.*

Pointing to the recent Boston engagement, in which he had performed during the day, recorded through the night, and played another concert the next day, Van added: "An artist cannot be a machine, although some people seem to expect him to be one. I will be very happy to do either the recordings or the concerts, but trying to do both is too much." [176]

And still the roller coaster rode on. On Tuesday, December 16, Shreveport had its own "Van Cliburn Day." Here, too, there were proclamations, a dinner, testimonials, and of course a bit of performing, with Van playing the Liszt Twelfth Rhapsody to a crowd that hadn't expected him to perform but clearly hoped he would.[177]

And yet, Van wouldn't have missed it.

"In his talk," reported the *Kilgore News Herald,* "Mr. [Travis A.] White [head of the Shreveport Chamber of Commerce] pointed out that Shreveport was grateful to Van for something he did for them. 'He was under great pressure from the State Department to cancel his December engagements and make a trip to India, but he insisted on keeping this date.' " [178]

How did he do it? How did Van withstand the attention, adulation, pressure, and scrutiny of the spotlight that was put on him?

Surely no other classical musician had experienced the like, if only because, for the first time, television was making an artist instantly visible throughout the world. Add to that the political ramifications of Van's Cold War victory, and you have a scenario that easily could crush an artist's spirit.

"This was the first time that a musical performer had been propelled into that kind of really extraordinary limelight," says Joseph Silverstein, the violinist who is also music director of the Utah Symphony. "It was beyond anything anybody had ever seen at that point. And it did put on Van a level of responsibility about his career that I think would have been daunting for anybody. Plus, at the very moment he was making that big splash, pianists such as Rubinstein, Horowitz, Serkin were all at the peak of their careers, so it was an incredible situation." [179]

Some observers were canny enough to notice that it all took its toll. "Van was affected, no question about it," says his longtime record producer at RCA, John Pfeiffer. "He was occasionally panicky—he occasionally got very uptight about everything. I knew that he immediately would be surrounded by a lot of people who would want to grab onto his coattails and fly along with him. I wondered if he would be able to shake them off and go on his own way, and not be too influenced.

"I saw evidences of people doing just that. Of course, I made no comment, but I was very glad when I saw that he just pushed them away—not in a bad way, but little by little, getting rid of them. And I think that after a little time, he managed to settle down, and it was sort of a day-by-day affair. I think he decided, 'Well, I have to take one day at a time.'

"I know his family was a big support at the time. Both his mother and father were there, not pushing him, not pressing him to do anything, as much as just saying, 'We're here when you need us.' " [180]

Perhaps the most important message Van received from his parents was a message of faith and deep love.

"There's a great quotation that my mother told me, and I think it was her original," says Van. "She said, 'Van, if you have a gift, that's from God. But if you have a career, that is a gift from the public—treasure it.' It is so true.

"Everything falls into place after that. I remember at the time [after winning the Tchaikovsky], someone said to me, 'Isn't this incredible that people know you here, know you there, and all that sort of thing?' And I said, 'No, not really.' I grew up in a small town. It was a lovely town, but its population was around ten thousand. My parents were nice people, and they were respected, and everybody knew everybody else. So to me, the really amazing thing was that as I grew up in Kilgore, some people in the next town actually knew of me.

"You see, I don't believe in 'overnight' success. There is no such thing. Yet, all of a sudden because of this wonderful thing called mass communication, somebody else now knew my name or knew little Van Cliburn from Kilgore. But I had been playing in public since I was three and had done various things on the stage from then on, either singing [as boy soprano from age eight to eleven] or speaking, whatever. So I knew what it was to be in public, and I love people. People were always a source of inspiration to me." [181]

As Van acknowledged in a piece he wrote for *Guideposts* magazine in 1960, as told to Sidney Fields: "With the sudden acclaim in Moscow, I should have been ecstatic, for the fragrance of fame is sweet. But I wasn't. All I saw ahead then was the desperate need to pray for the strength to continue whatever was meant for me." [182]

Or as pianist George Pappastavrou says, "Van is a very devout person and rather modest about his gifts. If he felt self-important at all, I think the magic would go out of his playing. In later years, whenever he played a concert, he also spoke to the audience. He has a very homespun kind of philosophy of what he's doing, and he has a little bit of the preacher about him." [183]

When Van won the Tchaikovsky competition, he also won a platform like no other American musician had had before him. Around the world, music lovers wanted to hear him, journalists wanted to talk to him, fans wanted to meet him.

Perhaps Van endured the glare of celebrity by choosing to use his newfound platform in a somewhat idiosyncratic way. In other words, at the instant he became internationally famous, he instinctively chose to turn around that fame, directing his message toward others. Certainly his subsequent actions suggest that's the case.

In the fall of 1958, Van donated to the City of New York the $1,250 prize money he had been allowed to take back with him from Moscow. The *New York Times* reported that

> . . . it was his wish the prize money be used to help all peoples find common understanding through "the universal language of the arts."
>
> At the same time, the 23-year-old pianist [sic] said that he had requested all of the orchestras in the cities in which he will give concerts this season to open the dress rehearsal of his performances to teenagers.

"I've wanted to do this sort of thing for a long time," Mr. Cliburn said at a press conference.[184]

Though he never would become the medical missionary his father originally had hoped he would, Van seemingly was applying a missionary's philosophy toward music. Virtually everywhere he went that first post-Tchaikovsky season, Van indeed insisted on throwing his rehearsals open to the teenagers, who flocked to attend them.

In New Haven, Connecticut, he "made a hit with 2,600 teenagers here," reported the Associated Press,

> . . . and they made a hit with him. As a consequence, he is thinking of offering repeated 50 cent rehearsals [to defray costs] just for youths.
>
> The 23-year-old [sic] winner of Moscow's Tchaikovsky piano competition, here for a public concert Tuesday night, took off his coat for the teenagers.
>
> More than 1,000 youths had to be turned away from the rehearsal. . . . Adults were not allowed.
>
> The audience cheered wildly, and Cliburn was pleased. "We are going to follow this thing up," he said. "It can bring on a new generation of music-loving Americans." [185]

Similarly, in Austin, Texas, Van won standing ovations at a morning dress rehearsal attended by 2,200 children and University of Texas students, reported the Kilgore News Herald.[186]

So Van was making music a kind of mission, an attitude that set the stage for the telling events of November 30, 1958. After playing the Schumann and Rachmaninoff Third piano concertos with the Dallas Symphony in Ft. Worth's Will Rogers Auditorium, Van "came down with nausea and fever after the performance, and barely felt well enough to go to the Ft. Worth Piano Teachers' Forum dinner [in Rildia Bee's honor]," reported the *Ft. Worth Star-Telegram* years later.

"If Cliburn hadn't come to the party, would erstwhile piano pedagogue Irl Allison have had the nerve to stand up and announce, with nothing but gumption to back him up, that there would be a piano competition founded soon, named for Cliburn?

"Allison, with the help of a lot of people in Ft. Worth, managed to make his spur-of-the-moment dream a reality and managed to coax Cliburn back for a recital to raise money in 1961," [187] a year before the first Van Cliburn International Piano Competition.

This was the same Irl Allison who, as a judge of the national piano playing auditions, had written of the young Van: "Your piano-playing proclivities will undoubtedly carry you far." [188]

When Allison made his impromptu announcement, "Van was stunned," recalled Grace Ward Lankford, chairman of the competition, years later. "I was sitting right next to him, and he had something right up to his lips to eat, and he just dropped it." [189]

As Van later explained, "I came back to Ft. Worth in 1958, and at a dinner for my mother, [Allison] suggested a competition, named for me and offered ten thousand dollars toward starting it. I'm a Texan till I die, and I wanted the people here to have what they want. We didn't begin, though, until 1962. Texans won't do it unless they can do it right." [190]

Though it would have been impossible to know at the time, it seems obvious today that there was no way Van would oppose a competition such as the one Allison proposed. The idea clearly appealed to the rising sense of mission in him.

Eventually, the competition would become not only the foremost in the Western hemisphere but a central artistic expression and personal statement for Van.

A couple of years after the colossal events of 1958, Van said, "Today we live in a world of many mixed emotions—fear, struggle, beauty, power, gigantic enterprises, financial uncertainty, high taxes—as well as the age-old problems of death, heartbreak and the very unglamorous everyday problems.

"Through it all, music is certainly a 'balm of Gilead' that soothes the soul. When great music is entered into with this purpose and with this very realistic attitude, the real rewards are intangible and far removed from this world." [191]

9

Artist's Life

*T*hough the tidal wave of publicity receded after Van's historic homecoming, he remained news, his every ache and pain seeming to find its way into print or onto TV. When Van's tooth bothered him in the beginning of 1959, UPI sent the news worldwide.

Van discovered that there were nagging little problems with fame. After having been named one of the ten outstanding men of 1958 by the U.S. Junior Chamber of Commerce (Jaycees), Van was summarily dropped when his concert schedule conflicted with the awards ceremony.[1]

"It has been a long standing policy of the program that, barring extreme circumstances, winners must accept the awards personally at a national awards ceremony," intoned Jaycees president Robert Cox, whose organization quickly chose singer Pat Boone as Van's replacement.[2]

Van was not silent about what really was going on here.

At first, he offered a somewhat wry response, telling Associated Press, "I was very pleased to have been named for this distinguished honor. However, I was not aware that the award was predicated solely on personal appearance and not for accomplishment. Such are the personal sacrifices one is called upon to make in an artistic existence." [3]

Later, in Memphis, Van sounded off a bit more expansively. "An award for one's art that is premised on deadheading one's presence at the presentation ceremonies is promotion for the organization, and very little beside," Van told *Variety*. "They ride my publicity and expect me to cancel paid concerts and make a trip at their convenience. Who are they kidding with their gimmicked honors?" [4]

Certainly Van was in a whirlwind, though now with somewhat less hysteria than before.

In the capital, Soviet First Deputy Premier Anastas I. Mikoyan "brought his Washington visit to a close tonight [Jan. 19, 1959] to the strains of an impromptu concert by Van Cliburn," reported the *New York Times*.

> As the tall young man bounded up the red-carpeted stairs of the Embassy, he was kissed and embraced by Ambassador Mikhail A. Menshikov. A moment later he got a bear hug and a kiss on each cheek from Mr. Mikoyan.
>
> Mr. Mikoyan led Mr. Cliburn to the Embassy's grand piano. The musician struck up a popular Moscow song, "Evenings in the Suburbs of Moscow" [also known as "Moscow Nights"]. Mr. Mikoyan and other Russians joined in the chorus. [5]

In Philadelphia at the end of January, Van shared the bill with Maria Callas, Eugene Ormandy, and the Philadelphia Orchestra for the 102nd anniversary concert of the Academy of Music.

"Last night's playing was not all compounded of flaunting youth and bravura," wrote the *Philadelphia Inquirer* critic of Van's return performance of the Rachmaninoff Third. "The young man who seemed to be on the verge of full bloom eight months ago has matured still further. The lyric moments of last night's performance had the tenderness of maturity." [6]

In San Francisco early in February, Van's reading of the Prokofiev Third Piano Concerto was deemed "fabulous" by Arthur Bloomfield in *Musical America*. And his performance there of Mozart's Piano Concerto in C Major, K. 503, prompted Bloomfield to write: "The young Texan will be a greater Mozart player with time, but there was no question that he realized that this composer's piano music must be played with well-sculptured evenness of phrase and unpushed tone." [7]

And in New York, Van played a herculean three concertos in a pension fund concert for the New York Philharmonic, raising about $40,000, at the time an imposing sum. Noted Howard Taubman in the *New York Times*:

> Since that memorable triumph [in Moscow] Mr. Cliburn has shown an instinct for turning his renown to the good of music. His eagerness to play for youngsters and to make his rehearsals available to them show his good will. His generosity in contributing his services to the Philharmonic pension fund is another example. But he had better beware of being too generous.
>
> It was a gesture far beyond the call of duty to undertake three concertos that he does not have under complete control.[8]

Not all the critics chided Van for his musical ambition, however. In the *New Yorker,* Winthrop Sergeant wrote:

> One cannot but admire the gallantry and impetuousness of the gesture, and the generosity of the young performer in attracting a capacity crowd to the auditorium, at twenty dollars an orchestra seat, for the benefit of the Philharmonic's pension fund.[9]

Still, Sargeant added that the Mozart "was simply not well done," either by pianist or conductor, that both Van and Bernstein "felt much more comfortable in this frankly emotional music" of the Schumann, and that the Prokofiev was "brilliant." [10]

Such was Van's rising popularity that his success became the grist for comics, such as the great musical anarchist Victor Borge, who quipped, "Tchaikovsky was born in 1840 and was a rather obscure musician until 1958 when he was discovered by a Texan." [11]

These heady times of sold-out performances and typically grand reviews came to an abrupt halt, however, when Van hit upon a series of catastrophes that very nearly cost him part of his right arm.

"He told me that he was riding in a taxi in San Francisco," recalls Fritz Steinway, of the famous piano family, "and he was manicuring his own fingernails. But the taxi went over a few bumps, and whatever he was manicuring himself with poked into his finger. And that poking under the skin, and his run-down condition, undoubtedly that's where the infection began. And then it developed, and he didn't pay any attention to it, in typical fashion, until it really got so bad that he came pretty close to losing [his arm]." [12]

The problem gruesomely came to a head in February, when Van, Steinway, and Skitch Henderson went to Atlantic City, where Van was scheduled to play for the American Association of School Administrators convention.

As soon as Van walked on stage, it was clear something was wrong. Associated Press reported,

> Cliburn told the audience that he was suffering from an inflamed finger on his right hand and was appearing, against his doctor's advice because "this is important to me.". . .
>
> When he had finished a hall crowd of more than 12,000 rose and thundered its approval.
>
> Cliburn ran backstage for a quick drink of water, squeezing his bandaged finger all the while with his left hand.

As he started to move back onstage, a friend
grabbed his arm.
"Don't use that hand any more," the friend told him.
"Just one more," Cliburn pleaded and went back
for an encore.[13]

By this point, Steinway was terribly worried about the risk
Van was taking by ignoring the pain to satisfy his audience.

"His finger hurt him so badly," recalls Fritz Steinway, who
had been backstage with Van, "that, charming as he was, he
announced from the stage that he had a little trouble with an
infected finger, and that he was going to play two pieces with
his left hand only [including the Scriabin Nocturne for the left
hand alone].[14]

"That didn't make the slightest bit of difference to the audience; they were there to see Van Cliburn and be able to go
home and tell everybody that they heard Van Cliburn play the
piano. That was the start of the trouble." [15]

After the painful performance, Van accepted an award,[16]
then began to realize he had a serious problem. By February
23, he had entered the Hospital for Special Surgery of New York
Hospital,[17] and on the 27th he underwent surgery "to drain an
abscess on the middle finger of his right hand," reported the
New York Times. [18]

Five physicians worked on the finger for half an hour, first
cutting through a callus an eighth of an inch thick. Normally,
Van was told, doctors removed the entire fingernail during
such a procedure, but in his case, a third of the nail had been
taken off in hopes it would grow back normally.[19]

Medical wisdom in those days confined Van to his bed from
Friday, February 27, the day of the operation, to the following
Wednesday, March 6. They were dreary, depressing days, as
were the weeks that followed, for Van had had to cancel more
than a dozen concerts, as well as a planned return engagement
to the Soviet Union.[20]

"The fact that I can't play is more injurious to my morale than the [physical] pain," Van told an AP reporter from the hospital.[21]

So Van watched TV, "something I never had much time for before. I've done a little reading too. Poetry, for the moment—poetry more than prose." [22] Scattered atop his bed were the score for Samuel Barber's Capricorn Concerto, a recording of Barber's opera *Vanessa,* and the like.[23]

As for several months' worth of canceled concerts, "Every concert is only postponed," Van said. "I don't believe in cancellations. Never close the door, you know.

"I have received several invitations to play with my good hand—some pieces like Ravel's Left Hand Concerto. . . . But the doctor thinks I should rest." [24]

Because Rildia Bee was swamped with students, who were preparing for a Bach Festival, she had to remain in Kilgore during Van's operation. It wasn't until Van was on the mend that she or he found out how grave his situation was.

"When the doctors told me I couldn't play for three months, it seemed like an eternity," Van told the *Dallas Morning News.* "It could have been a lot worse though. If I'd delayed another 48 hours I might have lost the finger." [25]

Associated Press later reported that the operation "narrowly averted the need for amputation of his right hand and possibly other portions of his arm. . . . He had not been informed about the danger 'until the operation was all over and the surgeon was sure I would recover completely.' " [26]

Released from the hospital, Van headed to Tucson to relax in the sun. Characteristically, Rildia Bee saw the bright side of a nearly tragic scenario. "He's terribly disappointed," she conceded to AP. "It just breaks his heart to cancel a concert—any concert. . . . He's so anxious to please and the audiences are so gracious to him that he never wants to take a rest. He certainly needs one, though." [27]

By the end of April, doctors gave Van the okay to resume full-time practicing,[28] and quickly he was off and running with a European tour in June. Again, reviews in cities as far-flung as London and Milan were enthusiastic.[29]

Yet, even on the overseas tour, Van remained deeply attached to Kilgore and all it represented.

"After he won the competition, he traveled a lot," recalls James Dickson, who was a piano student of Rildia Bee's at the time. "I remember that the telephone would ring in the middle of the lesson, and because Mrs. Cliburn was still having some back problems, she always had her students go answer the phone for her. Invariably it would be Van calling from Madrid or Paris or somewhere like that." [30]

Though Van had had to cancel the Soviet return tour, the Russian people had not forgotten him. Visiting the Soviet exhibition at the Coliseum in New York in July of 1959, he "was astonished yesterday to find his face on a box of chocolates," reported the *New York Times.* " 'My goodness, it's me,' Mr. Cliburn said when he spotted the exhibit. . . .

"Yuri Volsky, Soviet press officer at the exhibition, told Mr. Cliburn that it was the best-selling candy in the Soviet Union." [31]

Of course, the mere sight of Van in a Soviet setting delighted newsmen, who urged him to play the piano (though it probably didn't take many requests). After he played two pieces, "An American cameraman begged, 'All right, Van, go through one more routine,' " reported the *New York Times.* [32]

Though two books on Van were published in 1959, *The Van Cliburn Legend* by Abram Chasins (long since out of print) and a Russian language propaganda piece that discussed "the difficulties he encountered in winning recognition [in the United States]," [33] Van's own work drew the most attention.

His RCA Victor recording of Rachmaninoff's Third Piano Concerto, taped during his Carnegie Hall concert of May 19, 1958 [34] won sustained praise.

"It represents a truly extraordinary performance, even a great one," wrote Ray Ericson in *High Fidelity.*

> Diametrically opposed to the dazzling [Vladimir]
> Horowitz version [Ericson refers here to Horowitz's

second recording of the piece, with the RCA Symphony and conductor Fritz Reiner], working from within rather than without, and even more striking for what it achieves, this performance of the long, rhapsodic score is constantly lyrical, intimate, and introspective, without ever becoming small-scaled or static. Cliburn has a pianissimo tone that is as ravishing as Rachmaninoff's, a big tone that never loses its singing qualities.[35]

Not that it was easy to get Van to release the recording. "When Van decided [initially] not to approve the performance [of both the Tchaikovsky and Rachmaninoff] I got very upset," recalls RCA producer John Pfeiffer. "But I knew at the time that he had to be in control, and so if he wanted to redo it [the Tchaikovsky], fine, we would redo it [which was exactly what they did in the famous midnight Carnegie Hall session].

"But the Rachmaninoff Three, I made quite a stand on that one because I thought, *He cannot improve that,* and I don't think he could. He could do it differently, but to me, that performance is head and shoulders above everyone else's.

"I had worked with Horowitz on his Rachmaninoff Three, but it was a totally different sort of thing, as far as I was concerned. He was a well-established artist who knew Rachmaninoff, and with Reiner [conducting], the whole atmosphere was totally different.

"But here was Van, a young artist really taking this music and looking at it in a fresh way, and coming up with something that was totally new and very exciting.

"It was just a tape from that Carnegie Hall performance, there was no makeup session, no touching up of that—it was the concert complete," adds Pfeiffer. "And if you listen very carefully, there might be one or two little slips somewhere. And it took us a long time to talk Van into ignoring those little slips, but he finally realized that the overall performance was just what he wanted.

"I remember he was spending some time in Tucson, so we sent equipment out to the house that he had rented—we sent a turntable and speakers and amplifier and had them installed in the house, just so he could listen to it.

"Fortunately it was my hometown, so I stayed at home while I was working with him. We spent a lot of time at the home of a friend of his, a minister, a wonderful person, who had a house not too far from Van's. We spent most of the time there, listening to the record, and so I never hear that record without looking out and seeing the Catalina Mountains [in my mind's eye]. As we listened, we could see those mountains, it was almost overwhelming, and it seemed to suggest the breadth and the scope of the whole performance, a massive presence.

"Then later in New York, I remember walking with Van up Third Avenue, from the [RCA] studio, after we had listened to the tape for about the 90th or 110th time. And he was uncertain. Van has a great feeling for timing. If something isn't timed just right, you don't do it. But if the time is right and if all the little tumblers fall into place, then it's fine.

"But he still wasn't sure, so I walked him up Third Avenue, and we walked all the way from 24th Street to 72nd Street. When we got to about 59th street, he said, 'All right.'

"That performance is almost like chamber music, it really is. Just the blend of musicianship that you feel both from the orchestra and from Van is unique—that's the only way I can describe it. It's a total oneness of feeling and mind. And even if you ignore all of that and just listen to the sound and the technique, it's still phenomenal." [36]

Slowly and inexorably, Van was becoming a major and sustaining force in the American recording industry. *Billboard* affirmed as much in August of 1959, reporting: "Currently, of the top 50 monophonic LPs, only two are classical items—both of them played by young Cliburn. Three classical numbers appear on the stereo LP chart, of which Cliburn's albums are two." [37]

As Van acknowledged in the *Billboard* piece, his RCA recording contract was unique, to say the least.

His agreement commits him to record two albums per year. The rub, however, is that he is not committed to approving them for release. While this arrangement undoubtedly causes some agonizing hours in the label's private offices, it has its payoff. The prerogatives given to Cliburn are the foundation of his apparent happiness with his attachment to the label.[38]

The other unusual aspect of the contract was that, as originally conceived, it ran for twenty-five years, a remarkable commitment for a man in his early twenties. No doubt this arrangement (which was later renegotiated) had its advantages and disadvantages.

Recalls Max Wilcox, who produced various Van recordings, "If Van had just gone out and made the records, they would have sold like gangbusters and everything would have been fine. But the problem with the contract was that Van always was very slow on approving anything. He was just so fussy.

"So, of course, the contract was exaggerated. It would have been better if it were for ten years, but I think RCA didn't want to risk losing him. I guess you could say the record company had a lot of faith in Van. On the other hand, you could say, 'Why would he want to lock himself up for twenty-five years?'

"RCA Victor Red Seal in the '50s was still the king, and that was where you wanted to be. And if you got a twenty-five-year contract with the most prestigious record company in the world, why would you want to turn it down? But I don't think that kind of contract would ever happen again." [39]

There were other reasons behind the remarkable contract.

"Those terms all evolved out of the negotiations," says retired RCA executive Alan Kayes, who was intimately involved with those deliberations. "It was indeed a long-term contract, but it was structured from a tax standpoint as well as anything else. We had made contractual arrangements of that nature, though admittedly on a smaller scale and on a shorter duration, previously [with other artists] for the same reason, for tax purposes, to spread out the income. But I don't think it was excessive." [40]

As for Van's fussiness about releasing his recordings, "that's what he was like from the very beginning," says Pfeiffer, who was there from the beginning, in 1958. "His whole approach, the solidity of his preparation, his attention to every little detail. He wanted everything to be in its place, so there was no possibility of any kind of distraction—I think that was his primary interest. Although I think he imagined that all of the Juilliard students were saying, 'Ah-ha, he made a mistake.' I used to kid him so much about that, and he would laugh about it.

"I told him, 'You're only saying that because that's what you used to do. When you were at Juilliard you used to listen to Horowitz's recordings and say, 'Listen, listen to that slip.' And then he blushed.

"Van did a marvelous Schumann Concerto with [conductor Charles] Munch and the Boston Symphony that got pretty close to being approved. But then he finally got more interested in working with [conductor Fritz] Reiner, and when it came up that Reiner was interested in doing the Schumann, then Van did it with him, so the one with Munch was pushed aside." [41]

For the moment, all was well in that Van's first two records were shaping up as major successes, both critically and commercially. Through it all, Van seemed aware that many different constituencies were demanding different things from him. The record company wanted a lot of product as soon as possible; the general audience wanted to hear their old favorites; the critics seemed to want different repertoire for every performance. Van wanted to take matters at his own pace and in his own style and apparently was determined to do just that.

Van told an interviewer that summer of 1959, "People really do believe that Rome was built in a day. As soon as you've made a splash, everybody wants you to do everything at once, at any cost." [42]

Then Van took pains to set the record straight regarding specifics. After pointing out that he just had played solo recitals in London and Paris, he added, "My next engagement is a two-night stand in Hollywood in September, with the Los Angeles Philharmonic. I'll do the Beethoven 'Emperor' and the Prokofiev Third Concerto the first night and the Schumann Concerto and the Rachmaninoff Third the next. I don't know where some people get the notion that I play only Rachmaninoff and Tchaikovsky. I played all sorts of solo stuff in Englewood and Summit last year." [43]

All the while, Van adored the artist's life, though on his terms, preferring to use his name and box office power to champion causes dear to him. In Los Angeles that September, he played the four concertos over two nights at the Hollywood Bowl, raising money for the projected Los Angeles Music Center and winning critical acclaim in the process.[44]

When Khrushchev came to visit President Eisenhower in Washington, D.C., in September, it became apparent once again which superpower leader was in touch with Van's popular appeal and which one wasn't. Maxine Cheshire wrote in the *Washington Post*:

> Many music-lovers feel that President Eisenhower ignored the logical choice and hit a sour note when he booked popular music for his state dinner for Soviet Premier Nikita Khrushchev instead of [Van] Cliburn. . . .
>
> Now Cliburn, . . . has been invited to the Soviet Embassy here next week.
>
> Cliburn has accepted the bid to attend the Soviet Embassy reception Ambassador Mikhail Menshikov is giving on Sept. 24 for Premier and Mrs. Khrushchev when they return to Washington from their cross-country tour.[45]

Sure enough, in a now-familiar image, Khrushchev reached up to embrace Van during the reception, the resultant photo wired around the world. In the background, an orchestra rang out the strains of the Tchaikovsky Concerto.[46] After the embrace, Khrushchev told Van, "When you come to Moscow again you'll be our guest," reported the *New York Times.* [47]

Not content to wait until then, however, Khrushchev hastened to invite Van to take a look at his private plane.

"Premier Khrushchev's plane has luxurious cabins for six, a full kitchen and a dining room, Van Cliburn, the pianist, said today," reported Associated Press. "Mr. Cliburn, a favorite with the Soviet authorities on the strength of concert appearances in Russia, is one of the few Americans who has been permitted aboard the Tupolev V-114 turb-prop plane in which Mr. Khrushchev flew here Sept. 15." [48]

Artistically, Van ended the year rather boldly, venturing into Brahms's Piano Concerto no. 2, in B-flat Major, among the most profound and musically demanding pieces in the repertoire.

"Van Cliburn need no longer be regarded as half post-teenager and half-genius," wrote Edwin H. Schloss in the *Philadelphia Inquirer* in December, following Van's performance of the Brahms. "His art has mellowed in the past year." [49]

Wrote Max de Schauensee in the *Philadelphia Evening Bulletin,* "It is astounding how this 25-year-old pianist has matured in the last two years. . . . The massive aspects of the concerto were completely realized; so were the poignant questionings of the second movement." [50]

The other revelation of that last month of 1959 was the news that, on November 19, Van had signed with the manager he had always dreamed of working with, Sol Hurok.[51]

"Starting next season Van Cliburn will be managed by S. Hurok Attractions instead of Columbia Artists Management," reported the *New York Times.* "Mr. Cliburn has signed a contract with the Hurok management but will fill a handful of engagements booked by Columbia Artists this winter and spring." [52]

For several reasons, this would be a dream match. Born April 9, 1888, in Russia, self-made, impulsive, impetuous—everything about Hurok, including his illustrious reputation, appealed to Van. When the Moiseyev Ballet became the first Soviet company to visit the United States since World War II, it was Hurok who had brought them over. That they made their bow on April 14, 1958, just as Van won the Tchaikovsky, reflected the parallel courses of Van's and Hurok's careers.

Even then, Hurok was called "one of the last survivors of a nearly extinct breed, the fur-collar impresario," in the words of the *New York Times.* [53] In a musical world that already was increasingly defined by corporations and conglomerates, Hurok was one of the few remaining one-man bands, an impresario in the original meaning of the word, risking his own money to present artists he believed in.

In 1938, for instance, Hurok decided to woo Paris-based pianist Arthur Rubinstein for an American tour, even though his previous one, at the beginning of the century, had been a flop.

"You'll lose your shirt, Mr. Hurok," Rubinstein said. "I can borrow another one," said Hurok,[54] who proceeded to launch Rubinstein's sensational American career.[55]

"Hurok would go so far out on a limb for his artists, until he'd put one foot in the poorhouse. Van admired that," says Susan Tilley. "I think part of the attraction was Hurok's being Russian. And, of course, he was *the* presenter in those days." [56]

Beyond Van's desire to be linked with the grandest name among arts presenters, he also was ready to leave Columbia Artists Management. Just before his triumph in Moscow, the firm had seemed at least ambivalent toward him, failing to so much as list his name in its 1958 catalog.[57]

"After the ticker tape parade and so on, I was sitting in the office when Mr. Hurok brought Van Cliburn in," recalls Martin Feinstein, who was Hurok's vice president in charge of publicity at the time. "We knew already that Van was going to be added to our list, that he was now one of our artists, so we had a very nice and cordial conversation. At the end of it, as Van got up to leave, I said to him, 'Mr. Cliburn, we'll do our very best to make you famous,' and we all laughed heartily because that about summed up the situation." [58]

From the beginning, Van and Hurok hit it off famously. "They were both unique, they were both bigger than life," recalls

Doug Steinriede, Hurok's West Coast manager in the 1960s. "They both had worked very, very hard to get where they were. Hurok came over here in 1906 with either four or six rubles, depending on whose story you hear, and he did it. He came up with music for the masses, and it worked.

"He saw in Van a great talent that he wanted to represent. Van saw in him a great manager he would be proud to be with.

"You have to remember, this was really toward the end of the Hurok era [Hurok died in 1974], and you could see the whole industry changing [to a corporate approach]. It was kind of sad that it happened. But as far as Mr. Hurok and Van Cliburn went, Van probably was the most important artist in the end of the Hurok era. Rubinstein was already there, and Horowitz, but Cliburn was this great star who was born on the stage at the end of the Hurok era, and for that reason, among others, I think he meant a lot to Hurok." [59]

Buoyed by his new, promising relationship with Hurok, Van seemed to flower in 1960. Still inspired to nurture musical causes, he donated $5,000 to establish an annual Rosina Lhevinne Award at Juilliard;[60] $4,000 to the Dallas Symphony Orchestra, with no strings—and not so much as a cover letter—attached.[61]

Van was nostalgically reunited with the Moscow State Symphony at Madison Square Garden in New York in a program that also featured Valery Klimov, who had won the Tchaikovsky Violin Competition of 1958. The performance of the Prokofiev Third Piano Concerto, before 16,100 listeners, was warmly received.[62]

More important, in the middle of the year Van launched both a recital tour in the United States and further performances of the Brahms Second Piano Concerto in B-flat.

The recital tour drew both positive and mixed reviews. In Philadelphia, critic Edwin H. Schloss wrote, "It is pleasant to be able to report that this enormously gifted and engaging young Texan met the test triumphantly. While at the age of 26 [sic] no artist, however talented, can be expected to fill the interpretative frame down to the last depth or nuance,

Cliburn's performance had the virtues as well as the limitations of his years." [63]

In Dallas, *Morning News* critic John Rosenfield wrote,

> Cliburn of the recital was more aggressively impressive than Cliburn of the several concerto appearances with the orchestra, probably because he was in control of everything. . . .
>
> Cliburn's is husky Chopin, pushed to the tolerable limits of marked accents, rubato and the capacities of the modern piano. There have been no such liberties with him since Paderewski and more recently, Malcuzynski. From them we have learned that that is the way Poland likes it.[64]

In Chicago, his recital debut at the Civic Opera House prompted Claudia Cassidy of the *Chicago Tribune* to express reservations. "A sweeping Brahms intermezzo he carries off, but not the G Minor Ballade. Beethoven's 'Les Adieux' had passages both beautiful and powerful, but not the structure of its backbone, mind and heart." The Prokofiev Sixth Sonata, however, represented "a big, virtuoso performance, and the second movement in particular caught the precision of tart diablerie." [65]

In April, however, Van was back to make his Chicago Symphony Orchestra debut, playing the Brahms B-flat Concerto with no less than CSO music director Fritz Reiner conducting. Instantly, it seemed, a remarkable new musical partnership was forged.

Cassidy opened her review, in fact, with this line: "Memo to myself: Don't underestimate Van Cliburn. . . . It was a big evening, not just in that the house was packed—it usually is—but in that a brilliant young pianist took another long step forward, and that Mr. Reiner and the orchestra gave him the gift no one can pay for, that of unstinting support." [66]

For Van, meeting Reiner was predictably daunting. The great Hungarian conductor was at the peak of his career in Chicago, his tenure there (from 1953-62) reestablishing the Chicago Symphony Orchestra among the world's best.

"Reiner had this encyclopedic, computer kind of mind, a great insight, a penetrating insight into situations, music or whatever it was," says Van. "He was awfully nice, and I was scared to death the first time I played with him, which also was the first time I ever met him, right onstage at Orchestra Hall in Chicago, for the rehearsal of the Brahms B-flat. And I was scared to death. I thought, *Well, we'll probably start and stop and start and stop and start again.*

"We had a Thursday afternoon rehearsal [April 7, 1960], and at the time they still had open rehearsals Friday morning. I just dreaded that, to have to play a rehearsal Thursday afternoon, a performance Thursday evening, get up and do a rehearsal Friday morning and then play a Friday afternoon performance.

"So, there I am in Orchestra Hall, wondering what's going to happen, and right away he said, 'Vell, come up, Van Cliburn.' Almost before I could even address him, the orchestra was playing and we were doing the opening of the concerto.

"I had thought he would stop and say something to me, but the next thing I knew he was signaling for me to start the next movement. And we went sailing right through the whole thing.

"Finally, at the end, he said to me, 'Vell, you can sleep in the morning.' That was it—I wouldn't have to come to the next rehearsal. I was so grateful.

"He was so fabulous to play with. He had the most incredible stick technique. This economy of motion, but that's really what conducting has to be. It's just not necessary to have all this exaggeration. That's what Dr. [Bruno] Walter and Fritz Reiner and Eugene Ormandy, all three, taught me. As well as Kondrashin—he was economical in conducting too." [67]

From this moment on, "Van kept playing with the orchestra as long as Reiner was here," recalls former *Chicago Tribune* critic Cassidy, "because he really worshiped working with him. I think Reiner recognized Van's talent—he knew talent when he heard it, and he obviously worked with Van with great pleasure.

"I also think Reiner had an authority that was overriding, and it carried Van, in a way. In fact, I sort of wonder sometimes what happened to the great tidal flow of the great [orchestral] accompaniment, so a pianist could ride it. I'd like to hear that again, but you don't hear it anymore." [68]

There were a few lighter moments in the Cliburn-Reiner collaboration, as well. "I remember once, we went out at a break, and Van was a health food nut at that time," recalls Seymour Raven, who was in Chicago Symphony management. "So we went to one of those vegetarian bars or fruit juice places around the corner from Orchestra Hall, and he ordered something made out of sassafras and carrots—one of those liquid cocktails. And he was sipping it with a straw, and he said, 'Do you think Dr. Reiner would like some of this?' And to be mischievous, I said yes.

"Now, you understand, Reiner had a Hungarian appetite. He'd eat steak tartare with an egg on it—he broke all the rules. So Van got a carton full of this stuff, with a straw, and brought it back to the dressing room to present it to Reiner. Reiner took one sip out of it, and he made with his cheeks like a French horn player who can't breathe.

"But, still, they really were very good friends." [69]

Van played the Schumann Piano Concerto with Reiner and the CSO a few days after the Brahms, and Cassidy wrote, "He has the big, surging warmth for it, the enkindling imagination, the ranging technique, and the cresting wealth of tone to soar over the orchestra when the time comes. This was extraordinary Schumann in the grand manner." [70]

If there were any doubt as to whether the Russians still remembered Van, it quickly was erased during May and June, when he made his first return to the U.S.S.R. When he landed at the airport in Moscow on May 26, "a crowd of noisy teenagers and a sprinkling of middle-aged women cheered," reported UPI. "Americans [in the U.S.S.R.] were amazed at his reception. The 25-year-old pianist from Kilgore, Tex., was abashed. Celebrities usually come and go without fanfare in Russia. . . . About 200 shouting, cheering teen-agers at the airport—and the older women too—looked enraptured, giggled, and smiled." [71]

When it came time for Van to play the Prokofiev Third and Brahms Second Piano Concertos with the Moscow State Symphony, on June 3, the excitement turned into hysteria.

UPI reported it this way:

> In an unprecedented Moscow scene, about 1,000 persons crowded round the conservatory and another 1,500 jammed into neighboring blocks.
>
> Teams of militia worked to keep them under control, aided by conservatory students wearing red armbands. There also were loudspeakers urging the throng to move along, but no one paid any attention until well after the concert started. . . .
>
> Inside for the concert, every seat plus the aisles were jammed. At the end the crowd refused to leave and Cliburn was forced to come back from his dressing room to sign dozens of autographs for persons who stormed the stage.[72]

Gennady Rozhdestvensky, who conducted the orchestra, remembers the performance as if it happened yesterday. "He made a great impression," says Rozhdestvensky. "When we played Brahms's Second Concerto and the Prokofiev Third, it was a very natural contact between us, it was very easy to play with him, very easy to follow him, and very easy to cooperate with him. His playing felt like a kind of artistic improvisation, so free.

"I will not agree with those who said he can only play Russian music. He proved that was not true [with the Brahms] in this concert." [73]

Roberta Peters, the American soprano, had gone to the U.S.S.R. with Van and Hurok, to perform and to attend Van's concerts. She did not expect what she saw. "It was unbelievable," she says today. "They put flowers on his bench before

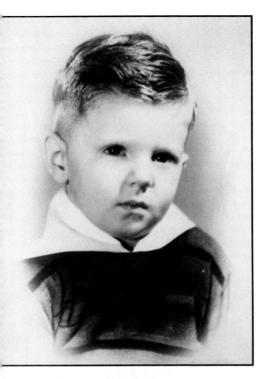

(Top left) Van at age four and (top right) at a public performance at age nine.

(Lower left) Age twelve at his Houston Symphony Orchestra debut, which was broadcast live. Conductor Ernest Hoffman stands behind him. (Lower right) With his parents, Rildia Bee and Harvey Lavan, after Van won the Tchaikovsky Competition in 1958.

(Left) 1958, Van in Paris following the Tchaikovsky Competition — the reviews for his first European tour were unanimously enthusiastic. (Right) Van with his graduating class at the Juilliard School, 1954. He almost missed the historic photo shoot.

(Left)With Rosina Lhevinne, his inspired piano teacher at Juilliard. (Right) Van playing for his adoring fans in the Great Hall of the Moscow Conservatory during the Tchaikovsky Competition.

The photo that was beamed around the world: Khrushchev embracing Van, East reaching out to West, after Van won the Tchaikovsky Competition.

(Left) President Harry S. Truman presenting Van with the State of Israel Medallion of Valor in 1962. (Right) Van and Kiril Kondrashin visiting the grave of Sergei Rachmaninoff in Valhalla, New York, 1958.

Van's ticker tape parade on Broadway. New York had not seen anything like it since Charles A. Lindbergh was so honored a generation earlier.

*Left) Van with Luci Baines Johnson and Dr.
Joseph E. Maddy, at the Interlochen National
Music Camp in Michigan, where Van performed
annually to overflow crowds. (Right) Backstage
at the Academy of Music in Philadelphia with
conductor Eugene Ormandy and opera star
Maria Callas.*

*(Left) In Ft. Worth with pianist Alicia de Larrocha, who was a
judge for the Van Cliburn International Piano Competition in
1966. (Right) An impromptu singalong in Washington, D.C., in
1959. Soviet First Deputy Premier Anastas I. Mikoyan and
Russian Embassy officials gather around their favorite pianist.*

(Left) With Barry Douglas, who won third prize in the Van Cliburn Competition in 1985 and went on to win the Tchaikovsky Competition the following year. (Right) Van surrounded by reporters during a break in the Cliburn Competition in Ft. Worth.

(Left) Van with the 1985 Cliburn Competition finalists: first-prize winner Jose Feghali is left of Van, Barry Douglas right of Van. (Right) Van with the official poster for the 1985 Cliburn Competition.

(Left) Embraced by Soviet leader Mikhail Gorbachev following Van's triumphant 1987 White House recital, his first performance in more than a decade. (Right) Receiving accolades with conductor Zubin Mehta in Carnegie Hall, after a 1991 concert with the New York Philharmonic. (Bottom) Van at the keyboard during the celebrated Moscow return, Van's first appearance in the Soviet Union in 17 years.

Van with Rildia Bee at her 92nd birthday party in Ft. Worth, 1989 — mutual inspiration.

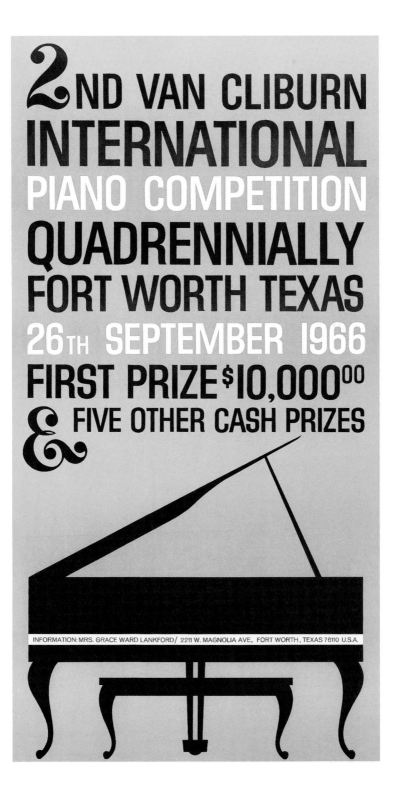

3rd VAN CLIBURN INTERNATIONAL PIANO COMPETITION

FORT WORTH, TEXAS

SEPTEMBER 29 - OCTOBER 12, 1969

FIRST PRIZE $10,000^{00}

&OTHER CASH PRIZES

INFORMATION: VAN CLIBURN FOUNDATION, P. O. BOX 17421, FORT WORTH, TEXAS 76102 U.S.A.

4.TH VAN CLIBURN INTERNATIONAL PIANO COMPETITION

FORT WORTH, TEXAS
17-30 SEPTEMBER, 1973
FIRST PRIZE $10,000⁰⁰
& OTHER CASH PRIZES

INFORMATION: VAN CLIBURN FOUNDATION, P. O. BOX 17421, FORT WORTH, TEXAS 76102 U.S.A.

5ᵀᴴ VAN CLIBURN INTERNATIONAL PIANO COMPETITION

FIRST PRIZE $10,000.00
& MAJOR ENGAGEMENTS

SEPTEMBER 12-25, 1977
FORT WORTH, TEXAS USA

FOR ADDITIONAL INFORMATION
VAN CLIBURN INTERNATIONAL QUADRENNIAL PIANO COMPETITION
3505 WEST LANCASTER   FORT WORTH, TEXAS 76107
(817) 738-6536

SIXTH VAN CLIBURN INTERNATIONAL PIANO COMPETITION

MAY 17 TO 31, 1981 FORT WORTH TEXAS

3505 WEST LANCASTER, FORT WORTH, TEXAS 76107

 Seventh Van Cliburn International Piano Competition

May 18 – June 2, 1985

8ᵀᴴ VAN CLIBURN INTERNATIONAL. PIANO COMPETITION - MAY 27 - JUNE 11 FORT WORTH. TEXAS - 1989

Ninth Van Cliburn
International Piano Competition
May 22–June 6, 1993
Fort Worth, Texas

he came out, and at the end, they ran down the aisle just like the bobby-soxers in the United States.

"It was a little strange to be over there at that time. President Eisenhower had asked us to go—Van, myself, and Isaac Stern. We were going to be inside the Kremlin—we were supposed to do a concert there, which was most unusual. Our spouses were not even invited.

"The recital was just for twenty-five people, something like that. But it never happened because that was when they blared in the street: 'Amerikanski, Amerikanski,' and they asked Eisenhower to stay home at that time. So Eisenhower never came, but we still were able to do our concerts.

"I think the Russian people still didn't know much about Americans. They kept asking us, 'Does America want war?' But I think the people themselves loved us, I mean all of us, Isaac Stern and Van and Hurok.

"That year we had dinner in Hurok's suite at the National Hotel. He had Lenin's suite, which overlooked Red Square, and Van was there. It was quite a wonderful evening of camaraderie and friendship and warmth.

"Of course, the Russian people adored Van, and they always started that unison clapping for him. It was an unbelievable experience." [74]

Interestingly, Moscow's critics were mixed in their reviews at the start of this tour (though never before or since). Associated Press noted that they were "lukewarm over his performance of Prokofiev's [Third] Concerto and Brahms's Second." [75]

Yet Van received a particular accolade that probably meant more to him than the others.

Alexander Goldenweiser, the dean of the Russian pianists, said in a Moscow newspaper article: "Like many others, I was anxiously looking forward to Van Cliburn's appearance on the stage after a two-year interval. I wondered if the charm of his inimitable skill would be preserved or if it would die away and Cliburn would turn into no more than an excellent pianist, of which there are many. Now we can see that Cliburn's wonderful gift has remained just as unique as it had been before." [76]

Beyond the concerts, though, the tour was a reunion, a chance to see once again the Russian friends who had meant so much to Van in 1958.

"I remember that he and his interpreter, Henrietta Belayaeva, came to my grandfather's place in the country," says Ashchen Mikoyan, whose grandfather was Soviet First Deputy Premier Anastas I. Mikoyan. "After almost every concert, he came to my parents' flat, where I lived. And lots of people gathered there after each concert—friends, musicians, pianists. First we would have dinner, and then we would sit down to the piano and play into the early hours of the morning. Sometimes neighbors complained, but they didn't know who was playing. If only they knew!

"And some of his fans who followed him all over Moscow, they knew the way to our house already. So even though he was more or less smuggled in my father's car after his concert —he had to double up in the back of the car and flowers were piled on his back so that he wouldn't be seen by the crowd—still some of the fans knew the route.

"Sometimes, at four in the morning, I would look out the window of my bedroom and see those fans sitting on the bench in the courtyard outside our flat." [77]

As Van's tour picked up momentum, so did critical assessment. Pianist-critic Sergei Dorensky, writing in *Trud,* said Van's playing was "absolutely inimitable. . . . In every piece he manages to show his individuality. It is superfluous to speak of Van Cliburn's technical mastery." Mikhail Sokolovsky, in *Literary Gazette* wrote: "He has matured as an artist and now plays with much greater ease, determination and self-confidence. His career is only beginning; he has not yet solved many artistic problems but he is growing to be one of the most outstanding pianists of the time." [78]

Meanwhile, the hysteria kept mounting. In Leningrad, "a crowd of 2,000 in the Philharmonic Hall applauded his playing for upwards of an hour," reported Associated Press, "then swarmed down the aisles to give him a flock of souvenirs, including a live pigeon. The bird bounced out of his arms and flew to the ceiling of the auditorium.

"Outside the hall, about 1,000 persons had assembled to follow him to his hotel, where they continued cheering until an hour after midnight.

"He gave an impromptu speech from the balcony, in which his appeal for friendship [between Russia and America] sent the crowd into renewed applause." [79]

On American Independence Day, July 4, Van played for Soviet and U.S. dignitaries at the American Embassy, but the tour's grand finale was a standing-room-only performance for 20,000 Russians who packed Moscow's Lenin Sports Palace, where Khrushchev often gave his speeches. With Kiril Kondrashin conducting the U.S.S.R. State Symphony Orchestra and Van playing the Tchaikovsky First, UPI reported, "More than a thousand teen-age Russian girls stampeded down the aisles. They crowded around the stage and threw bouquets at the lanky, grinning pianist. . . . At times during the concert, the teen-agers sighed in unison or wept. When it finished, the entire audience kept Cliburn coming back for curtain calls for at least half an hour." [80]

Lost amid the sheer spectacle of the tour was the salient fact that Van had played the MacDowell Piano Concerto no. 2 in what was surely the Soviet premiere of the piece. As Van later told the *Dallas Morning News,* "the Russians seemed to go wild over this piece of American music. I had to repeat the last movement." [81]

And despite the communist state's opinion of religion, Van donated 80,000 rubles (roughly $8,000 at the time) of his tour money to the Baptist Church in Moscow.

By the end of August, Van had returned from his Russian visit, and, of course, was weighed down by a variety of gifts, among them a three-week-old puppy.

There was a slight rumble in the Cliburn family late in 1960, in that the oil company where Van's father worked transferred him once again to Shreveport. The firm now was known as Mobil Oil Company, and Van's father worked as area representative for the new crude oil and gas liquids department. So Van's parents packed up and moved to 455 Wilder Place.[82]

Artistically, Van continued to extend his reach by bringing more repertoire into a series of recital and concert dates. In Boston he played a solo program holding three of the biggest sonatas in the repertory, the Liszt B Minor, the Barber, and the Rachmaninoff Second; [83] in Chicago, he played the MacDowell Second and Prokofiev Third concertos with the Chicago Symphony in Orchestra Hall, a noteworthy event in that Prokofiev himself had given the piece its world premiere in the same hall on December 16, 1921.[84]

But the signal performance was in December in Los Angeles, where Van and Bruno Walter, at age eighty-four, offered the Brahms Second Piano Concerto. The performance would be Walter's last.

Albert Goldberg wrote in the *Los Angeles Times,*

> One had the feeling that Cliburn must have studied the concerto carefully with the conductor, for their viewpoints coincided in an exceptionally unified interpretation. If anyone had the idea that Cliburn's fame was wedded to Tchaikovsky and Rachmaninoff this was ample proof of the depth of his musicianship and the comprehensiveness of his pianistic equipment. . . .
>
> It was all first rate Brahms, and it gave Cliburn a new stature among pianists.[85]

That Van and Walter fared so well was not a surprise, for Van had gotten to know the maestro in the years since winning the Tchaikovsky prize in Moscow. By studying conducting with Walter, by analyzing scores with him, Van had come to terms with one of the master conductors of the era.

"The first thing I had wanted to do when I got back from Moscow was study with Bruno Walter," remembers Van, "and to me that was such a thrill, seeing eye to eye, talking with him.

"I studied conducting with him. I remember when I first heard Bruno play, I found him intellectual, but not pseudo-intellectual. He was very spiritual, [there was] a very classic simplicity about him and his performances. This other-world came through, and Bruno had such warmth. Of course, he talked with me about stick technique too.

"But most important, he was one of those marvelous, saintly people whom you feel it's just God's blessing that you're in the presence of. I'd always adored him and his concerts. I would go whenever I could, every time I knew that he was conducting. When I began going to school [at Juilliard] he was doing guest conducting, and that's when I realized I hoped to study with him someday." [86]

By the early 1960s, Rildia Bee had joined Sol Hurok's payroll as a kind of touring manager for Van. By all accounts, she and Hurok got on famously, and for Van, having Rildia Bee on the road was a comfort.

"In those days, his mother was actually his personal manager," recalls Doug Steinriede, who was Hurok's West Coast representative in the '60s. "Mr. Hurok was his manager, and Rildia Bee handled the day-to-day things. She did a lot of the making sure that Van got there on time, and she was a mentor to him. She had this sense of what was the right thing to do at the right time. She was very savvy.

"A lot of times my wife would go with us to concerts, and she would stay backstage with Rildia Bee while Van played. I'd sit up in the box listening. And afterward, my wife would tell me, 'Rildia Bee went through that whole concert with him. She sat there with her eyes closed, and she didn't miss a note. It was as if she were almost playing that concert herself.' " [87]

Surely Rildia Bee was one of the few people who was not in awe of Van, who could tell him exactly what she thought, straight on.

"Rildia Bee kept Van on the road and showing up at rehearsals and so forth," says Max Wilcox, who had produced recordings for Van at RCA. "But if anyone thinks Van would do anything that Mrs. Cliburn told him to do—forget it. He was his own man. Yet, she was really important to the whole thing.

"She had a famous statement that she said constantly, and I'll never forget it: 'Well, he's a nice boy, but sometimes I could just wring his neck.' " [88]

Like Van, she generally had a sense of humor about life, even in the most rarefied places.

"I'd go to concerts that Van was giving," recalls his old Texas friend, pianist Ivan Davis, "and then I'd go backstage afterward. And Rildia Bee would say, 'Oh, Ivan, we're so lucky he didn't fall off the piano bench.'

"She'd say that every time, and I'd burst out laughing. It was so funny to hear that after he had given an incredible performance." [89]

Beneath the humor, though, Rildia Bee apparently knew precisely what was happening.

"I think Rildia Bee's role was even more than we realize," says RCA producer John Pfeiffer, "because even though Van is a very strong personality, and he knows pretty much what he wants, and he will not always follow what someone says, he *will* listen.

"He always listened to Rildia Bee very carefully. Maybe it would be six months later before he would decide: 'She was right, and I agree with her.'

"Now, he would never tell her that—he would just do it, whatever 'it' happened to be. And I think that she has played a major role in his career, even just in small ways, just being there and keeping him somehow aware of his roots. Because while she was there, she was in effect the root, the tap root that kept him going, whether he realized it or not. I think in a way he does now, but I don't know if he realizes how really important she has been to him all these years.

"For instance, I'm sure that he would play things for her [recordings before he decided whether to release them], and she would make some comment. Now she wouldn't really have any direct influence on him as far as choosing repertoire [to record] or anything like that. But I'm sure that underneath, she exerted her influence.

"So I think she was always a reassurance and a kind of reinforcement of his own values, and that, I think, kept him on the straight and narrow." [90]

Specifically, "I can tell you that Van had and has great respect for her musicianship, and also for her judgment," says Raymond Boswell, a longtime family friend who still lives next door to the Cliburn property in Shreveport. "I have known Rildia Bee closely—she is like a mother to me—and I know she has the ability to look right through a situation and understand exactly the meaning of it.

"I think her savvy has always been a tremendous part of his career. Her advice has proven correct time and time and time again, it would be hard to go against that." [91]

Naturally, Van was acutely aware of Rildia Bee's power in his life and in their relationship. "She worked for Mr. Hurok," says Van, "and he just adored her. [Sometimes] I thought it was they against me and me against the world. They would conspire to get me to do some things. And she knew that she could always talk me into something.

"Hurok would call her and say, 'Rildia Bee, I think so-and-so needs to have this and that.' Now, if she really thought it was not right, she'd tell him, and I think he'd accept it. But if she thought it really would be right for me, she'd try to put me in. She always succeeded, of course. And she really was right on in those times that she had a *real* feeling that something should be done. She was very intuitive. She could see through a situation so clearly." [92]

There was one other remarkable feature of Van and Rildia Bee's life on the road. Already, they were accustomed to staying up into the wee hours, a habit Van had picked up in earnest during his Juilliard years, when he found practicing most productive after everyone else had gone to sleep.

"He's always been that way, for as long as I've known him," says Doug Steinriede, whose friendship with Van dates to the early 1960s. "His mother used to stay up to all hours too. I'll never forget when I first met them, it was at the Hotel Utah in Salt Lake City. And that first time we met, the three of us sat up all night. I thought, *Gosh, do these people ever sleep?*" [93]

John Shenaut, the Shreveport conductor who has known Van since the early teen years, explains it this way: "He always has had a powerful belief in his privacy. And he also believes, I think, in the protectiveness of music making. That's what enables him to practice at 2 A.M. It isn't simply because he needs to practice at two in the morning or because he wants to turn his life-style upside down. The point is that when he goes into music like that, it offers a kind of protection for him. It's a time and a place for him that's safe and protected from the outside world, which is constantly trying to get at him." [94]

In 1961, three years after winning the Tchaikovsky Competition, Van was still regarded by the U.S. State Department as a living symbol of culture in America, an association he seemed to cherish. Thus he was asked by the State Department to launch a goodwill tour of Mexico in early February, under the sponsorship of the Mexican Ministry of Culture.

"His Mexican visit is widely regarded as the first move in a stepped-up cultural exchange program between the U.S. and Latin America," reported *Piano Guild Notes.* [95]

If so, Van seemed to fulfill his end of the bargain. After his two sold-out appearances at the Fine Arts Palace in Mexico City, with the National Symphony Orchestra of Mexico led by Luis Herrera, the Mexican critics called Van a "second Rubinstein" and a "keyboard giant." [96]

In some ways, the Mexican enthusiasm for Van surpassed anything that had been seen yet.

"I remember thinking at the time that the reception was absolutely unbelievable," recalled former Hurok publicist Lillian Libman, who accompanied Van on the tour (she died in

1992). "The only other thing it compared with was the way they had received Stravinsky, whom I also had brought there.

"I had gone down a few days before Van was due to arrive, and the concerts were sold out way before we came. In fact, the *Excelsior*, which is the big paper in Mexico City, had this big cartoon that took up almost the whole of the front page. And it showed a man on his knees offering his wife a box of silver and what-not. And in this cartoon, she said, 'I don't want any of that—get me a ticket to Van Cliburn.' It was wonderful.

"It was extraordinary—we couldn't walk in the streets. And yet I thought Van dealt with it extremely well. He really approached everything very modestly; that was part of his whole charm. For instance, there was a bullfight that he wanted to go to—he wanted it for the experience of having been to one. And we went, and it was the height of the season, and the greatest of the fighters was on. Van and I came in quietly through one of the under-entrances. And the whole stadium stood up and yelled, 'Cliburn, Cliburn, Cliburn!' It was extraordinary and frightening at the same time. Van didn't know what to do.

"I made him stand up and wave, and that was it; he did not know what to do. His face was scarlet, and the bull was dedicated to him, and so on. It was quite an event.

"Ever since that tour, I always thought Van was quite a mystical sort of person.

"Before he played a concert, he seemed to be completely oblivious of the fact that an audience was waiting for him.

"Most of the time, or a good portion of the time, Van was lost in his own thoughts. I believe he was thinking about the music. He played two big concerts, and the preparation for them I think was difficult because of the altitude—you know, Mexico City is at 8,200 feet.

"I think before a performance, Van was nervous. Of course, I worked with [pianist] Glenn Gould at one point, and he was almost sick before he went on stage.

"With Van, I think that was the reason for a lot of the delays [for the start of a concert].

"Of course, I remember handling Lily Pons—she used to throw up backstage before every performance.

"Van would lock himself in his dressing room, and I wouldn't dare to approach him. I think he was praying inside. I think that he would be sick to death before he came on to the stage, and there was something inside that gave him comfort and finally made him come out. But he waited until that happened." [97]

Shortly after Van returned to the United States, *Variety* announced some startling news:

> Pianist Van Cliburn will make his debut March 5 in Carnegie Hall, N.Y., as a conductor-soloist playing Prokofiev's Third Concerto at the Dimitri Mitropoulos Memorial Concert. To prepare himself for his new role Cliburn personally expended $1,800 to rehearse the number three hours with the Los Angeles Philharmonic.
>
> This concerto was long identified with the late Mitropoulos [who had died of a fall while conducting a rehearsal at La Scala, Milan, on Nov. 2, 1960], who subbed for an indisposed Egon Petri at the original Berlin premiere in 1924 and ever afterwards conducted the piece from the keyboard, as Cliburn is now essaying.[98]

Not that Van originally had intended to conduct this performance. "After Mitropoulos had died," recalls Van, "they called and asked me to perform the Liszt 'Totentantz' with [Leopold] Stokowski for the memorial concert, which was going to be held in March in 1961, and it was going to be a huge program.

"About two months before the concert, in January, they were preparing for the new *Turandot* [at the Metropolitan Opera in New York] for [Birgitt] Nilsson, and Stokowski was the conductor. He was playing with his two little boys that he had by Gloria Vanderbilt, and he fell and broke his hip.

"I assured the people at the Musicians' Aid Society, which was sponsoring the concert, that I would still participate. I told them on the phone, 'Don't worry, I will be there. I have a recital to play that afternoon in Washington, but I'll come back to New York in time. They wanted me to speak also, so I said, 'I will speak.'

"About ten days after the announcement that Stokowski was off the concert, they called me again and said, 'Would you do a memorial gesture?' And I said, 'What do you mean?' And they said, 'Would you play and conduct the Third Prokofiev [Piano Concerto]?'

"Well, I had studied conducting with Bruno Walter, but I never had done a concert that was conducted from the piano —with me playing the piano and conducting. I was scared half out of my mind.

"So I called Dr. Walter [for advice], and he said, 'My dearrr, you must trrry to do this because Mitropoulos was a great conductor.' And I said, 'Oh, but Herr Professor, I can't do that.' And he said, 'You can doo eeet—but you must try to do eet.'

"So I rented the Los Angeles Philharmonic. And to show you what a great man Dr. Walter was—and only great people can do this—this is what happened. I called him back up and said, 'Herr Professor, I will pick you up, and we'll go to Pasadena,' because the orchestra was going to a concert that night, but they could give me a three-hour service.

"Dr. Walter said, 'I vant you to please bring the orchestra score. I don't think I know the Third Prokofiev as well as I should.'

"Now can you imagine that humility coming from one of the great conductors? This was such a big man, he had such great qualities. It was awesome to be in his presence. You felt the greatness, the extraordinary qualities that are not often seen." [99]

So Walter coached Van during the rehearsal, and when Sunday, March 5, 1961, arrived, Van had a day like none other. It began with his afternoon recital in Constitution Hall, in Washington, D.C., which for nonmusical reasons did not get off to precisely a smooth start.

"The first item on Van Cliburn's Constitution Hall concert yesterday afternoon was the intermission," reported Paul

Hume in the *Washington Post,* noting that Van arrived on stage
twenty-two minutes late.

> What had held him up? It turned out that the door-
> man at his hotel had dismissed the limousine that was
> waiting to take him to the hall because the limousine
> was holding up a bus that wanted to unload some pas-
> sengers. A delay in getting a cab, and Sunday after-
> noon traffic did the rest. They call it "Artist's Life." [100]

By 5:16 P.M., Van dashed out of Constitution Hall, jumped
into a waiting cab and sped to the airport, a policeman on
motorcycle clearing traffic with siren and whistle.

For Van, of course, the frenetic day was only half over.
Landing in New York, he similarly hastened to Carnegie Hall to
conduct and play the Prokofiev Third Piano Concerto publicly
for the first time in his life.

Reported *Variety,* in reviewing the March 5 concert:

> Piano Cliburn used had a plastic lid built for such a
> performance by Steinway in 1953 when Mitropoulos
> was playing and conducting Prokofiev's 3rd Piano
> Concerto at the N.Y. Philharmonic. Cliburn took a
> chance if not with the audience at least with the New
> York critics. But his performance, showmanship and
> obvious communication to the orchestra and public
> leaves no doubt that here is a conductor in the mak-
> ing (though he will need a great deal of practice and
> experience to realize fully his inherent capacities).[101]

John Ardoin noted in *Musical America:* "Mr. Cliburn has
been studying conducting with no less a master than Bruno
Walter, and brought off his performance in a highly professional manner. The savage drive and bravura of his playing
brought the evening's most enthusiastic and prolonged ovation." [102]

Even with the Mitropoulos tribute finished, Van was not running out of causes to champion.

The piano competition that Irl Allison had dreamed of just a year ago was gathering momentum, with Van planning a benefit recital in Ft. Worth for March 27, 1961, to raise money for the event. It was not going to be just another piano contest.

"What is perhaps the largest prize yet offered in a performers contest, $10,000, awaits the pianist who wins a new competition to be held in Fort Worth, Texas, in September 1962," reported *Musical America* in March of 1961. "Co-sponsored by the Fort Worth Piano Teacher's Forum and Texas Christian University, the competition is planned to be held every four years and will be called the Van Cliburn International Piano Competition." [103]

Van's recital, in a crowded Will Rogers Auditorium, led *Dallas Morning News* critic John Rosenfield to write that Beethoven's "Les Adieux" Sonata, op. 81a, "has been seldom performed with such introspective searching, an approach which did wonders for the first two movements." [104]

And *Musical Courier* critic Serge Saxe wrote: "Highlight of a brilliant concert was a performance of Rachmaninoff's Sonata in B-flat minor, a work which has been lost for many years and which Cliburn introduced in Moscow three years ago. It is a showpiece, full of surging sonorities, melodic wealth, and bravura passages." [105]

The incipient competition got another boost later in the year, when Sol Hurok's office threw its support behind it, announcing that the winner "will be placed under its management for concert and orchestra appearances." [106]

With the competition apparently on its way, Van gave his attention to the Interlochen National Music Camp in Michigan—that is, with a little gentle persuasion from Rildia Bee.

"Rildia Bee had made a commitment that Van would perform at Interlochen," remembers Roger E. Jacobi, former Interlochen president. "It all had started when [Interlochen founder] Joseph E. Maddy met Rildia Bee, and they got along very finely." [107]

As Van once recalled,

> In the winter of 1961, while I was in Chicago mak-
> ing a recording, my mother telephoned me to ask a
> special favor. . . . I didn't know Dr. Maddy. Tele-
> phone bill was mounting. I finally compromised,
> with great reluctance. "I'll do it for you," I said. . . . So
> it was with the greatest trepidation and bewilder-
> ment that I sat down for our first rehearsal, taking my
> place at the piano in front of those earnest and silent
> hundred and eighty youngsters in their blue corduroy
> uniforms.
>
> When it was finished, I knew that here was some-
> thing quite extraordinary. These young musicians,
> still in their teens, would do credit to some of our pro-
> fessional symphony orchestras. I felt like sitting down
> and immediately writing recommendations for some
> of them.[108]

Obviously, appearances by Van worked wonders for the
Interlochen box office. "In 1961 we took in at the door
$13,000, which in 1961 was a lot of money," says Jacobi. "In
addition, Van paid his own expenses, paid for himself, for his
mother, for about twenty years.

"And he always had a pretty taxing time at Interlochen from
a standpoint of work because he usually got in just the day
before, had a rehearsal in the morning, and went through the
concerto once or twice, then did a dress performance in the
afternoon for the camp family—all the students, all the staffers
and everyone admitted free. And then in the evening there
would be a sold-out performance for the public. So he would
end up doing the concerto three times in one day. Sometimes
he would play two concertos, plus he'd do as many as six
encores.

"If someone said, 'You played just wonderfully,' he'd say,
'Really, did you like it?'

"Now, for the kids, this was an opportunity to meet a real live great artist who'll sit and schmooze with them, sign their autographs, and give them a memory they'll never forget." [109]

Everyone needs a rest now and then, and for those increasingly rare moments Van quietly bought himself a spacious adobe home—with built-in swimming pool—in Tucson in 1961.

Clearly, though Van was working hard, he was enjoying the perks of success—when he had the time.

For the remainder of 1961, however, he was still jetting around the world, playing to 20,000 listeners in Lewisohn Stadium, [110] a German debut with the Radio Free Berlin Symphony in West Berlin, [111] and most significant, the Beethoven "Emperor" Concerto with the Symphony of the Air in November, launching Carnegie Hall's seven-concert Beethoven series.

Wrote Ross Parmenter in the *New York Times,*

> The young Texas pianist can make great chords ring out as well as anyone, so last night the massive sonorities of this challenging concerto were no hazard to him. But they were not what distinguished his performance. The elements that did were the introspective slow movement, the beautiful transition to the third movement, and the passages of filigree that laced through the bigger moments of the opening movement and the final Rondo. [112]

By contrast, Harold C. Schonberg, covering a subsequent performance of the "Emperor" for the *New York Times,* was ambivalent: "Pianistically there was much to admire. Interpretively there were some reservations. From whence came the clanging, hard tone in the opening cadenza and elsewhere?" [113]

As if to provide holiday cheer, the end of 1961 brought the news that Van's recording of the Tchaikovsky First Piano

Concerto had sold 1 million copies, the first classical record ever to do so.[114]

"At a special ceremony in RCA headquarters in New York, Cliburn was presented with two plaques in token of this record," reported the *Dallas Morning News.* "One was the historic gold record millionth pressing awarded by RCA Victor, and the [other] award representing sales of over $1,000,000 in manufacturer's billing given by the Record Industry Association of America. Attending the ceremony were his mother, Mrs. Rildia Bee O'Bryan Cliburn, and his manager, impresario Sol Hurok." [115]

Van remembers, "When my recording of the Tchaikovsky Concerto sold a million copies, and it was the first classical record to do that, General [David] Sarnoff at RCA told me they never had an experience at all like that with a classical record since Jose Iturbi." Considering that Iturbi had been one of the first celebrated artists to encourage Van, "that was a really satisfying thing to hear." [116]

As the news reports stated, "In addition to the now historical recording, Van Cliburn has also recorded for RCA Victor the following best-selling albums: Schumann's Concerto in A minor, Op. 54 [with Reiner]; Rachmaninoff's Concerto No. 3 in D Minor, Op. 30 [with Kondrashin]; Prokofiev's Concerto No. 3 in C, Op. 26, coupled with MacDowell's Concerto No. 2 in D Minor, Op. 23 [with Walter Hendl]; Beethoven's Concerto No. 5 in E-flat, Op. 73 ('Emperor') [with Reiner]; and 'My Favorite Chopin.' " [117]

Clearly, Reiner had become Van's conductor of choice, and it's easy to hear why. The intelligence, clarity, and weight of Reiner's orchestral accompaniments represent a peak in Van's recorded concerto repertoire.[118]

"Reiner was always delighted to work with Van," remembers Richard Mohr, who produced the recordings Van and Reiner made with the Chicago Symphony Orchestra. "Van would say he would like to record such and such a concerto, for example, and Reiner was always glad to. So Fritz would engage him for appearances in Chicago, so that the concertos would be prior-rehearsed, and then they would be recorded.

"The last [live] performance would be on Saturday [in Chicago's Orchestra Hall], and then we'd record it on the Monday following.

"On the whole, Van was very serious and applied himself to the job at hand, although sometimes he would go off to talk on the phone for forty-five minutes. Of course, time is a sometime thing with him. We had to call for him in the morning because the sessions usually began at ten A.M., and Van is a night owl. Otherwise, he just wouldn't get to the session on time, and there was an orchestra waiting there and getting paid to wait.

"Van and Reiner worked together beautifully. Fritz's reputation as an ogre is highly exaggerated. Yes, he was a perfectionist, and he demanded perfection of others. There were very few retakes.

"The recording sessions usually went extremely well, not any hitches, and of course the recording of the Beethoven Fourth Concerto, with Van as soloist, was Reiner's last recording with the Chicago Symphony.

"I remember that [1962] session well because I had asked Fritz for an autographed picture after working with him for years, and he gave me one. He died the following year.

"Van was always almost excessively polite to everybody, and you never really knew what he was really thinking. He had a marvelous sense of humor, but underneath it all, he was definitely his own person. Nobody could get him to change his mind on anything if he had it made up." [119]

He also knew how to help out an old friend.

"Van was very sweet to me," recalls James Mathis. "When I won the National Federation of Music Clubs Steinway Award, the prize was a recital and a debut in Town Hall. Van and Rildia Bee didn't think that was nearly exciting enough, so they upped the ante and insisted that I make my debut in Carnegie Hall. That was, of course, much more fun, and I'll never forget that." [120]

In general, says Mathis, "Van was full of good will toward his colleagues. I think part of it is that he just knew he was so good, and he didn't have to worry. And I think Van loved his position in the world." [121]

Indeed, Van found himself befriended by some remarkable people. "The first time I encountered Frank Sinatra was sort of by accident, and I was so thrilled I couldn't stand it," recalls Van. "Before I met him, I played in Miami with the Philadelphia Orchestra and Ormandy, and Mr. Sinatra came to the concert. He sent word back[stage] that he was there but had to rush out. Well, of course, I'm sure I knew why he rushed out— because he would have been mobbed to death. He probably almost got run over as it was.

"I actually *met* him later because of Rosalind Russell and [her husband] Freddie Brisson. They loved Mr. Sinatra. Rosalind had been telling me, 'Van, I so want you to meet Frank Sinatra. Next time you're out in Los Angeles, I want to have a dinner, and I want to invite Frank Sinatra. You will love him.'

"Well, time passed, and we kept saying that we were all going to get together. And she'd say, 'I talked to Frank, and he wants to get together too.' We finally got everyone together, and it was delightful because I found he has a very serious mind.

"But the time I'll really never forget is the night that I introduced Placido Domingo to Frank Sinatra. I wish I had had a movie camera because Placido is an old friend of ours, and I had known Placido much longer than Mr. Sinatra. I really can't say that I know Mr. Sinatra because really we're just social acquaintances, and I'm a big fan of his.

"When I introduced them to each other, I thought both of those gentlemen would just die because each loved the other. It was the most fabulous thing because I just felt like an outsider—I was gone and forgotten, and those two were just like old buddies." [122]

Van and Rildia Bee also became good friends with America's most beloved comic of the era, Red Skelton, who remembers, "I went backstage to say hello after one of his performances, and we really hit it off. In fact, we became business partners." [123]

Van clarifies, "Well, that's a nice way of putting it. He loaned me money to buy a building, and eventually I paid him back. But that's typical of him to say we were partners; what a sweet man. We used to love spending time with him because he's so brilliant and funny, and Mother adored him. His knowledge of the theater in America was overwhelming." [124]

Musically, Van was as busy as ever, almost always receiving warm reviews for his concerto performances, but drawing mixed reviews for his recital programs. Perhaps Albert Goldberg summed up the prevailing critical sentiment best in reviewing a Los Angeles recital: "While he is certainly musical to an exceptional degree, the amount of emotional communication was variable; sometimes it was arresting, sometimes it only skimmed over the surface." [125]

In Chicago in March of 1962, Van rejoined Reiner for Rachmaninoff's Second Piano Concerto. Cassidy wrote: "It was a beautiful, wonderfully lyrical, almost hypnotic performance, but it will be more nearly the real thing when Cliburn plunges heart and soul into the electrifying climaxes. With luck, in time for the [pending] recording." [126]

By spring, Van was globetrotting again, playing in the U.S.S.R. in mid-June and, as usual, startling listeners with the unexpected. In Moscow, after his performance and several encores, "Cliburn further delighted the audience by leading his mother onto the stage to the piano and letting her play some numbers herself," reported UPI. [127] In rapid succession, she fired off Liszt's Hungarian Rhapsody no. 2 and a Moszkowski waltz. [128]

And after playing the Tchaikovsky First and Beethoven "Emperor" concertos, Khrushchev himself "stood in the aisle applauding and beckoning Cliburn to come to him," reported Associated Press. Van declined.

"Instead," added AP, "Cliburn stepped forward and said in Russian, 'I am going to play Chopin's Fantaisie in F Minor for Nikita Sergeivich Khrushchev.' He did, and Khrushchev seemed immensely pleased." [129]

Along the way, Van heard a young Russian pianist named Vladimir Ashkenazy, who had just won the second Tchaikovsky International Piano Competition (in a tie with British pianist John Ogdon).[130]

"Ashkenazy was fantastic," recalls Van. "That was probably one of the greatest piano techniques I have ever heard. In fact, when I heard him play, I thought, *That's it—I might as well pack up and start selling shoes.*"[131]

Ashkenazy, however, had had no intention of entering the Tchaikovsky Competition in the first place. "I never wanted to participate in it—I was blackmailed by the Soviet authorities," he says. "I had married a foreigner [Icelandic pianist Thorunn Tryggvason, who had competed in the 1958 Tchaikovsky Competition], and the Soviet authorities were very displeased. Plus I went to the States for the first time in '58, and after I came back, my 'companion,' from the ministry of culture, wrote a very negative report on my ideological image, so to speak, labeling me anti-Soviet and heaven knows what.

"Therefore they said in '62: 'Unless you participate in the competition, you might as well forget about your career.' That's why I played. And the Tchaikovsky Concerto is not my piece. I never liked it that much, but I was forced to play it, and I was lucky that I turned out to be first.

"This helped me as far as Soviet authorities were concerned. Otherwise they wouldn't let me go abroad."[132]

After Van's Russian tour, he traveled to Vienna, playing in Musikvereins Hall before one of the most discriminating audiences in the world. His reading of Beethoven's "Emperor" Concerto, with Karl Böhm conducting the Vienna Philharmonic, inspired an unusual outburst. He was called back seven times for bows, and, "Music fans compared the ovation he received to that for Soviet Pianist Sviatoslav Richter earlier in the festival," noted AP.[133]

But the most uninhibited reception came with Van's Israeli debut in September, with concerts in Tel Aviv, Haifa, and Jerusalem.

For one thing, "His press conference was the first in Israeli history where representatives of both the American and the Soviet embassies were present," reported *Variety*. "The Russian attache was later heard complaining that he couldn't get a ticket for Cliburn's concert." [134]

The Israelis responded to Van as only the Russian public had before.

Albert Goldberg covered Israel's second Music and Drama Festival for the *Los Angeles Times:*

> Whenever he appeared on the teeming boulevards, he was swamped by admirers and autograph seekers and charmed them as well as the press by his Texan courtesy and boyish naivete. . . .
>
> After Cliburn had finished his program of sonatas by Beethoven, Prokofiev and Liszt, the public rushed en masse to the edge of the stage and stood entranced while he played popular encores that extended the program for another half hour. There was no doubt that he had captured the fancy of the Israeli public, but musicians and critics were a shade more reserved in their approval. [135]

On September 24, 1962, Irl Allison's dream came to life, as the first Van Cliburn International Piano Competition opened in Ft. Worth, with 54 pianists competing for a first prize that included $10,000, a Carnegie Hall debut, and various dates across the United States and Europe. The judges were some of the most distinguished names in music, among them pianists Leopold Mannes, Rudolph Ganz, Lili Kraus, Jorge Bolet, and Lev Oborin. [136]

"One of the reasons the competition even took place was because Grace [Ward Lankford] had this tremendous energy, and somehow she convinced the Chamber of Commerce in Ft. Worth, Texas, that they really should back this thing," recalls Martha Hyder, who has been involved in various facets of the event since its inception. "She originally was going to start out and just have a small competition. But somehow she got the

Chamber of Commerce in on it," persuading the C.O.C. to pay any deficit up to $15,000.

"Then we got the local music teachers and teenagers to put together all our mailings, and I had my mother's bridge group putting together the files of information on each of the contestants.

"Sol Hurok helped us enormously because he made sure that we had a really good jury. People started noticing this competition of ours because we had four Russian contestants that first year, and they were among the first Russians to come to this country, outside of a few sports figures. That got everybody's attention, and the whole city got completely behind it. People started volunteering to put up contestants in their own home.

"Each contestant lived with a family, and each family thought that their contestant should win. They were the rooting section for that contestant, and that, of course, revved up lots of interest. Leopold Mannes used to say, 'This could never happen in New York City or anywhere else.' " [137]

Though Van stayed in Ft. Worth during most of the competition, he did have to fly to New York briefly to play with the Philadelphia Orchestra in Philharmonic Hall.

When the first Van Cliburn International Piano Competition prizes were handed out in early October, twenty-eight-year-old Van (who had contributed $4,600 toward the prize money)[138] congratulated twenty-three-year-old Ralph Votapek, of Milwaukee, Wisconsin.

For Votapek, a veteran prize-winner who had studied with Rosina Lhevinne at Juilliard, the victory was a decidedly mixed blessing. "Before the competition started, I think I would have been very happy just to get fourth or fifth prize, just knowing that Russians were going to be in it," says Votapek. "I had this idea that Russian pianists were like gods.

"When I got to Ft. Worth and found that two of them were eliminated in the semifinals, and then the two that I heard in the finals had their problems, I thought, *Well, they're human too.*

"Throughout the competition Van always had a big smile and a big handshake for everybody, and he made us feel like we were important. And when I won he was very nice to me. I think he maybe secretly would have preferred a Russian to win as a sort of return-the-favor kind of thing, but he never let on to me, and he was very gracious.

"I guess if I thought about it, Van seemed a lot more than five years older than I, in what he had accomplished and his reputation and everything. He seemed older than just twenty-eight. I suppose I thought that maybe if I won this [Van Cliburn Competition], that kind of thing would happen to me, but within a few months I realized that wasn't going to be the case.

"Now, I didn't want or expect any kind of career like Van Cliburn, but I guess, in my naivete, I was thinking of some kind of stable career from here on. You know, from Sol Hurok, who I thought would say, 'So here it is, forty or fifty concerts a year.' I found out quite rapidly that after fifty concerts the first year there were going to be fifteen the next, and that I would have to sweat each season.

"So the competition gives you a big boost, but I lost a lot of opportunities, I wasn't smart. I was determined that I wasn't going to be locked into a few concertos, so I went the other extreme and played concertos I probably shouldn't have played. I remember a conductor telling me, 'If you present a repertoire list of forty concertos, that arouses suspicion. The conductor thinks, *Well, he can't play that.*' So he said, 'Limit it, you'd be smart to.'

"This was about two years after [winning the Cliburn]. That came as a shock to me. I had thought, somehow, the more [repertoire you have], the more impressive. So it was a disappointment. But I appreciated the things I did get [from the Cliburn prize], and I still do." [139]

By 1963, Van's career was still growing in a variety of ways, with several critics noting artistic advance over the years.

In January of 1963, he played Brahms's Second with William Steinberg and the superb Pittsburgh Symphony Orchestra. *Pittsburgh Post-Gazette* music critic Donald Steinfirst noted, "Young Mr. Cliburn, still in his twenties, has grown enormously in pianistic stature since his pre-Moscow days. . . . He seemed resolved, last night, to a performance that eschewed any hint of romanticism, except for the third movement. And he was enormously convincing." [140]

When Van played the Brahms Second the following month with eighty-eight-year-old Pierre Monteux and the Los Angeles Philharmonic Orchestra, the *Los Angeles Times*'s Albert Goldberg wrote, "Mr. Cliburn had played the concerto here once before, with Bruno Walter conducting, but he has grown into it immeasurably since then. He now takes it in stride like a young giant, with an old giant's perspective. He sees the piece as a whole, and there were no gaps anywhere." [141]

In Chicago the following month, Van ventured the most elusive of the five Beethoven piano concertos—No. 4, with its deceptively difficult opening passage for solo piano.

Claudia Cassidy wrote in the *Chicago Tribune,* "It was his own performance, dreamy and mysterious, with a flooding lyricism that came from the very roots of the music. It was a deeply articulate performance, with the imagination to match the orchestra, the virtuosity to set it apart." [142]

And in Carnegie Hall Van played the Mozart Piano Concerto no. 25 in C Major (K. 503) and the Liszt Piano Concerto no. 1 with the Symphony of the Air, Alfred Wallenstein conducting. "In the Mozart," reported Henry W. Levinger in *Musical America,* "Mr. Cliburn completely forgot that he is one of the most celebrated virtuosos of the instrument and age, and played with restraint and sensitivity. All stops were pulled out in an electrifying performance of the Liszt, with thundering octaves and glittering runs." [143]

And though some critics had expressed reservations about Van's work as recitalist, even in this arena the tide was beginning to turn.

Albert Goldberg wrote in the *Los Angeles Times,* "His playing of a formidable program of major works was in the grand manner; it placed him unmistakably in the ranks of the greatest pianists of this or any other era. It was playing of eloquence and maturity, of poetic insight, of character and individuality, and of grandiose power and technical command." [144]

Similar opinions met Van's recitals in Cleveland,[145] Philadelphia,[146] Washington, D.C.,[147] and elsewhere.

As conductor, too, Van began to spread his wings, with plans to direct a full orchestral program (as opposed to the concerto-only performance he had conducted in the 1961 Mitropoulos memorial concert). The ensemble was no less than the Philadelphia Orchestra, the setting Robin Hood Dell, the orchestra's summer home.

This time he prepared at the Interlochen National Music Camp, where he had become a regular visitor.

"It came out in Van's conversations with Dr. Maddy that the following week he was going to conduct Tchaikovsky's 'Romeo and Juliet,'" recalls H. Charles Smith, then conductor of the Interlochen orchestra. "And it so happened that just a week or two before, my orchestra [at Interlochen] had played the 'Romeo and Juliet,' so the kids knew it—it was in the fingers and in the air. So one afternoon, for about two hours or maybe a little more, we gave Van an opportunity to conduct the orchestra here, just as preparation for the following week with the Philadelphia Orchestra.

"We all met in a very hot rehearsal hall, and, of course, everybody on campus was curious about it, so we had to lock the doors to keep the mobs out. He obviously knew the basics of conducting, and I found his approach to the orchestra actually quite interesting. He is so gentle on a one-to-one basis that I tried to convince him that he should be more determined to exert his musical will on the group." [148]

Unfortunately for Van, a torrential downpour interrupted his first attempt at conducting the Philadelphia Orchestra. "We have just received word that within 10 minutes the heavens will fall upon us," Van told the audience during the first half of the program. "We'll be back tomorrow night." [149]

Based on what he did hear, however, *Inquirer* critic Samuel L. Singer wrote:

> He has an easy baton beat. He is no podium dancer. Sometimes he keeps his left arm at his side; at other times, his left hand gives cues accurately and forcefully.
>
> He got into the spirit of Kabalevsky's Overture to "Colas Breugnon," conveying the general lightheartedness and humor. The Rachmaninoff "Symphonic Dances" is obviously a favorite work of Cliburn's, and the pianist-conductor was presenting a well-conceived and admirably balanced reading when the rains came. [150]

The following night, Van, who donated his fee to the Musicians' Pension Fund, [151] "seemed much freer with his baton the second time, watching the scores less closely and lashing out dramatically with his long arms," reported James Felton in the *Philadelphia Evening Bulletin.* [152]

The *New York Times* reported that, "The applause brought the young pianist back to the stage three times. On each occasion he tried in vain to get the members of the Dell orchestra to rise, but they refused, giving him full credit for the performance." [153]

The following summer, Van's New York debut as conductor of a complete orchestral program was received in similar fashion. Writing of the Lewisohn Stadium program, Raymond Ericson noted in the *New York Times,* "Using an eclectic collection of gestures—his long arms sometimes swinging wildly, sometimes relaxed in mere time-beating and occasionally giving visual shape to a phrase with his left hand—Mr. Cliburn came close to getting the results he wanted from his players." [154]

When Van and seventeen-year-old Luci Baines Johnson, President Lyndon B. Johnson's daughter, performed Prokofiev's "Peter and the Wolf" at Interlochen in the summer of 1964 (Luci read the narration), most of the media went for the celebrity angle. At least one critic, however, offered a serious evaluation of the concert.

Cleveland Plain Dealer music critic Robert Finn wrote:

> His platform manner is calm, with no acrobatics, and only a limited repertory of long, looping gestures. But he gets what he wants from an orchestra, and that is what counts.[155]

Later in the summer, Interlochen expressed its thanks by awarding Van an honorary doctor of music degree,[156] and at the end of the year he was given the Churchman of the Year award from the lay associates of Southern Baptist Theological Seminary in Louisville, Kentucky.[157]

The following year, 1965, Van's recital work won over even Claudia Cassidy, who had admired his concerto appearances but had not been persuaded by his solo performances. This time, she wrote:

> Van Cliburn has come a long, long way in the four years since his last stage-filled recital in Orchestra Hall. True, he came 20 minutes late yesterday afternoon, perhaps a bit lost to time in a world of dreams and storms, but I find that preferable to the best of time-keepers with nothing to say. Mr. Cliburn had plenty to say—so much, in fact, that he tackled Chopin's Sonata in B-flat minor and Liszt's in B minor, with only an intermission to hold them apart.
>
> These were big, dreamy, stormy performances typical of Cliburn the rhapsodist, but this time they had the backbone of character.[158]

By the spring of 1965, it had been three years since Van's last visit to the Soviet Union; predictably, his third return generated standing-room only crowds in Kiev,[159] flowers and near-riots in Moscow.

After his Moscow conducting debut, "his audience in Tchaikovsky Hall cheered him for 30 minutes and covered the stage with lilacs and lilies," reported AP, even if Tass did not match the enthusiasm. " 'His [conducting] debut did not add any new laurels to the fame of Cliburn the pianist,' Tass wrote." [160]

Back in the United States, Van continued to annoy some listeners and to amuse most others with his difficulty in keeping time—offstage.

Due to play the MacDowell Piano Concerto no. 2 with Howard Mitchell and the National Symphony in Constitution Hall in Washington, D.C., Van failed to appear after the program-opening Schubert Overture. Following a few moments of awkward silence, orchestra manager M. Robert Rogers took the stage.

" 'It's not what you think,' he began," reported Paul Hume in the *Washington Post.* " 'Because Mr. Cliburn is late, Dr. Mitchell has agreed to play the Tchaikovsky Fifth Symphony next. And then, after the intermission, we will hear Mr. Cliburn.'

"That, however, was far from the entire story," wrote Hume. "In actual fact, Cliburn was backstage all of the time. The real crux of the matter was the old business of who was upstaging whom. Cliburn did not like the preintermission spot assigned to him. He wanted to play last on the program where Mitchell had put the popular symphony. In the tug-of-war that ensued, Cliburn won." [161]

Hume, however, had failed to offer readers proof or any verification that Van was backstage "in actual fact."

The next day, Associated Press pieced together exactly what had happened:

> Cliburn really thought he was to be last on the pro-
> gram, as he was last year. . . . A phone call to his
> hotel prompted him to tear himself away from his

practice piano, summon his chauffeur and speed toward the hall.

But traffic being what it is, Tchaikovsky's Fifth Symphony had to be shifted into Van Cliburn's spot on the program, and he wound up playing MacDowell for the finale. . . .

"I will make amends," he told orchestra director Mitchell later. "I will come back next year and play before the overture if you want me." [162]

No verification, clarification, correction, or apology was forthcoming from Hume.

Van, true to his word, and then some, the following year opened his National Symphony performance "by singing 'The Star-Spangled Banner' on stage at Constitution Hall before a sellout audience that included President and Mrs. Johnson," reported UPI.

"Cliburn was making up for last year's opening concert with the National Symphony orchestra in which he showed up late and told Conductor Howard Mitchell, 'I'll do anything to make it up. I'll even sing 'The Star-Spangled Banner.' " [163]

In the summer of 1966, Van was reunited with Kondrashin at Philadelphia's Robin Hood Dell, their performance of the Tchaikovsky First prompting *Philadelphia Inquirer* music critic Daniel Webster to write, "The conductor matched the soloist in note and mood easily in what appeared to be an almost ideal collaboration." [164]

In Los Angeles's Hollywood Bowl, however, critic Martin Bernheimer found their work on Rachmaninoff's Second Piano Concerto disappointing: "It is difficult to ascertain who is more to blame for this, conductor or soloist, especially when the piano is as badly amplified as the Bowl's." [165]

In any event, the warm reunion between Van and Kondrashin represented a stark contrast to the relationship between the United States and the Soviet Union almost a decade after Van's triumph in 1958. Now, on the eve of the second Van Cliburn International Piano Competition (1966), it was becoming obvious that pianists from around the world would compete, with the notable exception of Soviet artists.

AP reported, "The absence of Russian entry was disappointing to competition officials, but came as no surprise. The Russians have not participated in any recent international competition with U.S. contestants, with the exception of a chess tournament. The earlier boycotts have been explained as a protest of U.S. involvement in Viet Nam." [166]

The prize that year went to twenty–year-old Romanian pianist Radu Lupu, who later would be integral to expanding the scope and stature of the Cliburn competition.

Van knew full well that he had a great deal to feel thankful for. In 1966 alone he had performed around the world, witnessed the second go-around for his piano competition, and appeared on national TV twice (in a CBS tribute to Sol Hurok and in a "Bell Telephone Hour" special).[167]

He could not have known at the time, though he would discover years later, that the man who had placed second to him at the Tchaikovsky Competition in 1958 was facing the tragedy of his life. The grim truth was that the Tchaikovsky Competition itself had contributed to his downfall.

"I had heard about the [Tchaikovsky] competition in the first place because the Russian government had informed the People's Republic of China about it," recalls Liu Shih Kun, a Chinese who had tied for second place with the Russian Lev Vlasenko. "And of course the PRC government selected some of its best pianists for this competition. The decision to compete wasn't very much up to me. It was a nomination from the government.

"After I won the second prize at the Tchaikovsky Competition, I was very well respected for this. But then came the Cultural Revolution [in which Mao joined forces with radicals to 'purge' the country of Western influences], and I was put into prison from 1967 to 1973, for six whole years.

"There were a host of reasons, but part of the reason was that I played Western music. And because I had been in Russia and had studied in Russia before, some people seized upon that fact to say I was a spy for Russia. And also because I was now quite famous in China, I became one of the popular targets for the movement.

"While I was in prison, I thought a lot about piano playing, and in particular Cliburn's style. I heard in his playing some new element which I think the Russian public did not expect. It was something new, something not traditional at all. His freshness just swept the crowd in Russia at the time. That was when I first picked up the message in Mr. Cliburn's playing.

"This may sound strange, but I would say there was an element of American jazz and American pop music in his playing, in the freedom of it. It sounded like improvising to me.

"So what I got most out of that competition was the message that Van Cliburn's playing gave me, and this is what I was thinking about and absorbing and trying to understand in the years while I was in prison.

"With the end of the cultural revolution in '76," says Liu, who now teaches in Hong Kong and concertizes in Asia and Europe, "that's when I really began to be able to pick up my life again." [168]

As the '60s drew to a close, Van continued to tour and record prolifically, sometimes seeming to make news at every turn.

He appeared in all the papers when, in October of '67, he left his white tie and tails on the plane and performed in Constitution Hall wearing a rather oversized set loaned to him by LBJ.[169] He made the papers, too, when he stopped in Ft. Worth to visit Grace Ward Lankford, by 1967 the honorary chairman of the Van Cliburn Competition, as she ailed in Ft. Worth's All Saints Hospital.[170]

When she died a month later, he called her loss "a very tragic thing . . . a great loss not only to Fort Worth but to so many people she has known around the world." [171]

All the while, he at once enjoyed much critical acclaim and faced some criticism for repeating particular concertos and solo pieces. For Van, works such as the Rachmaninoff Second and Third Piano Concertos, Beethoven Fourth and Fifth, Mozart Twenty-Fifth, Prokofiev Third, Liszt First and Second, MacDowell Second, and the Tchaikovsky First never grew old or tired. For Van, each time seemed new.

Still, he refreshed his repertoire with pieces he hadn't played before in public or had played only rarely.

In the late 1960s he played etudes of Karol Szymanowski,[172] Bach's Toccata in C Minor, Ravel's "Jeux d'eau," and excerpts from Albeniz's "Iberia" and Ravel's "Le Tombeau de Couperin" in Philadelphia;[173] the Chopin Scherzo in B-flat Minor and "one of the less-played pieces of Liszt's 'Années de Pelerinage,'" in the words of Boston critic Michael Steinberg;[174] Beethoven's Sonata op. 31, no. 3 in Cleveland;[175] Chopin's Piano Concerto no. 1 in E Minor in New York;[176] the Grieg Piano Concerto at Interlochen;[177] Beethoven's "Pathétique" Sonata, Brahms's Variations and Fugue on a Theme by Handel, and Taneyev's Prelude and Fugue in G-sharp Minor in Pittsburgh;[178] and Debussy's "Reflets dans l'eau" and "Feux d'artifice" in Boston.[179]

Still, newspaper reports of the late '60s suggest that the tide of critical opinion slowly began to turn against Van. The rate at which he introduced "new" pieces to his repertoire was not fast enough for some critics. And his sustained and growing popularity seemed to alienate some segments of the press.

After acknowledging that Van had sold three million albums and lavishing critical praise on his most recent Chopin Sonatas recording,[180] a tart *Time* magazine article on Van took him to task for running his life in his own way.

> To keep up the momentum that started in Moscow in 1958, Cliburn plays a punishing concert schedule of well over 100 appearances a year. At fees that start at $7,500 for a solo appearance, this means that he makes something like a million dollars a year, includ-

ing record royalties—although he coyly denies that he is rich ("Heavens, no!"). Furthermore, the travel, the friendship of the famous, the adoring crowds and the publicity are heady stimulation. . . .

But is this kind of headlong, exhausting career compatible with the study, reflection and artistic growth required by a talent such as Cliburn's?[181]

Thus the magazine that ten years earlier had depicted Van as a backwoods, unsophisticated Southerner now had a new complaint about him: too much money, too much fame, too much determination to run his career at his pace and not the pace preferred by the unnamed authors of the article.

It was a theme that other writers later would develop to a fantastic degree.

By the late 1960s, Van became more deeply involved with the competition named for him. In March of 1969, he played a benefit recital in Ft. Worth on behalf of the competition;[182] when the competitors arrived in Texas at the end of September, Van was on hand to greet them at a gala party at the Sheraton-Ft. Worth;[183] he and his parents hosted a Southern-style supper for the contestants during the run of the contest;[184] and he donated cash and counsel throughout the year (though not for the selection of the winners).[185]

Still, the third edition of the contest proved to be a difficult one in some ways.

"Ezra Rachlin was chairman of the jury," recalls Martha Hyder, "and he decided to make the repertory so difficult that we didn't have very many contestants applying, which was somewhat disastrous. Fortunately, we did have Cristina [Ortiz, the Brazilian pianist who won first prize] and Minoru [Nojima, who took second]." [186]

From this edition of competition forth, the repertoire options continually expanded, in hopes of attracting a wider field of top pianists.

❖   ❖   ❖

As the 1970s unfolded, Van's relationship with his public remained strong and growing.

A record 30,000 turned out to hear him with the Philadelphia Orchestra at Robin Hood Dell in July of 1970;[187] precisely 18,667 packed the Three Rivers Stadium in Pittsburgh in June of 1971, "the largest crowd ever to see a concert of this type in the city's history," reported *Variety.* [188]

In the summer of 1971, at the Interlochen National Music Camp, Van "rehearsed with [Interlochen's] highly talented 119-member World Youth Symphony Orchestra for two hours Saturday morning, then played two concertos with that orchestra in the afternoon and again in the evening, added three encores to the evening program and departed amidst cheers from a standing record crowd of 4,200, including 100 on benches on the lawn outside massive Kresge Auditorium," reported the *Muskegon Chronicle.* [189]

And in Philadelphia in the winter of '71, Van's drawing power inspired a local critic to write: "There may be differences of opinion about Van Cliburn's playing, but one fact will remain indisputable—he had the largest audience of the season at the Academy of Music Sunday afternoon. There were some 150 seats on the stage, and no other artist except Arthur Rubinstein commands such a following." [190]

To his fans, Van represented a different kind of classical pianist, one who disdained certain airs and pretensions often associated with the idiom. During a recital at the Shrine Mosque in Peoria, Illinois, for instance, his final piece drew a standing ovation from 2,000 listeners, at which point he sat down to play an encore and found the pedals had broken.

He "waited impatiently for a repairman to appear," reported the *Los Angeles Times.* "But finally Cliburn crawled under the concert grand, fixed the ailing pedal himself—and on with the show." [191]

He also devoted renewed energy and concentration to recording, releasing his album of the Barber Sonata and Prokofiev Sixth Sonata to exceptional critical praise.[192] His recordings of the Beethoven Third Piano Concerto; Beethoven Sonatas; Brahms Rhapsodies and other Brahms pieces; Liszt Piano Concerto No. 2 and Rachmaninoff's "Rhapsody on a Theme of Paganini"; and Prokofiev's Sixth Sonata and Mozart's Sonata in C Major, K. 330, enjoyed a similar response.

In looking over the burst of releases, Harris Goldsmith preferred some of the recordings to others but summed up in *High Fidelity:* "In many ways Cliburn's keyboard manner is akin to [Arthur] Rubinstein's: There is the same unforced tone, the same patient perfection of detail, the same down-to-earth, healthy style." [193]

From RCA producer John Pfeiffer's point of view, "Artistically, it was still thrilling to work with Van. In 1959 I had gone on sabbatical for a couple of years, then I worked with some other artists, and we started working together again in 1968, and it was absolutely like picking it up the next day. We'd get started recording on something, he was working on the Rachmaninoff Etude Tableau in E-flat Minor, and I would give him the announcement for that, and he would start. And then before I could stop him, he would go on to a Prelude in E-flat Minor, and then the second take of the Etude Tableau, then the second take of the Prelude, then [Debussy's] 'The Girl with the Flaxen Hair,' then his own piece, 'Nostalgia,' then a Chopin Nocturne, then a Chopin Scherzo. I finally had to stop because we ran out of tape. One thing just led to another, one thing suggested something else, and everything followed through. It was just like he was giving a performance. It all flowed from him so easily." [194]

One of the most vivid accounts of Van's working methods in the recording studio was written by Jack Somer, a record producer who filled in for Richard Mohr on certain sessions for

"My Favorite Chopin." In *Stereo Review,* he wrote of the struggle an artist faces in trying to represent himself on record:

> Cliburn begins to play. But he is apparently not warmed up enough. He drops some notes. After a few moments he stops.
>
> "Take two," I call. That's better.
>
> He plays again. Badly. Again he stops.
>
> "Take three."
>
> Some more dropped notes. I'm worried. It is *my* fault, I think. Despite our celestial harmony, I feel certain Cliburn is uncomfortable with a stranger in the booth. I begin to sense disaster.
>
> Again the cavernous hall fills with the sound of Chopin's towering "Winter Wind" Etude. First the somber theme; then the body of the piece with its torrential right-hand passages. But it is no go. After a few more frustrating minutes, Cliburn rises from the piano. I go out to talk to him. He apologizes for not being prepared and, seeing the terror in my face, assures me I am blameless. With a promise for better tomorrows, he bids me good night.
>
> Wednesday he arrives late again, but with energy in his step.
>
> "May we start with Opus Ten, Number Three?" he asks.
>
> Going to the piano, he plays the beautiful E Major Etude (the one made into the popular song "No Other Love"), but he has difficulty with its poetry. His playing is not nearly as tender as his original rendition. After a few takes he decides to drop the etude for something else.
>
> "Waltz in C-sharp Minor," he announces. He plays. It is fine; a clean, straightforward reading of the popular waltz. But halfway through, in the fast measures, he stumbles. He tries a few more takes, then quits the waltz.

"We will come back to it later," he says, an edge creeping into his voice. I glance at the clock, note the day, and wonder how much later "later" can be. I am deeply concerned, no longer for my [impending] vacation, but for Cliburn, whose struggle and gentle sincerity have won all my sympathy. I fear he will not reach the standard he has set for himself. But we go on.

He attacks a passage in the Scherzo, Number Three. He does it beautifully—but not to *his* satisfaction. After a few more takes he says he likes it, but he isn't sure.

"Can we go on to something else?" he asks. Then he skips restlessly from piece to piece, getting no satisfaction. His annoyance is rising. I suggest a break. He refuses. He adjusts the bench nervously. He plays, trying very hard to conquer himself. He doesn't. It is past four in the morning and he has tentatively approved only one brief excerpt. But he doggedly plunges back into the "Winter Wind," again getting tangled in its notes, still unable to loosen up.

Suddenly, after a particularly rough passage, he rises, angrily slams the cover down on the keyboard, *kicks* the piano, and turns his back on it. The noise, like two rifle shots, reverberates through the gaudy, mirrored hall as the engineers, the tuner and I swiftly converge to assuage Cliburn's anxiety. . . .

Thursday, the engineers and I meet early at my request. We darken the studio like a concert hall, hoping to reduce the rather mechanical ambiance of a recording session. We clamp a lone reading light to the piano's music rack to illuminate the keys. We turn out the lights in the control room. The piano glows like a distant galaxy on a summer night.

Cliburn arrives, on time and smiling. He seems happy and relaxed. He says, with warm pride, that he has practiced all day. He even approves the new dark atmosphere and sets right to work. In minutes we are recording, and the music reflects his lifted spirits.

He begins with the Waltz in C-sharp Minor, and in a few takes it is perfected. He moves on to a portion of the A-flat Polonaise that needs mending; it is repaired quickly. He corrects the scherzo and another waltz, then he turns to the tempestuous "Winter Wind."

Cliburn is torrid. His energy is boundless, his fingers under complete control. He plays two magnificent, tumultuous performances of the etude. He is playing so well that he decides he can afford to press on for musical perfection. . . .

But as the musical storm rages toward its conclusion there is an unexpected sharp crash, followed by the splintering of glass. The hall goes black. The music stops. . . . The infernal lamp has fallen to the keyboard from the explosive vibrations the piano has been subjected to. The bulb has burst! . . .

He calmly insists that another lamp be brought. It is fetched and installed, this time on a microphone boom independent of the piano's motion. The broken glass is swept away, and I return to the control room, shaking, drenched with sweat, and counting my blessings.

Cliburn resumes his passionate conquest of the "Winter Wind," and in half an hour only the tender E Major Etude remains unrealized. We start the tapes once more, and he starts to play.

It does not go well. Something is missing. Cliburn makes a few false starts. He gets halfway into the piece and halts to practice some vexing measures. . . .

I insist he take a break, and he does. While he sits musing at the piano I walk to a shadowy corner to stretch my tensed muscles. But soon I hear music. Cliburn is playing again. I run to the control room, but the senior engineer has gone to the men's room. I order the assistant to start the machines quickly anyway; we can't miss a precious note.

He pushes the buttons. The red "Recording" light pops on. The control room fills with sound. It is beautiful. But wait; it's *not* Chopin's lovely etude. It's "You and the Night and the Music," and Cliburn is *singing,* in a husky, torchy voice, accompanying himself in a wonderfully warm and easy style!

The unexpected but delightful "pops" concert continues for about fifteen minutes. Midway through it the engineer returns, relieved, but then shocked to hear what we are hearing. He juggles the knobs on his console, trying to pick up more of Cliburn's voice, but the microphones are too far away. At best he can get only a distant, somewhat spectral sound, not inappropriate to the misty mood the pianist has fallen into.

Cliburn sings six or seven songs. Then, almost without pause, he begins playing the etude. He plays with the introspection that has eluded him all week. He plays with several levels of Chopin's deceptively simple piece exquisitely balanced. He constructs Chopin's arch. At four o'clock Friday morning, after several completely sublime takes, the E Major Etude is completed, and, with it, the album. . . .

And somewhere in the vault at RCA there is a tape of Van Cliburn singing Dietz and Schwartz and Gershwin. Unless someone has erased it.[195]

In the spring of 1972, Van played a few more dates in the States before heading off to Moscow again, the most notable being two concerts honoring the 100th anniversary of the birth of Rachmaninoff. He chose to celebrate the event not in New York, Chicago, Los Angeles, Washington, or the other musical centers, but in Shreveport.

"To me, this was one of the events that seldom happens in a fellow's life," recalls Shreveport Symphony conductor emeritus John Shenaut. "We were going to celebrate the anniversary of Rachmaninoff's birth with concerts on the first and second of April [Rachmaninoff was born on April 1, 1872]. Van already had other dates with the Philadelphia Orchestra and the Boston Symphony, so he canceled those so in Shreveport, the town where he was born, he could play Rachmaninoff's Second and Third Piano Concertos on Rachmaninoff's birthday." [196]

Shortly thereafter, Van returned to the Soviet Union for the first time in seven years and, perhaps more significant, the last time in seventeen years. That President Richard Nixon would be in the Soviet Union at the same time seemed likely to heighten interest in the tour, which featured separate performance dates by Van and soprano Roberta Peters.

"Sol Hurok, the impresario who arranged for the appearances of the pianist and singer," reported the *New York Times,* "said yesterday that their concerts were scheduled four months ago and that it had not been arranged for the performances to coincide with the President's visit.

"Still, said Mr. Hurok, who will also be in Moscow, it is possible that Mr. Nixon will attend some of the 10 recitals that Mr. Cliburn is to give or the four operas in which Miss Peters will sing." [197]

Immediately after Van's opening Moscow concert, on May 23, it was obvious that the Russians held him in the same regard as always.

"Pianist Van Cliburn drew stormy applause from flower-throwing Muscovites at a concert Wednesday night, the news agency Tass reported today," read the first UPI report.[198]

During the tour, Nixon invited Van to perform for a party he gave at the home of the American ambassador,[199] and in every way Van remained the conquering hero.

"Things hadn't changed one bit since we were in the Soviet Union together in 1960," recalls Peters. "The people still adored Van, the country still seemed terribly sad. Even in places like beauty salons, it felt like the 1930s. The people didn't have anything. You certainly couldn't get something like caviar over there, but Van, the idol that he was, got us a four-liter can to take home. They loved him so much." [200]

By the end of Van's eight-city tour of the Soviet Union, he had reaffirmed his hold on the nation's musical public. The last performance, in Moscow, generated great enthusiasm, noted the *Shreveport Times*: "Cliburn returned to the same hall where, 14 years ago as a 23-year-old, he won the much-coveted Tchaikovsky Prize in an international contest which drew the most promising talent from many countries. . . .

"Outside his hotel, a 10-minute walk from the Conservatory, several hundred girls waited for him. They applauded him and shouted 'Vanya' and 'Vanyusha,' endearing Russian diminutives for Van." [201]

Perhaps as important to Van, on September 25, 1972, Kilgore celebrated Van Cliburn Day—for the third time. His sold-out concert in the Kilgore College Auditorium drew 1,800 listeners, many of whom had known Van since he was a boy.[202] Of all the people and places that had honored and thanked Van over the years, none did so more consistently, over as long a period of time, as the people of Kilgore.

Van seemed to savor the diplomatic and political circles in which he still traveled and performed. In February of 1973, he played at the White House for Israeli Prime Minister Golda Meir, acknowledging the link Van had made with the Israeli people in his earlier tour.[203]

And in April, he performed in Manila's Araneta Coliseum,[204] at the invitation of Imelda Marcos, who had asked him to help raise money for the training of young musicians.[205] Van had met Ferdinand and Imelda Marcos at the Nixon inaugural earlier in the year.[206]

Associated Press reported that "Van Cliburn's piano playing was a hit with Manila critics, but his clothes weren't.

" 'Only a person of his stature can get away with such an ill-fitting coat,' wrote columnist E. Aguilar Cruz.

" 'His arms are too long for his frame,' wrote Julie Y. Daza in the same paper. 'His legs are too long to fit under the piano. His pants are a bit short above his shoes.'

"But L. O. Goquingco, writing for the *Bulletin Today,* said Cliburn 'produces music that touches the mind, quickens the heart and moves the spirit beyond all description.' " [207]

In the early 1970s, the United States' attitude toward the Marcoses was somewhat different than it is today.

"I knew them a little bit," says pianist Gary Graffman, "and I played in Manila quite a bit. And I'm not ashamed to say it, because Ferdinand Marcos was elected and was a hero to everybody there at that time.

"Since Imelda was a music lover and dragged him [Ferdinand] to all the concerts, they were at every concert I gave every year. I suppose, eventually, power corrupts." [208]

In 1973 too, it was time for the fourth quadrennial Van Cliburn International Piano Competition. Again, Van played a benefit recital in Ft. Worth, in March, to help raise funds.[209]

Vladimir Viardo became the first Soviet winner of the competition,[210] and at first all appeared to be going well.

Unfortunately, Viardo subsequently was dealt a terrible defeat by the Soviet government. "At first, when I found out I won," Viardo recalls today, "my reaction was zero. It probably was similar to the reaction of my grandmother, who spent ten years in Stalin's prison as a political prisoner. People asked her, 'When you found out you were going to get out of prison, did your heart start beating fast?' She said, 'No, because I am going from a little prison to a bigger one.'

"But I still didn't comprehend then that the Soviet Union government could be so malicious toward musicians. I later found out, as did [Sviatoslav] Richter and 99 percent of them, who were not allowed to go abroad and sacrificed their careers because of it.

"For two-and-a-half years [after winning the competition] I started to really fly higher and higher in my career. But then it was my last tour, in 1975, with the Moscow Symphony Orchestra, in December. A month later I was supposed to come to the United States again and play Carnegie Hall and tour for two months. I would play the Pleyel [Hall] in Paris and make two records with [conductor] Lorin Maazel in London.

"Unfortunately," says Viardo, taking a deep, long breath, "the day before I was supposed to fly out, I was denied to receive foreign passport. And after that started a kind of theater of the absurd. Immediately, I was told, 'Tomorrow you can fly,' but of course tomorrow they didn't let me.

"The first years I tried to break the wall and tried to find out what was going on. I didn't realize that this was a general policy toward musicians because this was the main source of the bribes. You know, you go abroad, you must give not only 90 percent of your salary to the government, but you must make this secret bribe distribution [of gifts from the West] to them.

"So they want you to be really scared before you go, and that's what they did to musicians. They scared us so that in order to go abroad again, we would do anything. Of course, it was not really the Ministry of Culture that was doing this, but the KGB.

"So for twelve and a half years I was not allowed to leave," adds Viardo, who was not able to resume his performing career in the United States until 1989. "That's why it's so hard now [to restart a career], but I tried not to surrender. I spoke several times with Van over the telephone, and I spent my time trying to deepen my repertory. If I had five or six concertos before, at the end of this exile I had thirty-seven." [211]

For Van, too, there were sorrows yet to come, as he approached his fortieth birthday. Certainly no one would have predicted in the mid-1970s that his performing career would soon come to a halt for a very long time.

10

A Long Intermission

*T*he turning point came in two, swift blows at the start of 1974.

At 1:00 P.M. on January 12, Van's father, Harvey Lavan Cliburn, died in Shreveport's Highland Hospital at age seventy-five[1] after a gradual deterioration of his health.

"Even before he became ill," remembers Raymond Boswell, a longtime family friend and neighbor in Shreveport, "Mrs. Cliburn divided her time between being at home and traveling with Van. Yet Mr. Cliburn was so anxious about Van's career [that] he wanted Mrs. Cliburn to be with Van. So that's what they did. They traveled a good bit, and she was here [in Shreveport] some of the time. Of course, Van came in numerous times to visit. By the early 1970s, Mr. Cliburn started to fall into really bad health." [2]

While Van was on the road, with or without Rildia Bee, he continuously called home. James Mathis, his old friend, recalls meeting up with Van and Rildia Bee in Brussels, "where Van had played a beautiful concert, and they handed him all the money in cash! It was the wildest thing in the world. And Van and Rildia Bee just turned around and spent a lot of Van's fee to pay the telephone bill at the hotel because they called back home constantly. Mr. Cliburn was sick by then, and I remember they called home all the time." [3]

Even before then, Van and Rildia Bee were ever on the phone, as the *Shreveport Journal* noted in 1966:

> While his father, H. L. Cliburn, spends most of his time in the family home at 455 Wilder Place, the pianist's mother, Rildia Bee O'Bryan Cliburn, travels with him as his personal manager on all of his concert tours.
>
> The pianist and his mother chat with the elder Cliburn virtually every night, regardless of the miles which separate them from the red brick house of Georgian design and the man who misses his wife and son keenly during their absences. [4]

When Van's father began to fail, it hit Van about as hard as one might expect. "Van realized his dad's condition," says Raymond Boswell, "and on one visit up to the hospital, he left there and came down to Don's Restaurant and reckoned with himself that his dad was not going to last very long. He had just visited with his dad, and I guess the realization of all that was taking place really was on his heart and mind. This was less than a year before Van's father died. Somehow I think in an experience he had in the hospital room all alone with his father, he more or less recognized it and gave him up at that time.

"During the hospital confinement—Van's father was in the extended care area of Highland Hospital—Mr. and Mrs. Cliburn had their fiftieth anniversary [on June 6, 1973]. So we all celebrated that with Van's father up in the hospital room.

"One of the maids who had been sitting with him and I got him shaved and dressed with a coat and tie and so forth, as sort of a surprise for Van, so that when Van and Rildia Bee came in, we had him dressed. They had seen him in his bedclothes for so long that it was a pleasant surprise for them to celebrate their fiftieth under those circumstances, and we had a good visit there.

"Van had really looked forward to that. Now he said he didn't want anybody to know it was their fiftieth anniversary, but when he came that time he rented a gold car and gave his father a gold clock. I mean, he said 'golden anniversary' in every other way, but supposedly he was not going to call attention to their golden wedding anniversary!

"A few months later, in January of '74, Van was fixing to leave for Houston that afternoon, and I was going to get him up and off for that. But I checked with the hospital and found out that Mr. Cliburn had just passed away.

"So I went over and became the bearer of bad tidings for both Van and Mrs. Cliburn. The hospital had not yet called, and the doctor had not yet arrived. So I went over to share that news with them. It was difficult, and yet they knew his condition had deteriorated. He had held on a long time." [5]

Actually, Van had braced himself for this moment for some months. "I always felt very fortunate that in September 1973 I heard one of Leontyne Price's 'Madame Butterflys,'" Van later said, recalling how Price had helped him prepare. "At the dinner [after the performance], she and I talked about death because my father was very ill. I knew in my heart there was not much time left, and I said to her, 'I hope I'm up to what's coming.' Leontyne said, 'Oh, my dear, you won't have any problem at all because you're a believer, and the Lord will take care of you.' She was a great consolation to me that night." [6]

Ultimately, of course, the loss is of a magnitude for which no one can ever really prepare. The role Van's father had played in his life and career was quiet but unswerving. He was "the power behind the throne," in the words of longtime family friend Louise Jeter,[7] the man "who would go out and drive Van anywhere he needed to go for his music," remembers another family friend, Alice Whittlesey.[8]

Every Saturday afternoon, he set the radio dial to the Metropolitan Opera broadcasts,[9] surely one of the sources of Van's deep love of opera. He served as a deacon in the First Baptist

Church of Shreveport, setting an example of sustained faith during the heady years of Van's career.

If Rildia Bee was Van's chief adviser, his father probably played two different but related roles: a quietly fervent supporter early in Van's career and a kind of protector after Van became sought after and celebrated.

"When Van traveled to New York and back for school, he didn't want Van to fly," remembers Susan Tilley, Van's close friend and chairman of the Van Cliburn Foundation. "He got nervous at the thought of Van's flying, he worried the whole time [about Van's safety], so he [often] made Van ride the train." [10]

In many ways, Van's father "literally is the one who sacrificed, he's the one who stayed home," says Shreveport conductor John Shenaut. [11] Little wonder that Van's father once said, "One must make personal sacrifices when God has bestowed such a talent on one's son. It would be wrong not to share that gift, not to afford others pleasure by using it as widely as possible." [12]

At 2:00 P.M. January 16, Harvey Lavan Cliburn was buried in McGregor, Texas. [13]

Less than two months later, Van's dear friend and manager, Sol Hurok, who had directed his career virtually since the Tchaikovsky competition in 1958, died suddenly. On March 5, Hurok had lunch with guitarist Andres Segovia, whom he had presented on many occasions. Hurok then went to the offices of Chase Manhattan Bank president David Rockefeller, took the elevator to the seventeenth floor, and collapsed. He was pronounced dead at Beekman Downtown Hospital. [14]

Just ten months earlier, in May, 1,500 people had packed the Metropolitan Opera House to honor Hurok's sixty years of presenting performances, a program for which Van played piano, Isaac Stern played the violin, Margot Fonteyn danced in a *Swan Lake* excerpt, and Shirley Verrett sang Donizetti. [15]

Because Hurok was Russian, because he was one of the last great presenters in America, because he had struck a personal relationship with his young star, the loss to Van was immense.

"Hurok was really a paternal figure to Van," says Alan Kayes, of RCA, who had seen the relationship develop from the beginning. "He could counsel Van in a way that other people probably would not attempt to." [16]

Perhaps Hurok had Van's trust and so many other artists' because, "Hurok was in a category by himself," said Lillian Libman, who had worked for Hurok and with Van. "Mr. Hurok would have gone bankrupt to protect the artists, and he sometimes did. The dollar was not the bottom line to Mr. Hurok. Things have changed considerably since then. He was very, very careful in handling Van. He left a great deal of the [daily] management to Walter Prude, but Van's relationship to Mr. Hurok was quite close. At the funeral, Van was just beside himself." [17]

During the memorial service March 7 in Carnegie Hall, the great American contralto Marian Anderson gave the eulogy, saying, "He launched hundreds of careers. He magnified thousands more. And in the process, he brought joy and a larger life to millions. He made not ripples, but waves. He went beyond his own shores." [18]

Then Jan Peerce sang psalms, Isaac Stern played Bach's B Minor Partita for solo violin, and Rabbi Bernard Mandelbaum conducted the ceremony.[19] Among those who paid their respects were Leonard Bernstein, Agnes de Mille, Roberta Peters, Renata Tebaldi, Shirley Verrett, Montserrat Caballé, Sir Rudolf Bing, Byron Janis, Andres Segovia, and, of course, Van,[20] who grieved that he had barely missed a final opportunity to visit with Hurok not long before.

"I was supposed to see Mr. Hurok in New York in January," he later told *Newsday,* "but I canceled because of my father's death. So Mr. Hurok said, 'Oh, when you come next month we will talk.' But he was dead by the time I came back to New York." [21]

Predictably, the effect of these two personal losses, one expected, one not, was incalculably painful. "Ever since I was a child, I had been around older people; I had dreamed dreams with people much older than I was," says Van. "Because my parents always exposed me to their world as if I were part of it, some of my really good friends in life were twenty to thirty years older than I.

"It was terribly upsetting when, in the 1970s, so many of my old and early friends departed. In particular I was very, very upset in that month of January and then March, in '74, when first it was Daddy, and then almost two months to the day, Mr. Hurok. I thought, *This is too much. You've got to have more time so you can savor. There's a lifetime to go out on stage; there is not a lifetime with certain people.*"[22]

For Van, life essentially had been sixteen years of continuous performance since his Moscow triumph in 1958, twenty years of playing professionally since his Leventritt debut with the New York Philharmonic in 1954, nearly thirty years since his concerto debut with the Houston Symphony in 1947.

As Van later recalled in a *Vogue* interview,

> I had already been playing professionally since I was twelve. . . . I felt, well, stranded or dislocated. Friends and family were dying all over the place, and I still had never taken the time to have a life. I was tired of living out of a suitcase, flying nearly every day, never having a real home. I could never go to the opera, which I adore, or a friend's concert, or a movie. By 1978 I was ready to be bored for a while, to have a regular life. I wanted a house with all my things around me.[23]

It was time for a rest, all the more because of the kind of person Van is. As he later told *Newsday,* "I want some personal memories too, as well as the memories of meeting wonderful people in the concert halls and interesting times traveling. So I planned in 1974 to take some time off but never announced it."[24]

Or, as Van later put it, succinctly and a little more bleakly, "I love people, and that is a terrible thing because the study of classical music is so solitary you don't get to see your friends.

That, I think, was the most disappointing aspect of my profession." [25]

He expounded on the theme in a 1977 interview.

"'[Travel] is an unsatisfying part of a career,' he said. 'You don't get to see your colleagues. With all this travel, you begin to live vicariously, thinking about things happening someplace else, sometimes wishing you were someplace else.' " [26]

If he had been so inclined, Van could have canceled all his subsequent engagements, but his desire to communicate with an audience apparently still was intact, and his reluctance to disappoint those who already had signed him made him continue a bit longer.

Yet, to a degree, the strain of nearly two decades of racing around the globe, the grief of losing a father and various close friends, and the sense of missing out on the kind of life he needed began to show. Photographs of Van from the mid-1970s reveal him to be pale and quite thin.

His childhood friend Annette Davies Morgan remembers him looking "tired and drained." [27] Lottie Guttry, another longtime friend, says "he was gaunt, he was tired, . . . he looked like a driven man." [28]

Part of the reason surely had to do with the nature of the modern-day virtuoso's life. Like never before, the performer in the latter half of the twentieth century could squeeze more performances into a shorter period of time than his nineteenth-century counterparts, who traveled between continents by ship, between states by train. Everything was slower then and, presumably, easier on the nervous system.

"There's a lot of love and warmth that comes across from the audience when you do a performance, but there's a lot of nitty gritty bad warming of airplane seats and motel life and a lot of other things that go along with it that have a lot less charm," says Harold Shaw, who worked in the Hurok office during Van's years there.

"It's a very tough kind of life, and, particularly, for soloists. Van was fortunate that his mother was going with him because a lot of these people do it alone.

"But so many of these artists, if you say to them, 'Where is your town, where do you live?' they look at you and literally say: 'Europe and America.' " [29]

Edward Gordon, the former Ravinia Festival executive director who earlier toured as a concert pianist, says, "I was there, and I know what it feels like, and it's not always fun by a long shot. It's getting off a plane or a train and going to a town where you don't know a soul, and the hotels are not always the best, and the pianos usually are a disaster. They actually range from disaster to acceptable, and rarely a good one." [30]

Beyond these relatively minor irritations, there's the unique challenge a performing artist faces that most of us do not—constantly having to prove oneself.

"It's a very difficult career," says pianist Shura Cherkassky, "because every time you play you have to show to the audience that you still can do it, that you haven't gone down, and that alone is a great strain." [31] Cherkassky, an octogenarian, remains one of the glorious exceptions, busily performing around the world to this day.

For pianists, in particular, the problems can seem compounded, if only because the piano solo and concerto repertoire is huge, the demands for performances seemingly endless.

"Look at what happened to Horowitz," says John Browning, referring to the virtuoso who retired from the stage not once but at least three times.[32]

"With Horowitz [who spent some time coaching Browning], there was a curious psychological thing. It had nothing to do with his hands; his hands were fine. I think he had just burned out, and I think every performer can burn out.

"During one of the periods that Horowitz wasn't playing, apparently he thought his fingers were made out of glass and that if he went to the keyboard they would break. He would come down in the morning, look at the keyboard, turn around, go back up to bed.

"But he had had a history of ups and downs, and I think he stayed away from concerts until he felt pulled together again.

"You just repeat and repeat and repeat the work, concerts, travel, work, concerts, travel, work, concerts, travel. And there's so much summer work now [at the various music festivals] that you can easily get to the point where you are psychologically burned out, artistically burned out, or you do damage to yourself physically.

"The repertoire demands are so huge. Everybody knows the fiddlers carry a small repertoire, and they're not expected to have a huge one. I mean, how many concertos for fiddle are played very often? Eight at most.

"But there are forty piano concertos that are frequently played. And that's one of the troubles we all went through because we had to do Brahms D Minor on Wednesday and Mozart on Friday and Prokofiev Third on the following Monday, and it took its toll on many of us, one way or the other." [33]

Or as composer and former Juilliard president William Schuman put it shortly before his death, "You notice that conductors never seem to need long sabbaticals." [34]

Pianist Alexis Weissenberg, who was a kind of mentor to Van immediately following his Juilliard days, explains, "I stopped performing for several years because I wanted to become a better artist and a more profound musician, if possible. And I thought my career started too young—I'm not being egocentric, but I had the experience. I know what it's like. I won the Leventritt when I was seventeen-and-a-half, and immediately afterward there were great orchestras and great musicians in my life, a fantastic career for anyone that young. But after four or five years I realized I wanted to do other things, to finish my studies in philosophy, to get married, whatever. So I kept away from the stage.

"For Van, when he stopped playing [in 1978], he not only began to enjoy life, I think he *discovered* life at that point. He had been smothered by success." [35]

Then there's the issue of stage anxiety. Oxana Yablonskaya, the distinguished pianist, says, "I can tell you how it was for Gilels whenever he played in Carnegie Hall. He was always so nervous and so pale, it was frightening—and he was one of the absolutely great musicians. But the bigger your name, the more nervous you are." [36]

So in the devastating year of 1974, Van resolved to stop performing as soon as his signed engagements ran out. When offers came in, he simply said that he already had an engagement, thinking, *I have my own engagement.* [37] Though his managers suggested he make a formal announcement, he declined. As he explained in the *New York Times* years later, "But what if you call a press conference and then have to call up your manager three months later to say, 'I'm starving'?" [38]

There's no question that the wear and tear of many years took their toll.

"In the early '70s, I began to feel he wasn't as enthusiastic about everything as he had been," recalls RCA's John Pfeiffer, "and even though we were recording, the old bite wasn't there. It was missing, and I thought he was getting tired, and he knew it. He knew at some point he was just going to have to stop." [39]

By the mid-'70s, Van began to tell his closest friends that he finally planned to take a rest. "At one point," recalls Raymond Boswell, "he came over here to play at Louisiana Tech, which is about seventy miles from Shreveport. I was driving him over, and he said, 'You may be seeing and hearing the last recital I'm going to do. I'm just absolutely worn out.'

"So we knew the time had come. We could see that the pace was just more than anybody could take. And Van has always enjoyed the measure of good health, but the schedule of just crisscrossing the country for so long was just too much. I'll put it this way: It was not like he was playing in Seattle one night, then going down to San Francisco two or three nights later and San Diego a week later. It was Seattle to Miami to Buffalo and wherever. It was the kind of a schedule that would take its toll on anyone. By the mid- to late-'70s, we could see that he really was wearing thin, and he was just exhausted." [40]

Even taking into account the weariness that was beginning to tell in Van's performances, the mid-'70s yielded a wide range of critical reaction.

In Philadelphia in 1974, his Tchaikovsky First prompted *Philadelphia Inquirer* music critic Daniel Webster to write, "There is an aristocracy in his playing of this work, the feeling that it is his as much as anyone's." [41] In Shreveport, he honored the memory of his father by playing his father's two favorite concertos, the Brahms Second and Tchaikovsky First, for the season opening concert of the Shreveport Symphony.

Reported *High Fidelity/Musical America,* "Cliburn, looking tired and drawn, ambled to the piano and attacked the Brahms. After a measured first movement, where Cliburn was rather tentative in some thorny passagework, things began to pick up. The second movement had snap and fire—nothing tentative here. . . . The familiar Tchaikovsky found Cliburn at the top of his form." [42]

In Washington, D.C., in March of 1975, *Washington Post* critic Joseph McLellan found that in Beethoven's Sonata in E-flat op. 31, no. 3, "Cliburn grasped this structure . . . and his pointed accentuation of it made the movement a beautiful experience." [43]

And in Philadelphia in 1976, his reading of Liszt's First Concerto "caught the romantic sweep of the work. . . . The playing led to an ovation and Cliburn responded with five encores." [44]

On the other hand, his performance of the Tchaikovsky First in Philadelphia the following year prompted Daniel Webster to note, "The season's largest crowd was on hand to hear the pianist play the Tchaikovsky Concerto No. 1 again. . . . The piece does not, however, receive a fresh and explorative performance from Cliburn now. There is still the surging technical sweep in those long fingers, but much of the playing sounds mechanical now. There is a flatness in the sound of the instrument, of keys struck but not of notes formed." [45]

His performance of Beethoven's "Emperor" Concerto in Los Angeles in 1975 led *Los Angeles Times* music critic Martin Bernheimer to write: "The magnetic soloist of the evening was none less than Van Cliburn, who did rather strange things to the 'Emperor' Concerto. He managed a graceful, nicely shaded, limpid, agreeably sentimental Adagio. But in the noble bravura

of the outer movements, he tended to play in a detached—sometimes even leaden and mechanical—manner." [46]

There were distressing moments in Van's performance at the
Ravinia Festival in the Chicago suburb of Highland Park, when
he suffered a memory slip in the last movement of the
Rachmaninoff Second.[47] And there was a bizarre moment when
Van was playing a recital in Miami during the "streaking" craze.
"With 200 members of the sold-out audience in the Dade
County Auditorium sitting behind his grand piano onstage,
[Van] was midway through an encore, Chopin's Polonaise,
when a naked fellow pranced across the stage and made a clean
getaway," reported the *New York Times.* "Consummate artist
that he is, Mr. Cliburn didn't miss a beat." [48]

But perhaps the most striking aspect of the critical coverage
of Van during the mid-1970s and even in the early 1980s, after
he had stopped performing, was the sharpness of tone that
some articles began to convey.

Reviewing Van's performance of Brahms's Second Piano
Concerto with the Cleveland Orchestra in 1975, *Cleveland
Plain Dealer* music critic Robert Finn wrote:

> Yet the critics—myself included—have never really
> taken Cliburn seriously as a musician. After the first
> flush of newsworthiness wore off in 1958 and critics
> began listening objectively, he began to receive
> highly critical reviews—which the public blithely ig-
> nored in its eagerness to hear him play.
>
> He became the most glaring contemporary exam-
> ple in the serious music field of the public brushing
> aside the objections of critics. . . .
>
> Part of the problem may be that Cliburn has never
> been a "scholarly" musician. . . .
>
> His approach to music has always been intuitive
> and basically unsophisticated.[49]

Here was a remarkable piece of historical revisionism.
Though the writer claimed that "the critics—myself included—

have never really taken Cliburn seriously as a musician," in 1964 he had applauded Van's conducting and pianism with these words:

His platform manner is calm, with no acrobatics, and only a limited repertory of long, looping gestures. But he gets what he wants from an orchestra, and that is what counts. . . .

The MacDowell Concerto is well under Van Cliburn's fingers by now also, for he has made a sparkling recording of it. Its old-fashioned thundering and blazing display passages would tempt any pianist. Cliburn, who must have been tired after conducting two major scores just previously, played it with fiery brilliance.[50]

And in an article the following week, Finn had lavished more praise on Van:

Cliburn showed his devotion to Interlochen by throwing himself into an iron-man schedule for its benefit.

He played the MacDowell Second Concerto *three* times (once at rehearsal and twice in concert), conducted "Peter and the Wolf" and Howard Hanson's "Romantic" Symphony twice each, went through a long and frustrating morning rehearsal session, played a total of five encores at the two benefit concerts—and ended the day by attending a student-run party honoring him and Luci Baines Johnson.

Greater love than this hath no musician.[51]

Other critics were positively slipshod in reviewing Van. In covering a Washington, D.C., recital in March of 1975, *Washington Post* critic Joseph McLellan wrote:

Curiously, in Chopin's C Minor Scherzo, built on a similar quality between what might be called a light and a heavy theme, the reading was slack, failing to come to grips with the tensions in the interacting themes. [The Scherzo is in C-sharp Minor.]

The effect was better in the more purely lyrical ballade in A-flat, superb in two tight-packed miniatures by Brahms, adequate in Debussy's "Jeux d'eau" ["Jeux d'eau" is by Ravel].[52]

And as late as 1981, bizarrely inaccurate and exaggerated commentary on Van's career continued to surface, as in Harold C. Schonberg's comments in the *New York Times:* "There was never any argument about his talent. But where was the talent going? How long could a pianist go on playing only the Tchaikovsky First and Rachmaninoff Third Concertos?" [53]

Evidently Schonberg didn't know, or didn't care to know, that Van also prolifically played Beethoven's Third, Fourth, and Fifth Concertos, Rachmaninoff's Second and "Rhapsody on a Theme of Paganini," Mozart's K. 503, both Liszt concertos, the Grieg, both Brahms concertos, Chopin's First, Schumann's Concerto, and MacDowell's Second. Beyond concertos, Van had played the long list of solo repertoire detailed in previous pages.

Five years later, Donal Henahan wrote in the *New York Times,* "My guess would be that a lack of intellectual curiosity contributed most importantly to Mr. Cliburn's inability to sustain a public career." [54]

Inability to sustain a career? For fully twenty years after his Tchaikovsky win, Van sold out houses, broke attendance records, and released critically applauded albums. Only by refusing to accept engagements for four years, from 1974-78, while working through already booked dates, could he find free time for himself. Many soloists probably would kill to have such an inability to sustain a public career.

Despite such misrepresentations, Van's recordings continued to be released to wide critical praise. His recording of

Rachmaninoff solo works, including the then rarely performed Second Sonata, drew a rave from Igor Kipnis in Stereo Review. [55] His Brahms album prompted Larry Kart to write in the *Chicago Tribune:* "Never the slam-bang virtuoso one expects a contest winner to be, Cliburn is an introspective, sometimes dreamily romantic player who is rarely at his best in the war-horse concertos. But when he undertakes a program that suits his temperament—as he does on 'Van Cliburn Plays Brahms' (RCA)—the results can be remarkable." [56]

It was not by coincidence that Van's recordings were widely admired. He was remarkably finicky about releasing them.

"I remember skipping two weeks of my vacation, which was all I had in one summer, to sort of play around with individual chords and notes in Van's recording of the two Chopin Sonatas and the Barber Sonata, which were superlative performances," remembers former RCA producer Max Wilcox. "And he was extra fussy about the recordings. As I look back on it, in this day of digital editing, back then there wasn't much to it, but he'd want to diddle around with this, edit that a little bit more, try a few more things. He would find it almost impossible to just say, 'Okay.' And finally, after all this work over two weeks of my vacation, he said to me, 'Well, I guess it's all right.' And I said, 'Van, it really is a pile of fun to work with you, now that my wife and three children and I couldn't do what we wanted to do.' I was so mad, but I knew him well enough to be able to say that to him." [57]

From Van's point of view, there was a reason to be picky. As he once told the *New York Times,* "The [record] companies would always say, 'Just go ahead and release it. It's good for five years. Then you can re-record it.' I never thought of recording that way. I held up many records because I wanted to be sure before I said yes. When something is published, it's like the written word, and you want to be able to say, 'I'll live with that until I'm dead.' " [58]

On balance, says Guenter Hensler, who took over as head of BMG Classics (RCA Victor's parent company) in 1989, "I don't know if the pressure was such a bad thing. His records speak for themselves; maybe he needs a little pressure." [59]

Even while winding down his performing career from 1974-78, Van remained in almost perpetual motion. He received an honorary doctor of music degree, while Rildia Bee won a Distinguished Alumna Award, from Cincinnati College Conservatory of Music in May 1974, just as Van established a continuing scholarship program at the school.[60] He was named to the National Council on the Arts in September of 1974.[61]

Then he grieved the loss of another longtime friend, Rosina Lhevinne, who died November 9, 1976, at age ninety-six.[62]

And Van made musical history of sorts as late as 1976, performing as soloist for the first "Live from Lincoln Center" telecast, a series that continues to this day. Though a videotape of the program shows Van looking gaunt and pale, he turned in a reading of the Grieg Piano Concerto, with Andre Previn conducting the New York Philharmonic, that was by turns grandly dramatic and intimately lyric.

On the eve of his sabbatical, he remained closely involved with the fifth quadrennial Van Cliburn competition in September 1977, which produced South African pianist Steven de Groote as gold medalist and Soviet pianist Alexander Toradze as silver medalist.

"Tell 'em back East what we're doing here," Van told the *New York Times* while the competition was under way. "All they think about is the Leventritt. I love it—I won it—but we have something bigger going here." [63]

The 1977 edition of the contest caused a bit of a stir, however, because of comments in that *New York Times* piece, which had been written by the *Dallas Morning News'* John Ardoin. He wrote: "The award caused considerable disagreement among the judges and the audience—many felt that the first prize really belonged to second-prize winner Alexander Toradze, a 25-year-old Russian pianist." [64]

These remarks inspired a quick rebuttal from juror Leon Fleisher and jury chairman John Giordano. "I feel compelled to correct a misstatement of fact in John Ardoin's report of the

Van Cliburn Competition," wrote Fleisher, in a letter published three weeks later in the *New York Times.* "Notwithstanding Mr. Ardoin's sources, the fact is that Steven de Groote was chosen as winner of the first prize on the first ballot, cast by secret vote, by 12 of the 13 judges. How this can be interpreted as a jury being 'in considerable disagreement' is quite beyond me." [65]

In the same issue, Giordano wrote:

> Unfortunately, Mr. Ardoin was unable to attend the competition until the second day of the semifinals, and I would like to comment on his statement that Steven de Groote was "possibly a compromise choice for first prize by the jury."
>
> The decision to award Steven de Groote the Grand Prize was under no circumstances a "compromise" or "controversial" one on the part of the jury. The jury was instructed verbally and in the jury handbook that it was *not* to award a first prize unless it found an artist of exceptional ability. [66]

As Van approached his last performances before a long sabbatical still received some unabashedly enthusiastic reviews.

Opening Denver's new Boettcher Concert Hall in March of 1978, he persuaded *Denver Post* music editor Glen Giffin that "he of all people can rip through this concerto [Tchaikovsky no.1] with a presence and conception few can match." [67]

Van's final public performance before the sabbatical was a concerto appearance for the September 29 season-opener of the Toledo Symphony. Veteran *Toledo Blade* music critic Boris Nelson reviewed this performance of the MacDowell Second thus: "His technique is big. He produces a big resonant, lustrous tone and plays the music as writ, i.e. he takes no liberties with the score, although he can wax imaginatively lyrical and burst out with bravura brilliance. But primarily, his is a very engaging, conservative approach." [68]

Why some critics had become openly hostile to Van, to the point of bending the truth of his record, is subject to interpretation. Perhaps it has something to do with the popular American pastime of building up a star only to tear him down later. Perhaps the magnitude of Van's success and growing popularity simply rubbed some people the wrong way: Remember Robert Finn's indignant assertion, expressed in the *Cleveland Plain Dealer,* that Van "became the most glaring contemporary example in the serious music field of the public brushing aside the objections of critics." [69]

As for the most frequent complaint about Van's work in the '70s—the size of his repertoire—it's true that some artists had a far larger repertoire than he. But others, such as Vladimir Horowitz, did not. Through most of his career, Horowitz had recorded but four piano concertos (Beethoven's "Emperor," Brahms's Second, Rachmaninoff's Third, and Tchaikovsky's First). Only in the final years of his life did he add to that Mozart's Piano Concerto no. 23.

In recital, too, Horowitz's repertoire remained narrower than other pianists' (such as Arthur Rubinstein). Again and again, the same Scarlatti sonatas, Schumann Concerto Without Orchestra, Moszkowski etudes, and the like turned up on his programs.

But "when Horowitz walked out and played the Rachmaninoff Third," says RCA's John Pfeiffer, who produced Horowitz's recording of the piece with Fritz Reiner and the RCA Symphony Orchestra, "nobody said, 'Well, why doesn't he do the Bartok Second?' Who cares? I've always felt that an artist should play and record the things that he absolutely feels he needs to record.

"I once asked Jascha Heifetz about doing a Fritz Kreisler album. And he said, 'Come on, that's for Benno Rabinof to do.' Of course, Heifetz would have done it wonderfully, but he just didn't feel it, and it wasn't his style. And Van was the same. He had a certain repertoire, and for someone to say, 'You should have done this, and you should play that,' is not fair.

"Maybe because Van was an American, a young American, they thought, *He should be doing this, and we know better than he does.* The critics always know better. Of course, we all do that. There are things I would love to hear Van play. There are things I'd love to hear Heifetz or Horowitz or Rubinstein play. But you have to take what you can get." [70]

Van was not alone in being cornered by some critics. "If you really think back carefully, the critics have slashed all the good ones, all the big ones," says John Browning. "Toscanini got terrible reviews in New York—people forget. Horowitz got scathing reviews. Bernstein got murderous reviews—until he announced his retirement." [71]

And through most of his career, no less than Arthur Rubinstein received far less enthusiastic reviews for his Beethoven and Mozart than his Chopin and Albeniz.

Like any important artist, Van had built his career and his audience on repertoire that moved him, and that was the music he played, regardless.

As he once told an interviewer, in speaking of the Tchaikovsky First, "I love it; it's just a great piece. I was telling friends the other day that the concerto is 102 years old. Well, there's a reason [pianists still play it]; it's just great music, so classical, so succinct. You know, that's the beauty of classical music: What I learn, I enjoy, and what I enjoy, I play—I play it to death.

"It's like a great painting, really. You see one, and you know it will never be for sale like a piece of real estate. A great musical 'painting' you carry all your life. It's forever." [72]

Or, as Van later said at a Ft. Worth news conference, "From the day I was born, I gravitated toward certain repertoire. In music, no matter how familiar, there are no twice-told tales." [73]

So Van stopped performing. For the first time in several decades, there was not another concert to prepare for, another plane to board.

To Van's friends and colleagues, the rest seemed overdue. "He knew he was tired, and I think he put it off as long as he could, or as long as he was sure that he could maintain his lifestyle," says RCA's John Pfeiffer.[74]

John Giordano says, "Frankly, I was surprised that Van lasted as long as he did. Everybody advised him that he needed to take a break, to take some time off." [75]

As James Mathis says, "I think there's a kind of pianist who just will go on until they drop. And I was never certain that Van ever wanted to do that, even in the beginning. He had made his mark, he had made his money, and he was not somebody who knows nothing but music and music alone. His interests are varied, and for once in his life he wanted to pursue them." [76]

Naomi Graffman, who had first met Van at the Leventritt auditions, puts the issue in perspective when she says of her husband, pianist Gary Graffman, "He played for thirty years, not even at Van's pace, and his fingers wore out [today, Graffman performs works only for the left hand]. And looking back on it, we had had enough, both of us. The point is that you're really doing the same thing over and over again. No matter how much different repertoire you play, there are only so many places you can go to, only so many parties you can attend. For a long time, I think Van enjoyed the life. He enjoyed all of this very much. It was wonderful for him, and he loved his mother's company.

"I remember he was in Monte Carlo in the late '60s, and both he and Gary played in a festival there, so we all took the same plane. When we got off the plane in Nice, the luggage that came off for him was incredible. I think there were about forty-two pieces. And he said, 'Why don't I arrive in Monte Carlo with you, and we'll send the luggage with my parents.'

"So that's what happened. We drove from Nice to Monte Carlo together, and then he played this wonderful concert, and there was a big party afterward. It was all very glamorous. But after twenty years, that gets a little old. And imagine concertizing at the rate Van did, which is unprecedented." [77]

Indeed, there were moments when Van simply had to get off the plane, and the treadmill, even if briefly.

"I remember a wonderful moment in Minnesota," recalls Skitch Henderson, "and it was a typical airport scene. I was going to get on the airplane, and Vaniel was getting off. He had a recital that night in St. Paul, and I had just left a guest stint with the Minnesota Orchestra.

"So Van was ready to just step on the next plane when we spotted each other. And immediately Van thought it would be a wonderful idea if either one of us broke off our trip and just sat and talked. That wonderful, total candor he had about the world—I wish I had some of that. It's not unhealthy." [78]

Clearly a tremendous demand for Van's service existed across the United States and around the world. The question is whether the Hurok office overbooked Van and whether he accepted too many engagements for his own good.

Martin Feinstein, who worked in the Hurok office, says, "The pace Van was on was a normal and natural one at that time.

"He wasn't a young beginning artist studying repertory. When Van won the Tchaikovsky, he was already a seasoned artist, and he already had the repertory to go with it.

"It wasn't like the concert life was alien to him. Van was used to the routine of receptions and being charming to everyone. He was and is a naturally charming and gregarious person, so all these things weren't really a problem for him.

"He must have loved it—a lot of artists do. I remember talking to Rubinstein once after a concert in Cleveland, and I said to him, 'Why do you do it?' He said, 'I come into town a stranger, and when I walk out, everybody loves me.' " [79]

Even so, Van was under a unique kind of pressure.

"There would be times blocked off in the summer for Van to get a break," says Harold Shaw, who worked in the Hurok office. "All of a sudden Ormandy would call him up and say, 'Will you please come to the Dell, Van, just for me?' I think he felt caught. How do you turn down the offer from a guy who records for you? It was difficult. I think there was probably more pressure on Van than on any artist I've known.

"I think Van tried to accommodate people as much as he possibly could. For example, I think he found it very difficult to say no to Ormandy. If Ormandy asked him to do something, he tried his best to accommodate him because they had a good relationship." [80]

Somehow, Van endured and flourished through most of those twenty post-Tchaikovsky years, his recorded legacy and volumes of critical praise attesting to that. His peers, too, felt that he carried the burdens of his career about as well as one could hope to.

"Considering that most managers are greedy," says pianist Earl Wild, who knew Van in the Juilliard days, "that the record companies constantly want to press more and more records, that Van was playing with the world's greatest conductors —considering the stress and strain of all that, he handled it rather well." [81]

So well, in fact, that Schuyler Chapin recalls, "It almost seemed as if the success didn't come as any surprise to Van. It may have come a little sooner than he thought, but his mother and father were around, of course, to help.

"It was as if either he had read a lot of books about Hollywood, and this is how he believed world-famous people behaved, or else it came to him by instinct, which I suspect is the case. He simply felt this was something that was going to happen to him, and therefore he had a sort of built-in procedure for it, which was calm and cool and charming." [82]

To pianist Eugene Istomin, who had first heard and met Van at the Leventritt auditions, "I think he felt that he had a kind of destiny to fulfill, and that destiny meant that he had to play and had to reach the people that wanted to hear him. That was the most important thing to him." [83]

That Van finally stopped performing publicly "actually was not a surprise to me," says violinist-conductor Alexander Schneider, who coached Van at the Marlboro Music Festival in Vermont. "Everyone, every musician—and it's true in every profession in the arts—you come to a certain age when you suddenly realize that whatever you were doing doesn't mean anything at all.

"In music, you know that you play the piano—so what? You suddenly realize that it's not the instrument. What is the piano? It's a piece of wood with strings attached. What is important is who you are and what you do to it. I used to go to [pianist Artur] Schnabel's classes, and I remember he always said to his pupils, 'Don't forget, this is a piece of wood. It has nothing to do with anything at all. You make the music, not the piano.'

"And so you come to a certain age, everyone of us suddenly realizes, 'I don't know anything and I have to relearn.' That was my feeling with Van, just like with Yehudi Menuhin, with Jascha Heifetz and Horowitz.

"It happened with me too, and I'm very proud of it. Luckily I met [cellist-conductor Pablo] Casals and his assistant. Without them, I would be just nothing artistically; I wouldn't have anything now. I realized that music is what you are, and you have to learn. You have to learn literature, you have to go to museums, you have to become a human being." [84]

Indeed, Van longed to hear concerts, attend opera, make music away from the stage, reflect, appraise his place in the world through which he had raced for so long.

As he told an interviewer in 1983, "I think one of the nicest things about this period has been the feeling of relaxation, the ability to work quietly without pressure. Chamber music has always been a great interest of mine even though I didn't play much . . . in public. But now I have been playing with friends, for instance, the Brahms and Franck Quintets, and the Brahms C-minor trio." [85]

The opera, especially, loomed large in Van's sabbatical. "It's funny," says Van, "when I think about my life, I'm sure I've spent a great deal of it in the opera house. That's where some of my best memories are." [86]

Though Van stopped performing publicly in 1978, music remained an integral part of his life. "People don't understand that," says Ft. Worth Symphony conductor John Giordano, who saw Van regularly during his sabbatical. "They think that he just locked the lids on all the pianos and never played again in those years, but that's not true. During that period, several times we were over at his house and he played. People would sing and he would play. I often heard him playing at his house.

"Van is a better chamber music player than people realize in that, when he does not have the tune, when he's accompanying a flute solo, he's very sensitive to it, and Van doesn't try to force the player into doing what he thinks. He will literally accompany, and he's very good at it. People don't know that.

"And he's a real opera buff. He can put on a record or a laser disk of an opera and sing along with most operas. He knows them by heart. And in some ways that transfers to his concept of playing the piano, which is so lyrical and vocal." [87]

Not that Van's life was exactly idle during his time away from the stage. As Susan Tilley says, "There was so much going on in his life besides playing that, when he stopped playing, he still had more than enough that kept him and Rildia Bee almost frazzled. Awards and honors and honorary degrees and a speech here and there." [88]

In December of 1980, Van was in the audience for Juilliard's 75th anniversary jubilee,[89] in May and June of 1981 he was following the sixth quadrennial Van Cliburn International Piano Competition in Ft. Worth, when Andre-Michel Schub won.[90]

By 1982, Van's long absence from the performing stage had prompted all kinds of speculation.

"Rumors in the music world have indicated Cliburn was suffering from arthritis and would never play again," reported the *Ft. Worth Star-Telegram*'s New York columnist, Cissy Stewart.

> Another story going around is that he has given up the piano for all time.
>
> Judging from his appearance this week [at the Carnegie Hall performance of competition winner Andre-Michel Schub], Cliburn is in the best of health. In fact, he looks better than I ever remember him looking.[91]

For a while, it seemed as if everyone was using Van's newly found free time to give him awards. In May 1982, Van received another honorary doctorate, this one from Texas Christian University.[92] A year later, in April, Van received the 1983 Albert Schweitzer Award, "which is presented every four years in Schweitzer's memory to honor outstanding performers for humanitarian efforts in the music profession," reported *Music Clubs* magazine.[93] Previous winners had been Katharine Dunham and Isaac Stern.

Van was honored "for a life's work dedicated to music and devoted to humanity." Greer Garson presented the award in Carnegie Hall,[94] where Leontyne Price sang Samuel Barber's "Knoxville: Summer of 1915," at Van's request. She was an apt choice, for Van and Price not only had been Juilliard students at the same time, but both had made critical New York performances on the same day, November 14, 1954.[95]

The same month, the National Federation of Music Clubs presented him with its Presidential Citation;[96] and in May, he received the first outstanding alumnus award from Kilgore College.[97]

By now, the Van Cliburn International Piano Competition was coming around again, with Van donating $50,000 to that year's edition.[98] And yet, Van still hadn't returned to the stage. Everywhere he went, people wondered if he ever was coming back.

During a New York gathering at the Waldorf Astoria Hotel in March to promote the contest, Van tried to assure the crowd, "Oh, I haven't retired. I'm only on a sabbatical. I will play publicly again." [99]

When reporters pressed for details, he said, "I feel it is very important to stop for a while. I know certain friends who, in their lives, have not taken any reflection time at the right time. I didn't want to make that mistake." [100]

Still, Van tried to assuage his fans by noting that at least he was still practicing. "I try to keep fit," he said. "I work usually a couple of hours in the morning and about three hours in the afternoon." [101]

In June of 1985, Brazilian pianist Jose Feghali won the competition, with Barry Douglas from Ireland placing third. The next year, Douglas ventured to Moscow to win the eighth quadrennial Tchaikovsky Competition.

"As soon as I got to Moscow, people came up and asked me quite often about Van," recalls Douglas. "They assumed that because I was a Westerner I naturally would know Van. I had met him, but I didn't know him very well in those days.

"When this Russian TV crew came to film me, they brought some films they had of Van playing in 1958 because they wanted to film my reaction to watching Van play. And they had questions about Van, and when they found I'd been to Texas, they wanted to know more. People who came backstage constantly asked me, 'Any news of Van?' There were always people in the streets asking me.

"Even then, in 1986, there was no doubt about the impression that he made on the Moscow public and the Soviet public. It was still enormous." [102]

In October of 1985, after ten years of house-hunting in Ft. Worth, Van found, fell in love with, and bought the eighteen-acre Kimbell estate in the Westover Hills enclave of Ft. Worth. The mansion was previously owned by Kay Kimbell, who endowed the famous Kimbell Art Museum in Ft. Worth. [103]

In the years of his sabbatical, Van had been based in the Salisbury Hotel, in New York, visiting Texas regularly. Now the time had come for a permanent return home.

"When Van told me he was buying this house, I said, 'Well, that's wonderful,'" recalls RCA's John Pfeiffer. "And then I asked, 'But don't you have a house in Tucson?' He said, 'I know, but I wanted one that Rildia Bee would like.'

"I did remember her saying something once, when we were all sitting around talking in their apartment in the Salisbury Hotel: 'Well, I'm certainly glad my mother isn't still alive to see how I'm ending my days, sitting around in a hotel room,'" recalls Pfeiffer with a big laugh, considering that this "hotel room" was actually fourteen rooms that Van had taken over in the Salisbury.

"Van said, 'Mother, I'm going to get you a house, and you can pick out the house that you want.' And, of course, Texas was ideal.

"Over the years Van had collected antiques. Antique furniture, antique silver, all sorts of antiques, pictures—everything. They went into various apartments in the Salisbury Hotel. He'd fill one up, and then he'd move into another apartment. And he'd fill that up and move into another apartment.

"All of that furniture and everything fit so perfectly, into the new house in Texas, it was as if he had this house in mind when he collected all this stuff.

"And the house was so *him,* so much his style. It's solid, it's permanent, it has a great aura about it. It amazed me when I first saw the house, to see all of this stuff in one place because I had seen this furniture up there at the Salisbury in so many different apartments.

"Buying that house was good for Van because that whole atmosphere in Ft. Worth was so appealing for him in so many different ways. There are so many people around there who just have a great admiration for him. They're his people, and he feels very much at home there. And of course, Rildia Bee— that's her life right there." [104]

Rildia Bee—whom *Vogue* magazine described in 1990 as "a stately Texas matron who loves to entertain hordes of guests till the single-digit hours and is given to Adolfo suits, Belgian chocolates and her Maltese fluff ball of a dog, Baby Chops" [105]—fell in love with the house as soon as she saw it.

She told *Texas Monthly* magazine,

> "The first time Van brought me to see it, I told him, 'This is the house for me, *if*'—she held up a finger—'we can afford it.' If it was too much money, I didn't want him to buy it. . . .
>
> "Van has always been so good to me, and I give the credit for that to his father. When Van was just a little boy and his father was going on a trip, he would tell Van, 'Sonny Boy, you take care of your mother.' "Yes,

Daddy!" she mimicked a high-pitched voice and laughed to herself.[106]

Van, too, seemed thankful to be heading to Ft. Worth. "I think he felt it was like a little nest here, a protected nest," says John Giordano. "That's my theory, because the people here love him and are very supportive of him. This was where he belonged." [107]

Not that the move was easy. "The moving vans were packed, about to depart for Texas a few years ago," reported the *Ft. Worth Star-Telegram*, "when Cliburn remembered a piano stored at the Steinway offices [in Manhattan]. He and a friend dashed off to retrieve it, rolling it right through the middle of Manhattan." [108]

As family friend Tom Zaremba recalled in a *Dallas Morning News* article, "To tell you how much stuff Van had collected, the moving company told us it was the largest commercial move in the company's entire history." [109]

The house that Van bought for Rildia Bee and himself is a splendid place, decorated with exquisite antiques, graced by several grand pianos. The heart of the house, its living center, is the library, where a grand piano takes up a single corner. The walls are lined with books, and between the shelves and tucked into corners are photos of Van with Rildia Bee, with Mikhail Gorbachev, with President Ronald Reagan.

Adjacent to it is the huge family room, and off of that is a nearby hallway with a lifesize, perhaps larger than lifesize, oil portrait of Rildia Bee. The house seems to go on and on. At every turn, there is a sentimental keepsake of some concert, some party, some contact with an old friend.

Van once explained his tendency to hold onto things this way: "When I had my first apartment, I saved lunch money to go out and buy things for it. I never parted with anything. Whatever I have will be with me for the rest of my life because I'm the most sentimental person that ever drew breath." [110]

The *Dallas Morning News* underscored the point in covering a party at the Cliburn home:

The house is filled with family keepsakes and mementos of Van's career. This is a very sentimental family. In fact, Van and Rildia Bee sometimes can't bear
to take down their Christmas decorations until April.
And there are still signs of Rildia Bee's 90th-birthday
party, which took place more than two years ago.[111]

By 1987, Van still had made no hint of specifically when he
was going to return to the stage.

Victor Borge recalls, "I ran into him at the Plaza Hotel [in New
York], and he came over to my table. So I asked when he was
going to continue his concertizing, because we missed him. He
said, 'Not a minute before my canned soup runs out.' " [112]

Yet even if it was still unknown when, or if, Van would ever
return to the stage, it's worth remembering what his labors had
yielded. Beyond the millions who had heard his music in
concert and on television and radio broadcasts, beyond the
life's work that was documented in his recordings, beyond the
competition that helped launch many careers, there were
other, secondary effects of Van's work.

"For one thing, it raised pianist's fees," says pianist Leon
Fleisher. "With Van getting such high fees, people like Horowitz and Rubinstein would not accept less. I could see it even
in my own fees because everyone was getting on that band-
wagon. It was wonderful because it gave us all a kind of
recognition that really hadn't been there before." [113]

Edward Gordon, who worked both as touring pianist and,
later, as executive director of the Ravinia Festival, concurs,
saying, "Even somebody whose name nobody knew but who
played very well and had been getting $750, $1,000, $1,200
fees, suddenly it went to $2,500.

"It happened probably because now there was a bigger
audience for pianists and piano concerti, and so every concert
presenter, every orchestra manager said, 'Well, let's kick the
ticket prices up.' And when the ticket prices went up, the fees
had to go up." [114]

More important, Van's contribution "made people think that a musician was also capable of having some value [in society]," says violinist Yehudi Menuhin, "all the more because he maintained that position." [115]

Van's example, in winning the Tchaikovsky competition and building a formidable career after it, "lent a lot of wings to a lot of ambition, including mine," says pianist Garrick Ohlsson. "I thought that if he could become the first American to win the Tchaikovsky, maybe I could become the first American to win the Chopin Competition in Warsaw." [116] Indeed he did, in 1970.

Beyond the piano, Van's work helped "show that America could have a cultural identity in the world," says composer Ned Rorem. "A few years later, when [artist] Robert Rauschenberg was the center of the Venice Biennale, suddenly Europe was no longer the focal point for painting." [117]

When Van won the Tchaikovsky in 1958, pianist Eugene Istomin recalls, "There was a kind of feeling that this was going to do great things for the American awareness of our own artists, and Van felt that way himself. He told me, 'You'll see, this will be good for everyone.' " [118]

Thirty-five long years later, American opera singers, to use one example, are the most sought-after in the world. A generation ago, they had to go to Europe for recognition and acceptance. Similarly, pianist Olga Samaroff, who taught at Juilliard before her death in 1948, was actually Lucy Hickenlooper of San Antonio, Texas.[119] The European affectation was a way of gaining acceptance in the world of classical music.

Van alone did not change this scenario, but he was among the first who proved it could be otherwise.

As for the backlash against him from a few critics, that may simply be the price he paid for the nature and degree of his popularity.

"Considering everything he went through, he could easily have been embittered by events," says pianist Barry Douglas. "Of course, he's had his problems, as anyone does, but he's done very well because he's got an enormous capacity for giving. That's what's really important to him." [120]

As Vladimir Ashkenazy sees it, it didn't matter what some detractors might say, simply because "Van is what he is; he is not pretending to be anything else. And there are not so many people in the world, especially in the artistic world, who are just as they are. More often the people pretend to be something, or go after their own image and forget what they really are, but not Van." [121]

Through it all, Van seemed secure enough in his understanding of himself to realize there was no point in trying to be anyone else, to fulfill anyone else's vision of what he should do.

As early as 1983, six years before he finally returned to the stage, he presciently told an interviewer, "When I do return there won't be a 'new' Cliburn—I don't see anything wrong with the old one." [122]

11

On Music

At the center of Van's music, of course, is Rildia Bee, his first teacher and predominant influence.

Van says, "One of the first things my mother taught me when I first started playing in public was 'You must always make it look easy, whether it is or not. Don't make it look like a hazardous health problem.'

"And this is the same, I'd say, for anybody on the stage—conductor, instrumentalist, or whatever. If it begins to look hazardous, don't do it, because performing music is also visual, I think. You try to do something, you try to create certain motions that are not distracting, that do not inflict your effort on the public. They don't need to be aware of it. They're there for some kind of enjoyment.

"Now I hate the word *entertainer*. Somebody called me once and said, 'Oh, you're such a wonderful entertainer.' I said, 'No. What I do is not for entertainment. If you derive pleasure from it, thank you. But classical music is not entertainment,' and I feel viciously strong about that. Classical music is forever. It is not entertainment. Entertainment is something that is here today and may be gone tomorrow. So if you derive pleasure from my work, I'm grateful. But I'm not there to entertain you." [1]

As for repertoire, "There were certain things that my mother felt were a must. I had to go through all the Chopin Etudes, but also all of the Liszt Transcendental Etudes, such as 'Feux-follets,' which I never thought I played that well. That was a stymying thing. In fact, I was going to play it one night in recital, and I pulled it off the program and never played it in public again." [2]

And what of the Liszt Twelfth Hungarian Rhapsody, which long ago became a Cliburn signature piece? "I first played it when I was ten," says Van. "Mother had wanted me to play it. Actually, she wanted me to sightread all the rhapsodies, and she was particularly fond of the eleventh. She sat down and played through the piece, and then the thirteenth, and we finally settled on the twelfth. I subsequently did the sixth, but it wasn't the piece for me. The twelfth was the one. I felt an affinity for that piece almost immediately, and it was on my first Carnegie Hall program, when I was thirteen.

"When we got to Carnegie Hall, I couldn't believe it. We drove up from Kilgore. New York wasn't new for me because I had been there the year before and studied for three months in the summertime. But it was so exciting to be on the stage there.

"The next night, we had seats for Mr. Rubinstein's all-Chopin recital. I had met him the year before, and we got to go backstage to say hello. His playing made a tremendous impression on me.

"At one recital he played the Chopin F-sharp Minor Polonaise, and it was the most stunning performance of it I ever heard, live or anywhere. It was magic, and I don't even remember the next four or five pieces because I was so enthralled with that performance. He made music. His first intention was not simply to hit the notes. Most of the notes were there—but his first intention was to make music, and that, for me, is the most admirable thing.

"So many times you go to performances, and you have this feeling that the person is trying to hit the right notes. And, in your mind, you feel like saying to the pianist, 'It doesn't matter—go ahead, strike a wrong note, and then you'll be fine.' Nowadays, there is such a mass audience that has been brought up on recordings, and we're so recording-oriented, that we feel each performance is like a recording. It is not.

"This is why I always had a little friendly dispute with [pianist] Glenn Gould, whom I loved very much. He thought that live music making would be passé, and we'd all stay home and listen to recordings.

"I said, 'How can you say that? When I go to hear you, you're groaning and moaning in the performance.' And he said, 'Well, it isn't very much fun to hear, is it?' I said, 'That's not the point.' The point is that every time you hear it, for whatever it is, it's live. And each time you play, it's different. You'll hear things differently tomorrow than you heard today and yesterday. You'll be a different person tomorrow than you were yesterday, and that all comes through. You go back and restudy and rethink, and you'll hear something or see something that you didn't see before. That's what makes classical music live forever because it stands endless revisitation.

"Now another great pianist . . . was Gilels. He played [Stravinsky's] 'Petrouchka.' I was learning it at the time I heard him come through the States and play it in recital in the early '50s. His program was marvelous. He did Schumann F-sharp Minor Sonata, which I adore, and both books of Debussy's 'Images,' and he closed the program with 'Petrouchka.'

"And it was *his* 'Petrouchka.' It had his sound because he brought so much color and fantasy to the piece. After that performance I went right back to my little apartment and put that on the shelf, and I've never again brought it down.

"A lot of artists struck me like that. Eleanor Steber, who recently died, was one of our great American sopranos. I have some of her early recordings. She was a great 'Marschallin' [in Richard Strauss' opera *Der Rosenkavalier*], and I saw her only *Tosca* that she did at the Met. She was unbelievable.

"Another great one was Ormandy, who was a dream. The first time I met him was in Russia, when he and the Philadelphia Orchestra were on tour [immediately after Van won the Tchaikovsky Competition in 1958]. Freddie and Silvia Mann [lifelong musical philanthropists] were traveling with the Ormandys and the orchestra, and we all got to be together in Moscow.

"And Eugene Ormandy said to me, 'You've got to play with me in Amsterdam at the Concertgebouw.' I wanted more than life to play with him because I just adored him. I mean, I would enjoy the Philadelphia Orchestra with Eugene Ormandy if they played in a saloon. I often have thought, *Well, maybe Mr. Rachmaninoff was right when he called it the world's greatest orchestra. It really sounded overwhelming.*

"But the Chicago Symphony is overwhelming too, so I guess you can't really say any one thing like that. But I do know that Mr. Rachmaninoff was emotionally involved with the Philadelphia.

"The world has Mr. Ormandy to thank for that, for the 44 or 46 or 47 years of consistent sound that orchestra gave forth. I know he was music director there for about 42 years, but his real total was greater than that because he had more concerts [before he became music director in 1938 and after he stepped down as music director in 1980]. That's the longest tenure, even longer than Karajan with the Berlin.

"Of course, Karajan built the Berlin into a major force. It had a great sound, fabulous. Everybody used to argue about Berlin versus Philadelphia. They'd say, 'Oh, you can't eclipse the brass and woodwinds of Berlin.' And then someone inevitably would say, 'But you can't eclipse Philadelphia's strings.'

"I'd always remember those phrases going back and forth in the late '50s, but it was true. It is true.

"I always adored Karajan and the Berlin, and it's a great sadness that I never got to make the recording that we had all set up for November of '89, the Brahms B-flat [Piano Concerto] with the Berlin Philharmonic. It was thanks to [current RCA chief] Guenter Hensler that we even had that date. I loved the way Karajan drew such colors from the orchestra.

"Among pianists, of course, I adored Horowitz. I didn't get to know him well, but we were good corresponding friends, and I am so grateful that we had a fabulous time in April of 1988. I took him, Wanda, Rildia Bee, and Susan Tilley to dinner at La Côte Basque in New York. We arrived early and closed the place, and it was one of those magical experiences. You know, you can go along, and life can be just so-so, and then there's all of a sudden a magical evening.

"That was such an unforgettable evening, and I think it probably was unforgettable to the La Côte Basque, too, because they had never seen ordering like we did that night. We ordered everything on the menu, doubles and triples and all this, and getting carry-out packages.

"At first, when I called to invite Horowitz, Wanda said, 'No, we can't come out. We can't do it, Horowitz'—she always called him that—'Horowitz only eats sole and asparagus.' And I said, 'I think we can get that. Would you ask Volodya if he can come?' So she said, 'Well, wait a moment.' Then she came back to the phone and said, 'Horowitz said he would go. What time?' Well, I was shocked. And then she said, 'You will make certain they have sole and asparagus.'

"Horowitz was always so incredibly kind to me. We had a mutual friend, Jack Pfeiffer, and he and Horowitz would talk on the phone. We didn't get to see each other that often, but the things he would say to Jack about me were so really touching. He was charming, a raconteur par excellence, so warm and outgoing, a gentleman and a gentle man. An excellent person." [3]

How did Rildia Bee go about teaching Van? "She never asked me to do anything she couldn't do herself," says Van. "And that was true even right up until I was seventeen and going to Juilliard.

"She believed greatly in scales—doing scales, scales, and scales, and playing them with a beautiful legato. She always said that even if you don't want to practice but you've absolutely got to, the scales are a great way to get into it. You hear the sound, the colors, the line—and suddenly you're listening. You're involved.

"So when I really have to work—first of all, I don't do this nighttime schedule," explains Van, referring to his longtime habit of sleeping by day and rising by night. "When I really need to work, I have to be at the piano at 9:00 A.M., and I start with the scales, and immediately I'm listening.

"Mother also had me practice arpeggios. And Mother always told me, 'Don't bang, don't bang' [when Van was a child].

"For exercise, it was mostly scales, but then she had some special exercises she had gotten from Dr. Friedheim. She would talk to me a great deal about her studies with Friedheim, and he would tell her about studying with Liszt—I mean, specific things, like: 'Liszt pedaled this way here and did this there.' Score markings, phrasings, structure, architecture—Mother was able to pass it all along to me."

Or, as Rildia Bee herself once put it, "When I was teaching Van, I told him that he got the Hungarian Rhapsody no. 12 third-hand. I got it second-hand, from Liszt to Friedheim to me." [4]

Van adds, "And because Friedheim had studied with Anton Rubinstein, I really was getting all these ideas from the source of the Russian piano school too.

"Now if there was some piece that I wanted to learn, I'd say, 'Mother, I heard that concerto, and I want to play it.' And she would say, 'Then go get it and learn it.'

"She treated me like an adult. Later, I remember, she always would say, 'He was very teachable.'

"Another thing, Mother always talked about the structure, the architecture of a piece, of thinking of the last note when you play the first. That was important to her.

"She also talked a great deal about pedaling because Dr. Friedheim always used to talk about the proper approach to the pedal and all about the gradations of pedaling, and how they must be so geared and coordinated with what you're doing on the keyboard.

"She talked about the middle pedal at times, when it would be a help, but it was to be used very discreetly. And she talked about the left pedal.

"Another thing my mother was interested in was inner voices. When I was seven, we had great discussions about the first movement of Beethoven's 'Pathétique' Sonata. I remember so many instances when I was little when she would talk about how each voice must stand alone.

"She also would tell me that when you're playing, you're a singer. Mother also studied voice when she was in New York studying piano with Dr. Friedheim. She had a very good voice. And when I was little I was a boy soprano and sang in a lot of concerts—that's when I first got accustomed to being on the stage.

"All of that was very helpful to me because when I started to sing, she knew bel canto technique and could teach me. And I had a natural voice, which improved. *That* I was very proud of, because I knew I had a nice voice, and that was a sad day when it left me [during adolescence]." [5]

Or, as Van told the *Ft. Worth Star-Telegram* in 1990, "I guess my favorite instrument is the human voice. . . . I thought my life had come to an early demise when I lost my [boy-soprano] voice. Piano is the consolation." [6]

Van continues, "When Mother was teaching me piano, she would say, 'You have to look for a human voice, a person singing.' And she would help me draw on my experience as a singer. She would say, 'When you want to sing softly, from where you are [on stage], it can't be too soft, or it won't be heard. And that's how it is with playing the piano. If it's too soft, it's not communicating.

"It must be [deep] in the keys, in the illusion of pianissimo. It's all illusion, even a singing line on a piano is an illusion. And that's where it's so important to have such a close coordination between pedaling and legato touch. So the idea is to bring out that human voice and the discreet and the very judicious use of the sostenuto pedal. She always cautioned me, 'You don't say the soft pedal,' although that is the vernacular. She'd always say, 'It's the *una corda,'* very precise. And even when you were playing arpeggios, you were supposed to bring out that singing line." [7]

Rildia Bee once said, "I always was waiting for the time to come when Van would want to go to another teacher, and sometimes I would suggest the possibility. 'I'll quit if you won't teach me,' he'd say. Then we would go on with the practicing." [8]

One of Rildia Bee's longtime students, Annette Davies Morgan, recalls other specifics of her teaching method. "I studied with her from when I was five until about fourteen," says Morgan, "and one of the things I remember most vividly was that she was very positive as a person and as a teacher, and very dynamic.

"She wanted you to sightread the music, and she wanted you to bring it back to her at each lesson in sections, learned and memorized. In other words, what she assigned, she wanted that much music to be learned and done. She was very disciplined about that. So there was no time you did not come prepared and were not serious about it because, to her, it was very, very serious. It was not a game; it was great art.

"She began your studies with the scales and arpeggios and the simple rudiments of theory. And as she explained that to you, she would assign little repertoire pieces, which would demonstrate the principles or the technique that she wanted you to master. And exercises such as Czerny were given along with the pieces. You were expected to do those, and you would play them at the beginning of the lesson.

"At each lesson, as you became more advanced, she gave you more studies, exercises, and etudes. Basically, I remember her emphasizing the Bach Inventions and Beethoven Sonatas. She never said, 'That's too hard.' She just would assign you something, and you were expected to learn it. Period.

"Only years later did I discover that a piece was really more advanced than perhaps I should have played, but I never had any indication from her. It was just always: 'You will now learn this.' I did it because I wanted to, and I wanted very much to please her.

"At lessons and in recitals, she would accompany you sometimes; she would just make up an accompaniment to go along with what you were playing. She would do arpeggios and chords and harmonies, and it would make you feel like you were playing with some big orchestra or something because it sounded so wonderful to have another piano playing alongside you. You felt like you were a star.

"And then she would hold meetings of the music clubs that she organized [comprised of her students], and she would have little drills in which you would learn rhythm and theory and have little question-and-answer quizzes. Now that was a game, but it was a game toward a goal.

"As for your hand position, she wanted your hands close to the keys, your fingers curved. She wanted your hands relaxed but firm, and she would not allow you to bang.

"She wanted you to practice very slowly. I never will forget how many times she wrote on my music: 'Slow practice gains speed.' She wrote that so many times, and she would not allow you to race through music. She did not want you to be sloppy; you had to pay close attention to the notes. She wanted it accurate; she would show you phrasing as well as accuracy.

"To get a beautiful tone, she told you to relax, to play more with your upper body, rather than from the elbow down. She wanted you to use your arm, especially from your shoulder all the way down, which is something that's still very difficult for me.

"She entered her students in the various Bach festivals and the Mozart festivals—she did all that kind of thing.

"Regarding repertoire, Bach and Beethoven were very important. We did not launch into the big romantic repertoire until we became older. Then we would learn pieces such as the easier Chopin Etudes and Nocturnes, the Chopin Waltzes, some of the Schumann 'Kinderscenen,' and Schubert Impromptus. In other words, things that were not as difficult as Rachmaninoff, Prokofiev, and so on.

"Specifically, I remember she had me learn a Bach Prelude and Fugue in C-sharp Major, from Book II [of 'The Well-Tempered Clavier'], three Bach Inventions, Chopin's Nocturne in E-flat Major, Grieg's 'Butterfly,' Scharwenka's 'Polish Dance,' Chopin's C-sharp Minor Waltz, Rachmaninoff's G Minor Prelude, Beethoven's 'Moonlight Sonata,' Liszt's 'Liebestraume,' the Polonaise by John Alden Carpenter, Brahms' G Minor Rhapsody, a Mozart Sonata, Beethoven's Sonatas op. 49, Chopin's Polonaise 'Militaire.' In concertos, she loved the Grieg. She loved the romantic ones very much.

"So, essentially, it was the romantic school, with a lot of the classics but not a lot of contemporary, which, frankly, I didn't miss at all.

"Also, one of her principles of teaching was that if someone asked you to play, you got up there like a little lady or gentleman and you played.

"And I'll never forget her telling us, 'When you get in a recital, you play, no matter what happens in the audience. If somebody falls through their chair or if the house burns down, you play like a professional. And I remember that was one thing that I always heard from Van's friends that Rosina Lhevinne had said. She would say, 'Whatever the weather, if Van had been asleep or awake, sick, nearly dead, exhausted, or feeling wonderful, he could always get up there and play,' and that I attribute to Mrs. Cliburn because that was her philosophy.

"But she was careful not to just exhibit Van as the shining star. She taught every little student as a separate person, and nobody was compared to Van. You were compared only to *your* best, nobody else's.

"I remember, I would play things and think, *How could Van play this?* But she would never tell you. I would ask her, 'Mrs. Cliburn, could Van really play in double-thirds by the time he was six?' And she would say. 'Let's hear what *you've* prepared for today.' We never did waste time on what Van could do and all that. But we kids sure would get together and talk about it. We were sometimes so jealous and wished we could do those things." [9]

Joyce Anne Goyne Stanley, who also studied with Rildia Bee, remembers that "she never reprimanded you in an ugly way.

You always felt good when you left Mrs. Cliburn. She has the same sense of humor that Van has, the same love of life, of people, and of being able to say serious things in a very nice way." [10]

That was the musical environment in which Van grew up, a warm, loving place that nevertheless made considerable artistic demands of the individual.

As performing musician, Van approaches a score with a certain sense of freedom and spontaneity.

"To me, Van is a game player," says Ft. Worth Symphony conductor John Giordano. "What I mean by that is that his rehearsals are fine, but he really turns on in the concert. In the rehearsal, he sort of gives a sketch of what he's going to do, and then he's very spontaneous in the concert.

"At the same time, he telegraphs musically what he is going to do, so that, as a conductor, you know when he is about to play something that's rubato, or when he's going to move ahead a little or hold back. Somehow, he telegraphs this information to you, though I don't really know if he does it consciously or if it's part of his talent or whatever, but he can do that, and some people can't." [11]

And H. Charles Smith, who conducted for Van frequently at Interlochen, says, "I've always had the feeling that the better they are, the easier they are to accompany because their musical ideas make so much sense, and they're so clear in laying them out. Van was always easy to accompany because you knew what was coming next, and it made sense in relation to what had just happened musically. He had such a clear concept of the piece that it was very easy to follow him and to give him his freedom.

"He also had a sense of when he followed the orchestra, and when the orchestra must follow him. I remember occasionally, more than occasionally, he would look at me and say, 'Feel free.'

Then I would do my thing with the orchestra, and then when it was time for us to lock in on him, we would do that." [12]

The freedom of Van's approach sometimes clashed with his conductor's philosophy, as in the case of maestro Erich Leinsdorf. "They got along well," says Rosario Mazzeo, who was personnel manager of the Boston Symphony during Leinsdorf's tenure as its music director, "but Leinsdorf tended to be impatient with people like Van. Leinsdorf was a meticulous governor who followed the printed word, and when he did something once, he could repeat it exactly.

"That wasn't always the case with Cliburn. His approach tended to be more rhapsodic, while Leinsdorf was right on the button every time. Leinsdorf's attitude was 'Let's sew it up, and let the sewing remain sewed.' Cliburn . . . his nature, as I understood it, was that the performance was an adventure, and it might vary from one performance to the next, but the journey was supposed to be a thrill." [13]

Van never recorded any chamber music, but he considered it on several occasions. Remembers RCA's John Pfeiffer, "Jascha Heifetz had recorded scads of trios with [cellist Gregor] Piatigorsky and [pianist Leonard] Pennario, and then he worked with [pianist Leon] Fleisher, so I thought it would be marvelous for Heifetz to record with Van. I knew that Piatigorsky liked Van very much, and I think Heifetz did too.

"But Heifetz," who had fled his native Russia after the Revolution of 1917, "could not get over the fact that he remembered Khrushchev kissing Van after the Tchaikovsky. That was too much for Heifetz. He always said, 'I can forget, but I can't forgive.'

"Heifetz never forgave Van for allowing himself to be kissed by Khrushchev. I suppose Jascha wasn't quite reconciled to the fact that here was someone who made friends with his enemies, these terrible people. He overlooked the whole point of it.

"Of course, he said that about Horowitz too. I had Horowitz out in California [where Heifetz lived], and I was traveling around recording him, and Horowitz wanted to see Jascha. I didn't know quite what the feeling was between them, so I went to see Heifetz. I said, 'Horowitz wants to see you.' And Heifetz said, 'No. I can forget, but I can't forgive.' And I said, 'What does that mean?' He said, 'Never mind.' Who knows? It was just one of those Russian things, so I had to make up a story to Horowitz.

"But getting back to Van, he especially wanted to do the Schubert B-flat Major Trio, and he talked about the [Beethoven] 'Archduke' also, which would have been wonderful. Of course, Heifetz had done those with Rubinstein and [cellist Emanuel] Fevermann. Heifetz never repeated any of those that he had recorded with Rubinstein and Fevermann.

"Then I tried to set up a recording with Van and Piatigorsky to do the Rachmaninoff Sonata [for cello and piano] and the Chopin Sonata [for cello and piano], and that never worked out either.

"That could have been an exciting recording. So would the ones with Van and Heifetz. When you got down to it, Van wanted to do things of that sort, but not casually. He wanted to do it with the giants—otherwise don't do it. I agreed with him because he wanted to be able to express himself along with people on the same level, and it would have worked very well, no doubt." [14]

When it came to recording Van in solo and concerto repertoire, "I don't recall making any special adjustments in recording technique," says Pfeiffer. "I had made enough recordings at that time with some pretty great artists to feel that what they were going to project could be brought out with a very simple, straightforward microphone placement. In concertos, we recorded the orchestra on three microphones, or four microphones at best, and the piano with one.

"Now the piano is one of the most difficult instruments to record, but I had learned something about it three or four years before because I had spent a whole summer experimenting with piano recording. I was with Ania Dorfmann down in Webster Hall [in New York], and we had a series of pianos brought in from Steinway. We also had a series of microphones set at a series of distances from the instrument. And I kept records of where the microphone was placed, what kind of piano it was, and did this for at least a couple of sessions a week for about six weeks.

"After all that study, I came to the conclusion that the biggest thing that matters is the pianist and the piano. Producers and engineers can't do things to create anything. All we can do, at best, is reproduce what is done at the piano.

"In choosing pianos, I think Van always looked for the singing quality and the warmth of the sound. But he wanted the excitement there too. He wanted the brilliance there. But if you listen to some of Rachmaninoff's recordings, you get some of the same feeling from his playing, even though they're older recordings and they don't sound exactly the same—just in the voicing, Rachmaninoff and Van sound similar. I think it has a lot to do with the size of their hands. After that, it's a mystery.

"I remember once Van was recording a piece of Chopin's, and I noticed in all cases he left out a certain grace note. So I thought, *Well, this is the way he plays it.*

"So when we got to editing, and he was watching the score carefully, he said, 'Oh, we have to find a take with the grace note.' And I said, 'There is none.' He said, 'You mean I didn't play it?' I said, 'Well, no, it's not important.' And he said, 'Well, yes, it's in the score; we've got to have a grace note here.'

"So the engineer, Edwin Begley, who was so adept at anything, said, 'Well, let me try something.' I don't know what he did, but he took a piece of tape, and then he started fiddling at a certain point, and it sounded exactly like a grace note.

"And Van said, 'It's marvelous; it's incredible.' And Ed Begley looked up and said, 'Yes, it's the amazing grace note.' " [15]

To Max Wilcox, who also produced several of Van's recordings, "One interesting thing about him is that he did have an instinct for playing with great conductors, and I admired him for it.

"I hate to say anything against my most famous artist, Arthur Rubinstein [whom Wilcox also produced], but Rubinstein entered a period where unless he played with George Szell, he'd just as soon have had a more routine conductor that he could control.

"But Van, on the other hand, wanted to play with really good conductors. And he loved playing with the Philadelphia Orchestra and, of course, Eugene Ormandy. Although Ormandy may not have been a great musician, he certainly was the most flexible and malleable of accompanists; everybody loved to play concertos with him.

"But Van had this instinct for that, and he also is one of the most naturally gifted musicians that I've ever run across. His ability to get a beautiful tone out of the piano is amazing, and he has a natural aristocracy in his playing. When he sits down, he's this really regal figure and plays with this enormous breadth and dignity and taste." [16]

One pianist who has seen Van build a performance from the first bars is James Mathis. "He was very into metaphysical things," says Mathis. "For instance, he had a whole myth that he imagined about the F Minor Fantaisie [of Chopin]. He told me about it—there was a funeral scene and things like that. And I think he used that approach quite a bit, so there was an enormous amount of fantasy about his playing.

"Now, that was not my way. I would think about colors and other things. But Van was into all of that. And it was kind of funny, but I enjoyed hearing him talk about it, and it does work for some pianists.

"It certainly did for him. His repertoire wasn't huge, but what he played, he played awfully well. And though people didn't always realize it or admit it, he could play Mozart quite well too. He played the Mozart C Major [Piano Concerto, K. 503] brilliantly.

"Of course, he tackled most of the major concertos, as well. He was more comfortable with the Rachmaninoff Third than the Rachmaninoff Second, which was surprising because most people are the other way around.

"For a while [after winning the Tchaikovsky], he got real slow in everything he played. I think maybe Kondrashin got him to play slower in Moscow. Although, really, it's true that Van has had that most of his life.

"Now at Juilliard, he played the most beautiful Ravel Toccata in the world. And still, when he wanted to, the best Liszt Twelfth Rhapsody. The Ravel Toccata was wonderful because although it was driven, as it should be, it also was musical. It wasn't just notes, as many pianists play it. Van always was musical, even when it was dynamite technically. I think that's what put him ahead in many ways. It was always more thàn just technical expertise. It was fabulous playing." [17]

Though technique and physical equipment alone cannot make an artist worth listening to, it plays a part in the work of any major performer. In Van's case, one of the most frequently noted facets of his pianism is the sheer size of his hands.

"For my birthday a while ago, [pianist] Claude Frank and his wife, Lillian, gave me a present," says Naomi Graffman.

"I opened up this box, and there was a plaster cast of the hand of Liszt, and it was really horrible; it gave me the chills. And I shrieked out, 'It's humongous!'

"And then Gary [Graffman, Naomi's husband] said, 'Oh, it's not so big.' So I said, 'Put your hand up against it.' Well, do you know that Liszt's hand was more than a knuckle bigger than Gary's? It was like the hand of a Martian or something.

"I've given this hand to the library at Curtis Institute, where we're going to put the dimensions on it, so the kids can go and look and see why they have so much trouble playing these pieces of Liszt's.

"But Van's hand is as near to that size as anything I've ever seen, which doesn't mean that everyone with a big hand could play the piano that well. But it has something to do with the elegance with which Van could get around the keyboard, and he always sounded so beautiful." [18]

The apparent ease of Van's pianism and the pervasive warmth of his sound were evident at Juilliard, where other students realized that Van's way around a keyboard was unique.

"You have to realize that there is musical talent, there is intellectual talent, and there is also physical talent," says Jeaneane Dowis. "Van had all three, but the physical talent, the ability to get around the keyboard, I give his mother credit for that because it was something that obviously had been inculcated from an early age.

"Van was not afraid to pick up his hands two feet off the keyboard and just let them drop. Most people are afraid to do that because they're afraid they'll hurt themselves. Van was not afraid of that, and because of that, and because of the fact that physically he had a marvelous hand—two ideal hands with tapered fingers that could get in between the keys and a big stretch that could get around them—he was just never afraid of the keyboard.

"So he would pick up his hands and let them fly with a sort of abandon that most people couldn't approach. Even if they might have a very fine technical ability, they didn't have that dash, that absolute lack of fear." [19]

Always at the forefront of Van's mind during a performance was the setting itself. Van once told *Contemporary Keyboard* magazine,

> You are *not* playing for yourself. You are there in a service capacity, so fifty percent of you must be involved with the music and fifty percent of you must be out listening in the audience. It's like being a good conductor. A conductor must of course be very involved in the music, but he must be listening to the whole sound and gauging the total effect of the orchestra from an organizational standpoint, so that he is ever aware of what the person in the farthest point in the hall is receiving. [20]

On musical matters apart from his own playing, Van has several dearly held convictions. Notable among them is his belief that, "Music is music. I don't like it when someone says, 'Well, he or she can play Mozart but not Beethoven.' I just don't look at music that way. It's not as important which piece you choose to play. When I'm listening to a performance, I want to see how this performance is going to convince me. It's what you do with the piece.

"Now, you may have a different idea about how a Beethoven sonata should be played, or I may view a Mozart sonata differently than someone else, but that doesn't mean that person can't play Mozart. What matters is what kind of musical expression you can bring out, what you can say.

"It's all music, and that's how Arthur Rubinstein, for example, regarded it. When he played, he was playing the piano. He wasn't afraid of the sound of the piano, even if he was playing Mozart. He had a classic simplicity when he played, but he wasn't afraid of the full sound of the instrument, as these so-called early music purists are. Why make a sound so thin [on the piano]? Imagine what Mozart or Beethoven would have done if they had a modern piano. Look at what Beethoven *did* do! He thundered. He wrote arpeggios up and down and up the keyboard. He wanted as big and beautiful a sound as he could get.

"Plus, I know it's sacrilege to say this, but not every single piece by Mozart and Brahms is a masterwork. There are piano pieces by Mozart that just don't work. Generally, I think the piano pieces that are vocal, operatic [in their style and influence] are often the best, the ones that sing—that is what Mozart did best.

"But some of Mozart, and some of Beethoven, I find too percussive. Not all the late sonatas of Beethoven are completely inspired.

"But don't say so aloud, for you will hear about it. These are sacred cows in music. Say anything you want about Telemann. Handel? No problem. Liszt? Make all the fun you want. But if it's by Beethoven or Mozart, it is automatically a masterwork, according to some people.

"I can remember being greeted with sneers, when I was growing up, because people used to laugh about the music of Liszt. And they forgot completely that had it not been for Liszt, there would not be the great symphonic tone poems because he really was the man who gave the emphasis to the tone poems. Without Liszt's advanced harmony, you wouldn't have Debussy and Ravel. In many ways, Liszt even led into Impressionism.

"But they just howled at Liszt, and this incensed me. And they'd make fun of certain other composers too. I hated having so many people make fun of certain composers that I held dear back in the '50s. The unspoken rule was that you don't make fun of certain icons, but it was time to spit in the face of some other great composers. That seemed to be so fashionable, but, frankly, I was never dictated by the fad of the moment.

"And I really think that the poseurs took over in the '60s, and they drove many people out of the concert hall. They intimidated so many people. I suppose I'm just very old-fashioned. I love refinement.

"It's just like with Hollywood and some of the vulgarity of today's films. If the intention in Hollywood was shock value, I think it has worn off. If anything, I think now it has gotten to such a level that, more than anything, it points up sometimes our inability to speak well. I was brought up to believe that if you had to use profanity or vulgarity, it represented an inability to speak in a cohesive and coherent way. And I was always afraid of being thought incoherent, so perhaps I was just brainwashed right there." [21]

Van, who has been alternately praised and excoriated for opening many of his recitals with a florid rendition of "The Star-Spangled Banner," once explained his purpose: "The younger set of reviewers wonder why I play it, but the older ones remember that during the war, it used to be the custom for the artist to play the 'Banner' before a performance. . . . And being a July baby, I just adore the national anthem, so I play it." [22]

No doubt it also offers Van a chance to get acclimated to the piano before the recital proper begins, to understand how the piano sounds with a room filled with people, and to gently ease into the work ahead.

In reminiscing on the world's great concert halls, Van cites "Orchestra Hall in Chicago—a great hall, I don't care where you are in the world. Symphony Hall in Boston, fabulous hall. The Academy of Music in Philadelphia. The Lyric Theatre in Baltimore, which is patterned after the Leipzig Gewandhaus, is fantastic. Constitution Hall in Washington, D.C., has wonderful acoustics; RCA used to do some recording there.

"When you're playing on these stages, you can hear very clearly how the sound of the piano travels through the hall." [23]

Among new compositions, he considers some pieces worthy of more respect than they receive. "I liked Paul McCartney's 'Liverpool Oratorio,'" says Van, "and I can hardly believe he can't read or write music." The piece was dictated by McCartney to conductor-composer Carl Davis. "I'm just amazed by what he did in that piece, essentially by ear." [24]

And among artists whose work he has admired, a few instantly leap to mind: "James Dick, who is one of the most erudite and thoughtful pianists. He came to Texas from Kansas, and he has dedicated himself to making his festival in Round Top [Texas] really work. By sheer force of will, he has made that festival happen. I admire that tremendously.

"Gennady Rozhdestvensky I consider a great conductor and a sweet, modest man. Selfless.

"Naum Shtarkman [who placed third in the Tchaikovsky Competition in 1958 and whose son, Alexander, was a finalist at the Van Cliburn Piano Competition in 1989] is a wonderful pianist, very elegant, beautiful sound, of course technically fine. He could do a Chopin F Minor Concerto and E Minor Concerto gorgeously.

"When you talk about people I've been privileged to meet, such as Rubinstein, Horowitz, Walter, Ormandy, Reiner, Kondrashin, and many more, I consider them more than legends. They're incredible people, incredible musicians, great minds, great thinkers, great artists.

"When I think back on these people, I realize they're the ones who have been my inspiration. They are people that we, in the United States, have been blessed to have in our midst, to inspire us and to teach us.

"I consider myself a tiny mirror of the great legends that I have known." [25]

12

Return to the Spotlight

*T*o those close to Van in Ft. Worth, Kilgore, and Shreveport, it slowly became apparent in the late 1980s that Van was eyeing a return to the stage. Rested for more than ten years, caught up on performances and reunions he had missed, refreshed after two decades of constant world travel, Van began to drop hints about a possible comeback.

"Just as he desperately needed that time off, I think that after a while he desperately needed to get back into making music again," says Ft. Worth Symphony conductor John Giordano. "In 1986 at the latest, possibly earlier, it seemed that he was hinting that he wanted to come back again. You could tell he really wanted to play. He went to concerts, and he seemed so interested in what was going on. Afterward he had receptions for the artists at his house, or we all went out after a concert, and I could tell he was itching to perform again.

"It's hard to put my finger on it, but he would say, 'Do you think I should ever play again?' Or, 'That [recital] was so good maybe I should never play again.' He just seemed to be looking for the opportunity, the right time. Van has always been one for timing, and I think he was waiting for the right moment." [1]

No doubt a variety of factors persuaded Van to make the move. "For one thing, his mother was getting older," says family friend Martha Hyder, "and I think he wanted to play again on the stage for her. I think that had something to do with it, and I think she wanted to see him play again." [2]

Says Susan Tilley, "There's no question about it: Rildia Bee really wanted to hear him play again because he is her legacy, and he also feels a responsibility to carry on for her.

"She always wants him to go in and practice and let her hear him. She adores for him to play. He'll go in late at night and practice a little bit, and she will sit there absolutely mesmerized." [3]

Said Lillian Libman, shortly before her death in 1992, "Knowing Van, I believe he had a desire to be in touch with the public again, and I believe he also wanted to see if he still had that power of inspiration." [4]

Perhaps most important, a decade's rest and contemplation in his home in Ft. Worth rejuvenated him. By all indications, they were profoundly recuperative years.

"He has been happier in Ft. Worth than he has at any time since he left [his childhood home in Kilgore]," said John Pfeiffer in *Aura* magazine, which had selected Van as its "1990 Person of the Year." "It [Ft. Worth] has contributed a great deal to his peace of mind, to his outlook on his career, his life and everything else." [5]

Still, returning to the stage would not be so easy. Ten years away is an enormous amount of time for an artist. "If I stayed away for six months," says flute virtuoso Jean-Pierre Rampal, "I never would be able to come back again. It would seem impossible." [6]

Van had last performed publicly on September 29, 1978, in Toledo. In the interim, he had left New York, reestablished his Texas roots, redefined his life, and helped change Ft. Worth in the process. For instance, many people knew that Van had "poured a fortune into the arts in this community," as Ft. Worth Symphony conductor John Giordano once said.[7]

And as the *Ft. Worth Star-Telegram* noted,

> Since Cliburn's arrival, Broadway Baptist [Church] has become a center of classical-music performance, with numerous choral-orchestral services and concerts of a sort not generally associated with the Baptist tradition. Church officials openly credit the direction to Cliburn's moral support.[8]

Hardly a mysterious figure in his adopted hometown,

> His behavior in Ft. Worth has belied the general reputation for shyness—even reclusiveness—that has grown up around Cliburn during the past decade. He appears frequently, though with a tendency to arrive late, at ballet performances, orchestra concerts, opera productions and concerts on the Cliburn Foundations's concert series.[9]

After establishing this new, peaceful life for himself in Ft. Worth, after so many years away from public performance, would Van be able to return to the stage, to play at his peak level, to live up to the legend that had accrued even during his absence?

The opportunity to find out presented itself in the summer of 1987, when the White House came calling.

"There really hadn't been any calls before then because everybody just assumed that Van was never going to play again," says Susan Tilley. "So in June the White House contacted us because they knew there was going to be a summit [between U.S. President Ronald Reagan and Soviet leader Mikhail Gorbachev], but they didn't know when. They wanted to do something big for Gorbachev's visit, which was going to be the first visit of a Soviet head of state in years. Gorbachev, meanwhile, had actually asked if Van could come and play, so it seemed like a natural idea all around.

"So they wanted to know if there was any possibility that Van would do this. There was a rumor that the summit would be in August or September, and that was even announced on the radio, but that turned out to be false. It wasn't until the middle of November[10] that they finally called us with a definite invitation for a concrete date.

"It definitely appealed to Van's sentimentality and his heart and his soul to play for our country and for the Russians. He likes to play for sentimental reasons.

"Now, he did not come right out and say to me he was going to do it. But I think in concept he embraced the idea. And yet, naturally, he was torn, as well, because the question was: Does he want to take this step in his life at this time? Does he want to start playing again?

"But he certainly never rejected the idea out of hand. When the White House called back in November, he took about two or three days to think it over before he finally told them yes.

"But even when the possibility first came up that he might be invited to play at the White House, I think he knew that if he did that, he was opening up the door to doing more, that it probably wasn't going to be just a one-shot deal. He knew that once he played the White House, everyone would be asking again." [11]

Indeed, even before Van actually played the White House, the offers began coming in.

"I'm definitely interested in some proposals I've had," Van told the *Ft. Worth Star-Telegram* in November of 1987. "Zubin Mehta called up recently about playing with the New York Philharmonic. I told him I was thrilled that he even remembered me." [12] How could he forget?

"I had many things to be grateful to Van for," remembers Mehta. "My first visit to Carnegie Hall with the Los Angeles Philharmonic—would have gone completely unnoticed had it not been for Van's playing with us.

"I also played with him in '67 at the Montreal Expo. We played there, and then we did the Brahms [Piano Concerto no. 2] at Carnegie Hall, which really gave the Los Angeles Philharmonic a great boost. It gave the concert a personality, and we were grateful." [13]

Why did Van accept the White House offer?

"I just thought I'd like to do this," he told the *Ft. Worth Star-Telegram*. "I'm optimistic about the world these days, and about people getting together.

"Emil Gilels was gifted with second sight. He told me that he felt that when I did play again, it would have something to do with Russia and America. . . .

"You may be sure that before I agreed to go to the White House, I went to play for my mother. And she said to go ahead," noted Van, adding, "My mother is one of my greatest critics." [14]

Before the performance, "once Van had decided to go back [to the stage], he just locked himself in the house and really woodshedded for awhile," recalls Ft. Worth Symphony conductor John Giordano. [15]

Raymond Boswell, the Cliburn family friend from Shreveport, also remembers that "Van spent a great deal of time in his home in Ft. Worth preparing. Actually, he would play for hours, until his fingers bled, because he was really preparing to get back in the swing of it.

"He had played some before then, both at his house in Ft. Worth and when he visited our home here [in Shreveport]. But the serious rehearsal did not come along until preparation for the White House performance. And he had to be dead serious because that was an incredible kind of exposure, so he just closeted himself up in his living room and worked." [16]

Meanwhile, Associated Press reached Van, asking whether this engagement signaled a full-fledged return to the concert hall. "Let's wait and see how it goes," said Van. "All I can tell you now is that I'm ready and will do my best." [17]

To better prepare for the White House engagement, and to simultaneously bolster the piano competition named for him, Van gave a private performance for Van Cliburn Foundation contributors at his home on December 3.[18]

Then it was off to Washington, D.C. Van's nine-foot Steinway concert grand Model D headed there via Allied Van Lines,[19] while Van, Rildia Bee, and Susan Tilley took a plane.

Susan Tilley never will forget the flight to Washington, D.C., for the December 8 performance. "Van and his mother were in two seats," she says, "and then I was across the aisle.

"And the minute we took off, Van started looking out the window, and he never stopped, not once during the whole flight.

"My heart just bled for him because I knew what he was going through. He knew this was the end [of the intermission], or the beginning, depending on how you look at it." [20]

In more ways than one, Van's performance was historic. As a videotape of the concert shows, he opened the evening unconventionally, with a performance of the Russian National Anthem followed by its American counterpart.

"The White House had been very explicit that his program was to be no more than twenty minutes, absolute maximum, and that's not easy to do," says Susan Tilley. "Gorbachev had specified that he and his entourage wanted to be out of the White House by ten o'clock [at night] because they had lots of meetings and all.

"So Van had played around with the program to try to meet those time frames. He would play a program for me, and I had to time him with a stopwatch and send the exact timings of every piece, down to the second, to the White House.

"I asked them if he could make a little introductory statement or something at the beginning, and they said yes. So I assured them it wouldn't be very long. I didn't tell them he was going to play the national anthems because they probably wouldn't have let him do it. But that was his statement, even if it did make his program last a bit longer than twenty minutes." [21]

As Van walked out onto the small stage—really more of a platform—he instantly made eye contact with Gorbachev.

"The General-Secretary [Gorbachev] was exceedingly hospitable and gracious," Van later told the Chicago Tribune, "and when I came out to bow, he flashed me a really dazzling smile. He was just very kind. Mrs. Gorbachev was very sweet, too." [22]

When Van launched into the anthems, the audience in the East Room of the White House[23] gradually rose to its feet. In attendance were Ronald and Nancy Reagan; Mikhail and Raisa Gorbachev; Vice President George and Barbara Bush; Senate Minority Leader Bob Dole and his wife, former Transportation Secretary Elizabeth Dole; the Reverend Billy Graham; former U.N. Ambassador Jeane Kirkpatrick; former Secretary of State Henry Kissinger; Occidental Petroleum chief Armand Hammer; actress Claudette Colbert; baseball legend Joe DiMaggio; actor James Stewart; author Saul Bellow; singer Pearl Bailey and her husband, drummer Louie Bellson; jazz pianist Dave Brubeck; cellist Mstislav Rostropovich and his wife, singer Galina Vishnevskaya; conductor Zubin Mehta; and, of course, smiling euphorically through it all, Rildia Bee.[24]

After the anthems, Van proceeded to the serious portion of the program, opening with Brahms's Intermezzo, op. 118, no. 6. It was a fervently lyric performance, large in scale, slow in tempo, profound in its musical expression. Then came the Rachmaninoff Etude Tableau, op. 39, no. 5, a rush of sound beneath a singing melodic line in the right hand.

The Schumann-Liszt "Widmung" sustained the melodic thrust of the program, which ended with Claude Debussy's spectacular study in color, "L'isle joyeuse." Van's performance was brisk in tempo, inexorable in its drive toward the climax. Such was Van's enthusiasm in reaching the final notes of the piece, which lie low in the keyboard, that he very nearly lost his balance upon striking them, then quickly regained his equilibrium on his way up to take a bow.

The audience reaction was instantaneous, as was Van's—with the applause still roaring, he bounded off the stage to give Gorbachev a huge hug.

Once the crowd settled down, President Reagan took to the microphone: "The American poet Longfellow once wrote that music is the universal language of mankind," he said. "We've certainly seen that confirmed here tonight. There was no need to translate this magnificent performance by Van Cliburn. Van Cliburn is a musician that is known almost as well perhaps in the Soviet Union as he is here in the United States," continued Reagan, as Gorbachev nodded his agreement.

"For young Van Cliburn won the hearts of the Soviet people and the critics during the Tchaikovsky competition, which he won in 1958. The tickets to his auditions in Moscow were in such demand that people lined up for three and four days in advance. And when the competition ended, Mr. Cliburn performed for Premier Khrushchev, and then for a number of sold-out conferences [sic] in Moscow." As Reagan completed that sentence, Van, who was standing alongside him, shook his head to concur.

"Back home in the United States, he began his career, the career that established him as one of America's most respected musicians. And he continued to take that role in the international—take a role, I should say, in the international competition that is named in his honor.

"Since going on a sabbatical in 1978, Van Cliburn has not performed in public. And so for this, your first public appearance, I believe, in nine years," said Reagan, as Van smiled and the audience began to applaud again, "you are once again speaking in that language of music. I think I can say for everyone here, we thank you from the bottom of our hearts."

After a few moments, Van asked the president, "May I respond?" Reagan welcomed him to speak, and Van said, "Mr. President and First Lady, I'm so grateful for the invitation to get to play. I think there comes a time in one's life when one feels one wants to have relaxation and to enjoy life. And I know the fabulous, inimitable, and incomparable Russian pianist Emil Gilels once told me, 'You are very smart to realize that because we all need enjoyment, we must enjoy life and smell the flowers.'

"So, unfortunately, I've thought about him so often, since he left us recently. And, when this opportunity came, I said, 'You know, there are very few things that are as meaningful to me—first, of course, I love my home country. And some people like to tease me, Mr. General Secretary, and say that sometimes they think I love Texas better than all the rest of the United States. But we want to have Texas, you know, very healthy.

"But in addition to that, I think you know my constancy, how very deeply I love the Russian people, and your culture and your art." As Van spoke, Gorbachev beamed. "And you go with me always in my life.

"And it is for both my beloved president, and for you, that I am so happy to do this. Thank you."

More applause—and then matters started getting really interesting. Van left the platform to kiss Nancy Reagan and Raisa Gorbachev, at which point Raisa made with her fingers as if playing on an imaginary piano and said to Van: "What a pity there is no orchestra because if we did [have an orchestra present] you could play Tchaikovsky." [25]

Van responded instantly: "We have no orchestra, but if you'll help me, I will do something."

And with that, Van loped back up to the platform, sat himself down at the keyboard, and before he had unrolled more than an arpeggio or two, the Gorbachevs had joined him singing—in Russian—the beloved Soviet song "Moscow Nights." Without so much as looking at the keyboard, Van sang and played, making eye contact with the superpower leaders, and their wives, who stood before him. This, of course, was the same nostalgic song Van had learned and performed during his first, incredible journey to Moscow in 1958. The room rapidly dissolved into tears.

When Van finished, the place seemed to go up for grabs. Kisses flew in all directions among Van, the Gorbachevs, and the Reagans. Camera bulbs flashed incessantly, the room was abuzz.

"She asked me to play more," Van told someone who asked him, in the confusion of the moment, what precisely was going on.

Thus did an already intriguing concert turn into an event. Once again, even despite a long absence, Van proved that he had not lost his innate gift for making the world sit up and take notice.

Quipped Reagan to Van, "Maybe I can be your agent. I'll see if I can get you some dates." [26]

The next morning, December 9, newspapers across the country ran with the story. Lisa Anderson and Michael Kilian reported on the front page of the *Chicago Tribune:*

> The melancholy of a Russian song about the romance of "Moscow Nights" brought tears to the eyes of the Soviet summit delegation Tuesday night and capped a state dinner with an impromptu and emotional sing-along in the East Room of the White House. . . .
>
> A beaming Gorbachev, who had been visibly tired from his first full day of summit meetings, burst into applause. He and his wife began singing with Cliburn, and soon all the Soviets in the room were singing.
>
> At the conclusion of the song, Gorbachev leaped to his feet and embraced the pianist with a bear hug, kissing him on both cheeks.[27]

So what prompted Van to venture a pop encore? "There had already been speeches and the atmosphere was very warm," he told the *Ft. Worth Star-Telegram.* "I took my life in my hands and played and sang a little Russian song. . . . It was a very exciting evening. Very emotional and nostalgic for me. It brought so many memories of evenings in Russia." [28]

Later, Van told the *Chicago Tribune,*

when Mrs. Gorbachev asked me to play something
else, I didn't feel that anything else classical would be
appropriate, and I thought of this song, "Moscow
Nights.". . .

After I got back to the hotel that night, though, I
thought, *Goodness, this is terrible,* because I was
sorry that there had been nothing on television of my
playing of classical music, only this little song! [29]

Zubin Mehta remembers of that night, "It was the first time
that I heard him after so many years, and I was very, very happy
for him, that he had this exposure and that he did so beautifully.
Of course, he has this natural habit of charming everybody off
their feet. This is him, it's not put on. That's how he is.

"That night, I kept asking him to play with us. I even asked
him to come to Russia with us [the New York Philharmonic],
which he very nearly came close to doing. But I wanted to
encourage him to start playing again because Van is really an
important artist. He's not just one of those virtuosos who came
and went. He has that very rare and important thing, staying
power." [30]

Later in the evening, pianist Dave Brubeck told the *Ft. Worth
Star-Telegram,* "I thought his playing was remarkable. His
choice of program was just right. He still had all the power and
emotion and strength that you need. He played from the heart,
and that's what counts." [31]

While Van was still in Washington, invitations for future
engagements began to reach him. Most notably, he was asked
to perform for the opening of the Bob Hope Cultural Center in
Palm Springs, California. The program would be taped and
broadcast nationally a couple months later, but Van wasn't
interested.

From Washington, D.C., Van flew on to New York to see
opera performances and visit old friends.[32] Now the producers
of the Bob Hope Cultural Center program continued to call.
Tilley remembers, "They even went so far as to have President
Reagan fax Van a personal request to do the show because

Reagan was going to be there. So in this fax on presidential letterhead that Reagan sent to the hotel, he wrote, 'Well, I told you I was going to try to get you some dates.' Then the producers just kept on and on and on, and they just finally wore Van down, so he said he would do it, but not until he said no about twenty-five times." [33]

The program was taped in January, and shortly thereafter Van reflected on the events of the past few weeks, and the years that led up to them. Van told the *Dallas Morning News:*

> To be honest, I never thought the "intermission" would go on for 10 years. I guess it went on so long because I felt relaxed and was having such a good time simply living. . . . I don't think I can ever go back to the schedule I once maintained. Frankly, I want a more normal life, but at the same time I want to have the wonderful contact that comes with an audience. . . . I never felt that music was something just for me. I always had to share it. I had to play something for someone. [34]

Throughout the beginning of 1988, unconfirmed reports that Van was planning a tour of the Soviet Union with Zubin Mehta and the New York Philharmonic continued to surface. [35] But by March Van had decided against the idea, saying in a prepared statement, "I'm extremely disappointed that the scheduling did not work, especially because I love the New York Philharmonic, and Zubin Mehta is a wonderful friend of mine—and a great artist." [36]

Not long after, however, the Dallas Symphony announced that Van had accepted an invitation to play for the first public performance the following year in the new Morton S. Meyerson Symphony Center, a spectacular, glass-and-steel concert hall built at a cost of 79 million dollars. [37] In effect, this would be one of Van's first public performances since his sabbatical, since the White House and Bob Hope Cultural Center events were private affairs.

"We all held our breath about the Meyerson [and its potential acoustics]," recalls Van. "They had called me about doing the first concert about a year-and-a-half before it opened. Well, they made me an offer I couldn't refuse. So I thought, *Well, let's just pray* [that the hall would turn out all right].

"And at one point I called Susan [Tilley] in the middle of the night and said, 'Do you really think that they're going to have a good hall?' Mother just said, 'Oh, well, I can't worry about that. At least it'll pay the bills.' " [38]

Until then, Van made private appearances at special events, such as the dedication of the Nancy Lee and Perry R. Bass Concert Hall at the University of Texas at Austin.[39]

By the start of 1989, he was making headlines again, when the Mann Music Center in Philadelphia announced that Van would perform with the Philadelphia Orchestra that summer to benefit the outdoor music festival.

"My husband had been dead just a short time when I went down to a spa down in Ft. Worth, and while I was there I called Van," remembers Silvia Mann, who with her late husband, Fredric R. Mann, had known Van since 1958.

"Van asked me if I wanted to come over for dinner. So he sent a car. This enormous car pulled up, and it had a TV and everything else. We had dinner at about 10 or 10:30 that night, and we talked about so many things.

"The [financial] condition of things at the Mann Center was just awful, and we knew we just had to have a fundraiser. So I just asked Van if he would play one for us. We just thought we needed someone very, very special. It couldn't be just another artist. Right away, Van said yes. There was no hesitation, absolutely none. And he did it so that we could really sell the tickets and make some money. He wanted to do that in memory of my husband.

"I knew that would be great for the Mann Center because there's no one like him. And I hoped this might start him off performing publicly again." [40]

Indeed it did. A few months later, Van announced that negotiations were under way for his return to the Soviet Union.

After a Ft. Worth news conference in May, and on the eve of the eighth quadrennial Van Cliburn International Piano Competition, the *Ft. Worth Star-Telegram* reported, "Cliburn elaborated only briefly and somewhat reluctantly, saying the negotiations began after an invitation from Raisa Gorbachev, wife of Soviet President Mikhail Gorbachev, for whom he performed at the White House after a December 1987 state dinner. He said his Soviet performances probably will include engagements in Moscow, Leningrad and Novosibirsk." [41]

A few weeks later, on May 27, 1989, the eighth Van Cliburn International Piano Competition began in Ft. Worth, but other, related events were in the air.

Specifically, a tragic story unfolded just as the competition commenced, with the news that Steven De Groote, winner of the Cliburn competition in 1977, had died in Johannesburg, South Africa, at age thirty-six. In 1985, De Groote, who had a passion for flying, was seriously injured in a crash near Phoenix, on the Gila Indian Reservation.[42] He was practicing stunt landings with an instructor at the time of the accident, which left him with a punctured aorta and lung and a lacerated liver, among other serious injuries.

"It was a horrible plane crash," Van recalls. "He was an excellent pilot, and many times he would fly here [to Ft. Worth] for a benefit performance. Now, before one particular benefit, he accepted an offer to do some stunt flying. He was a real daredevil, he really was. So he took on to do this stunt flying, and he got together with a man in Phoenix who was a stunt flyer, and they were going to do this trick together. But Steven's plane stalled, and he couldn't get out of it, and he dropped into a ghastly crash.

"This was in January of '85. He had a severed aorta, and in the first day they gave him a 2 percent chance of surviving. And then in forty-eight hours it went to 7 percent, and 15—but nobody ever dreamed he would live.

"We were planning a funeral, really, when they called me. I was just waiting for the death announcement—and nothing came. And then they told me, 'Van, he's getting along better.'

"But Steven really wanted to live, and for four years he did. He was very heroic because the daredevil in him also gave him that zeal for life.

"In late April of '89, he had just been with us in Ft. Worth and played gorgeously. He said he had a cold or something. Then he got ill on the plane back to South Africa. When the plane landed, his father was there, and they rushed him to the hospital." [43] De Groote died in the Brenthurst Clinic in Johannesburg on May 22, the cause of death listed as "inflammation of the liver." [44]

In one of the most moving moments of that year's competition, a memorial service for De Groote was held in Ed Landreth Auditorium at Texas Christian University. One of the jurors, Ralph Votapek, eloquently played a Schubert four-hand piece with his wife, Tina. Van spoke lovingly of his memories of De Groote.

Away from the limelight, Van practiced hard for his impending Philadelphia appearance, his first public performance in roughly eleven years.

"I remember talking to him at the time," says pianist Ralph Votapek. "It was about three weeks before he played with the Philadelphia Orchestra, and he admitted that he was scared to death. He said, 'Oh, I'm just so nervous, why am I doing this?' " [45]

And though Rildia Bee was ninety-two at the time, she was involved in Van's musical preparation. " 'I want your Philadelphia selections again,' Tom [Zaremba] says she announced to her son," reported the *Dallas Morning News*. " 'And when you're finished with that, let's hear what you're considering for your encores.' " [46]

On June 11, nineteen-year-old Soviet pianist Alexei Sultanov was chosen winner of the competition, and a few days later, Van headed for Philadelphia.

"The rehearsal was in the afternoon, the day before the performance [of June 19], and I sat in the audience for that," says Susan Tilley. "I have a tendency to be more uptight than I let myself realize, and the next morning I got up, and I was sore all over. I said to myself, 'I can't understand this—I didn't do anything.' And Van said, 'I know what it was: You were so tense during my rehearsal that it was like doing isometrics the whole time.'

"I guess I was nervous, but I didn't realize it. It was a tense moment. Here you're talking eleven years away from performance. I knew Van was going to be wonderful because he had really worked, and I know what he is capable of doing. Still, you always worry that there could be some little mishap or something.

"And another thing: It would be wonderful if everybody could simply come to grips with the fact that there probably will be a few dropped notes. That doesn't matter so much in music. It's the overall that counts.

"Before the performance, Van and I didn't talk about who would be in the audience. I knew Andre Watts would be there, for instance, people like that. But I didn't discuss it with Van, and I know Van well enough to know that he probably suspected [that various major figures in the music world would attend].

"If he wanted to know, he would have asked me, and I didn't see any need to volunteer with more pressure.

"And sure enough, Andre Watts came back to see Van after the performance. And Van said, 'If I'd known you were here, I never would have been able to play a note,' which is not true of course, but he didn't need the extra pressure. There's enough pressure there already." [47]

"It was a very special experience and, of course, I realized Van's tension," recalls Stanislaw Skrowaczewski, who conducted the rehearsal and the performance. "Of course, he had his preoccupations—how people will take him, and how his playing will be. I think he was very conscious about all of his possibilities.

"Actually, even during the competition in Ft. Worth, we had a get-together where he played me the tempi and everything, and he played beautifully. I was very pleased to hear him in very fine shape, after all these years of not playing. Listening to him, I felt he was much more mature as a musician now. I had played with him right after the Moscow competition many times, when I was music director of the Minneapolis Symphony. He came there every several years, and it was fine. It was exciting. But this time it was much more mature.

"And so now we met again with the orchestra in Philadelphia. The rehearsal went beautifully, and he was extremely quiet and controlled at the rehearsal. We didn't have much time, so we hardly repeated anything. It wasn't really necessary, though.

"Just before the concert, of course, I realized how nervous he could be. However, he didn't really show his nerves. And neither did I, of course. I tried to be sort of fatherly, you know. Just to take it easy, not to aggravate his tension, but on the contrary, to diminish it and help him to take it more easy.

"So we talked a lot, about his future concerts in America. He just had an offer to go back to Moscow and to some other places. So we talked about his future and tried to build certain relaxation into this difficult moment." [48]

No doubt the moment was all the more difficult because Van had decided to play not one but two concertos—the Tchaikovsky First and the Liszt First—before an audience of 10,000.[49]

From Skrowaczewski's vantage point, "The concert went absolutely beautifully, and I was very relieved because I realized what it was for him. It's pleasant to be part of somebody's success. The orchestra seemed happy too, and everything went very well.

"Musically, I would say his tempi were somehow more quiet than before, his phrasing was very carefully done. He operated with long periods of a phrase, long breaths you might say. His touch was very strong, very beautiful, exquisite, really, both in lyrical and in dramatic moments." [50]

The audience seemed to concur, calling Van back to the stage thirteen times after the concert ended,[51] which, in turn, inspired him to play several encores.

Though the reviews wouldn't be in until the next morning, a sense of relief already was apparent.

"There must have been I don't know how many hundreds of people backstage wanting autographs and wanting to see Van," recalls Susan Tilley, "and we could have been backstage for four or five hours. But the people in Philadelphia charged high prices for those gala tickets and for the party afterward, and Van was supposed to be there, and they were just about to go crazy because Van wasn't there yet. He was still backstage signing autographs.

"So this was where I just had turn into a person I don't like to be and say to visitors, 'That's it; leave, right now.' I hate that, but somebody had to do it or he would have been there till the next day.

"So then we went on over to the party, and it was a lovely event, but the same thing: hundreds of people all over him. I have a wonderful photo from there that sort of expresses the way we felt: 'Whew, what a wonderful feeling—we're through it, and it was good, and it's over.' " [52]

Silvia Mann remembers the evening for "an incredible performance that was just like something out of a beautiful dream. Then we had a tremendous party, and the combination of that concert and that party was the most popular thing we've ever had there. The money it raised saved us that year.

"Van seemed pleased—actually, he couldn't have looked or seemed happier. He was in a wonderful mood afterward; he had so many of his friends there and his mother and her friends. And they came in from different states—they didn't all come in from Philadelphia by any means. In fact, there was quite a nice contingent from Texas." [53]

At the very least, Van seemed to be pleased with the piano he played.

"Before the performance," recalls Steinway chief technician and Van's longtime tuner, Franz Mohr, "Van called me and said, 'Franz, please prepare a piano there that you think I might like in Philadelphia, from the concert stock.'

"So I went a day ahead, and I prepared a piano because I know what he likes. And he fell in love with that piano—so he played it, and he bought it from Steinway right then and there." [54]

The morning after the performance, the reviews came in, and they were virtually unanimous in their assessment.

"Yes, to end the suspense, Van Cliburn can still play the piano," wrote Donal Henahan in the opening of his *New York Times* review.

> The Liszt showpiece went off especially well and put the listener immediately at ease: Mr. Cliburn, it was clear, had been practicing. . . .
> Many observers of the concert scene predicted he would never set foot on stage again. Now he has, and he can take great satisfaction in having overcome great odds.[55]

Other reviews echoed these sentiments. Joseph McLellan wrote in the *Washington Post* that

> it would be hard to find a pianist anywhere who can communicate with an audience as powerfully, who can generate the kind of excitement that was witnessed here. This is partly because he is a legend, but it is also part of the reason why he became a legend.[56]

Beyond Van's playing, there was something else that inspired critical commentary: his words to the audience.

"Cliburn strode onto the stage and did what no other pianist does: He talked to the audience," noted one reviewer. "He gave a touching remembrance of Eugene Ormandy and Fredric Mann, paid homage to their wives, and delivered an anecdote about Beethoven, information on the choice of concertos and a recitation of an Italian sonnet before re-emerging to play." [57]

Afterward too, Van addressed his audience.

"Even in the midst of his standing ovation," reported the *Dallas Morning News,* "Van didn't forget Rildia Bee. After his encores, he made a speech that ended with an impassioned poem. It was a sonnet he wrote for his mother when he was 14." [58]

Henahan in the *New York Times,* however, did not respond to Van's words in quite the same way. "His coda, the recitation of a long inspirational poem, was a reminder that playing the piano is still Mr. Cliburn's forte." [59]

If there was a disturbing element to the reviews, it was the still lingering condescension toward the repertoire Van chose to play. Just as he found some people sneering at Liszt when he was coming of age musically in the early '50s, so too were they sneering at Liszt and Tchaikovsky on the eve of the '90s. In that regard, not much had changed.

Henahan, in a positive review, nevertheless complained that neither the Liszt nor Tchaikovsky concertos "were the repertory's sternest tests of artistic maturity or intellectual growth." [60]

And McLellan, in his otherwise enthusiastic *Washington Post* review, wrote, with some condescension,

> We may have to hear him in a few Mozart concer-
> tos to answer some questions about what has hap-
> pened to him since 1978. On the other hand, he
> clearly will never need to play a note of Mozart to
> pack concert halls and make large audiences happy.[61]

Once again, the narrow notion that only works by Austro-Germanic composers such as Beethoven, Brahms, and Mozart represent a worthy test of a pianist's mettle was being put forth as law. If the score is by the Russian Tchaikovsky or the Hungarian Liszt—or, for that matter, by a French or American composer—it simply doesn't rate, even if it suffices to "make large audiences happy."

Nevertheless, the Philadelphia comeback remained a popular and critical success, setting the stage for Van's return to Moscow a week later.

"I think in his mind Van held the option to cancel the Soviet tour, but by the time he played in Philadelphia, it had to be done because everything was set up already," says Susan Tilley.

"Rildia Bee planned to do the Moscow trip all along. Of course, there's always that possibility when someone is elderly that something could happen and she wouldn't feel like going. Van always said, 'If she doesn't go, I'm not going,' and I think he really meant it. But it never did seem to be a real possibility that she wouldn't. She was doing really well." [62]

Indomitably, Rildia Bee boarded the chartered jet with Van at Ft. Worth's Meacham Field just before midnight on June 28.[63] The plane had been officially christened the *Rildia Bee O'Bryan Cliburn*, and the American flag and the Lone Star flag had been painted on its side. Along for the ride were Tilley; Van's cook, Nanette Leeper, of Ft. Worth; friends Raymond Boswell of Shreveport and Tom Zaremba of Detroit;[64] and forty-seven boxes and crates including a microwave oven, a case of Campbell's chicken noodle soup, various goodies from Van's seemingly inexhaustible personal kitchen, all neatly packaged in Tupperware, several cases of Evian water,[65] and one small rehearsal piano.

Heading east, the plane stopped in Newark to pick up two more family friends, Clara and Ernest Menaldino, then flew on to Keflavik, Iceland, to refuel. While on the ground, Van and friends rushed into the shop to pick up gifts for friends in Russia. Then the refueled jet took off again, landing in Moscow four hours later, at 2:30 A.M. June 30.[66]

Several television cameras and a large crowd awaited Van on the tarmac, and when everyone had gotten off the plane, Van and entourage were brought into the airport, "where they [the Soviets] had arranged a tea, in an unairconditioned room," recalls Tilley. "Now, at two o'clock in the morning, when you've flown for fourteen hours, you don't exactly want to have a tea party. But Van, ever gracious, went and had tea with these people, and they had the press interview there." [67]

After that, "we headed for town," wrote Tilley in her tour diary, "making a stop to see St. Basil's Cathedral and take a short walk around Red Square," just as Van had done the first time he had arrived in Moscow, thirty-one years earlier, and on each return thereafter. At the National Hotel, "there was a large crowd of admirers waiting for Van with flowers and gifts. It was very touching. As it turned out, these people were omnipresent at rehearsals, in front of the hotel, backstage, everywhere." [68]

Van told one of the reporters awaiting his arrival, "I feel so close to this town that I sometimes walk the streets in my dreams." [69]

Of the many admirers awaiting Van, still cherishing memories of 1958, Irina Barmash, said, "We would have waited all night." She had brought for her vigil treasured photos of Van from his last Moscow visit—in 1972. [70]

Inside the National, Van, his small entourage, and various officials ascended a marble staircase and headed to his luxury suite, the same one that Lenin had used a generation ago. Gold mirrors, magnificent pieces of furniture, and the like graced the rooms, which led to a balcony overlooking Red Square. [71]

Then four men carried into the suite the piano Van had brought from Ft. Worth. The *Dallas Morning News* reported,

> "This is a small rehearsal piano," the pianist said. "You can mute the sound as low as you want. We had 12 seats on our [rented] jet. I had them take out four so we could put in the piano. I practiced during the long trip, but the sound was turned off so I didn't disturb anyone else."
>
> He said that as the plane approached the Soviet Union, he became very emotional.
>
> "When the crew announced we had at last flown into Russian airspace, I was so overcome," he said, "I sat down and played the Russian national anthem." [72]

Susan Tilley's diary picked up the story: "Since the sun comes up about 3:30 in the morning in the summer in Moscow, we got to bed long after sunrise. . . .

"When Van arose he asked me to call room service and order breakfast for him. He wanted kefir, hard-boiled eggs, blue-gray caviar, black bread and butter, coffee, and almond cookies.

That night, there were many, many callers—Russian friends of long standing who came to see Van." [73]

Among them, was Ashchen Mikoyan, whose grandfather was Soviet First Deputy Premier Anastas I. Mikoyan. "We hadn't seen Van for seventeen years," she says. "And my mother and I and Henrietta Belayaeva, who used to be his interpreter, all wondered whether he remembered us at all, and whether we should go to the airport to meet him.

"But then my mother and I decided we wouldn't go because we thought he probably didn't remember us, or want to see us or something. He was not a great correspondent, so we never really heard from him, except for occasional hellos passed by word of mouth. Then again, we didn't really believe he would come until he actually arrived. Before that, several times in fact, there had been rumors that he might come.

"And then when he finally did come [in 1989], he flew in during the middle of the night, so we didn't hear from him until the next day. In fact, on his first full day in Moscow, my mother rang my door—we live in the same block of flats, but she was too excited to use the telephone. She came to my apartment, and when I opened the door, she was very flustered and said, 'I just got a phone call from Van from his hotel room, and he said come immediately, rush here, why aren't you here already?'

"So we ran to his old suite at the National Hotel, and it was just like the old days. And then we spent every day together; we went to all of his concerts.

"It was a sentimental journey because he always seemed to like Russia very much, and he had so many good friends there, people who really loved him as a person and as a musician, as a friend.

"And he didn't really look older. He was very much the same. You know how it is when you meet somebody you haven't seen for a long time. The first instant, your first visual impression, you see the difference. But in a minute you forget about it, and you find the same person. And Van is very much the same person I remembered, in terms of his personal qualities.

"And all through the day people kept on coming to visit. Lev Vlasenko, his fellow competitor from the Tchaikovsky Competition, came and the sons of [the late] Kiril Kondrashin.

"And Van remembered many of his fans—he actually remembered the names of some people in the crowd, you know, those fans who really were there all the time. He would say, 'Hello, Tanya, how are you?' And I would ask him, 'How come you remember all those names?' And he said, 'Well, of course, I remember the names of my friends.' These were not the people who would go to the parties to his hotel room. They were just the people who hung around the stage doors." [74]

The next day, Saturday, July 1, "There was a rehearsal at noon," Tilley wrote in her tour diary. "There was a mob outside the rehearsal hall, and it was very difficult to get through. The rehearsal went beautifully, and there were quite a number of people who had managed to slip into the hall. After rehearsal it was back to the hotel and again crowds and crowds of friends and well-wishers. Among the visitors was the young Russian prodigy Evgeny Kissin, who came along with his mother and his piano teacher. That evening U.S. Ambassador and Mrs. Jack Matlock had invited us to the Ambassador's Residence, Spaso House, to meet them. Spaso House is truly a palace, and it was a thrill to see it." [75]

On Sunday, July 2, there was another rehearsal with the Moscow Philharmonic and conductor Dimitri Kitiaenko. "During those rehearsals, there were all these little babushka ladies that followed Van around," recalls Ed Wierzbowski, a filmmaker who had traveled to Moscow to document the event. "There was one particular woman who had lost both of her parents, and during that same period went and heard Van. Van's playing was such that she claimed that it took her out of her grief." [76]

Then, Sunday evening, came Van's first Moscow performance in seventeen years, in Tchaikovsky Hall.

"All the way up to this point, we were curious whether or not the Gorbachevs were coming," recalls Wierzbowski. "And Van did not know until he was there in the hall that they were coming. When I set up cameras two hours before [the perfor-mance], the KGB was everywhere. So I had to get introduced to all the KGB agents because I was going to be walking all around the room, and therefore, all around the Gorbachevs if they showed up. My Soviet partner wanted to make sure that I didn't get shot. So that's how we knew that the Gorbachevs would attend." [77]

Before Van played a note, he addressed the audience: "For thirty-one years, I have felt like I had two homes. I will soon ask permission from your distinguished President Gorbachev to buy an apartment in Moscow. I will be coming for much-needed visits for my music, for my soul, to Russia and to Moscow." [78]

Then Van offered a donation of $10,000, "wrapped in a bright ribbon," according to one news account, for the Soviet Culture Fund[79] (in addition, all proceeds from his concerts went to Soviet cultural organizations).[80]

And then Van played the Liszt and Tchaikovsky. When he finished, "The response of the audience was unbelievable," recalls Ed Wierzbowski. "But backstage he was not entirely pleased with himself. I mean, there's this level of perfection that he demands of himself. And it's not that he got too caught up in technical mistakes—what he gets caught up in is the architecture of the piece." [81]

Dallas Morning News critic John Ardoin, who covered the event, wrote:

> Mr. Cliburn re-shoed these two grand old war-horses and made one rethink them from top to bot-tom. I have always believed, for example, that the Tchaikovsky concerto has become so overly familiar that it is capable of exciting only if delivered as an out-and-out virtuoso romp. Wrong.
>
> In his hands, it became something noble and enno-bling, and he became not just a pianist but an elo-quent storyteller recounting absorbing tales of

epochs past, of cultures that long ago faded into the pages of history.[82]

Because the Gorbachevs were on a tight schedule, Van was limited to two encores—a Debussy Prelude and the Schumann-Liszt "Widmung"—at which point he was summoned for a meeting with his hosts.

"They were charming, absolutely charming," wrote Tilley, who attended the meeting, in her tour diary. "We had tea, Russian red wine, apple pie, fresh fruits, and a visit of about an hour or more. We talked of many subjects, and Gorbachev emphasized that he thought the world was tired of war. Van and Rildia Bee presented the Gorbachevs with a sterling silver Tiffany plate engraved to the Gorbachevs from them. Van also presented both of them with a set of Ft. Worth Club jogging clothes, including a T-shirt with block letters saying 'Ft. Worth Club' across the front, a pair of shorts and socks to match. Who knows, someday we may see them jogging along the Moscow River with their Ft. Worth Club outfits on.

"During the visit, Van proposed to Gorbachev that he would like to play in Leningrad," which was a problem, since the Leningrad Philharmonic was on a summer break, "to which Gorbachev immediately agreed and said he would arrange a charter flight for the Moscow Philharmonic to go with Van to Leningrad to play there on July 9." [83]

And when the Gorbachevs chuckled over Van's repeated proposal to buy an apartment in overcrowded Moscow, Van protested, "Mr. President, I was serious!" [84]

After meeting the Gorbachevs, "We had to make our way back to the dressing room through corridors absolutely jammed with people," wrote Susan Tilley in her tour journal. "It was extremely frightening. I was punched in the stomach. Rildia Bee's purse was knocked out from under my arm (but fortunately Van picked it up) and I seriously thought Richard Rodzinski [Van Cliburn Foundation executive director] was about to get in a fist fight with one determined fan. We owe a true debt of gratitude to Alexei Sultanov, who took it upon himself to deliver some modified kung fu blows and was of immeasurable assistance in getting us to our destination. This scene was truly indescribable and horrifying, but nonetheless, we all realized it came from a wellspring of love for Van. Beth Rodzinski [Richard's wife] summed it up very well when she said to one group of unruly fans, 'If you love him so much, why do you try to kill him?' " [85]

The next night, Monday, July 3, Van played in the Great Hall of the Moscow Conservatory, where he had triumphed in 1958. Whereas Sunday night's performance had been before a benefit audience of invited guests, Monday's was for the public.

Wrote John Ardoin in the *Dallas Morning News,*

> Even before Mr. Cliburn played a note, there were bouquets of flowers, and they continued to flow throughout the concert. There were simple bunches and huge baskets. . . .
>
> At the end of the Tchaikovsky concerto, a crowd pushed its way down front to ring the stage and fill the central aisle to bursting. They pelted the pianist with still more flowers; he gathered them up and threw them to the orchestra.[86]

As Wierzbowski recalls of that night, "after the main performance, Van played a couple of encores, then he literally would go back to his dressing room and relax for a few minutes. Apparently he had completely forgotten that he had left the orchestra still sitting on the stage. He asked everyone standing around, 'Do you think I should go out and play another encore?' I mean, he had gone back and had a cigarette, and they were still applauding!

"Then, even after the encores, when there was no way that he was going to come back on stage, there were these diehards, maybe fifty or sixty people, standing there clapping, hanging by the stage, hoping to get a glimpse of him. It was just a magical thing between him and the audience.

"Backstage there's a two-story stairway leading up to the dressing room, and in a matter of minutes, this stairway was full of people, dangerously full of people, running, somehow thinking that they were going to be able to get in this tiny little dressing room. And you couldn't get through the crowd to get in; you almost had to risk your life.

"And then to get him out, the police had to form this human barricade—it was a regular rock star kind of experience—and the police got around him and forged their way down through the stairs to get him out. Actually, he's lucky he got out with his clothes on." [87]

One Russian told Raymond Boswell, "We're in the midst of a lot of change that we don't understand; we don't know what's happening. But when Van comes, he makes us forget our troubles for a little while." [88]

The next day was July 4, which Van and friends spent at Spaso House, where Ambassador Matlock had invited two thousand people for the American Independence Day celebration. Van, of course, was ushered to the piano, where he offered listeners patriotic fare, including the American and Russian national anthems, "Moscow Nights," and "America, the Beautiful." [89]

Van spent the next few days visiting with friends, practicing, and grabbing snippets of rest where possible, between live-via-satellite interviews with ABC-TV's "Good Morning, America" and the "The CBS Morning News." [90]

Meanwhile, in the Soviet press, Van was lauded not only for music but for something broader than that. "The Soviet cultural newspaper *Sovetskaya Kultura,*" reported the *Ft. Worth Star-Telegram,* "was quick to emphasize that Cliburn had been not only loyal, but recognized the good in the Soviet Union before others did.

"An article quoted Cliburn at 24 in the depths of the Cold War between East and West as saying: 'I'm sure there are enormous unused potentials to achieve real understanding between East and West. . . . These potentials are unlimited.' Few Westerners thought that way in 1958." [91]

After a few days of reunions, practice and rest, Van and friends boarded the plane for Leningrad at about 2:00 P.M. July 9, then checked into the Pribaltiskaya Hotel, on the Bay of Finland. The performance would be in the Concert Hall of the Leningrad Philharmonic society, a room that Van called "imperially gorgeous." [92]

Says Wierzbowski, "After every performance that Van had done in Leningrad in years past, immediately thereafter people would queue up and get numbers for tickets for the next time that he would arrive.

"In 1972 he left and didn't return until seventeen years later. And what I found out when we were in Leningrad was that every year the concert hall updated this waiting list. And when he finally came back, even though no one yet knew for sure whether he was going to play Leningrad, the people continued to check in on availability for tickets. There were nineteen people from the original list who claimed their tickets after waiting seventeen years, and they got to sit in the first row." [93]

The response in Leningrad was similar to Moscow's, with Van's performance inspiring extended applause that, in turn, led to six encores.

"I added up the applause from the three concerts," recalls Wierzbowski, "and it was an hour-and-a-half of applause." [94]

The next day Van and crew flew back to Moscow for more personal get-togethers, a visit to the Moscow Baptist Church, where Van and Raymond Boswell took to the pulpit. "It was very touching," wrote Tilley in her Moscow report, "to see all the Russian people at church obviously devoutly religious and rich in spirit." [95]

Then it was time for some serious shopping.

" 'Shop till you drop' is not a phrase often heard in Russia," reported the *Dallas Morning News* of Van's trip to a Moscow grocery store. "But then Van Cliburn doesn't often come to Moscow. . . .

It's not that Mr. Cliburn was hoarding the pur-
chases for himself. He is a generous man who gives
away everything.

Friends aren't given one bottle of perfume, but
three. Russian visitors to his room are sent away with
pocket calculators, watches and soft drinks.

"Do you need any toilet paper?" he whispers in
their ears as they walk away.[96]

On July 12, Van's fifty-fifth birthday, he was to attend a party
in his honor at Spaso House. Before that, however, Van met
"the Metropolitan who is to the Russian Orthodox Church as
an archbishop is to the Roman Catholic Church," wrote Tilley
in her journal. "First we went to the monastery of St. Daniel,
which was built in the fourteenth century. There we had a short
tour and witnessed a beautiful Orthodox service." [97]

After the birthday party, "We went back to the hotel where
another large group of people was waiting for us. There was a big
cake from Gosconcert [the Soviet concert agency] and lots and
lots of flowers. The festivities went on until the wee hours." [98]

On Friday, July 14, the Moscow Conservatory awarded Van
a Master of Fine Arts degree—not an honorary one but a degree
representing studies completed. "Mr. Kulikov, who is the director of the Conservatory, made the presentation and gave
Van a beautiful diploma," wrote Tilley. "We were then escorted
into the Rachmaninoff Hall where the Conservatory choir sang
three pieces of Rachmaninoff in honor of Van, including two
selections from the Rachmaninoff Vespers. We were all in
tears, and Mr. Kulikov said to me, 'Is a Russian compliment.'
There are no words to describe the emotion of that event." [99]

Then the group rushed back to the hotel to "throw our effects
into suitcases and rush to the airport for our departure time
that had already been changed to two hours later than we had
intended," wrote Tilley. "As we exited the hotel there were the
familiar faces of Van's fans, who seemed to be everywhere he
was: the concert halls, the hotels, Leningrad, etc., and they
were the last faces we saw as we took off at the airport." [100]

The flight home was smooth—until the plane reached Newark, New Jersey, to drop off Clara and Ernest Menaldino.

"As we came in to land there, we circled and circled at about 4:30 in the morning; we just could not seem to land," recalls Raymond Boswell. "So we knew something was a problem. Then we got the word from the pilot that the right landing gear light did not indicate that it was down, so the pilot said he was going to fly very low over the control tower, and they were going to tell us if it was down.

"So we flew very low over the tower, and they indicated that the landing gear was down, but they had no idea whether it was locked or not.

"The pilot said, 'We're going to circle one more time, and I'm going to come down and bank the plane very much to the right. I'm going to hit that one wheel one time and take off immediately, and then you [in the control tower] tell me if that wheel seems to hold or if it buckled under, and then we'll know if we've got to make a bedded landing.'

"So we came in at a sharp angle, he hit that wheel one time and took off again sharply. And they indicated that the wheel seemed to be in place because it did not turn under or bend when we hit it.

"So then we came in a third time for a landing with all the fire trucks and the police and the ambulances and everything running down the runway. Van and everyone pretty much took it in stride. We all took our pillows and held on to them when we came down on the runway that third time because, while we thought it was going to be all right, we didn't know for sure. So we just held onto our pillows and bent over and landed safely and thanked the Lord.

"The plane came to a stop, and before they could open the door, the pilot discovered that two little wires had disconnected, which was why the panel didn't indicate that the wheels were locked in place. Let me tell you, that kind of thing will improve your prayer life." [101]

After dropping off the Menaldinos, the plane flew on to Ft. Worth, landing at about 8:00 A.M. Sunday, July 16.

"When we arrived back in Ft. Worth," wrote Tilley, "it was so wonderful to see Richard's [Rodzinski's] smiling face"—he and his wife had left the Soviet Union before Van—"to greet us with a sack of donuts and a half gallon of vanilla ice cream. We knew we were home!" [102]

Letters, packages, and gifts from Van's Russian fans followed him back to Texas. One letter in particular, sent to Susan Tilley, summed up the sentiment:

> Since year 1960 I did not miss his concerts in Moscow, Kiev and Leningrad. All these years I collected articles, reviews, photographs, recordings. I have a big collection of his photographs about 800, about 400 articles, recordings, although there were issued not so many.
>
> The influence of his talent for people is so great in our country that verses, portraits, sculptures appeared, and the press wrote much about the secret of his influence for the souls of the people. The sculptor Vasilyev created a very lyrical portrait Van in a wood.
>
> He has given the belief to the good and beauty thousands of people in our country.
>
> My best wishes to Rildia Bee and Van. Tell him that in Russia [people] remember, love and wait always for him.[103]

Van and Rildia Bee rested for a few days, before RCA announced at the end of July that Van would become the first classical pianist to receive a platinum record, signifying more than one million sales of his Tchaikovsky First Piano Concerto recording with Kondrashin.[104]

Actually, the recording had sold at least a million copies by 1961, two million by 1967, and 2.5 million by 1970.[105] RCA had given Van a gold record in 1961, but the distinction of platinum had not been officially made by RCA and the Recording Industry Association of America until July 10, 1989.[106]

To celebrate both Van's recording award and his homecoming from the Russian tour, two thousand fans turned out August 2 at the Round-Up Inn in Ft. Worth for a civic ceremony. Ft. Worth Mayor Bob Bolen presented Van with a plaque from the city, RCA Victor chief Guenter Hensler gave Van a platinum disk for his million-plus-selling Tchaikovsky recording and a gold disk for his 500,000-plus selling "My Favorite Chopin" recording.[107]

Reported the *Ft. Worth Star-Telegram:* "The assembled music and civic dignitaries let loose as enthusiastically as the rest of the crowd when it came to throwing colored streamers at a smiling Cliburn and a grinning Rildia Bee Cliburn, his mother, when the pair rode through the room in a red convertible, re-enacting Cliburn's famous ticker-tape parade in New York in 1958.

"Cliburn surprised the assembled throng with his rendition of 'Moscow Nights' with the Broadway Baptist Church Chancel Choir." [108]

While he was in town, RCA's Guenter Hensler visited with Van: "I just said to him, 'Look, I know we have to go at your pace [regarding new recordings]. Don't ever accuse me of not wanting what you have to say musically, but I think it's wrong to pressure you to give us records. You have to go at your own pace.'

"I think he actually appreciated that I didn't want to put him under any pressure because I noticed he breathed a sort of sigh of relief. I think maybe he thought, *Well, here is somebody who doesn't just say I have to go sell a million records tomorrow, but who understands.*" [109]

On September 8, Van offered his first Texas performance in more than a decade, playing for the first public performance of the new, Morton H. Meyerson Symphony Center in Dallas.

"He was very nervous, very apprehensive," recalls Dallas Symphony conductor Eduardo Mata, who led the performance, "but, still, he performed beautifully. He was in control of it." [110]

Wrote Wayne Lee Gay in the Ft. Worth Star-Telegram, "From the moment the grand opening chords rolled into the room like thunder, it was obvious that an extraordinary musical event was in progress. After the thunder, Cliburn's special magic with the lyrical sections took over, backed up responsibly by [conductor Eduardo] Mata and the [Dallas Symphony] orchestra." [111]

The following day, September 9, Van appeared at a Sound Warehouse record store in Dallas to sign records[112]—and was kept busy doing so from 3 P.M. to midnight.

"The only time I've ever seen anything like that," says Guenter Hensler, "was for Luciano Pavarotti, and that didn't last as long." [113]

And on December 9, Van renewed ties with his public one more time, traveling home to Kilgore to speak for the dedication of the Anne Dean Turk Fine Arts Center at Kilgore College. The building would house the new Van Cliburn Auditorium, to which Van donated a concert grand piano.

Van spoke at the event, and though the reunion with his lifelong Kilgore friends was an important one, it had its lighter moments too.

"Van and I have this tendency to laugh when we're not supposed to," says Joyce Anne Goyne Stanley, who has known Van since they were both children. "In fact, we always had this relationship in which, all we had to do was look at each other, and we'd start laughing, especially in serious situations.

"Well, Van was giving this speech at the dedication of the Anne Dean Turk building when he saw me sitting out in the audience. At first, I could tell he was trying hard to compose himself. But then he cracked up, right there on the podium!

"The local paper even reported it. It said, 'Cliburn, often laughing, almost uncontrollably, told the audience stories from his childhood in Kilgore.' " [114]

After the speech, everyone who knew Van from way back talked to him at the reception afterward. One by one, they asked him to come back and perform in Kilgore for the friends who knew him since he was knee-high.

Longtime family friend Annie Lou Ballard remembers, "I told him, 'Van, if you don't come back and play for us one more time, I'm not going to live to hear you.' And Annette [Davies Morgan] told me later, 'You know, I think that remark made him realize that many of his friends in Kilgore were getting older, and if he was ever going to play for them again, he ought to do it soon.' I think that planted an idea in his mind." [115]

For the meantime, though, Van savored his reunions. He traveled to Washington, D.C., in June of 1990, one of thirty guests at a luncheon for Americans in the arts and sciences given by Soviet President Mikhail and Raisa Gorbachev.

In September, Van played a short, private recital for the opening of the Fogelson Forum medical education center at Presbyterian Hospital in north Dallas. In the audience were Texas billionaire H. Ross Perot, U.S. Senator John Tower, and screen star Greer Garson, who had donated half the 6.3-million-dollar cost of the center in the memory of her late husband, Colonel E. E. "Buddy" Fogelson, a Texas wildcatter.

"They came expecting the best, and Cliburn obliged," reported the *Ft. Worth Star-Telegram,* "dazzling them with a brief, emotional performance.

"Unfamiliar with Cliburn's tendency toward tardiness, this most luminescent crowd was left for a time to contemplate its own sparkle." [116]

Shortly thereafter, Van left for Lincoln, Nebraska, for the opening of the sixty-fifth season of the Lincoln Symphony Orchestra in its new Lied Center for Performing Arts. He had played in Lincoln years before, appreciated the cultural traditions of the university town, and agreed to accept the engagement.

The performance was one of Van's most intriguing. Out of the media spotlight that focuses on him when he plays in major cities, he sounded relaxed and magisterial throughout. His tempos were audaciously slow, his tone characteristically warm, his phrases legato even in double-octave passages.

The day after the performance, Van surprised almost everyone by turning up at Memorial Stadium to play the game-opening "Star-Spangled Banner" for 76,000 Cornhusker football fans. Longtime friend and former University of Nebraska President D. B. "Woody" Varner had invited Van to play the anthem.

"Cliburn had never performed before a football game in his 32-year career as a pianist," the *Lincoln Sunday Journal-Star* soberly noted. "But he had played a musical instrument during a football game before.

" 'I was a clarinet player in the Kilgore (Texas) High School marching band,' he said. 'I have loved football all my life and have marched in so many games.'

"Cliburn said the Memorial Stadium audience was about the largest he has ever played for, surpassed only by an outdoor concert audience of 80,000 people in Chicago [at Grant Park in 1958]." [117]

Come October, it was time for Van's long-awaited return performance at Kilgore College, which would mark the tenth anniversary of the East Texas Oil Museum and the sixtieth anniversary of the discovery of the East Texas Oil Field.[118] The recital's proceeds would benefit the school's Harvey Lavan and Rildia Bee Cliburn Scholarship.[119]

Everyone, it seemed, wanted to attend this performance.

"Tickets sold out four hours after they went on sale," noted the *Chicago Tribune,*

> Crews from "Good Morning, America" and other TV shows flocked to Kilgore, Texas, and every cab driver in town (both of them) suddenly was talking Beethoven and Brahms.
>
> "You here for the Van Cliburn concert?" asked the cabbie, who looked more like a Houston Oilers fan.
>
> "Man, wish I could have gotten tickets to that. What a great pair of hands." [120]

Clearly, this performance was not going to be easy.

"I can assure you that I was very afraid," Van later told the *Flare,* the newspaper of Kilgore College. "It's always hardest to play before those who know you only too well. They expect more of you, and you hope that you won't disappoint.

"I have felt the same nervousness since the time I was three. My friends tell me that I have enough bravado to get on and off stage, and that's it." [121]

Wayne Lee Gay wrote in the *Ft. Worth Star-Telegram,* "The world had waited 10 years, and the 1,600 music-lovers who jammed Dodson Auditorium on the Kilgore Junior College campus in this town of 11,000 last night waited an extra 45 minutes before their favorite son finally arrived onstage at 8:45 p.m. to begin the concert, which had been scheduled for 8. It was worth the wait." [122]

After Van's signature performance of the national anthem, he launched into a formidable program, his nervousness most apparent in the incendiary tempos he took in Beethoven's "Appassionata" Sonata. After its rigors, he clearly calmed down, offering a rhapsodic "Funeral March" Sonata of Chopin, sensual colors in Szymanowski's Etude in B-flat Minor, subtle shadings in Debussy's "La terrasse des audiences du clair de lune" and "Reflets dans l'eau," and a brilliant "L'isle joyeuse."

Then came encore after encore, including the Schumann-Liszt "Widmung," a Rachmaninoff miniature, and Chopin's Polonaise in A-flat Major.

"Cliburn obviously was moved by the audience response," observed the *Chicago Tribune,* "for he offered no less than five encores. When he got to the main theme of Chopin's famous Polonaise in A-flat, some folks in the audience literally started whistling." [123]

Then came an encore that puzzled almost everybody.

"When he played his own 'Nostalgia' as an encore," says RCA's John Pfeiffer, one of the few listeners to recognize the piece, "everybody whispered, 'What is that? What is that?' And I thought, *You fox, you—playing something they never heard.* I had always wanted him to release that [recording], but he was always a little hesitant about it. He thought it was just too much chutzpah to put it on a record." [124]

The *Kilgore News Herald* summed up the evening best with a headline streaming across the front page of the next morning's newspaper: "Cliburn's Kilgore recital Vantastic." [125] The piece noted that,

> At the close of his program, the pianist was presented a bouquet of red roses by Annette Davies Morgan. . . .
> The tall pianist, about whom friends can still detect the boyish qualities that so endeared him to the world . . . surprised none of his hometown friends when he bounded out into the audience to present the flowers to his mother. . . .[126]

After the performance, it seemed almost as if all of Kilgore—population 10,904[127]—had decided to attend the post-recital celebration.

"At the reception in the library after the performance," reported the *Kilgore News Herald,* "Cliburn and his mother accepted the outpouring of love and friendship from those lucky enough to get close enough to the mercurial Cliburn and his mother, still happily at her son's side despite her advancing years." [128]

For Van, of course, the night was still young, so he and a few friends headed over to the First Presbyterian Church to hear an impromptu, mini-recital from the church's superb organist and longtime family friend Jimmy Culp.

Van, of course, stayed up through what little remained of the night, then dashed over to the East Texas Oil Museum, where "Good Morning, America" did a live interview with him.

A few hours later, he made another appearance, at a downtown civic celebration of the sixtieth anniversary of the East Texas Oil Field, with Texas Governor William P. Clements, Jr., among the dignitaries.

Though there were more performances to come—warmly reviewed performances at the Tilles Center on Long Island in October,[129] a marathon performance of the Liszt First, Tchaikovsky First, and Beethoven Fifth Concertos New Year's Eve in Ft. Worth—the Kilgore recital had to be the emotional high point of them all.

Along similar lines, on October 14 Van threw a grand ninety-fourth birthday party for Rildia Bee at the Ft. Worth Club. *New Yorker* magazine, which covered the weekend's festivities, noted, "When she founded a mission for the homeless in Shreveport, Louisiana, in 1937, she did it, she says, 'because it was the right thing to do and somebody had to do it.' " [130]

On Saturday, the night before the party, "Van had a few people to the house to honor Rildia Bee as she turned 94, at midnight. "The house looked as though an inauguration were about to take place," noted the *New Yorker*. "There were balloons and pots of roses everywhere. Rildia Bee came downstairs a few minutes before twelve, looking spectacular in a long red dress and with her silver-gold hair swept up à la Tebaldi. When Van seated himself at the piano to play 'Happy Birthday,' she said, 'Make it sing, honey.' " [131]

The next night, "Van had this gorgeous, glamorous party for her," recalls Mrs. Henry Miller, who has known Van since Kilgore days. "Everyone was dressed to the nines, with their great-grandmother's jewelry on. Van had the complete Ft. Worth Symphony Orchestra there, and Roberta Peters came to sing." [132]

The next year, 1991, Van played a recital for the first installment of the Irving S. Gilmore International Keyboard Festival on May 5, a few days earlier appearing with Zubin Mehta and the New York Philharmonic as part of Carnegie Hall's Centennial Festival.

The reviews were split.

Dallas Morning News critic John Ardoin wrote:

> The result was vintage Van, and one of the most exciting of his performances since he returned to concert life in 1989. There was daring yet suppleness to everything he did, and his sound was big and brawny.

The Philharmonic collaboration, however, was more sour and rough than not.[133]

James R. Oestreich wrote in the *New York Times:*

For all his volcanic octaves and moments of quiet poetry, the performance moved from event to event without much overall impetus.

Mr. Cliburn's sonority was also somewhat clangorous, in keeping with the quality of the orchestral playing. The horns set a crude tone at the outset of the Tchaikovsky, which prevailed for most of the evening.[134]

The fact remained, however, that Van was back.

"You know, some people say Van should have done this or should have done that," says pianist Gary Graffman. "He should have taken a shorter leave, he should have played this piece or that piece, whatever. But there's something much more important here. He has lived his life his way, the way he wanted to. As far as I'm concerned, everything else is beside the point." [135]

13

Coda

*I*f Van were never to play another note in public, which does not seem likely, he could rest assured that he has made his contribution.

His large catalog of individualistic recordings, his long years of concertizing around the world, his renowned piano competition, his role in raising the international profile of the American performing artist—these facets of his career affirm that his impact on both classical music and popular culture are felt to this moment. For those who doubt, consider that, to this day, his recordings sell briskly, his concerts sell out shortly after they are announced, and he is perpetually sought after for interviews, nearly all of which he declines.

Van has said, "An artist can be truly evaluated only after he is dead—at the very eleventh hour he might do something that will eclipse everything else." [1] Still, the work he has done thus far has been rich. His dramatic, sometimes turbulent career has reached millions and, by all appearances, has proved fulfilling to him, as well.

"I've run into him a few times over the years," says conductor Joseph Silverstein, "and it's obvious he's at peace with himself." [2]

Why not? Van survived success and acclaim that few performing artists will ever know.

"I experienced only a little taste of what he had, and I can tell you that it can be frightening," says pianist Andrei Gavrilov, who won the Tchaikovsky International Piano Competition in 1974. "I won the Tchaikovsky when I was eighteen—I had just entered conservatory. And I remember very well how it went. At three o'clock in the morning, the telephone rang. NBC was coming over with the camera for an interview, asking how I felt after I had won the first prize. I said, 'Did I? I didn't know.' It was euphoria.

"But then comes the difficult time, when you are becoming known, when you go under criticism, when, one day, they say good-bye to you charitably. And then you find that you are already losing the charm of youth, you are getting older, and it's so painful, it's indescribable. It could destroy you from inside. This is the hardest moment of artistic life. You must have not only intellectual and physical ability, you should have guts to go through this.

"In Van's case, it was a thousand times worse because he became something like Elvis Presley. I would put it this way: a nice, beautiful kid—a genius, which is what I consider him—with enormous success, an enormous set of coincidences: How do you handle this?" [3]

For Van, there was only one way: Be himself, play the music that meant the most to him, and, just as important, try to nurture classical music wherever possible.

No doubt there was in Van a little of his great-great-grandfather—the one who was Sam Houston's preacher. Consistently, without embarrassment and despite a certain degree of ridicule from some quarters, Van went about trying to inspire others to the music he revered.

"Of course, a lot of people felt like pouncing on Van because he doesn't follow what people think he ought to follow," says conductor Jorge Mester. "He doesn't play the pieces some people say he should play. When he breaks those 'rules,' a lot of people get mad." [4]

Naomi Graffman recalls, "The last time I heard Van before he stopped performing, he played the Grieg Concerto with the New York Philharmonic. And I remember particularly that it was utterly roasted in the [New York] *Times,* but I swear to you it was a beautiful performance of the Grieg Concerto. Yes, it definitely was on the slow side, but the slowest portions— such as the slow movement—were heavenly, lovely. And I believe if anybody but Van had played it, it would have been much better received. That kind of thing does happen.

"After his sabbatical, it's even more dangerous because there are these alligators out there waiting to get him. With someone as famous and as popular as Van, that's certainly the case." [5]

That was not news to Van, for it had been a central theme of his life for almost as long as he played the piano. Penalized for playing a performance when his school principal tried to stop him, ridiculed for preferring repertoire considered out of date in the 1950s, mocked by the Eastern press for being from the South, criticized for failing to stress the Austro-Germanic repertoire, put down for taking a long sabbatical—this list goes on and on.

The beauty of it is that Van never budged, never gave up the faith in his vision of his music or in music itself.

"You've always got to remember with Van that nobody has had a life like that, by a long shot—no one has even come close," says pianist Garrick Ohlsson, who also created a stir when he became the first American to win the Chopin International Piano Competition in 1970. "So my feeling is, God bless him. If he didn't want to make the usual decisions, run the usual kind of career, so what? And I wouldn't be surprised if it took a decade [away from the stage] to balance out those first twenty incredible years of his career. People have to live their lives, and because Van doesn't do it according to someone else's model, that will upset some people very much.

"Of course, we as a nation have a lot invested in him as a fantasy, but he's only a person, and he has to live too. He has to do what he needs to do.

"I was in Ft. Worth a few years ago playing with the orchestra. Van had just played at that Bob Hope Cultural Center event. I watched it on TV, and I thought, *Hey, that's Van Cliburn. He sure plays well. That's the way he's supposed to play.*

"And somebody else, who was not being very nice, said, 'Tell me—you're a pianist. Did he really play well? Can he still play the piano?' I said, 'You bet he can!'

"See, when you're that famous, you have people sniping at you, people who are dying to say, 'You're not what you once were.' But I say, 'Hey, I might have artistic differences with him, but that was splendid playing.' " [6]

Van's life today is very much the way he wants it to be. His spacious house sits on the cul-de-sac of a quiet, peaceful street in a quiet, peaceful neighborhood of Ft. Worth. Inside that house, he continuously talks to his friends on the phone, does as much as he can to make his mother comfortable and happy, looks after the piano competition that bears his name, and follows the TV news to see what's happening in the world.

After circling the globe more times in a year than most of us will in a lifetime, Van now prefers the world to come to him. Most of the best singers, pianists, and chamber ensembles visit Ft. Worth and Dallas, many under his direct sponsorship. Often, after the performance there's a through-the-night soiree at Van's house, outside the glare of publicity.

The Van Cliburn competition now stands as his chief artistic outlet, and it has taken a form like no other competition of its stature. Competitors no longer are required to perform from any list of repertoire. In acknowledging both the level of accomplishment of the contestants and the inarguable fact that every pianist has particular strengths, each young artist is free to perform any repertoire he or she wishes to play.

This, says Van, underscores his belief that the competition is "as much a festival as anything else, a festival of piano and piano music." [7]

Many critics have raised just concerns about the proliferation of piano competitions, and Van addressed these in an interview with *Contemporary Keyboard* magazine:

> I think it should always be borne in mind that competitions do not signify a life's career. A competition is only one of several doors to step through. . . . I think it's like Rudolf Serkin once said, you can have a career if you're able to live through the scars because musical development brings many scars, and you remember them all.[8]

❖   ❖   ❖

No doubt Van contemplates recording again. He would love to record the Mozart Piano Concerto in C Major, K. 503. RCA executives surely will record anything he wants the moment he says so.

Too, he knows that the vaults at RCA contain his unreleased recordings that the company wants to put out, if he so decides. His recording of the Schumann Piano Concerto with Charles Munch and the Boston Symphony Orchestra is said to be superb; there's a CD's worth of solo works that he never otherwise recorded, including pieces such as the two greatest Chopin Ballades—the First in G Minor and the Fourth in F Minor—the Beethoven Sonata op. 31, no. 3, Liszt's Twelfth Rhapsody (Van's signature solo piece), his own "Nostalgia," and more.[9]

In addition, Ed Wierzbowski's film of Van's return to Moscow in 1989 is virtually ready to be released, whenever Van chooses to have it out.

To those who care most about Van, how often he appears on stage these days is not the point. "I don't care whether he goes back to the stage or not," John Pfeiffer said in the *Aura* magazine profile. "I want him to be happy. I want him to be the kind of person he feels that he wants to be. Certainly his fulfillment as a person is the important thing. I know that is very closely tied in with his music." [10]

For now, Van's interests are more contemplative than commercial, more driven by philosophical thought than career ambition. "I was watching TV the other day, and Daniel Boorstin gave this fascinating talk—he is the librarian emeritus of the Library of Congress," says Van. "He decried that we are forgetting in America who we are, that we come from every place on the face of the earth, that that is what differentiated America, the United States, from any other place on the face of the earth. We came here from every place, and each of us, all of us, can enjoy everything—we can enjoy the world.

"And I think he said that to fractionalize our population, as some do today, is really to do us a disservice. And he couched all of this in the most beautiful language. It seemed to be the most uncontroversial thing in the world, coming from a learned, intelligent person and sounding like the most logical thing.

"And I said, 'Right on,' as I listened to him because it's true: That's what made America so wonderful. . . . We have this freedom—we still have freedom, and we can do things. We can wake up one morning, have an idea, try to put it into progress, and we can do something. We yearn to have something in life; that's the beauty and the spirit of America.

"But now we're dividing as people, and I don't want that to happen. I don't want this kind of thinking to cramp the dreams of young people—they may be stymied by divisiveness.

"You know, maybe I'm hopelessly old-fashioned, maybe I'm living my life in the nineteenth century, in a way. But I don't think we have to give up all the hope and optimism and values of that time. I know I haven't." [11]

APPENDIX

Van Cliburn's Complete Discography

Following is an annotated discography of the complete Van Cliburn (on compact disc). All recordings are on RCA, with the exception of the last entry, on Melodiya.

RACHMANINOFF: Piano Concerto no. 3 in D Minor, op. 30, Symphony of the Air, Kiril Kondrashin conducting (recorded 1958); Prokofiev: Piano Concerto no. 3 in C, op. 26, Chicago Symphony Orchestra, Walter Hendl conducting (recorded 1960).

This stands as the definitive recording of Rachmaninoff's Third Piano Concerto. Vladimir Horowitz's recording with Fritz Reiner conducting the RCA Symphony Orchestra and Rachmaninoff's recording with the Philadelphia Orchestra remain its only rivals, though the latter sounds more like Cliburn's than the former. Cliburn emphasizes the lyric impulse of this score throughout. His tone, even as captured by comparatively primitive 1958 technology, sounds meltingly beautiful, particularly in the ethereal opening statement of the first movement.

Cliburn plays the first, more difficult cadenza Rachmaninoff wrote for the movement (and which the composer himself cut for performance and recording, as did Horowitz). The cadenza in particular shows that Cliburn, even at age twenty-three, when this recording was made, was a formidable Rachmaninoff interpreter. He offers an epic, heroic performance, ringing out with lyricism, yet fresh with a feeling of improvisation and spontaneity. Even the recapitulation of the first movement sheds light on the meaning and structure of the music, with Cliburn and Kondrashin understating the case, the recap trailing off to almost a whisper.

The pianist rides from one lyric climax to the next in the second movement and presses forward with great momentum in the finale.

Cliburn made most of his best concerto recordings with conductor Fritz Reiner and the Chicago Symphony Orchestra; and even though Walter Hendl, rather than Reiner, conducts Cliburn's recording of the Prokofiev Third, orchestra and soloist communicate vividly. Cliburn's piano sounds more biting and bracing than usual, which also makes it a fascinating anomaly.

TCHAIKOVSKY: Concerto no. 1 in B-flat Minor, op. 23, RCA Symphony Orchestra, Kiril Kondrashin conducting (recorded 1958); Rachmaninoff: Concerto no. 2 in C Minor, op. 18, Chicago Symphony Orchestra, Fritz Reiner conducting (recorded 1962).

The most popular classical piano recording ever made, Cliburn's Tchaikovsky First sounds worthy of its acclaim more than three decades after its release. Cliburn plays a swift, dashing, and youthful performance, direct in its expression, uninhibited in its lyric warmth and, quite often, emotionally impulsive.

In the end, this performance suggests the spirit and the unique rhythmic lilt of Russian folk music, as expressed in a concerto setting.

In Rachmaninoff's Second Piano Concerto, Cliburn establishes the grand scale of the performance in the opening measures. After only a chord or two, his deep and resonant sound epitomizes the grand manner of so much of his pianism. Though Fritz Reiner is often thought of as a kind of classicist, the swell and sweep of his orchestral accompaniment sound idiomatically romantic.

RACHMANINOFF: Sonata no. 2, op. 36, in B-flat Minor (recorded 1960); Prokofiev: Sonata no. 6, op. 82 (recorded 1970); Rachmaninoff: Prelude, op. 23, no. 4, in D Major; Etude-tableau, op. 39, no. 5, in E-flat Minor (recorded 1970 and 1972).

This is the premier recording of the Rachmaninoff Second Sonata, for only Vladimir Horowitz recorded a similarly epic-scaled reading. And yet the immensity of the conception of each artist's performance remains the only parallel between the two, for Horowitz's overwhelming virtuosity differs from Cliburn's more refined and more sonically resplendent approach to the keyboard. In the finale especially, Cliburn creates tremendous rhythmic and sonic excitement yet without forcing the tempo.

The approach is quite different, though appropriately so, in Prokofiev's Sixth Sonata. First, Cliburn addresses the main theme with a dryness of touch and ferocity of attack that sharply defines the difference between Rachmaninoff's neo-Romanticism and Prokofiev's more angular modernism. More important, Cliburn dispatches the score with equal parts keyboard virtuosity, architectural clarity, and intellectual insight.

The warmth and radiance of Cliburn's singing tone pervade his reading of Rachmaninoff's Prelude in D Major, op. 23, no. 4, as does his ability to project the inner workings of a Rachmaninoff score by weighting each melodic line differently.

Cliburn offers a sweeping, though not hasty, performance of the heroic Etude-tableau in E-flat Minor, op. 39, no. 5.

"MY FAVORITE CHOPIN": Polonaise in A-flat Major, op. 53,
"Heroic"; Nocturne in B Major, op. 62, no. 1; Fantaisie in
F Minor, op. 49; Etude in A Minor, op. 25, no. 11, "Winter
Wind"; Etude in E Major, op. 10, no. 3; Ballade no. 3 in A-
flat Major, op. 47; Waltz in C-sharp Minor, op. 64, no. 2;
Scherzo no. 3 in C-sharp Minor, op. 39; Bacarolle in F-
sharp Major, op. 60; Waltz in D-flat Major, op. 64, no. 1,
"Minute" (recorded 1961, 1971, and 1975).

Cliburn's full-bodied approach to Chopin resembles Arthur Rubinstein's conception, rather than the light and ethereal Chopin favored by earlier generations of pianists.

There's nothing dainty or precious about this tack, with Cliburn stating his case boldly and forthrightly.

BRAHMS: Piano Concerto no. 2, in B-flat Major, op. 83, Chi-
cago Symphony Orchestra, Fritz Reiner conducting (re-
corded 1961); Brahms: Intermezzi, op. 117, no. 1, in
E-flat Major, no. 2 in B-flat Minor; op. 119 no. 1 in B
Minor, no. 2 in E Minor, no. 3 in C Major (recorded
1970, 1972, and 1975).

Cliburn's recording of the Brahms Second Piano Concerto represents an epic performance befitting the scale of one of the monumental works in the repertoire. Reiner and Cliburn communicate extremely well, even if their musical tempera-ments seem slightly different. Somehow, the clarity and classi-cism of Reiner's Brahms proves to be the perfect underpinning for the romantic expansiveness of so much of Cliburn's pia-nism. In this instance, however, Cliburn slightly tapers this aspect of his playing to match Reiner's lucid orchestral accom-paniment.

The dramatic intensity doesn't let up in the series of Brahms Intermezzi that follows, with Cliburn offering a vibrant tone, moderate tempo, and fervent lyricism in op. 117, no. 1; a tender, confiding sound in op. 117, no. 2; a bejewelled touch and misterioso opening in op. 119, no. 1; a fascinating and gloriously impetuous, if idiosyncratic, reading of op. 119, no. 2, with a certain instability of tempo that underscores the rhythmic and harmonic volatility of the piece; a robust, thoroughly extroverted performance of op. 119, no. 3.

CHOPIN: Piano Sonatas no. 2, in B-flat Minor, op. 35 ("Funeral March"); no. 3 in B Minor, op. 58; Liszt: "Un Sospiro"; Sonetto del Petrarca no. 123; "Mephisto" Waltz (recorded 1967-75).

Cliburn's performance of Chopin's two greatest sonatas remains astonishing for the individuality of the conception. He opens the "Funeral March" Sonata at a daredevil tempo, capturing the fevered passions of its early pages with hyperdramatic intensity.

Many pianists go for speed in the scherzo movement, but Cliburn opts for thunder instead, in the form of hammered, repeated octave notes and massive repeated chords. Once again, in the lyric trio section, Cliburn revels in a bold, vibrant tone where other pianists prefer a softer, melting legato. He plays the "Funeral March" third movement with great deliberation and an almost unyielding rhythms, underscoring the darkest, tragic undercurrents of the piece.

Cliburn brings much more rhythmic elasticity to the Third Sonata, as befits his conception of the piece as a more typically Chopinesque piece of writing. The first movement sounds heroic in every way, a reading fashioned for a large and brightly colored canvas.

The flowing arpeggios of Liszt's "Un Sospiro" provide an alluring setting for the top line in Cliburn's recording. The album concludes with Liszt's Sonetto del Petrarca no. 123, performed with a clarity of line and architectural detail to which Liszt's solo works are not always subjected; and the "Mephisto" Waltz, played with a heightened sense of color, a clear and animated sense of narrative.

LISZT: Piano Concerto no. 1 in E-flat Major; Grieg: Piano Concerto in A Minor, op. 16; Liszt: Piano Concerto no. 2 in A Major; Philadelphia Orchestra, Eugene Ormandy conducting (recorded in 1968 and 1970).

Cliburn's Liszt differs from many other pianists', if only in the depth of sound he chooses to use. Where other artists tend to play Liszt with a somewhat lighter touch, thereby making Liszt's technical demands easier to finesse gracefully, Cliburn reaches unusually deep into the keys.

The best case in point is his reading of the more widely performed of the Liszt Concertos, the no. 1 in E-flat Major. Though Cliburn occasionally tosses off a quick scalar passage racing up the keyboard, he more often prefers a plush, cushioned sound. Combine that approach with some audaciously fast tempos, and you have a galvanic Liszt First. Eugene Ormandy represents a different kind of counterbalance to Cliburn's pianism than Fritz Reiner: Ormandy's orchestra sounds full-voiced, rhapsodic in gesture, sensual in nearly everything it plays.

Cliburn treats the Grieg Concerto, too, with a majesty, dignity, and seriousness that it does not always receive. The deliberation of some of the tempos, the fastidiousness of the phrasing, the variety of attack and color say a great deal for Cliburn's regard for this piece.

BEETHOVEN: Piano Concerto no. 4 in G Major, op. 58; Piano Concerto no. 5 in E-flat Major, op. 73, "Emperor"; Chicago Symphony Orchestra, Fritz Reiner conducting (recorded in 1961 and 1963).

In the deceptively difficult solo passage that opens the Fourth Concerto, Cliburn manages to subtly stretch the rhythm for expressive purpose and voice the chords to maximum lyric effect. Reiner, again, represents the perfect foil to Cliburn in this repertoire, the classical conception of his reading bringing out similar qualities in Cliburn's playing. In this most chamber-like of Beethoven's piano concertos, Cliburn's piano and Reiner's orchestra trade phrases with ease and grace.

In Beethoven's "Emperor" Piano Concerto, pianist and conductor forge a single, cohesive interpretation with classical structure at its base. Cliburn's playing is notable for its breadth of expression, from the grandiosity of massive double octave passages to the hushed lyricism of contrasting episodes.

CHOPIN: Piano Concerto no. 1 in E Minor, op. 10; Rachmaninoff: "Rhapsody on a Theme of Paganini," Philadelphia Orchestra, Eugene Ormandy conducting (recorded 1969 and 1970).

Cliburn offers a lovely, aria-like performance of the Chopin Piano Concerto no. 1, with Ormandy providing a warm, if somewhat unfocused orchestral accompaniment. The grace and taste of Cliburn's reading of the slow movement epitomizes the differences between musical expression and its more frequently encountered substitute, sentimentality.

Power and depth of sound seem more important to Cliburn than fast tempos in Rachmaninoff's "Rhapsody on a Theme of Paganini." Where other pianists go for speed and dash, Cliburn tends to press deep into the keys, bringing out an immense well of sound that's appropriate for the Russian idiom.

BRAHMS: Piano Concerto no. 1 in D Minor, op. 15, Boston Symphony Orchestra, Erich Leinsdorf conducting; Variations and Fugue on a Theme by Handel, op. 24 (recorded 1964, 1974).

Cliburn's performance of the Brahms First Concerto with Leinsdorf stands as an eccentric, unusual, and uneven affair, starting with the remarkably hurried tempo of the first movement. The grandeur of the music does not surface at this pace;

whether the tempo owes to Leinsdorf or Cliburn remains open to speculation, though Cliburn's lifelong tendency toward leisurely tempos suggests he's following the conductor's lead.

The steadfastness of Cliburn's tempos, combined with his reluctance to indulge in all but the slightest hint of rubato, speak to his respect for the classical underpinnings of Brahms's "Variations on a Theme of Handel." Still, the beauty of his lyric lines and the uncommonly wrought legato make this one of the most fluid performance of a piece that lies awkwardly on the keyboard.

SCHUMANN: Piano Concerto in A Minor, op. 54, Chicago Symphony Orchestra, Fritz Reiner conducting; MacDowell: Piano Concerto no. 2 in D Minor, op. 23, Chicago Symphony Orchestra, Walter Hendl conducting (recorded 1960); MacDowell: "To a Wild Rose" (no. 1 of "Woodland Sketches," op. 51, recorded 1972).

From the opening notes of the first movement of the Schumann Concerto, Cliburn's tone commands attention both for its sonic beauty and its sheer presence, even at a soft dynamic level. In heroic octave passages, Cliburn makes music—rather than mere display—of the thematic ideas at hand. No doubt Reiner's intelligent phrasing and imposing conception of the orchestral accompaniment inspires Cliburn.

The MacDowell Second Piano Concerto owes a great deal to the Grieg Piano Concerto, in both the boldness of the opening theme and the rhapsodic nature of subsequent ones, as well as sometimes inflated rhetorical gestures. Cliburn argues as persuasively as one could for this piece, reveling in its technical challenge and dramatically charged atmosphere.

The lovely closing work, MacDowell's solo piece "To a Wild Rose," represents a kind of softly lyric counterbalance to the concerto.

BEETHOVEN: Piano Concerto no. 3 in C Minor, op. 37, Phil-
adelphia Orchestra, Eugene Ormandy conducting;
Brahms: Rhapsody in B Minor, op. 79, no. 1; Rhapsody in
G Minor, op. 79, no. 2; Intermezzo in A Minor, op. 118,
no. 1; Intermezzo in A Major, op. 118, no. 2; Ballade in G
Minor, op. 118, no. 3; Capriccio in G Minor, op. 116, no. 3;
Intermezzo in E Major, op. 116, no. 6 (recorded 1970-71).

Ormandy and Cliburn provide a solid account of the first movement of the Beethoven Third Concerto, though it doesn't really rise above that until the cadenza, which Cliburn plays with equal parts majesty and clarity. The songful piano writing of the second movement brings out Cliburn's best playing of the performance, his reading defined by a melodic intensity tempered by classical restraint. In various passages, Cliburn proves that it is possible to play Beethoven's staccato and portato passages correctly without becoming percussive or brusque. In other words, he will not sacrifice beauty of tone, even in middle-period Beethoven.

Like the first movement, the finale is straightforward but not on a par with Cliburn's recordings of Beethoven's Piano Concertos nos. 4 and 5 with Reiner and the Chicago Symphony Orchestra.

The Brahms solo pieces that complete this disk are far more effective, as in the quick tempo and dark emotional stirrings of the Rhapsody in B Minor, op. 79, no. 1, in which Cliburn emphasizes unresolved harmonies and turbulent phrasings. It's the lyric and dramatic intensity of Cliburn's Brahms that is so striking, witness his account of op. 79, no. 2. As ever, he plays deep into the keys, offering up a ravishingly symphonic sound; the resonant bass notes, the magnificent block chords, and the sweeping way with a line help make this a definitive performance.

Other pianists may approach the Intermezzi with a lighter tone and mood, but Cliburn brings a deeper insight to the op. 118, no. 1, in which his sound is immense, his statement imposing. Even in the comparatively tender and lyric op. 118 no. 2, every note has depth of sound and dramatic purpose.

The motivic repetition of the main theme of the Ballade in G Minor, op. 118, no. 3, proves wearing to the ear in some performances, but Cliburn gets around the problem by subtly varying the arch of a phrase in its every recurrence.

"MY FAVORITE ENCORES." CHOPIN: Scherzo no. 2 in B-flat Minor, op. 31; Debussy: "Reflets dans l'eau" from "Images" Book I; Szymanowski: Etude in B-flat Minor, op. 4, no. 3; Chopin: "Revolutionary" Etude in C Minor, op. 10, no. 12; Debussy: "La plus que lente," "La fille aux cheveux de lin"; Chopin: Nocturne in E Major, op. 62, no. 2; Schumann/Liszt: "Widmung"; Scriabin: Etude in D-sharp Minor, op. 8, no. 12; Debussy: "Clair de lune," "L'isle joyeuse"; Rachmaninoff: Etude tableau in E-flat Minor, op. 39, no. 5 (recorded 1970 and 1972).

From its first notes, this performance of Chopin's Scherzo no. 2 in B-flat Minor, op. 31, establishes its individuality. The unusual legato phrasing, the nearly languid tempo, the well of tone show that Cliburn views the Second Scherzo as a long, lyric tone poem more than a dramatic virtuoso showpiece.

Cliburn's gifts as interpreter of French music were generally overshadowed by his work in other repertoire, but as this recording attests, he plays this music superbly. For one, his control of tone, touch, and shading eminently suit the gradations of sound required. Even beyond the exquisite, shimmering sonorities he draws from the keyboard, the control of line, and the emphasis on structure yield thoughtful, ravishing performances. And Cliburn's idiomatically French phrasing in the spare and elusive "La plus que lente" reiterates his affinity for this repertoire.

In Chopin's "Revolutionary" Etude, Cliburn prefers grandeur to speed, taking the piece slower than most pianists, but thereby allowing its phrases to expand, its rumbling, perpetual-motion bass line to ring out with every note.

Elsewhere in the album, he offers great melodic warmth in Chopin's Nocturne in E Major, op. 62, no. 2; and exquisite melodic ideas cast above a swirling accompaniment in the Schubert/Liszt "Widmung," which Cliburn builds from a whisper to a tremendously swelling climax.

With the exception of Sviatoslav Richter, no living pianist today plays the Scriabin-Rachmaninoff repertoire as persuasively and idiomatically as Cliburn, his recording of the Etude in D-sharp Minor, op. 8, no. 12, affirming as much. The ineffable poetry of the melody line, the tremendous warmth of sound, the epic scope of the interpretation represent a definitive performance by any measure.

Cliburn's reading of "L'isle joyeuse" drives inexorably toward a fantastic, orgiastic finale.

LISZT: Sonata in B Minor; Consolation no. 3; Brahms: Rhapsody in E-flat, op. 119, no. 4; Schumann: Romance, op. 28, no. 2; Tchaikovsky: "Chant de l'alouette" from "The Seasons"; Granados: "The Maiden and the Nightingale"; Ravel: Toccata; "Pavane for a Dead Princess"; Rachmaninoff: Prelude in G-sharp Minor, op. 32, no. 12 (recorded 1971-75).

One of the most stunning of Cliburn's recordings remains his version of the Liszt Sonata in B Minor, a whirlwind performance cast in startling colors and tempos. Beyond the force and power of the huge chords and the whirring speed of the virtuoso passages, consider the shape of the interpretation, which flows naturally from nightmarish, nearly expressionistic passages to lyrically inspired ones. Technically, the performance offers Horowitzian octave passages, as well as rapid-fire figurations played with consistent clarity. Interpretively, the performance adroitly balances the themes of light and dark, demon and angel, one against the other. By way of contrast, Cliburn offers a feeling of repose and lyric contemplation in Liszt's Consolation no. 3.

Cliburn puts more tone and substance into the march-like chords of the Brahms Rhapsody in E-flat, op. 119, no. 4, than virtually any other pianist who comes to mind; voices chords delicately in Schumann's Romance; brings out an element of pathos in his phrasing of the main theme of Tchaikovsky's "Chant de l'alouette" ("Song of the Lark"); and emphasizes romantic ardor and a fervent lyric tone in Granados' "The Maiden and the Nightingale." He also breaks utterly with tradition in his reading of Ravel's Toccata, from "Le tombeau de Couperin," declining to push the tempo, refusing to be locked into a metronomical beat, and daring to breathe at the end of a phrase or pause at a structural turning point.

MOZART: Piano Sonata in C Major, K. 330; Debussy: "La soiree dans Grenade"; Etude in Octaves; "La terrasse des audiences du clair de lune"; "Jardins sous la pluie"; "Reflets dans l'eau"; "Feux d'artifice"; Barber: Sonata, op. 26 (recorded 1965-72).

This remains the only major work of Mozart's that Cliburn recorded, and it piques one's interest in hearing his further thoughts on the composer. Neither dry and airy, along the lines of the early music performers, nor bejewelled, à la Alicia de Larrocha and Murray Perahia, Cliburn's Mozart more closely resembles the approach of Claudio Arrau, with a clear and weighted tone, moderate to slow tempos, and an undeniable sense of contemplation. It stands as an important performance if not a traditional one, with particularly beautiful and sometimes profound lyric playing in the arietta second movement.

Cliburn's Debussy group opens with a richly atmospheric "La soiree dans Grenade" ("Evening in Granada"), a performance built on constantly shifting colors, tones, and attacks; but at the core of this reading is the singing line, even when ensconced deep in the pianistic texture. The massive scale, depth of tone, and rhapsody of phrase in Cliburn's reading of the Etude in Octaves add up to a striking performance.

Cliburn's account of "Jardins sous la pluie" ("Gardens in the Rain") epitomizes what listeners mean when they refer to the sweep of Cliburn's playing—it shows an irrepressible sense of forward drive but without sacrificing clarity of tone or structural turning points in the score. In "Feux d'artifice" ("Fireworks"), Cliburn offers more precision in the right-hand figurations and more projection of motivic ideas than one is used to hearing.

Finally, Cliburn's recording of the Barber Sonata remains the definitive one on record. Though it's a slight exaggeration, one is tempted to say that Horowitz's recording captures the brilliance of Horowitz, while Cliburn's captures the brilliance of Barber. Cliburn takes pains to bring out contrapuntal ideas and oft-submerged themes, as in his underscoring of the two-note motif in the final pages of the first movement that later will dominate the third movement. In the slightly tipsy waltz of the second movement Cliburn's piano sounds light, genteel, and pristine of texture. In the final pages, Cliburn lets loose with the stunning virtuosity of which he is capable. The force of his tone, the forward drive of his rhythm, and the sheer profusion of sound still stun the ear.

BEETHOVEN: Piano Sonata in C-sharp Minor, op. 27, no. 2, "Moonlight"; Piano Sonata in C Minor, op. 13, "Pathétique"; Piano Sonata in E-flat Major, op. 81a, "Les Adieux"; Piano Sonata in F Minor, op. 57, "Appassionata" (recorded 1966, 1970).

Cliburn opens the "Moonlight" Sonata in unusual fashion, with a rather quick reading of the first movement that sounds a bit breathless. He takes a more moderate approach in the middle movement minuet, which he plays with lyric grace and only a hint of the storms to come. Even in the last movement, Cliburn offers a finale of moderate tempo and digital clarity; at times, he even seems to be holding back the tempo a shade, the better to build to the tension and release of the final pages.

The pianist gives the "Pathétique" more credit than other performers, playing the introductory section with a great sense of occasion and importance. The succeeding material of the first movement follows along these lines, as Cliburn shapes themes with high melodic profile, rhythmic crispness, and a forcefulness of gesture pointing toward middle-period Beethoven.

The "Les Adieux" Sonata suits Cliburn's lyric gifts, as in the opening measures, in which Beethoven portrays emotions felt at the departure of a beloved friend. The sureness of this reading, the depth of Cliburn's understanding of this material, and the way one theme evolves into the next argues convincingly for his affinity for this repertoire.

Cliburn's reading of the "Appassionata" Sonata differs from most others in its pervasive interest in a sustained musical line. In other words, even as he brings out the tremendous dramatic contrasts of this music, the melodic profile of the score remains always in the forefront. Thus when, on rare occasion, Cliburn turns from his characteristically warm tone to a sharper, more dramatic attack, the effect is all the more striking. Ultimately, this "Appassionata" looks forward to the romantic age that it helped usher in. Cliburn makes no apologies for this in his performance, which nevertheless remains mindful of classical style.

BEETHOVEN: Piano Sonata in F Minor, "Appassionata," op. 57; Liszt: "Liebestraume" no. 3; Tchaikovsky: Piano Concerto no. 1 in B-flat Minor, op. 23, Moscow Philharmonic Symphony Orchestra, Kiril Kondrashin conducting (recorded in 1958; Melodiya).

This recently reissued Melodiya performance, recorded in Moscow during Cliburn's Tchaikovsky competition triumph in 1958, technologically does not match Cliburn's RCA recordings made in the U.S. And yet it provides a fascinating glimpse at an historic moment in Cliburn's life and music.

Cliburn takes the "Appassionata" at a more aggressive tempo and with more striking contrasts of dynamics than in his familiar RCA recording. Even if the biggest passages have been muddled by the live-performance recording, the reading has drama and drive that are not easily resisted.

The way Cliburn unfolds a melodic line in Liszt's "Liebestraume" no. 3 suggests the work of a fine singer. Playing of this level of romance and melodic ardor hardly exists anymore, but it remains an integral part of Cliburn's pianism.

Why did Cliburn's performance of the Tchaikovsky First Concerto thrill his Russian listeners? In the double octave passages at the bottom of the keyboard, Cliburn brings out an explosive roar of sound that must have epitomized to his audience what Russian keyboard virtuosity is all about. The first big solo passage of the first movement, in particular, offers an exquisite dialogue between the hands and underscores the operatic elements of Cliburn's performance. And in the cadenza Cliburn brings a level of fantasy to this music that can't help but heighten its impact.

Cliburn and Kondrashin play a brightly animated, second movement, the tempo moving along steadily, the phrases unfolding easily. Again, Cliburn draws fantastic colors from the keyboard, even while keeping trills and other figurations pristinely clear.

"THE WORLD'S FAVORITE PIANO MUSIC."
Liszt: "Liebestraume" no. 3; Rachmaninoff: Prelude in G Minor, op. 23, no. 5; Beethoven: "Fur Elise"; Mozart: third movement of Piano Sonata in A Minor, K. 330 ("Rondo alla turca"); Rachmaninoff: Prelude in E-Flat, op. 23, no. 6; Debussy: "Reverie"; Rachmaninoff: Prelude in C-sharp Minor, op. 3, no. 2; Prelude in G, op. 32, no. 5; Brahms: Waltz in A-flat, op. 39, no. 15; Liszt: Consolation no. 5; Schubert: "Moment musical" in F Minor, no. 3; Brahms: Intermezzo in E-flat Minor, op. 118, no. 6; Schumann: "Traumerie"; Tchaikovsky: Bacarolle; Brahms: Inter-

mezzo in C-sharp Minor, op. 117, no. 3; Rachmaninoff: Prelude in C Minor, op. 23, no. 7; Chopin: Fantaisie-Impromptu in C-sharp Minor, op. 66 (recorded 1970-75).

Though ostensibly a collection of unrelated miniatures, this actually happens to be one of Cliburn's most appealing discs, as it documents the expressive and stylistic range of his pianism. The grandeur he brings to Rachmaninoff's Prelude in G Minor, the remarkable legato playing of his reading of Beethoven's "Fur Elise," the element of fantasy he finds in the third movement of Mozart's Piano Sonata in A Minor each attest to Cliburn's communicative power in even the smallest musical forms. Chopin's Fantaisie-Impromptu in C-sharp Minor makes a particularly strong impression, with Cliburn managing a romantic swell of sound without sacrificing clarity of individual notes.

NOTES

FOREWORD

1. Andrei Gavrilov interviewed by Howard Reich, Oct. 1991.

CHAPTER ONE

1. John Davidson, "Every Good Boy Does Fine," *Texas Monthly*, May 1987.
2. Abram Chasins with Villa Stiles, *The Van Cliburn Legend (Garden City, NY: Doubleday, 1959), p. 36.*
3. Ibid.
4. "Baylor Conquered by Cliburn, Cleric," *Dallas Morning News,* Nov. 8, 1958; "Van Cliburn Talks," *Newsweek,* Aug. 4, 1958; "Man of the Month," *Shreveport Times,* Nov. 3, 1958; Abram Chasins with Villa Stiles, *The Van Cliburn Legend,* p. 36.
5. Marice Richter, "Van Cliburn's Mother Always Demanded the Best," *Dallas Morning News,* Nov. 8, 1987.
6. "H. L. Cliburn Dies After Long Illness," *Shreveport Times,* Jan. 13, 1974.
7. Van Cliburn interviewed by Howard Reich, 1991-92.
8. Abram Chasins with Villa Stiles, *The Van Cliburn Legend,* p. 36.
9. Ibid., p. 158.
10. "H. L. Cliburn Dies After Long Illness," *Shreveport Times,* Jan. 13, 1974.
11. Van Cliburn interviewed by Howard Reich, 1991-92.
12. Ibid.
13. Winston Gardner, "A Look at Kilgore's News-Making Personality: Life-Long Dedication Placed Cliburn Atop Heap," *Kilgore News Herald,* April 20, 1958.
14. Marice Richter, "Van Cliburn's Mother Always Demanded the Best," *Dallas Morning News,* Nov. 8, 1987.
15. Ibid.

16. John Davidson, "Every Good Boy Does Fine," *Texas Monthly,* May 1987.

17. Rildia Bee Cliburn, "How My Son Van Started to Play," *Music Journal,* Sept. 1958.

18. Marice Richter, "Van Cliburn's Mother Always Demanded the Best," *Dallas Morning News,* Nov. 8, 1987.

19. Harold C. Schonberg, *The Great Pianists: From Mozart to the Present* (New York: Simon & Schuster, 1987), pp. 178, 323.

20. Ibid., p. 323.

21. Ibid., p. 269.

22. Ibid., p. 278.

23. Van Cliburn and John Browning interviewed by Howard Reich, 1991-92 and July 1991, respectively.

24. Marice Richter, "Van Cliburn's Mother Always Demanded the Best," *Dallas Morning News,* Nov. 8, 1987.

25. Van Cliburn interviewed by Howard Reich, 1991-92.

26. Michael Fleming, "Van Cliburn Reflects on the Past and a Possible Future," *New York Times,* June 9, 1985.

27. Marice Richter, "Van Cliburn's Mother Always Demanded the Best," *Dallas Morning News,* Nov. 8, 1987.

28. Van Cliburn interviewed by Howard Reich, 1991-92.

29. Annette Davies Morgan interviewed by Howard Reich, July 1991.

30. Susan Tilley interviewed by Howard Reich, March 1992.

31. Ibid.

32. Van Cliburn interviewed by Howard Reich, 1991-92.

33. Ibid.

34. Abram Chasins with Villa Stiles, *The Van Cliburn Legend,* p. 34; "He Was Great Even 'Before Moscow': Van's Hometown Surprised the Least," *Kilgore News Herald,* Dec. 1, 1958.

35. Van Cliburn interviewed by Howard Reich, 1991-92.

36. Rildia Bee Cliburn, "How My Son Van Started to Play," *Music Journal,* Sept. 1958.

37. Van Cliburn interviewed by Howard Reich, 1991-92.

38. David Daniel, "Music: As he prepares for a rare concert appearance, Van Cliburn talks with David Daniel," *Vogue,* Oct. 1990.

39. "Pianist Cliburn to Return For Church Benefit Recital," *Shreveport Times,* Nov. 4, 1962.

40. Rildia Bee Cliburn, "How My Son Van Started to Play," *Music Journal,* Sept. 1958.

41. Ibid.

42. Ibid.

43. Van Cliburn interviewed by Howard Reich, 1991-92.

44. Paul Rowan, "Childish Whim: Cliburn Wanted to Drive a Taxi," *Ft. Worth Star-Telegram,* March 7, 1969.

45. Abram Chasins with Villa Stiles, *The Van Cliburn Legend,* p. 34.

46. Van Cliburn interviewed by Howard Reich, 1991-92.

CHAPTER TWO

1. "A Brief History of the East Texas Oil Field," from "East Texas Oil Museum at Kilgore College" booklet, produced by East Texas Oil Museum, Hwy. 259 at Ross St., Kilgore, Texas.

2. Ibid.

3. Ibid.

4. Mary Meador, "Museum celebration grand event," *Kilgore News Herald,* Oct. 4, 1990.

5. Doris Bolt and Bonnie Durning, *A History of Kilgore College, 1935-1981* (Kilgore, TX: Kilgore College Press, 1981), p. 19.

6. Mary Meador, "Museum celebration grand event," *Kilgore News Herald,* Oct. 4, 1990.

7. Van Cliburn interviewed by Howard Reich, 1991-92.

8. Doris Bolt and Bonnie Durning, *A History of Kilgore College, 1935-1981* (Kilgore, TX: Kilgore College Press, 1981), p. 90.

9. Gussie Nell Davis interviewed by Howard Reich, Aug. 1991.

10. "He Was Great Even 'Before Moscow': Van's Hometown Surprised the Least," *Kilgore News Herald,* Dec. 1, 1958.

11. Oleta Gray interviewed by Howard Reich, Aug. 1991.

12. Van Cliburn interviewed by Howard Reich, 1991-92.

13. Oleta Gray interviewed by Howard Reich, Aug. 1991.

14. Eloise Bean interviewed by Howard Reich, Aug. 1991.

15. Mrs. Henry S. Miller interviewed by Howard Reich, Aug. 1991.

16. Joyce Anne Goyne Stanley interviewed by Howard Reich, July 1991.

17. Van Cliburn interviewed by Howard Reich, 1991-92.

18. Lottie Guttry interviewed by Howard Reich, July 1991.

19. "Russians Cheer Cliburn Again at Awards Presentation Affair," *Kilgore News Herald,* April 15, 1958.

20. Ibid.

21. John Shenaut interviewed by Howard Reich, Aug. 1991.

22. Lottie Guttry interviewed by Howard Reich, July 1991.

23. Van Cliburn interviewed by Howard Reich, 1991-92.

24. John Ardoin, "World of Music: Pianist Cliburn—At Home in Dallas," *Dallas Morning News,* May 11, 1971.

25. Van Cliburn interviewed by Howard Reich, 1991-92.

26. Alice Morton interviewed by Howard Reich, Aug. 1991.

27. Reprinted by permission of Velma Dickson.

28. John Shenaut interviewed by Howard Reich, Aug. 1991.

29. Louise Jeter interviewed by Howard Reich, July 1991.

30. Joan Barthel, "Eight Years Later: Has Success Spoiled Van Cliburn?" *New York Times,* Oct. 9, 1966.

31. Joyce Anne Goyne Stanley, interviewed by Howard Reich, July 1991.

32. Jean Warner Stark, untitled, *American Music Teacher,* Nov./Dec. 1961.

33. Bill Hallman interviewed by Howard Reich, Aug. 1991.

34. Lottie Guttry interviewed by Howard Reich, July 1991.

35. Gerald Fitzgerald, "Vanyusha," *Opera News,* March 26, 1960.

36. Van Cliburn interviewed by Howard Reich, 1991-92.

37. Ibid.

38. Risë Stevens interviewed by Howard Reich, Dec. 1991.

39. "Red roses for Iturbi," *High Fidelity/Musical America,* Sept. 1974.

40. Van Cliburn interviewed by Howard Reich, 1991-92.

41. "Red roses for Iturbi," *High Fidelity/Musical America,* Sept. 1974.

42. *Kilgore News Herald* file material, dated April 5, 1953.

43. "Kilgore Boy Wins Praise of Critics; Played Bach at Five," *Shreveport Times,* Feb. 23, 1947.

44. Because spellings of foreign composers' names have changed continuously over the years, the author will use contemporary spellings throughout, including in quotations from newspaper articles, in the interests of clarity and consistency.

45. "Van Cliburn Is Acclaimed For Piano Concert Friday: 12-Year-Old Kilgore Pianist Is Presented By Kilgore Woman's Club," *Kilgore News Herald,* March 14, 1947.

46. "Woman's Club Will Present Van Cliburn Here March 14: Presentation To Be Highlight Of Spring Events," *Kilgore News Herald,* March 9, 1947.

47. "Concert To Be Given By Kilgore Piano Prodigy: Music Club To Present Van Cliburn Tuesday In High School Auditorium," *Kilgore News Herald,* April 25, 1948.

48. Ibid.

49. "He Was Great Even 'Before Moscow': Van's Hometown Surprised the Least," *Kilgore News Herald,* Dec. 1, 1958.

50. "Young Kilgore Pianist Wins Praise," *Kilgore News Herald,* April 27, 1947.

51. "Ex-Resident To Be Soloist At Musicale," *Shreveport Times,* April 13, 1952.

52. Abram Chasins with Villa Stiles, *The Van Cliburn Legend* (Garden City, NY: Doubleday, 1959), p. 45.

53. James Mathis interviewed by Howard Reich, Jan. 1992.

54. Van Cliburn interviewed by Howard Reich, 1991-92.

55. Ibid.

CHAPTER THREE

1. Flyer announcing Van Cliburn's Carnegie Hall debut.

2. "Former Local Boy To Play At Carnegie," *Shreveport Times,* Jan. 18, 1948.

3. Ibid.

4. Van Cliburn interviewed by Howard Reich, 1991-92.

5. Abram Chasins with Villa Stiles, *The Van Cliburn Legend* (Garden City, NY: Doubleday, 1959), p. 41.

6. Josef Raeiff interviewed by Howard Reich, March 1991.

7. Mitchell Andrews interviewed by Howard Reich, June 1991.

8. RCA Victor producer John Pfeiffer affirmed this when interviewed by Howard Reich, Nov. 1991.

9. Ivan Davis interviewed by Howard Reich, March 1992.

10. Annette Davies Morgan interviewed by Howard Reich, July 1991.

11. Maryln Schwartz, "Life with Van and Rildia Bee," *Dallas Morning News,* June 26, 1989.

12. Ibid.

13. Yale Youngblood, "Cliburn's star still shines: Pianist pleases East and West," *Shreveport Times,* April 13, 1988.

14. Lottie Guttry interviewed by Howard Reich, July 1991.

15. Alice Whittlesey interviewed by Howard Reich, Aug. 1991.

16. Van Cliburn interviewed by Howard Reich, 1991-92.

17. Susan Tilley interviewed by Howard Reich, March 1992.

18. Abram Chasins with Villa Stiles, *The Van Cliburn Legend,* p. 44.

19. Van Cliburn interviewed by Howard Reich, 1991-92.

20. Ibid.

21. Ibid.

22. Bob Waters interviewed by Howard Reich, July 1991.

23. Program from an early recital, the text including these words: "Kilgore Music Club Presents Van Cliburn, pianist in recital, Tuesday, March 13, 1951, 8 p.m."

24. Van Cliburn interviewed by Howard Reich, 1991-92.

25. Lottie Guttry interviewed by Howard Reich, July 1991.

CHAPTER FOUR

1. Harold C. Schonberg, "Lady in Room 412," *New York Times,* March 27, 1960.

2. Josef Raeiff interviewed by Howard Reich, March 1991.

3. Mark Schubart interviewed by Howard Reich, Nov. 1991.

4. Josef Raeiff interviewed by Howard Reich, March 1991.

5. Van Cliburn interviewed by Howard Reich, 1991-92.

6. Ibid.

7. Ibid.

8. Abram Chasins with Villa Stiles, *The Van Cliburn Legend* (Garden City, NY: Doubleday, 1959), p. 49.

9. John Browning interviewed by Howard Reich, July 1991.

10. George Pappastavrou interviewed by Howard Reich, May 1991.

11. Alexis Weissenberg interviewed by Howard Reich, June 1991.

12. George Pappastavrou interviewed by Howard Reich, May 1991.

13. Kay Kraber Lund, interviewed by Howard Reich, May 1991.

14. Daniel Pollack interviewed by Howard Reich, Feb. 1991.

15. Jeaneane Dowis interviewed by Howard Reich, May 1991.

16. According to John Browning, Jeaneane Dowis, Ivan Davis, and James Mathis, among others, as interviewed by Howard Reich.

17. John Browning interviewed by Howard Reich, July 1991.

18. Jeaneane Dowis interviewed by Howard Reich, May 1991.

19. John Browning interviewed by Howard Reich, July 1991.

20. Jeaneane Dowis interviewed by Howard Reich, May 1991.

21. James Mathis interviewed by Howard Reich, Jan. 1992.

22. Joan Brown interviewed by Howard Reich, May 1991.

23. Mark Schubart interviewed by Howard Reich, Nov. 1991.

24. John Browning interviewed by Howard Reich, July 1991.

25. Ibid.

26. Van Cliburn interviewed by Howard Reich, 1991-92.

27. Jeaneane Dowis interviewed by Howard Reich, May 1991.

28. Joan Brown interviewed by Howard Reich, May 1991.

29. Jeaneane Dowis interviewed by Howard Reich, May 1991.

30. Jorge Mester interviewed by Howard Reich, May 1991.

31. Kay Kraber Lund, interviewed by Howard Reich, May 1991.

32. Joan Brown interviewed by Howard Reich, May 1991.

33. John Browning interviewed by Howard Reich, July 1991.

34. George Katz interviewed by Howard Reich, May 1991.

35. Jerome Lowenthal interviewed by Howard Reich, March 1991.

36. George Pappastavrou interviewed by Howard Reich, May 1991.

37. Jeaneane Dowis interviewed by Howard Reich, May 1991.

38. Josef Raeiff interviewed by Howard Reich, March 1991.

39. John Browning interviewed by Howard Reich, July 1991.

40. Jeffrey Siegel interviewed by Howard Reich, Aug. 1991.

41. Ibid.

42. Robert Mann interviewed by Howard Reich, May 1991.

43. John Browning interviewed by Howard Reich, July 1991.

44. P. J. Wilson, "Pianist From Kilgore Wins Dealey Award," *Dallas Morning News,* April 10, 1952.

45. "Van Cliburn Wins Chopin Scholarship," *Shreveport Journal,* June 23, 1952.

46. Abram Chasins with Villa Stiles, *The Van Cliburn Legend,* pp. 22-23.

47. "Van Cliburn Wins Chopin Scholarship," *Shreveport Journal,* June 23, 1952.

48. Josef Raeiff interviewed by Howard Reich, March 1991.

49. John Rosenfield, "Concert in Review: Young Man With Talent and Hands," *Dallas Morning News,* Dec. 22, 1952.

50. "Shreveport Dates Dealey Winner," *Dallas Morning News,* March 19, 1953.

51. Cover story, *Southwestern Musician,* April 1953.

52. "Six-Foot Texas Artist," *Magnolia News,* April, 1953.

53. John Shenaut interviewed by Howard Reich, Aug. 1991.

54. He had played Bach's Toccata in C Minor; Mozart's Sonata in C Major, K. 330; Prokofiev's Sixth Sonata; Chopin's Etudes nos. 5 in E Minor and 11 in A Minor ("Winter Wind") from Op. 25; Chopin's Fantaisie in F Minor; Ravel's Toccata from "Le Tombeau de Couperin" and "Une barque sur l'océan" from "Miroirs"; plus encores. The program was detailed by Winston Gardner in "Hundreds Hear Concert: City Applauds Van Cliburn," *Kilgore News Herald,* April 10, 1953.

55. Winston Gardner, "Hundreds Hear Concert: City Applauds Van Cliburn," *Kilgore News Herald,* April 10, 1953.

56. Ibid.

57. Frank Gagnard, "Concert Review: Cliburn in Series Finale, Kilgore Pianist Is Last 'Young Artist,'" *Dallas Morning News,* April 13, 1953.

58. Untitled, *Chicago Tribune,* June 29, 1953.

59. Roger Dettmer, "Public is Invited: Large Audience in Grant Park Has Own Ideas About Contest Winner," *New York Times,* Aug. 10, 1958.

60. Roger Dettmer interviewed by Howard Reich, March 1992.

61. Ibid.

62. Tom Porter interviewed by Howard Reich, May 1991.

63. Abram Chasins with Villa Stiles, *The Van Cliburn Legend,* p. 58.

64. David Holden, "Tall Texan Given Ovation for 1953 New York Concert," *Chautauquan Daily,* Aug. 1953, as excerpted in *Kilgore News Herald,* Dec. 1, 1958.

65. "19 On Airliner Die In Crash On Coast: Craft From Australia Hits Peak Near San Francisco—Kapell, Noted Pianist, Is a Victim," *New York Times,* Oct. 30, 1953.

66. UPI, "I Shall Never Return," *New York Times,* Oct. 30, 1953.

67. AP, "Award Given Dealey Winner," *Dallas Morning News,* March 27, 1954; "Pianist, 19, Captures Leventritt Award," *New York Times,* March 27, 1954.

68. Ibid.; plus "Van Cliburn Wins Leventritt Award," *Musical Courier,* April 15, 1954.

69. Naomi Graffman interview by Howard Reich, July 1991.

70. Ibid.

71. Abram Chasins with Villa Stiles, *The Van Cliburn Legend,* pp. 24-25.

72. Ibid.

73. Ibid.

74. Eugene Istomin interviewed by Howard Reich, March 1991.

75. Gary Graffman interviewed by Howard Reich, July 1991.

76. Abram Chasins with Villa Stiles, *The Van Cliburn Legend,* pp. 25-26.

77. Ibid., pp. 26-27.

78. Claude Frank interviewed by Howard Reich, May 1991.

79. John Browning interviewed by Howard Reich, July 1991.

80. "Wins Highest Honor: Cliburn to Appear in Carnegie Hall," *Kilgore News Herald,* March 28, 1954.

81. "He Was Great Even 'Before Moscow': Van's Hometown Surprised the Least," *Kilgore News Herald,* Dec. 1, 1958.

82. "Van Cliburn Signs Concert Management," *Dallas Morning News,* June 11, 1954.

83. Van Cliburn interviewed by Howard Reich, 1991-92.

84. Josef Raeiff interviewed by Howard Reich, March 1991.

85. Ivan Davis interviewed by Howard Reich, March 1992.

86. Mark Schubart interviewed by Howard Reich, Nov. 1991.

87. Van Cliburn interviewed by Howard Reich, 1991-92.

88. James Mathis interviewed by Howard Reich, Jan. 1992.

CHAPTER FIVE

1. "Van Cliburn Gets Ovation At Chautauqua," *Chautauquan Daily,* as excerpted in *Kilgore News Herald,* Aug. 6, 1954.

2. Private letter from Van Cliburn to Juilliard dean Mark Schubart, dated Sept. 21, 1954. Used by permission.

3. Van Cliburn interviewed by Howard Reich, 1991-92.

4. Naomi Graffman interviewed by Howard Reich, July 1991.

5. Robert Sabin, *Musical America,* Dec. 1, 1954.

6. "N.Y. Hailed Van Back in 1954," *New York World-Telegram & Sun,* as reprinted in *Kilgore News Herald,* Dec. 1, 1958.

7. Harold C. Schonberg, "Symphonic Epigram," *New York Times,* Nov. 15, 1954.

8. "N.Y. Hailed Van Back in 1954," *New York Post,* as excerpted in *Kilgore News Herald,* Dec. 1, 1958.

9. "N.Y. Hailed Van Back in 1954," *New York Herald Tribune,* as excerpted in *Kilgore News Herald,* Dec. 1, 1958.

10. "N.Y. Hailed Van Back in 1954," *New York Journal-American,* as excerpted in *Kilgore News Herald,* Dec. 1, 1958.

11. Robert Sabin, *Musical America,* Dec. 1, 1954.

12. Henry W. Levinger, *Musical Courier,* Dec. 1, 1954.

13. Ross Parmenter, "Song Recital Given by Leontyne Price," *New York Times,* Nov. 15, 1954.

14. "N.Y. Hailed Van Back in 1954," *Kilgore News Herald,* Dec. 1, 1958.

15. Naomi Graffman interviewed by Howard Reich, July 1991.

16. "Van Cliburn Writes New Anthem," *Musical Courier,* Nov. 15, 1954.

17. Van Cliburn interviewed by Howard Reich, 1991-92.

18. Allen Young, *Denver Post,* as excerpted in the 16-page liner-note booklet accompanying Van Cliburn's first LP recording, Tchaikovsky Piano Concerto no. 1, in B-flat Minor, RCA Victor.

19. Abram Chasins and Villa Stiles, *The Van Cliburn Legend* (Garden City, NY: Doubleday, 1959), p. 28.

20. Ibid.

21. *Houston Post* review, as excerpted in the 16-page liner-note booklet accompanying Van Cliburn's first LP recording, Tchaikovsky Piano Concerto no. 1, in B-flat Minor, RCA Victor.

22. *Detroit News* review, ibid.

23. Van Cliburn interviewed by Howard Reich, 1991-92.

24. Alexis Weissenberg interviewed by Howard Reich, June 1991.

25. Schuyler Chapin interviewed by Howard Reich, March 1991.

26. Skitch Henderson interviewed by Howard Reich, March 1991.

27. Ibid.

28. Abram Chasins with Villa Stiles, *The Van Cliburn Legend,* p. 66.

29. Skitch Henderson interviewed by Howard Reich, March 1991.

30. AP, "Loose Pedal Foils Pianist," *Philadelphia Evening Bulletin,* March 14, 1955.

31. Van Cliburn interviewed by Howard Reich, 1991-92.

32. AP, "Loose Pedal Foils Pianist," *Philadelphia Evening Bulletin,* March 14, 1955.

33. Allen Young, "Cliburn Performance Impressive: Symphony Concert Marked by 'Fireworks,'" *Denver Post,* Nov. 16, 1955.

34. "Tall at the Keyboard: Van Cliburn," *New York Times,* April 14, 1958.

35. Alexander Schneider interviewed by Howard Reich, July 1991.

36. Joseph Esposito interviewed by Howard Reich, May 1991.

37. Rena C. Holtkamp review in *Cleveland Plain Dealer*, as excerpted in *The Van Cliburn Legend*, by Abram Chasins with Villa Stiles, p. 72.

38. Van Cliburn interviewed by Howard Reich, 1991-92.

39. Schuyler Chapin interviewed by Howard Reich, March 1991.

40. Van Cliburn interviewed by Howard Reich, 1991-92.

41. "Army Rejects Famous Young Texas Artist," *Dallas Morning News*, April 20, 1957. Reprinted with permission of the *Dallas Morning News*.

42. Abram Chasins with Villa Stiles, *The Van Cliburn Legend*, p. 86.

43. Ibid.

44. John Rosenfield, "Pianist Cliburn Returns Home After European Stint for U.S.," *Dallas Morning News*, Aug. 23, 1958.

45. Annette Davies Morgan interviewed by Howard Reich, July 1991.

46. Van Cliburn interviewed by Howard Reich, 1991-92.

47. Naomi Graffman interviewed by Howard Reich, July 1991.

48. Van Cliburn interviewed by Howard Reich, 1991-92.

CHAPTER SIX

1. Van Cliburn interviewed by Howard Reich, 1991-92.

2. Olegna Fuschi interviewed by Howard Reich, May 1991.

3. Fritz Steinway interviewed by Howard Reich, April 1991.

4. Mark Schubart interviewed by Howard Reich, Nov. 1991.

5. From the transcript of Van Cliburn's interview on radio station WQXR in New York, with Abram Chasins, broadcast during the intermission of Cliburn's Carnegie Hall performance on May 26, 1958.

6. Abram Chasins with Villa Stiles, *The Van Cliburn Legend* (Garden City, NY: Doubleday, 1959), p. 96.

7. Eugene Istomin interviewed by Howard Reich, March 1991.

8. Abram Chasins with Villa Stiles, *The Van Cliburn Legend*, p. 98.

9. Mark Schubart interviewed by Howard Reich, Nov. 1991.

10. Internal memo of the Institute of International Education.

11. Van Cliburn interviewed by Howard Reich, 1991-92.

12. Competition requirements taken from an original competition brochure, titled "International Chaikovsky [sic] Piano and Violin Competition: To Be Held In Moscow, March-April 1958."

13. Ibid.

14. Ibid.

15. Ibid.

16. Ibid. The official competition brochure also specified that: "The prize-winners undertake to participate gratis in two big concerts to be held within two weeks after the final audition. The winner of the first prize undertakes to give a solo recital. The winners of the first three prizes are guaranteed concert tours of the U.S.S.R. and gramophone recordings."

17. Mark Schubart interviewed by Howard Reich, Nov. 1991.

18. AP, "Reds Tell Plan To Probe Moon By Tank And TV," *Chicago Tribune,* April 26, 1955.

19. AP, "Sputniks Not Proof Of ICBM, Scientist Says," *Chicago Tribune,* Nov. 18, 1957.

20. George Katz interviewed by Howard Reich, May 1991.

21. William Schuman interviewed by Howard Reich, March 1991.

22. Van Cliburn interviewed by Howard Reich, 1991-92.

23. John Rosenfield, "Pianist Cliburn Returns Home After European Stint for U.S.," *Dallas Morning News,* Aug. 23, 1958.

24. Jeaneane Dowis interviewed by Howard Reich, May 1991.

25. Martin Canin interviewed by Howard Reich, May 1991.

26. Lucy Mann interviewed by Howard Reich, May 1991.

27. Josef Raeiff interviewed by Howard Reich, March 1991.

28. Henrietta Belayaeva interviewed by Howard Reich, Feb. 1992.

29. Harriet Wingreen interviewed by Howard Reich, May 1991.

30. Van Cliburn interviewed by Howard Reich, 1991-92.

31. Ibid.

32. Henrietta Belayaeva interviewed by Howard Reich, Feb. 1992.

33. Mark Schubart interviewed by Howard Reich, Nov. 1991.

34. Daniel Pollack interviewed by Howard Reich, Feb. 1991.

35. Ibid.

36. "Cliburn Continues As Toast Of Soviet," *New York Times,* April 16, 1958.

37. Abram Chasins with Villa Stiles, *The Van Cliburn Legend,* p. 102.

38. Gustav A. Alink, *International Piano Competitions, Book 3, The Results* (Hungary: Gustav A. Alink, 1990).

39. Biographical material on Goldenweiser from Nicolas Slonimsky, *Baker's Biographical Dictionary of Musicians* (New York: Schirmer Books, 1984, seventh ed.).

Information on organizing committe of the Tchaikovsky Competition from the original competition brochure, which lists the following organizing committee members: D. D. Shostakovich, composer, Chairman of the Organizing Committee; V. V. Tselikovsky, conductor, Vice-Chairman of the Organizing Committee; V. M. Ankudinov, Manager of Intourist; N. I. Bobrovnikov, Chairman of the Executive Committee of the Moscow City Soviet; G. V. Bryushkov, pianist, Director of the State Conservatoire in Leningrad; E. G. Gilels, pianist, professor; A. B. Goldenweiser, pianist, professor; A. I. Denisov, professor; D. B. Kabalevsky, composer, professor; D. F. Oistrakh, violinist, professor; G. A. Orvid, professor, Director of the State Conservatoire in Moscow; T. N. Khrennikov, composer, General Secretary of the Union of Soviet Composers.

40. Abram Chasins with Villa Stiles, *The Van Cliburn Legend,* p. 103.

41. Mary Meador, "Parents Besieged By Telephone Calls," *Kilgore News Herald,* April 14, 1958.

42. Abram Chasins with Villa Stiles, *The Van Cliburn Legend,* p. 105.

43. Igor Oistrakh interviewed by Howard Reich, Feb. 1992.

44. Sergei Dorensky interviewed by Howard Reich, March 1992.

45. Van Cliburn interviewed by Howard Reich, 1991-92.

46. Sequeira Costa interviewed by Howard Reich, March 1992.

47. Andrei Gavrilov interviewed by Howard Reich, Oct. 1991.

48. Sequeira Costa interviewed by Howard Reich, March 1992.

49. Ibid.

50. Abram Chasins with Villa Stiles, *The Van Cliburn Legend,* p. 106.

51. Gustav A. Alink, *International Piano Competitions, Book 3, The Results* (Hungary: Gustav A. Alink, 1990).

52. Naum Shtarkman interviewed by Howard Reich, Sept. 1991.

53. Thorunn Tryggvason interviewed by Howard Reich, July 1991.

54. Abram Chasins with Villa Stiles, *The Van Cliburn Legend,* p. 106 and Van Cliburn interviewed by Howard Reich, 1991-92.

55. Lev Naumov interviewed by Howard Reich, July 1991.

56. Lev Vlasenko interviewed by Howard Reich, July 1991.

57. Daniel Pollack interviewed by Howard Reich, Feb. 1991.

58. Mark Schubart interviewed by Howard Reich, Nov. 1991.

59. AP, "1952 Dealey Musician in USSR Finals," *Dallas Morning News,* April 11, 1958.

60. Vladimir Feltsman interviewed by Howard Reich, July 1991.

61. Alexander Toradze interviewed by Howard Reich, June 1991.

62. Henrietta Belayaeva interviewed by Howard Reich, Feb. 1992.

63. Van Cliburn interviewed by Howard Reich, 1991-92.

64. "Russians Cheer Cliburn Again At Awards Presentation Affair," *Kilgore News Herald,* April 15, 1958.

65. "Texan in Moscow," *Time,* April 21, 1958.

66. Edward L. Smith, AP wire report, dated March 12, 1959.

67. Oxana Yablonskaya interviewed by Howard Reich, March 1991.

68. Abram Chasins with Villa Stiles, *The Van Cliburn Legend,* p. 109.

69. "Russians Cheer Cliburn Again At Awards Presentation Affair," *Kilgore News Herald,* April 15, 1958.

70. Van Cliburn interviewed by Howard Reich, 1991-92.

71. Sequeira Costa interviewed by Howard Reich, March 1992.

72. Oxana Yablonskaya interviewed by Howard Reich, March 1991.
73. Van Cliburn interviewed by Howard Reich, 1991-92.
74. Max Frankel, "Russians Cheer U.S. Pianist, 23: Texan Wins Ovation for His Brilliance at Moscow Fete," *New York Times,* April 12, 1958. Copyright © 1958 by The New York Times Company. Reprinted by permission.
75. Sequeira Costa interviewed by Howard Reich, March 1992.
76. Maxim Shostakovich interviewed by Howard Reich, June 1991.
77. Sergei Dorensky interviewed by Howard Reich. This story is corroborated by Andrei Gavrilov, vis-à-vis Sviatoslav Richter, Maxim Shostakovich, Vladimir Ashkenazy, Soviet pianist Alexander Slobodyanik, and scholar Nicolas Slonimsky, among others.
78. Andrei Gavrilov interviewed by Howard Reich, Oct. 1991.
79. Vladimir Ashkenazy interviewed by Howard Reich, July 1991.
80. Henrietta Belayaeva interviewed by Howard Reich, Feb. 1992.
81. Alexander Slobodyanik interviewed by Howard Reich, Oct. 1991.
82. Max Frankel interviewed by Howard Reich, March 1992.
83. Telegram Sol Hurok sent to Mark Schubart, dated April 16, 1958. Used by permission.
84. John Pfeiffer interviewed by Howard Reich, Nov. 1991.
85. Alan Kayes interviewed by Howard Reich, March 1992.
86. AP, "Kilgore Pianist Rests After Wowing Moscow," *Shreveport Times,* April 13, 1958.
87. Max Frankel interviewed by Howard Reich, Nov. 1991.
88. Mark Schubart interviewed by Howard Reich, Nov. 1991.
89. Abram Chasins with Villa Stiles, *The Van Cliburn Legend,* p. 113.
90. Max Frankel, "U.S. Pianist, 23, Wins Soviet Contest," *New York Times,* April 14, 1958. Copyright © 1958 by The New York Times Company. Reprinted by permission.
91. Ibid.

92. "The Arts As Bridges," *New York Times,* April 14, 1958.
93. Annie Lou Ballard interviewed by Howard Reich, July 1991.
94. Naum Shtarkman interviewed by Howard Reich, Sept. 1991.
95. Alexander Slobodyanik interviewed by Howard Reich, Oct. 1991.
96. Claudia Cassidy interviewed by Howard Reich, March 1991.
97. Vladimir Viardo interviewed by Howard Reich, July 1991.
98. Vladimir Ashkenazy interviewed by Howard Reich, July 1991.
99. Viktoria Postnikova interviewed by Howard Reich, July 1991.
100. Ashchen Mikoyan interviewed by Howard Reich, March 1992.
101. Max Frankel interviewed by Howard Reich, March 1992.
102. Ibid.

CHAPTER SEVEN

1. Max Frankel, "U.S. Pianist Plays For Soviet Chiefs: Cliburn, 23, Performs for Notables After Triumph in Moscow Contest," *New York Times,* April 15, 1958.
2. Daniel Pollack interviewed by Howard Reich, Feb. 1991.
3. "Cliburn Selected Winner: Local Pianist Is Toast of Musical World," *Kilgore News Herald,* April 14, 1958.
4. Max Frankel, "U.S. Pianist Plays For Soviet Chiefs: Cliburn, 23, Performs for Notables After Triumph in Moscow Contest," *New York Times,* April 15, 1958.
5. "Cliburn Selected Winner: Local Pianist Is Toast of Musical World," *Kilgore News Herald,* April 14, 1958.
6. Van Cliburn interviewed by Howard Reich, 1991-92.
7. Harriet Wingreen interviewed by Howard Reich, May 1991.
8. James Roos, "Stalled Van: Pianist Cliburn, 'The Texan Who Conquered Russia,' continues a 4-1/2-year 'intermission,'" *Miami Herald,* as reprinted in the *New Orleans Times Picayune,* April 24, 1983.
9. Mary Meador, "Parents Besieged By Telephone Calls," *Kilgore News Herald,* April 14, 1958.

10. UP, "Word Leaks Out: Kilgore Pianist Wins Moscow Contest," *Shreveport Times,* April 14, 1958.

11. Ibid.

12. Ibid.

13. Ibid.

14. "Cliburn Selected Winner: Local Pianist Is Toast of Musical World," *Kilgore News Herald,* April 14, 1958.

15. UP, "Word Leaks Out: Kilgore Pianist Wins Moscow Contest," *Shreveport Times,* April 14, 1958.

16. Max Frankel interviewed by Howard Reich, March 1992.

17. Alexander Toradze interviewed by Howard Reich, June 1991.

18. Alexander Slobodyanik interviewed by Howard Reich, Oct. 1991.

19. Annette Davies Morgan interviewed by Howard Reich, July 1991.

20. "May Return After May 10: Dates In U.S., Abroad Shape Up For Cliburn," *Kilgore News Herald,* April 16, 1958.

21. Ibid.

22. "Van Cliburn: Test Of Greatness, An Editorial," *Kilgore News Herald,* April 14, 1958.

23. Bill Hallman interviewed by Howard Reich, Aug. 1991.

24. Jack Kilpatrick, "Russians Cheer Cliburn Again at Awards Presentation Affair," *Dallas Times-Herald*, as excerpted in *Kilgore News Herald,* April 15, 1958.

25. "Cliburn Selected Winner: Local Pianist Is Toast of Musical World," *Kilgore News Herald,* April 14, 1958.

26. "American *Sputnik,*" *Time,* April 28, 1958.

27. Josef Raeiff interviewed by Howard Reich, March 1991.

28. Gary Graffman interviewed by Howard Reich, July 1991.

29. Naomi Graffman interviewed by Howard Reich, July 1991.

30. "Cliburn Selected Winner: Local Pianist Is Toast of Musical World," *Kilgore News Herald,* April 14, 1958.

31. Yehudi Menuhin interviewed by Howard Reich, Oct. 1991.

32. Jerome Lowenthal interviewed by Howard Reich, March 1991.

33. Ivan Davis interviewed by Howard Reich, March 1992.

34. James Mathis interviewed by Howard Reich, Jan. 1992.

35. Max Frankel, "U.S. Pianist Plays For Soviet Chiefs: Cliburn, 23, Performs for Notables After Triumph in Moscow Contest," *New York Times,* April 15, 1958.

36. Ibid.

37. Abram Chasins with Villa Stiles, *The Van Cliburn Legend* (Garden City, NY: Doubleday, 1959), p. 114.

38. AP, "Champion Pianist: Capitalist Gets Hug From Nikita," *Dallas Morning News,* April 15, 1958.

39. "Van Admits Overlooking Punch Line," *Kilgore News Herald,* Dec. 1, 1958.

40. Irwin Weil interviewed by Howard Reich, March 1992.

41. Ibid.

42. James Roos, "Stalled Van: Pianist Cliburn, 'The Texan Who Conquered Russia,' continues a 4-1/2-year 'intermission,'" *Miami Herald,* as reprinted in the *New Orleans Times Picayune,* April 24, 1983.

43. From the transcript of Van Cliburn's interview on radio station WQXR in New York, with Abram Chasins, broadcast during the intermission of Cliburn's Carnegie Hall performance on May 26, 1958.

44. Lorin Maazel interviewed by Howard Reich, Aug. 1991.

45. Max Frankel, "U.S. Pianist Plays For Soviet Chiefs: Cliburn, 23, Performs for Notables After Triumph in Moscow Contest," *New York Times,* April 15, 1958.

46. B. J. Cutler, "Texas Pianist Wins Top Prize At Moscow Tchaikovsky Test," *New York Herald Tribune,* April 15, 1958.

47. Max Frankel, "U.S. Pianist Plays For Soviet Chiefs: Cliburn, 23, Performs for Notables After Triumph in Moscow Contest," *New York Times,* April 15, 1958.

48. B. J. Cutler, "Texas Pianist Wins Top Prize At Moscow Tchaikovsky Test," *New York Herald Tribune,* April 15, 1958.

49. Max Frankel, "U.S. Pianist Plays For Soviet Chiefs: Cliburn, 23, Performs for Notables After Triumph in Moscow Contest," *New York Times,* April 15, 1958.

50. "Cliburn Continues As Toast Of Soviet," *New York Times,* April 16, 1958.

51. AP, "Prize-Winner Van Cliburn May Give Concert in Dallas," *Dallas Morning News,* April 16, 1958.

52. "Winner in Moscow: Kilgore's Young Pianist Planned His Goals Early," *Dallas Morning News,* April 17, 1958.

53. Abram Chasins with Villa Stiles, *The Van Cliburn Legend,* p. 121.

54. "American *Sputnik,*" *Time,* April 28, 1958.

55. Carried in several newspapers, via UP, including: *Dallas Morning News,* "Music Has No 'Iron Curtains,' by Van Cliburn, via UP, April 18, 1958; *New Orleans States-Item,* "Cliburn Tells of Stay In Moscow," via UP, April 21, 1958.

56. Skitch Henderson interviewed by Howard Reich, March 1991.

57. AP, "Moscow Again Hails Cliburn," *New York Times,* April 19, 1958.

58. All of these engagements announced in "Dates Being Set For Van Cliburn," *Kilgore News Herald,* April 18, 1958.

59. "Ike Congratulates Kilgore Musician," *Dallas Morning News,* April 19, 1958.

60. Howard Taubman, "A Winner On His Merits," *New York Times,* April 20, 1958.

61. Lorin Maazel interviewed by Howard Reich, Aug. 1991.

62. Yehudi Menuhin interviewed by Howard Reich, Oct. 1991.

63. Radio broadcast by Patrick Hayes from Washington, D.C., on April 20, 1958, as excerpted in the 16-page liner-note booklet accompanying Van Cliburn's first LP recording, Tchaikovsky Piano Concerto no. 1 in B-flat Minor, RCA Victor.

64. Abram Chasins with Villa Stiles, *The Van Cliburn Legend,* p. 122.

65. Ibid.

66. AP, "Exhausted But Happy: Tired Van Cliburn Ends Soviet Tour," *Kilgore News Herald,* May 11, 1958.

67. As excerpted in the 16-page liner-note booklet accompanying Van Cliburn's first LP recording, Tchaikovsky Piano Concerto no. 1 in B-flat Minor, RCA Victor.

68. Abram Chasins with Villa Stiles, *The Van Cliburn Legend,* p. 118.

69. "Shostakovich Hails Cliburn's Success," *New York Times,* April 21, 1958.

70. Walter H. Waggoner, "U.S. Hopes To Sign Cliburn For Fair: Seeks Brussels Appearance by Pianist Who Captured First Prize in Moscow," *New York Times,* April 23, 1958.

71. Personal letter from Rosina Lhevinne to Mark Schubart, dated April 24, 1958. Used by permission.

72. Abram Chasins with Villa Stiles, *The Van Cliburn Legend,* pp. 125-126.

73. Van Cliburn interviewed by Howard Reich, 1991-92.

74. Abram Chasins with Villa Stiles, *The Van Cliburn Legend,* p. 127.

75. From the transcript of Van Cliburn's interview on radio station WQXR in New York, with Abram Chasins, broadcast during the intermission of Cliburn's Carnegie Hall performance on May 26, 1958.

76. AP, "Cliburn Leaves Soviet," *New York Times,* May 15, 1958.

77. "Tall at the Keyboard: Van Cliburn," *New York Times,* April 14, 1958.

78. "Tell Experiences: Shreveporters Encounter Van On Moscow Trip," *Shreveport* magazine, as excerpted in *Kilgore News Herald,* Dec. 1, 1958.

79. "Russian Vox Pop View of Cliburn," *Variety,* May 28, 1958.

80. "Hero's Return," *Soviet Culture*, as excerpted in *Time* magazine, June 2, 1958.

CHAPTER EIGHT

1. Van Cliburn interviewed by Howard Reich, 1991-92.

2. Michael Fleming, "Van Cliburn Reflects on the Past and a Possible Future," *New York Times,* June 9, 1985.

3. Van Cliburn interviewed by Howard Reich, 1991-92.

4. "The All-American Virtuoso," *Time,* May 19, 1958.

5. Frank Gagnard, "Cliburn Coup," *New Orleans Item,* May 18, 1958.

6. "The All-American Virtuoso," *Time*, May 19, 1958.

7. Ibid.

8. Ibid.

9. Ibid.

10. William A. Payne, "Forecasts: The Symphony, Van Cliburn Stories," *Dallas Morning News,* May 15, 1958.

11. Milton Bracker, "Jubilant Cliburn Arrives Here After Piano Triumph in Soviet," *New York Times,* May 17, 1958.

12. Van Cliburn interviewed by Howard Reich, 1991-92.

13. Robert E. Baskin, "Interlude At Idlewild: A Happy Cliburn Returns As Concert, Parade Await," *Dallas Morning News,* May 17, 1958.

14. "Carnegie Hall," *Musical Courier,* June 1958.

15. Milton Bracker, "Jubilant Cliburn Arrives Here After Piano Triumph in Soviet," *New York Times,* May 17, 1958.

16. Van Cliburn interviewed by Howard Reich, 1991-92.

17. Milton Bracker, "Jubilant Cliburn Arrives Here After Piano Triumph in Soviet," *New York Times*, May 17, 1958; Abram Chasins with Villa Stiles, *The Van Cliburn Legend* (Garden City, NY: Doubleday, 1959), pp. 123-124.

18. Milton Bracker, "Jubilant Cliburn Arrives Here After Piano Triumph in Soviet," *New York Times,* May 17, 1958.

19. Milton Bracker, "Cliburn Greets Soviet Conductor: Russian in New York to Lead Concert at Carnegie Hall by Pianist Tomorrow," *New York Times,* May 18, 1958.

20. AP, "Cliburn Greets Soviet Conductor," *Kilgore News Herald,* May 18, 1958.

21. Milton Bracker, "Cliburn Greets Soviet Conductor: Russian in New York to Lead Concert at Carnegie Hall by Pianist Tomorrow," *New York Times,* May 18, 1958.

22. "Kilgore Friend of Van's Shares New York Reception," *Kilgore News Herald,* May 25, 1958.

23. Ibid.

24. Charles Mercer, AP, "Next One More Expensive: Skitch Henderson Boosted Van Cliburn 'Back When ...'," *Kilgore News Herald,* May 19, 1958.

25. "Biggest in Carnegie Hall History: Cliburn Wows 'Em At Home; Given Thunderous Ovation," *Kilgore News Herald,* May 20, 1958.

26. "Young Man 'Goes on Trial,' Gets Ovation From 'Jury,'" *New York World-Telegram*, May 20, 1958, as excerpted in *Kilgore News Herald*, Dec. 1, 1958.

27. Virgil Miers, AP, "Cliburns Find Reception 'Overwhelming,'" *Kilgore News Herald*, May 25, 1958.

28. UP, "Van Cliburn's Homecoming Is Smash Hit," *Cleveland Plain Dealer*, May 20, 1958.

29. Ibid.

30. Mary Meador, "Kilgoround," *Kilgore News Herald*, May 21, 1958.

31. "Young Man 'Goes on Trial,' Gets Ovation From 'Jury,'" *New York World-Telegram*, May 20, 1958, as excerpted in *Kilgore News Herald*, Dec. 1, 1958.

32. Gilbert Millstein, "Great Moments at Carnegie Hall," *New York Times*, May 22, 1960.

33. Milton Bracker, "Cliburn Cheered In Packed House: 23-Year-Old Pianist Gets a Tumultuous Ovation as Parents Watch in Awe," *New York Times*, May 20, 1958.

34. "Young Man 'Goes on Trial,' Gets Ovation From 'Jury,'" *New York World-Telegram*, May 20, 1958, as excerpted in *Kilgore News Herald*, Dec. 1, 1958.

35. Milton Bracker, "Cliburn Cheered In Packed House: 23-Year-Old Pianist Gets a Tumultuous Ovation as Parents Watch in Awe," *New York Times*, May 20, 1958.

36. Gilbert Millstein, "Great Moments at Carnegie Hall," *New York Times*, May 22, 1960.

37. Milton Bracker, "Cliburn Cheered In Packed House: 23-Year-Old Pianist Gets a Tumultuous Ovation as Parents Watch in Awe," *New York Times*, May 20, 1958.

38. "Biggest in Carnegie Hall History: Cliburn Wows 'Em At Home; Given Thunderous Ovation," *Kilgore News Herald*, May 20, 1958.

39. Abram Chasins with Villa Stiles, *The Van Cliburn Legend*, p. 144.

40. Ross Parmenter, "Cliburn Proves Himself a Real Winner," *New York Times*, May 20, 1958.

41. Paul Henry Lang, *New York Herald-Tribune,* as excerpted in *Kilgore News Herald,* "Memorable Week: Van Cliburn Takes New York By Storm," May 25, 1958.

42. W. G. Rogers, AP, as excerpted in *Dallas Morning News,* "Van Cliburn Captures New Yorkers' Acclaim," May 20, 1958.

43. Douglas Watt, *New York Daily News,* as excerpted in *Kilgore News Herald,* "What The Critics Said," May 20, 1958.

44. The text of the proclamation, as seen in a surviving original program for the "American Music Day" festivities, reads thus:
The impact of Van Cliburn's triumph in the Moscow International Tchaikovsky Competition goes far beyond music and himself as an individual, and is a dramatic testimonial to American culture; and
WHEREAS: The United States has already recognized this genius and awarded him the highest honors in the world of music; and
WHEREAS: Winning the International Tchaikovsky Competition is the direct result of the superb American training and coaching of a performing artist and our recognition of his talent by fellow-Americans; and
WHEREAS: With his two hands Van Cliburn struck a chord which has resounded around the world, raising our prestige with artists and music-lovers everywhere,
NOW, THEREFORE I, Robert F. Wagner, Mayor of The City of New York, do hereby proclaim Tuesday, May 20th, 1958 as
AMERICAN MUSIC DAY
and do urge New Yorkers, young and old alike, to show their appreciation of this great talent and those who brought it to fruition, by filling the City's streets with people on American Music Day symbolized by Van Cliburn as he makes the historic ride up Lower Broadway; and further, by doing so to encourage other music students to aspire to the heights he attained in his profession.

45. AP, "100,000 Hail Van Cliburn in N.Y. Bow," *Chicago Tribune,* May 21, 1958.

46. "Van Cliburn Gets A Hero's Parade: 100,000 Line Broadway at First Musician to Take Triumphal Route," *New York Times,* May 21, 1958.

47. Abram Chasins with Villa Stiles, *The Van Cliburn Legend,* pp. 134-135.

48. Virgil Miers, AP, "Cliburns Find Reception 'Overwhelming,'" *Kilgore News Herald,* May 25, 1958.

49. "Van Cliburn Gets A Hero's Parade: 100,000 Line Broadway at First Musician to Take Triumphal Route," *New York Times,* May 21, 1958.

50. "Hero's Welcome: Gotham Cheers Pianist Cliburn," *Dallas Morning News,* May 21, 1958.

51. Van Cliburn interviewed by Howard Reich, 1991-92.

52. "Van Cliburn Gets A Hero's Parade: 100,000 Line Broadway at First Musician to Take Triumphal Route," *New York Times,* May 21, 1958.

53. AP, "100,000 Line Broadway: Cliburn and Ike Share Gotham Parade Honors," *Shreveport Times,* May 21, 1958.

54. Abram Chasins with Villa Stiles, *The Van Cliburn Legend,* p. 136.

55. Ibid.

56. "Tribute," *New Yorker,* May 31, 1958.

57. Ibid.

58. "Van Cliburn Gets A Hero's Parade: 100,000 Line Broadway at First Musician to Take Triumphal Route," *New York Times,* May 21, 1958.

59. Ibid.

60. *Ft. Worth Star-Telegram* editorial, as excerpted in "Van Cliburn Day In New York," *Kilgore News Herald,* May 25, 1958.

61. As noted in "Memorable Week: Van Cliburn Takes New York By Storm," *Kilgore News Herald,* May 25, 1958.

62. Ibid.

63. Ibid.

64. Joyce Flissler interviewed by Howard Reich, May 1991.

65. Harriet Wingreen interviewed by Howard Reich, May 1991.

66. Edwin H. Schloss, "Cliburn Captivates Audience With Sparkling Play," *Philadelphia Inquirer*, May 22, 1958.

67. Max de Schauensee, "Pianist Van Cliburn, Soviet Award Winner, Thrills Capacity Audience at Academy," *Philadelphia Evening Bulletin*, May 22, 1958.

68. Ibid.

69. Abram Chasins with Villa Stiles, *The Van Cliburn Legend*, p. 150.

70. Ibid., p. 149.

71. AP, "They Love Van In Washington, Too!" *Kilgore News Herald*, May 25, 1958.

72. Mary V. R. Thayer, "Van Cliburn Meets the Press: He'd Like to Play for Ike," *Washington Post*, May 24, 1958.

73. Paul Hume, "Van Cliburn Wins Wild Ovations Here," *Washington Post*, May 24, 1958.

74. Winzola McLendon, "Van Toasted in Vodka and Champagne," *Washington Post*, May 25, 1958.

75. Abram Chasins with Villa Stiles, *The Van Cliburn Legend*, p. 152.

76. Mary V. R. Thayer, "Why So 'Quiet' for Van?" *Washington Post*, May 26, 1958.

77. Schuyler Chapin interviewed by Howard Reich, March 1991.

78. Alan Kayes interviewed by Howard Reich, March 1992.

79. Schuyler Chapin interviewed by Howard Reich, March 1991.

80. Skitch Henderson interviewed by Howard Reich, March 1991.

81. Jack Gould, "TV: Van Cliburn Plays: Steve Allen Presents Young Pianist as Guest Star on Channel 4," *New York Times*, May 26, 1958.

82. Bob Bernstein, "Accent on Youth In Longhair Boom: Cliburn Impact Can Pave Way to Fat Era for Young, U.S. Talent," *Billboard*, May 26, 1958.

83. Ibid.

84. Alan Kayes interviewed by Howard Reich, March 1992.

85. John Pfeiffer interviewed by Howard Reich, Nov. 1991.

86. John M. Conly, untitled, *High Fidelity* magazine, Aug. 1958.

87. Jack Gould, "Live WQXR Broadcast of Cliburn Concert Is Outstanding Event of the Week," *New York Times,* June 1, 1958.

88. Edward Downes wrote ("Van Cliburn Repeats His Prize-Winning Program in Sold-Out Carnegie Hall," *New York Times,* May 27, 1958):

He showed again the superb accuracy and security of his technique. But he reinforced the impression made on his appearance here a week ago that he cares more for other qualities than brilliance.

He made the piano sing in the more intimate moments of both concertos and sometimes there was a hushed tone in his playings that almost matched the tone of the muted violins. The heartfelt sentiment, which is so much a part of the Slav temperament, seemed to come especially naturally to him.

89. Naomi Graffman interviewed by Howard Reich, July 1991.

90. John Pfeiffer interviewed by Howard Reich, Nov. 1991.

91. Ibid.

92. Ibid.

93. Van Cliburn, Edward R. Murrow's "Person to Person," May 30, 1958.

94. Ibid.

95. *Kilgore News Herald* photo caption, Dec. 1, 1958.

96. UPI, "European Tour Set by Cliburn," *Shreveport Times,* June 10, 1958.

97. Following his June 15 performance before 7,000 people in Royal Albert Hall, with Kondrashin conducting the London Philharmonic Orchestra, the *Times* of London reported that Van showed "a prodigious technique and all the vitality and eagerness of youth as a powerful driving force behind it." *The Daily Telegraph* said Van had "the unmistakable musician's instinct and a gift for refined lyrical playing which is probably his greatest asset." *The Daily Express* called Van a "prodigious artist" and added that he "merits fuss, even a touch of hysteria. He produced a controlled thunder of tone with the relaxed ease of a master twice his age." These reviews were quoted in a

Reuters story that appeared in the *Chicago Tribune*, June 17, 1958.

The London acclaim was noteworthy because "it was no foregone conclusion it would be so," wrote London correspondent Alan Prentice, in a piece for the *Kilgore News Herald* ("With Cliburns in London: Concert Is Great Success," June 21, 1958). "Because his story is essentially an 'American boy made good,' he had relatively little advance publicity in the English press, some of which is coloured in varying shades of anti-Americanism."

98. AP, "London Audience of 7,000 Hails Cliburn In Concert Conducted by Kondrashin," *New York Times,* May 16, 1958.

99. AP, "Gets Cheering Ovation: Van Cliburn Does It Again—In London," *Kilgore News Herald,* June 16, 1958.

100. UPI, "Cliburn Treats Dutch To Royal Performance," *New York Times,* June 23, 1958.

101. The newspaper *Figaro* called Van "a great success ... a born virtuoso"; *Parisien Libere* wrote that Van offered "the most brilliant work we have heard in a long time." (Both reviews excerpted by UPI in the *Dallas Morning News,* "Critics of Paris Hail Van Cliburn," June 28, 1958.)

102. Howard Taubman, "American Pianist Plays at the Final Concert of Philadelphia Orchestra," *New York Times,* July 6, 1958.

103. Abram Chasins with Villa Stiles, *The Van Cliburn Legend,* p. 160.

104. Signing date noted in Dosha Dowdy and Rene Devries, "Chicago," *Musical Courier,* Aug. 1958.

105. Edward Gordon interviewed by Howard Reich, July 1991.

106. *Dallas Morning News,* photo, July 17, 1958.

107. Barnard K. Letter, *Chicago Daily News,* as excerpted in *Kilgore News Herald,* "Wonder Boy: Windy City Had Crush On Cliburn," Dec. 1, 1958.

108. Louise Hutchinson, "Shriners Greet Cliburn," *Chicago Tribune,* July 16, 1958.

109. Jeffrey Siegel interviewed by Howard Reich, Aug. 1991.

110. The *Chicago Tribune*, in a Louise Hutchinson piece, announced "55,000 Strong, They Came To Hear Cliburn," July 17, 1958; UPI, in the *Shreveport Times*, put the number at 65,000, in a piece titled "Cliburn Greeted By Chicago Crowd," July 18, 1958; *Musical America*, in a Howard Talley article headlined "Van Cliburn Draws Crowd of 70,000 At Grant Park," Aug. 1958; *Musical Courier* estimated the number at 150,000 for two nights, with 70,000 for the first evening, 80,000 for the second, in a Dosha Dowdy and Rene Devries article titled "Chicago," Aug. 1958.

111. Louise Hutchinson, "55,000 Strong, They Came To Hear Cliburn," *Chicago Tribune*, July 17, 1958.

112. Edward Gordon interviewed by Howard Reich, July 1991.

113. Van Cliburn interviewed by Howard Reich, 1991-92.

114. Claudia Cassidy, "Cliburn Plays Stunning Rachmaninoff to Huge Lakefront Audience," Chicago Tribune, July 17, 1958.

115. Claudia Cassidy interviewed by Howard Reich, March 1991.

116. Donal Henahan, *Chicago Daily News* review, as excerpted in *Kilgore News Herald*, "Van Cliburn Grand At Concert Piano," Dec. 1, 1958. Information on encores from Dosha Dowdy and Rene Devries in *Musical Courier*, "Chicago," Aug. 1958.

117. Van Cliburn interviewed by Howard Reich, 1991-92.

118. Howard Talley, "Cliburn Draws Crowd of 70,000 At Grant Park," *Musical America*, Aug. 1958.

119. "Cliburn to Take Two Month Break From Concert Dates," *Dallas Morning News*, July 23, 1958.

120. Van Cliburn intrreviewed by Howard Reich, 1991-92.

121. Nicolas Slonimsky, *Baker's Biographical Dictionary of Musicians* (New York: Schirmer Books, 1984, seventh ed.).

122. Van Cliburn interviewed by Howard Reich, 1991-92.

123. Cliburn played the Tchaikovsky First Concerto, with Thor Johnson and the Los Angeles Philharmonic Orchestra on Wednesday, July 30, according to Albert Goldberg:

... to an assemblage that filled the vast acreage of the Bowl to its last seat at a special concert at advanced prices. The crowd was estimated at 20,000, with many more turned away.

Mr. Cliburn is a pianist of comprehensive abilities and strongly individualized outlook. Contest winners are very apt to be race horses, distinguished for their speed and endurance, but this one has considerably more than those qualities. He has personality and musical sensitiveness, in addition to the virtuosity that is indispensable to anyone who aspires to renown nowadays."

From Albert Goldberg, "Capacity Bowl Crowd Acclaims Van Cliburn," *Los Angeles Times,* July 31, 1958.

The following night, Thursday, July 31, Cliburn played the Rachmaninoff Third at the Hollywood Bowl, and Goldberg wrote:

For the first time in history, an American pianist filled the Hollywood Bowl to capacity on two consecutive nights. It was a stirring occasion and if Van Cliburn has become a hero to his fellow countrymen one can honestly say on the strength of his playing of Rachmaninoff's D Minor Concerto with the Los Angeles Philharmonic Orchestra under Thor Johnson's direction last night that he fully merits all the adulation.

. . .

The stupendous cadenza to the first movement which Rachmaninoff himself omitted in favor of an easier version was tossed off with reckless abandon.

From Albert Goldberg, "Cliburn Dazzles in Bowl Concert," *Los Angeles Times,* Aug. 1, 1958.

124. Dick Sands, "Van, at Home Again, Recalls Highlights," by *Kilgore News Herald,* Oct. 10, 1958.

125. Jean Warner Stark, untitled, *American Music Teacher,* Nov.-Dec. 1961; John Davidson, "Every Good Boy Does Fine," *Texas Monthly,* May 1987.

126. Van Cliburn interviewed by Howard Reich, 1991-92.

127. "Soviet Extends Bid To Pianist Cliburn," *New York Times*, Aug. 2, 1958.

128. Ross Parmenter, "Music: 22,500 Hear Cliburn at Stadium," *New York Times*, Aug. 5, 1958.

129. Ibid.

130. Ibid.

131. Ibid.

132. "Van Cliburn In Stadium Finale," *Musical America*, Aug. 1958.

133. Untitled, *Musical Courier*, Sept. 1958.

134. "Cliburn To Join Russian Concert," *New York Times*, Aug. 10, 1958.

135. "Cliburn, Russians In Concert At Fair," *New York Times*, Aug. 17, 1958.

136. Howard Taubman, "Musical 'Summit' In Belgian Accord," *New York Times*, Aug. 18, 1958.

137. H. I. Phillips, as quoted in *Musical Courier*, "Van Cliburn: Young Man with a Mission," by Chris Nelson, Sept. 1958.

138. "Cliburn Would Biopic Liszt 'If Plot Is Right,' " *Variety*, Sept. 10, 1958.

139. "Cliburn Album Sells Like Hot Single," *Billboard*, Aug. 18, 1958.

140. John Pfeiffer interviewed by Howard Reich, Nov. 1991.

141. John Rosenfield, "Pianist Cliburn Returns Home After European Stint for U.S.," *Dallas Morning News*, Aug. 23, 1958.

142. "Cliburn Would Biopic Liszt 'If Plot Is Right,'" *Variety*, Sept. 10, 1958.

143. "Cliburn Gives City $1,250 Soviet Prize," *New York Times*, Sept. 26, 1958.

144. UPI, "Boston to Hear Cliburn Twice," *New York Times*, Sept. 23, 1958.

145. "The most important aspect just now is the way he integrates a solo part with the orchestra. You feel he is not giving a solo to accompaniment but is playing as a somewhat more emphasized instrument of the orchestra. This is a portion of the true essence of music making."

From Cyrus Durgin, "Van Cliburn Gets Wild Ovation In Boston Debut at Symphony Hall," *Boston Globe,* Oct. 6, 1958.

146. Ibid.

147. Rosario Mazzeo interviewed by Howard Reich, March 1992.

148. John Pfeiffer interviewed by Howard Reich, Nov. 1991.

149. "Van's Big Year," *Time,* Oct. 6, 1958.

150. Don Freeman, "Cliburn Flies Here To See Ill Mother," *Dallas Morning News,* Oct. 9, 1958; AP, "Van Cliburn Flying Home; Mother Is Ill," *Kilgore News Herald,* Oct. 8, 1958.

151. AP, "Cliburn Flies in To Cheer Mother," *Kilgore News Herald,* Oct. 9, 1958.

152. Dick Sands, "Van, at Home Again, Recalls Highlights," *Kilgore News Herald,* Oct. 10, 1958.

153. Ross Parmenter, "3 'Grand Old Men' Of Music Honored," *New York Times,* Oct. 17, 1958; Howard Taubman, "Music: The New and Old," *New York Times,* Oct. 18, 1958.

154. Irving Kolodin, "Reiner Returns, also Cliburn, to Los Angeles, Simionata," *Saturday Review,* Nov. 1, 1958.

155. *Kilgore News Herald,* photo caption, Oct. 30, 1958.

156. AP, "Van Cliburn Gets Ovation At Newark," *Kilgore News Herald,* Nov. 3, 1958.

157. John Nussbaum, "Cliburn Concert Emotional Affair For 4,050 Fans," *Pittsburgh Post-Gazette,* Nov. 5, 1958.

158. "Cliburn Scores Mixing Of Politics, Art Here," *Dallas Morning News,* Nov. 6, 1958.

159. Ibid.

160. William B. Pope, "Big Gifts Cap Van Cliburn Concert," *Dallas Morning News,* Nov. 7, 1958.

161. Ibid.

162. AP, "Van Cliburn Adds Degree To Gold Medal," *Kilgore News Herald,* Nov. 7, 1958.

163. Charles L. Dufour, "Cliburn Shows Orleans Why He Won Contest," *New Orleans Times-Picayune,* Nov. 12, 1958.

164. Vaden Smith, "Kilgoround," *Kilgore News Herald,* Nov. 15, 1958.

165. Van Cliburn interviewed by Howard Reich, 1991-92.

166. Don Freeman, "Rayburn Praises Feats of Cliburn," *Dallas Morning News*, Nov. 29, 1958.

167. John Rosenfield, "Van Cliburn Cheered Here," *Dallas Morning News*, Nov. 30, 1958.

168. Charles Schulz, "Peanuts" comic strip, *Kilgore News Herald*, Dec. 1, 1958.

169. John Rosenfield, "Kilgore Ready to Fete Cliburn," *Dallas Morning News*, Dec. 2, 1958.

170. "Cliburn Day: Once Over Lightly," *Kilgore News Herald*, Dec. 3, 1958.

171. "'I'm Speechless,' Says Van," *Kilgore News Herald*, Dec. 2, 1958.

172. Pericles Alexander, "Van Cliburn Is Amazed By Kilgore Homecoming," *Shreveport Times*, Dec. 3, 1958.

173. "Noisy Ovation At Matinee: Youngsters Go Wild Over Van, Forget 'Rock,'" *Kilgore News Herald*, Dec. 3, 1958.

174. John Rosenfield, "Kilgore Evokes Best of Cliburn," *Dallas Morning News*, Dec. 3, 1958.

175. Dick Sands, "Gifted Pianist 'Gives All' As Climax at Homecoming," *Kilgore News Herald*, Dec. 3, 1958.

176. Rudy Rochelle, "Artist Wear: Fame's Demands Tiring to Cliburn," *Dallas Morning News*, Dec. 15, 1958.

177. Mary Meador, "Van Cliburn Paid Honor At Shreveport," *Kilgore News Herald*, Dec. 17, 1958.

178. Ibid.

179. Joseph Silverstein interviewed by Howard Reich, Aug. 1991.

180. John Pfeiffer interviewed by Howard Reich, Nov. 1991.

181. Van Cliburn interviewed by Howard Reich, 1991-92.

182. Van Cliburn, as told to Sidney Fields, "What Is Success?" *Guideposts*, Feb. 1959.

183. George Pappastavrou interviewed by Howard Reich, May 1991.

184. "Cliburn Gives City $1,250 Soviet Prize," *New York Times*, Sept. 26, 1958.

185. AP, "Van Cliburn Solid with Teen-Agers," *Chicago Tribune*, Oct. 1, 1958.

186. AP, "Van Plays To 17,000 In Austin," *Kilgore News Herald,* Nov. 14, 1958.

187. Wayne Lee Gay, *Ft. Worth Star-Telegram,* Dec. 30, 1990.

188. "Russians Cheer Cliburn Again at Awards Presentation Affair," *Kilgore News Herald,* April 15, 1958.

189. "Cliburn Contest Opens Tomorrow," *New York Times,* Sept. 23, 1962.

190. Bernard Holland, "Van Cliburn: Man Behind the Contest," *New York Times,* March 27, 1989.

191. "Van Cliburn the Man Was a Federation Boy," *Music Clubs* magazine, March/April 1960.

CHAPTER NINE

1. AP, "Van Cliburn Dropped Off List of 10," *Dallas Morning News,* Jan. 4, 1959.

2. Ibid.

3. AP, "Cliburn to Miss Award For Missing a Dinner," *New York Times,* Jan. 5, 1959.

4. "Cliburn Scores 'Gimmicked' Honor Revoked When He Wouldn't Do a Personal," *Variety,* Jan. 21, 1959.

5. Harrison E. Salisbury, "Cliburn A Guest At Mikoyan Fete: U.S. Pianist Plays at Soviet Reception Marking End of Soviet Leader's Trip," *New York Times,* Jan. 20. 1959.

6. Edwin H. Schloss, "Cliburn Superb," *Philadelphia Inquirer,* Jan. 25, 1959.

7. Arthur Bloomfield, "Jorda Revives Two Overtures For San Francisco Series," *Musical America,* March, 1959.

8. Howard Taubman, "Music: Three by Cliburn: Pianist in Concertos With Philharmonic," *New York Times,* Feb. 18, 1959.

9. Winthrop Sargeant, "Cliburn Plain," *New Yorker,* Feb. 28, 1959.

10. Ibid.

11. Abram Chasins with Villa Stiles, *The Van Cliburn Legend* (Garden City, NY: Doubleday, 1959), p. 171.

12. Fritz Steinway interviewed by Howard Reich, April 1991.

13. Andrew Meisels, AP wire copy, dated Feb. 19, 1959.

14. Ibid.

15. Fritz Steinway interviewed by Howard Reich, April 1991.

16. Andrew Meisels, AP wire copy, Feb. 19, 1959.

17. AP, "Pianist Cliburn Goes to Hospital," *Los Angeles Times,* Feb. 24, 1959.

18. "Cliburn Has Hand Surgery," *New York Times,* Feb. 28, 1959.

19. Edward L. Smith, AP wire copy, dated March 12, 1959.

20. AP, "Cliburn's Soviet Concert Off," *New York Times,* April 19, 1959.

21. Edward L. Smith, AP wire copy, dated March 12, 1959.

22. Ibid.

23. Ibid.

24. Ibid.

25. Sue Connally, "Cliburn Muses About Injury," *Dallas Morning News,* April 2, 1959.

26. AP, "Van Cliburn Tells Of Near Loss Of Hand," *Chicago Tribune,* May 19, 1959.

27. AP, "Van Cliburn Undergoes Operation on Finger," *Dallas Morning News,* March 1, 1959.

28. "Cliburn Allowed to Practice," *New York Times,* April 21, 1959.

29. In London, Van's recital was called a "triumph" and "brilliant," as quoted by UPI in the *Dallas Morning News,* "London Critics Give Texas Van Praise, Advice," June 9, 1959. In Milan he "got a resounding ovation" at the La Scala Opera house, as quoted by AP in the *Chicago Tribune,* "Pianist Van Cliburn Applauded at La Scala," June 17, 1959.

30. James Dickson interviewed by Howard Reich, July 1991.

31. Farnsworth Fowle, "Van Cliburn Sees Soviet Fair Here: Pianist Is Surprised to Find His Picture Being Used on Lid of Candy Box," *New York Times,* July 27, 1959.

32. Ibid.

33. Reuters, "Russian Book on Cliburn," *New York Times,* Aug. 1, 1959.

34. Ray Ericson, "Van Cliburn's Rachmaninoff: A Devotion Encompassing All," *High Fidelity,* Aug. 1959.

35. Ibid.

36. John Pfeiffer interviewed by Howard Reich, Nov. 1991.

37. Bernie Asbell, "Cliburn Mulls Next Classical Wax Entry," *Billboard,* Aug. 10, 1959.

38. Ibid.

39. Max Wilcox interviewed by Howard Reich, March 1992.

40. Alan Kayes interviewed by Howard Reich, March 1992.

41. John Pfeiffer interviewed by Howard Reich, Nov. 1991.

42. "Struggle," *New Yorker,* Aug. 22, 1959.

43. Ibid.

44. Walter Arlen, "Second Concert Yields Even Bigger Results: Gala Atmosphere Was Same, but Difference Was Famed Piano Soloist's Repertoire," *Los Angeles Times,* Sept. 5, 1959.

45. Maxine Cheshire, "Red-Letter Day," *Washington Post,* Sept. 20, 1959.

46. AP, "Khrushchev Hugs Cliburn and Invites Him to Soviet," *New York Times,* Sept. 25, 1959.

47. Ibid.

48. AP, "Cliburn Visits Plane: Khrushchev TU-114 Described by Pianist, Soviet Guest," *New York Times,* Sept. 26, 1959.

49. Edwin H. Schloss, "Pension Concert at Academy: Cliburn Shifts to Schumann, Brahms," *Philadelphia Inquirer*, Dec. 18, 1959.

50. Max de Schauensee, "Cliburn in Full Rapport With Orchestra, Wins Ovation With Schumann and Brahms Concertos," *Philadelphia Evening Bulletin,* Dec. 18, 1959.

51. "Death Called 'Passing of Era,'" *Shreveport Times,* March 6, 1974.

52. "Hurok Signs Cliburn: Pianist Switches Management From Columbia Artists," *New York Times,* Dec. 5, 1959.

53. "Fur-Collar Impresario: Solomon Hurok," *New York Times,* April 15, 1958.

54. Ibid.

55. Arthur Rubinstein, *My Many Years* (New York: Alfred A. Knopf, 1980), p. 599.

56. Susan Tilley interviewed by Howard Reich, March 1992.

57. Sim Myers, "Van Cliburn Returning as Recitalist," *Chicago Tribune,* Feb. 28, 1960.

58. Martin Feinstein interviewed by Howard Reich, April 1991.

59. Doug Steinriede interviewed by Howard Reich, March 1992.

60. "Piano Award Created: Van Cliburn Donates $5,000 for Rosina Lhevinne Prize," *New York Times,* Jan. 19, 1960; "Lhevinne Award Established by Pianist Cliburn," *Dallas Morning News,* Jan. 20, 1960; "Juilliard Lhevinne Award Established by Cliburn," *Musical Courier,* Feb. 1960.

61. "Van Presents $4,000 Gift To Symphony," *Dallas Morning News,* May 18, 1960.

62. John Briggs, "Moscow State Symphony and Cliburn Play for 16,100 at Madison Square Garden," *New York Times,* Feb. 15, 1960.

63. Edwin H. Schloss, "Van Cliburn Triumphs In First Phila. Recital," *Philadelphia Inquirer,* March 12, 1960. Specifically, Schloss noted that Van's reading of Brahms Intermezzi (op. 118, nos. 1 and 2) showed "lyric loveliness," his performance of Brahms' Ballade in G minor (op. 118, no. 3) was "impassioned."

64. John Rosenfield, "Texas Prodigy 'Informs' On Polish Master," *Dallas Morning News,* April 22, 1960.

65. Claudia Cassidy, "Van Cliburn's First Chicago Recital an Evening of Paradoxes," *Chicago Tribune,* March 9, 1960.

66. Claudia Cassidy, "Cliburn Proves Worth with Reiner in Stunning Brahms' Second," *Chicago Tribune,* April 8, 1960.

67. Van Cliburn interviewed by Howard Reich, 1991-92.

68. Claudia Cassidy interviewed by Howard Reich, March 1991.

69. Seymour Raven interviewed by Howard Reich, March 1992.

70. Claudia Cassidy, "Cliburn, Reiner, and the orchestra in Brilliant Tuesday Farewell," *Chicago Tribune,* April 13, 1960.

71. UPI, "Moscow Cheers Greet Cliburn: Flowers Tossed at U.S. Pianist," *Chicago Tribune,* May 27, 1960.

72. UPI, "Van Cliburn Mobbed by His Moscow Fans," *Chicago Tribune,* June 4, 1960.

73. Gennady Rozhdestvensky interviewed by Howard Reich, July 1991.

74. Roberta Peters interviewed by Howard Reich, March 1992.

75. AP, "Van Cliburn Mobbed by His Moscow Fans," *Chicago Tribune,* June 4, 1960.

76. AP, "Oldest Soviet Music Teacher Lauds Cliburn," *Shreveport Times,* June 4, 1960, quoting Tass.

77. Ashchen Mikoyan interviewed by Howard Reich, March 1992.

78. These remarks were quoted in two pieces: AP, "Van Cliburn Gets More Raves From Critics in Moscow," *Dallas Morning News,* June 12, 1960; Reuters, "Cliburn Lauded by Red Critics," *Chicago Tribune,* June 13, 1960.

79. AP, "More Cheers For Cliburn," *Pittsburgh Post-Gazette,* June 17, 1960.

80. UPI, "Red Teenagers Mob Van Cliburn At Final Concert," *Dallas Morning News,* July 20, 1960.

81. "Cliburn Plays Debut Concerto," *Dallas Morning News,* July 23, 1960.

82. Margaret McDonald, "Mobil Moves H. L. Cliburn To Shreveport," *Shreveport Journal,* Sept. 9, 1960; "Van Cliburn Lonely Man—of Necessity," *Shreveport Times,* Oct. 21, 1966.

83. Robert W. Dumm, "National Scene," *Musical Courier,* Dec. 1960; *Musical America,* Dec. 1960.

84. Thomas Willis, "Van Cliburn to Be Soloist with Symphony This Week," *Chicago Tribune,* Oct. 16, 1960.

85. Albert Goldberg, "Van Cliburn and Walter Show Brahms Mastery," *Los Angeles Times,* Dec. 5, 1960.

86. Van Cliburn interviewed by Howard Reich, 1991-92.

87. Doug Steinriede interviewed by Howard Reich, March 1992.

88. Max Wilcox interviewed by Howard Reich, March 1992.

89. Ivan Davis interviewed by Howard Reich, March 1992.

90. John Pfeiffer interviewed by Howard Reich, Nov. 1991.

91. Raymond Boswell interviewed by Howard Reich, July 1991.

92. Van Cliburn interviewed by Howard Reich, 1991-92.

93. Doug Steinriede interviewed by Howard Reich, March 1992.

94. John Shenaut interviewed by Howard Reich, Aug. 1991.

95. "Van Cliburn on Good-Will Mission," *Piano Guild Notes,* Jan./Feb. 1961.

96. "Mexicans Wild Over Van Cliburn," *Dallas Morning News,* Feb. 14, 1961.

97. Lillian Libman interviewed by Howard Reich, March 1992.

98. "Breaks In As Conductor: Van Cliburn Expends $1,800 to Privately Rehearse in L.A.," *Variety,* Feb. 22, 1961.

99. Van Cliburn interviewed by Howard Reich, 1991-92.

100. Paul Hume, "Autograph Hunters Disappointed: Cliburn, Tied Up in District Traffic, Keeps Audience Waiting 22 Minutes," *Washington Post,* March 6, 1961.

101. Trudy Goth, "Van Cliburn as Conductor, Touching Tributes Mark Mitropoulos Memorial," *Variety,* March 15, 1961.

102. John Ardoin, "Memorial Concert For Mitropoulos," *Musical America,* May 1961.

103. "$10,000 Prize Piano Competition Planned," *Musical America,* March 1961.

104. John Rosenfield, "Cliburn Gives Ft. Worth Lift," *Dallas Morning News,* March 28, 1961.

105. Serge Saxe, "Dallas-Fort Worth," *Musical Courier,* May 1961.

106. "Hurok Will Sign Cliburn Winner," *Dallas Morning News,* Sept. 22, 1961.

107. Roger E. Jacobi interviewed by Howard Reich, July 1991.

108. Van Cliburn, Foreword to Norma Lee Browning, *Joe Maddy of Interlochen* (New York: Henry Regnery Company, 1963).

109. Roger E. Jacobi interviewed by Howard Reich, July 1991.

110. John Ardoin, *Musical America,* Sept. 1961.

111. UPI, "Van Cliburn Plays For Free Berlin," *Dallas Morning News,* Aug. 31, 1961.

112. Ross Parmenter, "Music: Van Cliburn Plays: He Is Soloist in 'Emperor' Concerto With Symphony of the Air at Carnegie Hall," *New York Times,* Nov. 27, 1961.

113. Harold C. Schonberg, "Music: Van Cliburn With Philadelphia Orchestra: Work by Beethoven Played by Pianist," *New York Times,* Dec. 13, 1961.

114. William A. Payne, "Cliburn Makes Classical Album History," *Dallas Morning News,* Dec. 29, 1961.

115. Ibid.

116. Van Cliburn interviewed by Howard Reich, 1991-92.

117. William A. Payne, "Cliburn Makes Classical Album History," *Dallas Morning News,* Dec. 29, 1961.

118. See the discography section of this book for a fuller analysis of Van's recorded output.

119. Richard Mohr interviewed by Howard Reich, March 1992.

120. James Mathis interviewed by Howard Reich, Jan. 1992.

121. Ibid.

122. Van Cliburn interviewed by Howard Reich, 1991-92.

123. Red Skelton interviewed by Howard Reich, Oct. 1992.

124. Van Cliburn interviewed by Howard Reich, 1991-92.

125. Albert Goldberg, "Cliburn's Concert Variable," *Los Angeles Times,* Feb. 26, 1962.

126. Claudia Cassidy, "Superb Sound, Dreamy Rachmaninoff and Rich, Autumnal Brahms," *Chicago Tribune,* March 30, 1962.

127. UPI, "Moscow Cheers Cliburn Return," *Dallas Morning News,* June 14, 1962.

128. "Rildia Bee," *New Yorker,* Dec. 17, 1990.

129. AP, "Nikita Joins In Applause For Cliburn," *Chicago Tribune,* June 15, 1962.

130. Gustav A. Alink, *International Piano Competitions, Book 3, The Results* (Hungary: Gustav A. Alink, 1990).

131. Van Cliburn interviewed by Howard Reich, 1991-92.

132. Vladimir Ashkenazy interviewed by Howard Reich, July 1991.

133. AP, "Cliburn Given Vienna Ovation," *Dallas Morning News,* June 25, 1962.

134. Joseph Lapid, "Cliburn's Texas-Size Ovations In Israel," *Variety,* Sept. 5, 1962.

135. Albert Goldberg, "Israelis Acclaim Pianist Van Cliburn," *Los Angeles Times,* Sept. 6, 1962.

136. "Cliburn Contest Opens Tomorrow: Fort Worth Event Honoring Pianist Has $10,000 Prize," *New York Times,* Sept. 23, 1962.

137. Martha Hyder interviewed by Howard Reich, March 1992.

138. "Cliburn Contest Opens Tomorrow: Fort Worth Event Honoring Pianist Has $10,000 Prize," *New York Times,* Sept. 23, 1962.

139. Ralph Votapek interviewed by Howard Reich, Feb. 1991.

140. Donald Steinfirst, "Van Cliburn Features Concert by Symphony: Pianist Departs from Usual Custom In Program; Orchestra in Good Form," *Pittsburgh Post-Gazette,* Jan. 5, 1963.

141. Albert Goldberg, "Cliburn, Monteux Triumph in Brahms Piano concerto," *Los Angeles Times,* Feb. 23, 1963.

142. Claudia Cassidy, "Reiner, Cliburn and the Orchestra on a Night Rich in Music," *Chicago Tribune,* April 20, 1963.

143. Henry W. Levinger, *Musical America,* June 1963.

144. Albert Goldberg, "Van Cliburn Proves His Greatness," *Los Angeles Times,* Oct. 3, 1963.

145. Herbert Elwell, "Cliburn Performs With Force, Skill," *Cleveland Plain Dealer,* Feb. 17, 1964.

146. Daniel Webster, "At the Academy: Van Cliburn Crown Remains Untarnished," *Philadelphia Inquirer,* March 2, 1964.

147. Paul Hume, "4000 Persons Jam Constitution Hall to Hear Van Cliburn," *Washington Post,* Nov. 20, 1964.

148. H. Charles Smith interviewed by Howard Reich, July 1991.

149. Samuel L. Singer, "At Robin Hood Dell: Van Cliburn Podium Debut Rained Out," *Philadelphia Inquirer,* Aug. 2, 1963.

150. Ibid.

151. James Felton, "Cliburn Wins Ovation As Conductor and Pianist," *Philadelphia Evening Bulletin,* Aug. 3, 1963.

152. Ibid.

153. "Concert At Dell Is Led By Cliburn: Pianist Conducts Orchestra in Season's Last Program," *New York Times,* Aug. 4, 1963.

154. Raymond Ericson, "Cliburn Conducts at Stadium: Pianist Also Soloist in Prokofiev Concerto," *New York Times,* July 20, 1964.

155. Robert Finn, "Pert Luci Shows Her Pluck at Interlochen," *Cleveland Plain Dealer,* July 24, 1964.

156. "It's Dr. Cliburn Now," *Dallas Morning News,* Aug. 26, 1964.

157. AP, "Van Cliburn Is Named Churchman of the Year," *Ft. Worth Star-Telegram,* Nov. 13, 1964; "Churchman of Year," *New Orleans Times-Picayune,* Nov. 19, 1964.

158. Claudia Cassidy, "Cliburn Comes Late, but in a Long Stride Since His Last Recital," *Chicago Tribune,* March 15, 1965.

159. AP, "Cliburn Scores Again in Russia," *Pittsburgh Post-Gazette,* June 7, 1965.

160. AP, "Red Audience Likes Cliburn as Conductor," *Ft. Worth Star-Telegram,* June 14, 1965.

161. Paul Hume, "Cliburn Plays for Time in Feud Over His Billing," *Washington Post,* Oct. 20, 1965.

162. AP, "At Concert Time, Where's Cliburn?" *Chicago Tribune,* Oct. 21, 1965; AP, "Cliburn's Better Late Than Never in Mixup," *Ft. Worth Star-Telegram,* Oct. 21, 1966.

163. UPI, "President Hears Van Cliburn Sing National Anthem," *Chicago Tribune,* Oct. 13, 1966.

164. Daniel Webster, "Cliburn Cheered by 30,000, Plays 6 Encores," *Philadelphia Inquirer,* July 26, 1966.

165. Martin Bernheimer, "Cliburn-Kondrashin Reunion at Bowl a Disappointing One," *Los Angeles Times,* Aug. 4, 1966.

166. AP, "Russians Boycott Cliburn Contest," *Shreveport Times,* Sept. 18, 1966.

167. Norma Lee Browning, "Unspoiled Van Cliburn Hasn't 'Gone Hollywood,'" *Chicago Tribune,* April 29, 1966; Jack Gould, "TV: Van Cliburn Portrait," *New York Times,* Oct. 17, 1966.

168. Liu Shih Kun interviewed by Howard Reich, Oct. 1991.

169. "Cliburn Takes LBJ's Measure: A Tall Pianist Suits Up at White House," *Washington Post,* Oct. 15, 1967.

170. "Van Cliburn Here to Visit Mrs. Lankford," *Ft. Worth Star-Telegram,* Sept. 21, 1967.

171. "Van Cliburn Expresses Sympathy," *Ft. Worth Star-Telegram,* Oct. 31, 1967.

172. Daniel Webster, "At the Academy: Cliburn 'Proves' Repertory," *Philadelphia Inquirer,* Feb. 24, 1967.

173. Samuel L. Singer, "At the Academy: Van Cliburn Presents Combination Recital To Overflow Audience," *Philadelphia Inquirer,* March 11, 1968.

174. Michael Steinberg, "Cliburn: Great, but Could Do Better," *Boston Globe,* April 3, 1967.

175. Robert Finn, "Barber Sonata Is Top Van Cliburn Event," *Cleveland Plain Dealer,* April 6, 1968.

176. Harold C. Schonberg, "Music: Steinberg Leads Philharmonic in New Sessions Work: Van Cliburn Performs Concerto by Chopin," *New York Times,* May 3, 1968.

177. "Van Cliburn at Interlochen ... It's Unforgettable," *Muskegon Chronicle,* July 15, 1968.

178. Donald Steinfirst, "Cliburn Impressive in Recital," *Pittsburgh Post-Gazette,* May 19, 1969.

179. Harry Neville, "Concert-goers hear new Cliburn classic," *Boston Globe,* March 3, 1969.

180. "Pianists: The Artist as Culture Hero," *Time* magazine, Nov. 22, 1968.

181. Ibid.

182. "Packed House Exhilarated By Performance of Cliburn," *Ft. Worth Star-Telegram,* March 25, 1969.

183. Claire Eyrich, "Cliburn Greets Artists," *Ft. Worth Star-Telegram,* Sept. 29, 1969.

184. *Ft. Worth Star-Telegram,* Oct. 6, 1969.

185. *Ft. Worth Star-Telegram,* Feb. 9, 1969.

186. Martha Hyder interviewed by Howard Reich, March 1992.

187. Samuel L. Singer, "Van Cliburn Plays Weather—and Wins," *Philadelphia Inquirer,* July 24, 1970.

188. "Cliburn Draws 18,667; Next Follows Rock," *Variety,* June 23, 1967.

189. "Record Crowd of 4,200 Hears Cliburn Perform At Inter-lochen," *Muskegon Chronicle,* July 19, 1971.

190. "Capacity Crowd Applauds Cliburn at Academy," *Philadelphia Inquirer,* Dec. 6, 1971.

191. *Los Angeles Times,* April 8, 1971.

192. Donal Henahan wrote in *High Fidelity* magazine, "Cliburn's Barber [Piano Sonata], more nearly than [John] Browning's, fits the Horowitz mold. He solves the complications of the fugue particularly well, RCA's piano sound (and Cliburn's, of course) is rich at bottom and evenly distributed all the way up, losing out only at the top octave where the best piano recordings take on overtones of sheen and shimmer. . . . Under the circumstances, considering recorded sound as well as interpretative and more technical command, one can happily recommend the Cliburn."

From Donal Henahan "Barber's Piano Sonata Revisited—Cliburn and Browning vs. Horowitz," *High Fidelity,* Jan. 1972.

Paul Hume wrote in the *Washington Post,* "Van Cliburn has hit every kind of jackpot with his newest Victor recording, 3229. It combines his finest playing in every department in the sonatas of Samuel Barber and the Sixth Sonata of Prokofiev, the latter being the one for which he was so highly praised in his Constitution Hall concert last week."

From Paul Hume, "Van Cliburn's Finest Playing," *Washington Post,* Jan. 2, 1972.

193. Harris Goldsmith, "Van Cliburn—True to Form on Six New Releases," *High Fidelity,* March 1972.

194. John Pfeiffer interviewed by Howard Reich, Nov. 1991.

195. Copyright © 1973 Hachette Magazines, Inc. All rights reserved. Excerpted from Jack Somer, "Tales from the Studio: Van Cliburn, Crooner," *Stereo Review,* Dec. 1973, with permission.

196. John Shenaut interviewed by Howard Reich, Aug. 1991.

197. "U.S. Stars Due in Soviet At Same Time as Nixon," *New York Times,* May 15, 1972.

198. UPI, "Cliburn Scores a Hit," *Shreveport Journal,* May 23, 1972.

199. Robert B. Semple, Jr., "President Honors Leningrad Dead; Calls For Peace," *New York Times*, May 28, 1972.

200. Roberta Peters interviewed by Howard Reich, March 1992.

201. UPI, "Van Cliburn Completes Soviet Tour," *Shreveport Times*, June 10, 1972.

202. AP, "Kilgore Honors Van Cliburn," *Ft. Worth Star-Telegram*, Sept. 25, 1972.

203. *New York Times*, Feb. 24, 1973; UPI, "Van Cliburn to play at White House," *Chicago Tribune*, Feb. 24, 1973.

204. *New York Times*, April 5, 1973.

205. Martin Bernheimer, "The Merchandising of an Artist," *Los Angeles Times*, June 15, 1973.

206. Ibid.

207. AP, "Critics like Van's music, not his garb," *Chicago Tribune*, June 18, 1973.

208. Gary Graffman interviewed by Howard Reich, July 1991.

209. Leonard Eureka, "Cliburn Benefit Pulls Near Sell-Out Crowd," *Ft. Worth Star-Telegram*, March 17, 1973.

210. AP, "Cliburn Prize Goes To Soviet," *Shreveport Times*, Oct. 1, 1973.

211. Vladimir Viardo interviewed by Howard Reich, July 1991.

CHAPTER TEN

1. AP, "Harvey Cliburn, Pianist's Father, Dies At Age 75," *Ft. Worth Star-Telegram*, Jan. 13, 1974.

2. Raymond Boswell interviewed by Howard Reich, July 1991.

3. James Mathis interviewed by Howard Reich, Jan. 1992.

4. Margaret McDonald, "Van Cliburn Lonely Man—of Necessity," *Shreveport Journal*, Oct. 21, 1966.

5. Raymond Boswell interviewed by Howard Reich, July 1991.

6. "In Praise of Leontyne," *Opera News*, Jan. 23, 1982.

7. Louise Jeter interviewed by Howard Reich, July 1991.

8. Alice Whittlesey interviewed by Howard Reich, Aug. 1991.

9. James Dickson interviewed by Howard Reich, July 1991.

10. Susan Tilley interviewed by Howard Reich, March 1992.

11. John Shenaut interviewed by Howard Reich, Aug. 1991.

12. Margaret McDonald, "Van Cliburn Lonely Man—of Necessity," *Shreveport Journal,* Oct. 21, 1966.

13. "H. L. Cliburn Dies After Long Illness," *Shreveport Times,* Jan. 13, 1974.

14. Alden Whitman, "Sol Hurok, the Impresario, Dies at 85," *New York Times,* March 6, 1974.

15. Ibid.

16. Alan Kayes interviewed by Howard Reich, March 1992.

17. Lillian Libman interviewed by Howard Reich, March 1992.

18. Deirdre Carmody, "Hurok Rites Fill Carnegie Hall," *New York Times,* March 9, 1974.

19. Ibid.

20. Ibid.

21. Tim Page, "The Lone Star Pianist," *Newsday,* June 11, 1989.

22. Van Cliburn interviewed by Howard Reich, 1991-92.

23. David Daniel, "Music: As he prepares for a rare concert appearance, Van Cliburn talks with David Daniel," *Vogue,* Oct. 1990.

24. Tim Page, "The Lone Star Pianist," *Newsday,* June 11, 1989.

25. Mary Meador, "Cliburn feels he has been privileged," *Kilgore News Herald,* Oct. 4, 1990.

26. Daniel Webster, "Cliburn: Same old requests but played with good grace," *Philadelphia Inquirer,* July 31, 1977.

27. Annette Davies Morgan interviewed by Howard Reich, July 1991.

28. Lottie Guttry interviewed by Howard Reich, July 1991.

29. Harold Shaw interviewed by Howard Reich, May 1991.

30. Edward Gordon interviewed by Howard Reich, July 1991.

31. Shura Cherkassky interviewed by Howard Reich, June 1991.

32. Glenn Plaskin, *Horowitz: A Biography of Vladimir Horowitz* (New York: Quill, 1983), pp. 178, 183-90, 277-283, 382-387.

33. John Browning interviewed by Howard Reich, July 1991.

34. William Schuman interviewed by Howard Reich, March 1991.

35. Alexis Weissenberg interviewed by Howard Reich, June 1991.

36. Oxana Yablonskaya interviewed by Howard Reich, March 1991.

37. Van Cliburn interviewed by Howard Reich, 1991-92.

38. Michael Fleming, "Van Cliburn Reflects on the Past and a Possible Future," *New York Times*, June 9, 1985.

39. John Pfeiffer interviewed by Howard Reich, Nov. 1991.

40. Raymond Boswell interviewed by Howard Reich, July 1991.

41. Daniel Webster, "Cliburn Works Magic at Dell," *Philadelphia Inquirer*, July 26, 1974.

42. "Shreveport Symphony, Cliburn," *High Fidelity/Musical America*, Jan. 1975.

43. Joseph McLellan, "Deserved Applause for Van Cliburn," *Washington Post*, March 22, 1975.

44. Daniel Webster, "Cliburn's play vigorous, lively in new Dell," *Philadelphia Inquirer*, June 22, 1976.

45. Daniel Webster, "Cliburn mystique strong, but recitation is flat," *Philadelphia Inquirer*, Aug. 3, 1977.

46. Martin Bernheimer, "Nostalgia, Beethoven in Daisy Dell," *Los Angeles Times*, Aug. 11, 1975.

47. Thomas Willis, "When the mind wanders so do the fingers," *Chicago Tribune*, July 18, 1974.

48. Albin Krebs, *New York Times*, April 13, 1974.

49. Robert Finn, "Study in keyboard contrasts," *Cleveland Plain Dealer*, Sept. 7, 1975.

50. Robert Finn, "Van Cliburn Conducts: Pert Luci Shows Her Pluck at Interlochen," *Cleveland Plain Dealer*, July 24, 1964.

51. Robert Finn, "Gray Day Project for Cliburn: Opera," *Cleveland Plain Dealer*, Aug. 2, 1964.

52. Joseph McLellan, "Deserved Applause for Van Cliburn," *Washington Post*, March 22, 1975.

53. Harold C. Schonberg, "Cliburn Recalls '58 Event As Piano Semifinals Start," *New York Times*, May 26, 1981.

54. Donal Henahan, "What Makes a Gifted Artist Drop Out in Mid-Career?" *New York Times*, Aug. 17, 1986.

55. Igor Kipnis, "Rachmaninoff By Cliburn: An album of works for solo piano reveals a decided flair for a virtuoso repertoire," *Stereo Review,* May, 1974.

56. Larry Kart, "Just for the record, Brahms thrives in the hands of Cliburn," *Chicago Tribune,* June 5, 1977.

57. Max Wilcox interviewed by Howard Reich, March 1992.

58. Michael Fleming, "Van Cliburn Reflects on the Past and a Possible Future," *New York Times,* June 9, 1885.

59. Guenter Hensler interviewed by Howard Reich, Nov. 1991.

60. "Van Cliburn Establishes Scholarship," *Dallas Morning News,* May 30, 1974.

61. Jean M. White, "The Arts Council, Plus 10," *Washington Post,* Sept. 4, 1974.

62. Raymond Ericson, "Rosina Lhevinne, Pianist, Is Dead; Juilliard Teacher of Noted Students," *New York Times,* Nov. 11, 1976.

63. John Ardoin, "Triumphs and Turmoil at the Cliburn Competition," *New York Times,* Oct. 9, 1977.

64. Ibid.

65. Leon Fleisher and John Giordano, "Music Mailbag: Winners And Sinners at The Cliburn," *New York Times,* Oct. 30, 1977.

66. Ibid.

67. Glenn Giffin, "Concert Hall a Winner in First Test," *Denver Post,* March 5, 1978.

68. Boris Nelson, "Van Cliburn Guest: Toledo Symphony Opens 35th Season At Masonic," *Toledo Blade,* Oct. 1, 1978.

69. Robert Finn, "Study in keyboard contrasts," *Cleveland Plain Dealer,* Sept. 7, 1975.

70. John Pfeiffer interviewed by Howard Reich, Nov. 1991.

71. John Browning interviewed by Howard Reich, July 1991.

72. Daniel Webster, "Cliburn: Same old requests but played with good grace," *Philadelphia Inquirer,* July 31, 1977.

73. Wayne Lee Gay, *Ft. Worth Star-Telegram,* May 4, 1989.

74. John Pfeiffer interviewed by Howard Reich, Nov. 1991.

75. John Giordano interviewed by Howard Reich, March 1992.

76. James Mathis interviewed by Howard Reich, Jan. 1992.

77. Naomi Graffman interviewed by Howard Reich, July 1991.

78. Skitch Henderson interviewed by Howard Reich, March 1991.

79. Martin Feinstein interviewed by Howard Reich, April 1991.

80. Harold Shaw interviewed by Howard Reich, May 1991.

81. Earl Wild interviewed by Howard Reich, March 1991.

82. Schuyler Chapin interviewed by Howard Reich, March 1991.

83. Eugene Istomin interviewed by Howard Reich, March 1991.

84. Alexander Schneider interviewed by Howard Reich, July 1991.

85. James Roos, "Stalled Van: Pianist Cliburn, 'The Texan Who Conquered Russia,' continues a 4-1/2-year 'intermission,'" *Miami Herald,* as reprinted in *New Orleans Times-Picayune,* April 24, 1983.

86. Van Cliburn interviewed by Howard Reich, 1991-92.

87. John Giordano interviewed by Howard Reich, March 1992.

88. Susan Tilley interviewed by Howard Reich, March 1992.

89. Glenn Collins, "At Juilliard's 75th Jubilee, A Harmony of Gratitude," *New York Times,* Dec. 19, 1980.

90. Harold C. Schonberg, "Schub Wins Cliburn Piano Competition," New York Times, June 1, 1981.

91. Cissy Stewart, "Van Cliburn in the pink," *Ft. Worth Star-Telegram,* March 10, 1982.

92. "Pianist, physician to get TCU honor," *Ft. Worth Star-Telegram,* May 8, 1982.

93. "National Citations To Outstanding Individuals and Organizations," *Music Clubs* magazine, Summer 1983.

94. Cissy Stewart, "Cliburn parties exhausting and fascinating," *Ft. Worth Star-Telegram,* April 24, 1983.

95. Ross Parmenter, "Song Recital Given by Leontyne Price," *New York Times,* Nov. 15, 1954; Harold C. Schonberg, "Symphonic Epigram," *New York Times,* Nov. 15, 1954.

96. "National Citations To Outstanding Individuals and Organizations," *Music Clubs* magazine, Summer 1983.

97. Claire Eyrich, "Kilgore College to honor Cliburn," *Ft. Worth Star-Telegram,* May 5, 1985; Perry Stewart, "Cliburn takes a bow again," *Ft. Worth Star-Telegram,* May 12, 1985.

98. "Van Cliburn: Sheds shyness for competition," *Ft. Worth Star-Telegram,* March 18, 1985.

99. Michael Fleming, "Van Cliburn Reflects on the Past and a Possible Future," *New York Times,* June 9, 1985.

100. Ibid.

101. Ibid.

102. Barry Douglas interviewed by Howard Reich, Aug. 1991.

103. Cissy Stewart, "Cliburn to make Westover Hills his new home," *Ft. Worth Star-Telegram,* Oct. 21, 1985.

104. John Pfeiffer interviewed by Howard Reich, Nov. 1991.

105. David Daniel, "Music: As he prepares for a rare concert appearance, Van Cliburn talks with David Daniel," *Vogue,* Oct. 1990.

106. John Davidson, "Every Good Boy Does Fine," *Texas Monthly,* May 1987.

107. John Giordano interviewed by Howard Reich.

108. Carol Nuckols, *Ft. Worth Star-Telegram,* Jan. 10, 1990.

109. Maryln Schwartz, "Life with Van and Rildia Bee," *Dallas Morning News,* June 26, 1989.

110. Joan Barthel, "Eight Years Later: Has Success Spoiled Van Cliburn?" *New York Times,* Oct. 9, 1966.

111. John Ardoin, "The Return Of Van Cliburn: Pianist says he never expected his 'intermission' to last 10 years," *Dallas Morning News,* Feb. 21, 1988.

112. Victor Borge interviewed by Howard Reich, April 1991.

113. Leon Fleisher interviewed by Howard Reich, June 1991.

114. Edward Gordon interviewed by Howard Reich, July 1991.

115. Yehudi Menuhin interviewed by Howard Reich, Oct. 1991.

116. Garrick Ohlssen interviewed by Howard Reich, Oct. 1991.

117. Ned Rorem interviewed by Howard Reich, Oct. 1991.

118. Eugene Istomin interviewed by Howard Reich, March 1991.

119. Nicolas Slonimsky, *Baker's Biographical Dictionary of Musicians* (New York: Schirmer Books, 1984, seventh ed.), p. 1,980.

120. Barry Douglas interviewed by Howard Reich, Aug. 1991.

121. Vladimir Ashkenazy interviewed by Howard Reich, July 1991.

122. James Roos, "Stalled Van: Pianist Cliburn, 'The Texan Who Conquered Russia,' continues a 4-1/2-year 'intermission,'" *Miami Herald*, as reprinted in the *New Orleans Times-Picayune*, by James Roos, April 24, 1983.

CHAPTER ELEVEN

1. Van Cliburn interviewed by Howard Reich, 1991-92.
2. Ibid.
3. Ibid.
4. Marice Richter, "Van Cliburn's Mother Always Demanded The Best," *Dallas Morning News*, Nov. 8, 1987.
5. Van Cliburn interviewed by Howard Reich, 1991-92.
6. Carol Nuckols, *Ft. Worth Star-Telegram*, Jan. 10, 1990.
7. Van Cliburn interviewed by Howard Reich, 1991-92.
8. Jean Warner Stark, *American Music Teacher*, Nov./Dec. 1961.
9. Annette Davies Morgan interviewed by Howard Reich, July 1991.
10. Joyce Anne Goyne Stanley interviewed by Howard Reich, July 1991.
11. John Giordano interviewed by Howard Reich, March 1992.
12. H. Charles Smith interviewed by Howard Reich, July 1991.
13. Rosario Mazzeo interviewed by Howard Reich, March 1992.
14. John Pfeiffer interviewed by Howard Reich, Nov. 1991.
15. Ibid.
16. Max Wilcox interviewed by Howard Reich, March 1992.
17. James Mathis interviewed by Howard Reich, Jan. 1992.
18. Naomi Graffman interviewed by Howard Reich, July 1991.
19. Jeaneane Dowis interviewed by Howard Reich, May 1991.
20. Bob Doerschuk, "Van Cliburn," *Contemporary Keyboard*, April 1978.21. Van Cliburn interviewed by Howard Reich, 1991-92.
22. Joan Barthel, "Eight Years Later: Has Success Spoiled Van Cliburn?" *New York Times*, Oct. 9, 1966.
23. Van Cliburn interviewed by Howard Reich, 1991-92.

24. Ibid.
25. Ibid.

CHAPTER TWELVE

1. John Giordano interviewed by Howard Reich, March 1992.
2. Martha Hyder interviewed by Howard Reich, March 1992.
3. Susan Tilley interviewed by Howard Reich, March 1992.
4. Lillian Libman interviewed by Howard Reich, March 1992.
5. Rita Wolf, "Van Cliburn and Forth Worth: In Harmony," *Aura,* Jan./Feb. 1991.
6. Jean-Pierre Rampal interviewed by Howard Reich, Aug. 1991.
7. Wayne Lee Gay, "As Fort Worth applauds the echoes of his Moscow triumph, the world waits for the sound of Cliburn's fingers," *Ft. Worth Star-Telegram,* May 21, 1989.
8. Ibid.
9. Ibid.
10. Wayne Lee Gay, "A maestro's encore: Van Cliburn says he'll play at summit to end long hiatus," *Ft. Worth Star-Telegram,* Nov. 27, 1987.
11. Susan Tilley interviewed by Howard Reich, March 1992.
12. Wayne Lee Gay, "A maestro's encore: Van Cliburn says he'll play at summit to end long hiatus," *Ft. Worth Star-Telegram,* Nov. 27, 1987.
13. Zubin Mehta interviewed by Howard Reich, March 1992.
14. Wayne Lee Gay, "A maestro's encore: Van Cliburn says he'll play at summit to end long hiatus," *Ft. Worth Star-Telegram,* Nov. 27, 1987; Wayne Lee Gay, "Pianist is an old hand at thawing Soviet hearts," *Ft. Worth Star-Telegram,* Nov. 27, 1987.
15. John Giordano interviewed by Howard Reich, March 1992.
16. Raymond Boswell interviewed by Howard Reich, July 1991.
17. AP, "Cliburn to play at Gorbachev dinner: Dec. 8 performance will be his first in public since 1978," *Shreveport Times,* Nov. 17, 1987.
18. Wayne Lee Gay, "Cliburn might play in Soviet Union, sources say," *Ft. Worth Star-Telegram,* Jan. 21, 1988.

19. Wayne Lee Gay, "A Cliburn piano goes grandly," *Ft. Worth Star-Telegram,* Dec. 5, 1987.

20. Susan Tilley interviewed by Howard Reich, March 1992.

21. Ibid.

22. Howard Reich, "Power playing: After 10 years, Van Cliburn returns to the center of the world's stage," *Chicago Tribune,* March 6, 1988.

23. Michael Kilian and Lisa Anderson, "White House Glitter Caps Historic Day," *Chicago Tribune,* Dec. 9, 1987.

24. Ibid; and Wayne Lee Gay, "Cliburn returns in grand style," *Ft. Worth Star-Telegram,* Dec. 9, 1987.

25. Howard Reich, "Power playing: After 10 years, Van Cliburn returns to the center of the world's stage," *Chicago Tribune,* March 6, 1988.

26. Susan Tilley interviewed by Howard Reich, March 1992.

27. Michael Kilian and Lisa Anderson, "White House Glitter Caps Historic Day," *Chicago Tribune,* Dec. 9, 1987.

28. Wayne Lee Gay, "Cliburn returns in grand style," *Ft. Worth Star-Telegram,* Dec. 9, 1987.

29. Howard Reich, "Power playing: After 10 years, Van Cliburn returns to the center of the world's stage," *Chicago Tribune,* March 6, 1988.

30. Zubin Mehta interviewed by Howard Reich, March 1992.

31. Wayne Lee Gay, "Cliburn returns in grand style," *Ft. Worth Star-Telegram,* Dec. 9, 1987.

32. Susan Tilley interviewed by Howard Reich, March 1992.

33. Ibid.

34. John Ardoin, "The Return Of Van Cliburn," *Dallas Morning News,* Feb. 21, 1988.

35. Wayne Lee Gay, "Cliburn might play in Soviet Union, sources say," *Ft. Worth Star-Telegram,* Jan. 21, 1988.

36. Wayne Lee Gay, "Cliburn declining tour offer," *Ft. Worth Star-Telegram,* March 24, 1988.

37. Wayne Lee Gay, "Dallas center to feature Cliburn, sources say," *Ft. Worth Star-Telegram,* June 10, 1988.

38. Van Cliburn interviewed by Howard Reich, 1991-92.

39. John Hawkins, "Van Cliburn Steps Out To Honor Bass Family," *Dallas Morning News,* Sept. 23, 1988.

40. Silvia Mann interviewed by Howard Reich, March 1992.

41. Wayne Lee Gay, "Tuning up," *Ft. Worth Star-Telegram,* May 4, 1989.

42. *New York Times* News Service, "South African Pianist Steven de Groote," *Chicago Tribune,* May 28, 1989.

43. Van Cliburn interviewed by Howard Reich, 1991-92.

44. *New York Times* News Service, "South African Pianist Steven de Groote," *Chicago Tribune*, May 28, 1989.

45. Ralph Votapek interviewed by Howard Reich, Feb. 1991.

46. Marlyn Schwartz, "Life with Van and Rildia Bee," *Dallas Morning News,* June 26, 1989.

47. Susan Tilley interviewed by Howard Reich, March 1992.

48. Stanislaw Skrowaczewski interviewed by Howard Reich, July 1991.

49. Joseph McLellan, "Van Cliburn's Triumphant Return: After an 11-Year Absence, Wowing a Crowd of 10,000," *Washington Post,* June 21, 1989.

50. Stanislaw Skrowaczewski interviewed by Howard Reich, July 1991.

51. AP, "Van Cliburn makes triumphant return after 11-year hiatus," *Pitt-sburgh Post-Gazette,* June 20, 1989.

52. Susan Tilley interviewed by Howard Reich, March 1992.

53. Silvia Mann interviewed by Howard Reich, March 1992.

54. Franz Mohr interviewed by Howard Reich, May 1991.

55. Donal Henahan, "Cliburn, With Orchestra, Returns in Concert Pitch," *New York Times,* June 21, 1989.

56. Joseph McLellan, "Van Cliburn's Triumphant Return: After an 11-Year Absence, Wowing a Crowd of 10,000," *Washington Post,* June 21, 1989.

57. Tom Di Nardo, Knight-Ridder Newspapers, "Van Cliburn's return to concert stage rewarding," *Chicago Tribune,* June 21, 1989.

58. Maryln Schwartz, "Life with Van and Rildia Bee," *Dallas Morning News,* June 26, 1989.

59. Donal Henahan, "Cliburn, With Orchestra, Returns in Concert Pitch," *New York Times,* June 21, 1989.

60. Ibid.

61. Joseph McLellan, "Van Cliburn's Triumphant Return: After an 11-Year Absence, Wowing a Crowd of 10,000," *Washington Post,* June 21, 1989.

62. Susan Tilley interviewed by Howard Reich, March 1992.

63. From a private document, "Trip Report—Moscow," by Susan Tilley, June 28-July 14, 1989. Used by permission.

64. Wayne Lee Gay, "Cliburn off to perform in Moscow," *Ft. Worth Star-Telegram,* June 28, 1989.

65. Maryln Schwartz, "Van Cliburn returns to scene of triumph: Pianist arrives in Moscow to gifts, groupies," *Dallas Morning News,* July 1, 1989.

66. From a private document, "Trip Report—Moscow," by Susan Tilley, June 28-July 14, 1989. Used by permission.

67. Susan Tilley interviewed by Howard Reich, March 1992.

68. From a private document, "Trip Report—Moscow," by Susan Tilley, June 28-July 14, 1989. Used by permission.

69. "Cliburn is in Moscow for a pair of concerts," *Ft. Worth Star-Telegram,* June 30, 1989.

70. Ibid.

71. "Cliburn goes to Russia with music," *Ft. Worth Star-Telegram,* July 1, 1989.

72. Maryln Schwartz, "Van Cliburn returns to scene of triumph: Pianist arrives in Moscow to gifts, groupies," *Dallas Morning News,* July 1, 1989.

73. From a private document, "Trip Report—Moscow," by Susan Tilley, June 28-July 14, 1989. Used by permission.

74. Ashchen Mikoyan interviewed by Howard Reich, March 1992.

75. From a private document, "Trip Report—Moscow," by Susan Tilley, June 28-July 14, 1989. Used by permission.

76. Ed Wierzbowski interviewed by Howard Reich, March 1992.

77. Ibid.

78. AP, "Cliburn Plays In Moscow," *New York Times,* July 3, 1989.

79. Vincent J. Schodolski, "Van Cliburn, Soviets renew their love affair," *Chicago Tribune,* July 4, 1989.

80. T. Elaine Carey, Cox News Service, "To Vanya with love: The Soviet people welcomed back Van Cliburn with open arms. 'In my heart I never left,' he said," *Ft. Worth Star-Telegram,* July 7, 1989.

81. Ed Wierzbowski interviewed by Howard Reich, March 1992.

82. John Ardoin, "Cliburn soars beyond musical limits: Long-awaited Soviet concert takes legend status one step further," *Dallas Morning News,* July 3, 1989.

83. From a private document, "Trip Report—Moscow," by Susan Tilley, June 28-July 14, 1989. Used by permission.

84. Ann Imse, "Encore," AP, *Ft. Worth Star-Telegram,* July 3, 1989.

85. From a private document, "Trip Report—Moscow," by Susan Tilley, June 28-July 14, 1989. Used by permission.

86. John Ardoin, "Cliburn scores a sentimental triumph in Soviet concert," *Dallas Morning News,* July 4, 1989.

87. Ed Wierzbowski interviewed by Howard Reich, March 1992.

88. Raymond Boswell interviewed by Howard Reich, July 1991.

89. From a private document, "Trip Report—Moscow," by Susan Tilley, June 28-July 14, 1989. Used by permission.

90. Ibid.

91. T. Elaine Carey, Cox News Service, "To Vanya with love: The Soviet people welcomed back Van Cliburn with open arms. 'In my heart I never left,' he said," *Ft. Worth Star-Telegram,* July 7, 1989.

92. From a private document, "Trip Report—Moscow," by Susan Tilley, June 28-July 14, 1989. Used by permission.

93. Ed Wierzbowski interviewed by Howard Reich, March 1992.

94. Ibid.

95. From a private document, "Trip Report—Moscow," by Susan Tilley, June 28-July 14, 1989. Used by permission.

96. Maryln Schwartz, "Van Cliburn's buying spree fills the bill," *Dallas Morning News*, July 11, 1989.

97. From a private document, "Trip Report—Moscow," by Susan Tilley, June 28-July 14, 1989. Used by permission.

98. Ibid.

99. Ibid.

100. Ibid.

101. Raymond Boswell interviewed by Howard Reich, July 1991.

102. From a private document, "Trip Report—Moscow," by Susan Tilley, June 28-July 14, 1989. Used by permission.

103. Handwritten letter from Russian fan.

104. Wayne Lee Gay, "Platinum record to come to Cliburn after long skip," *Ft. Worth Star-Telegram*, Aug. 2, 1989.

105. Ibid.

106. Ibid.

107. Wayne Lee Gay, "Heavy metal: Cliburn finally receives platinum, gold records," *Ft. Worth Star-Telegram*, Aug. 3, 1989.

108. "Arts Organizations Honor Van Cliburn," *Ft. Worth Star-Telegram*, Aug. 4, 1989.

109. Guenter Hensler interviewed by Howard Reich, Nov. 1991.

110. Eduardo Mata interviewed by Howard Reich, July 1991.

111. Wayne Lee Gay, "Forth Worth's Cliburn opens Meyerson in Dallas," *Ft. Worth Star-Telegram*, Sept. 9, 1989.

112. Wayne Lee Gay, "Cliburn gives signs of his appreciation," *Ft. Worth Star-Telegram*, Sept. 10, 1989.

113. Guenter Hensler interviewed by Howard Reich, Nov. 1991.

114. Joyce Anne Goyne Stanley interviewed by Howard Reich, July 1991.

115. Annie Lou Ballard interviewed by Howard Reich, July 1991.

116. James Vincent Brady, "Cliburn helps open medical unit in Dallas," *Ft. Worth Star-Telegram,* Sept. 9, 1990.

117. Ed Russo, "Van Cliburn plays Memorial Stadium," *Lincoln Sunday Journal-Star,* Sept. 23, 1990.

118. Mary Meador, "Cliburn's Kilgore recital Vantastic," *Kilgore News Herald,* Oct. 3, 1990.

119. "Van Cliburn is back on the concert trail," *Shreveport Times,* Oct. 4, 1990.

120. Howard Reich, "To Van Cliburn, There's Still No Place Like Home," *Chicago Tribune,* Oct. 14, 1990.

121. "Cliburn the Man," *The Flare* (newspaper of Kilgore College), Oct. 5, 1990.

122. Wayne Lee Gay, "Home on the stage: Van Cliburn returns to Kilgore for solo recital," *Ft. Worth Star-Telegram,* Oct. 3, 1990.

123. Howard Reich, "To Van Cliburn, There's Still No Place Like Home," *Chicago Tribune,* Oct. 14, 1990.

124. John Pfeiffer interviewed by Howard Reich, Nov. 1991.

125. Mary Meador, "Cliburn's Kilgore recital Vantastic," *Kilgore News Herald,* Oct. 3, 1990.

126. Ibid.

127. Howard Reich, "To Van Cliburn, There's Still No Place Like Home," *Chicago Tribune,* Oct. 14, 1990.

128. Mary Meador, "Cliburn's Kilgore recital Vantastic," *Kilgore News Herald,* Oct. 3, 1990.

129. Wayne Lee Gay, "Cliburn once again unfurls brilliance at gala concert," *Ft. Worth Star-Telegram,* Oct. 28, 1990; Bernard Holland, "Leningrad Philharmonic With an American Hero," *New York Times,* Oct. 29, 1990.

130. "Rildia Bee," *New Yorker,* Dec. 17, 1990.

131. Ibid.

132. Mrs. Henry Miller interviewed by Howard Reich, Aug. 1991.

133. John Ardoin, "Fitting tribute to Carnegie Hall," *Dallas Morning News,* May 12, 1991.

134. James R. Oestreich, "Van Cliburn with remembrance of things past," *New York Times,* May 4, 1991.

135. Gary Graffman interviewed by Howard Reich, July 1991.

CHAPTER THIRTEEN

1. Michael Fleming, "Van Cliburn Reflects on the Past and a Possible Future," *New York Times,* June 9, 1985.
2. Joseph Silverstein interviewed by Howard Reich, Aug. 1991.
3. Andrei Gavrilov interviewed by Howard Reich, Oct. 1991.
4. Jorge Mester interviewed by Howard Reich, May 1991.
5. Naomi Graffman interviewed by Howard Reich, July 1991.
6. Garrick Ohlsson interviewed by Howard Reich, Oct. 1991.
7. Van Cliburn interviewed by Howard Reich, 1991-92.
8. Bob Doerschuk, "Van Cliburn," *Contemporary Keyboard,* April 1978.
9. RCA producer John Pfeiffer interviewed by Howard Reich, Nov. 1991.
10. Rita Wolf, "Van Cliburn and Forth Worth: In Harmony," *Aura,* Jan./Feb. 1991.
11. Van Cliburn interviewed by Howard Reich, 1991-92.

About the Author

Howard Reich is arts critic of the *Chicago Tribune* and winner of the *Tribune*'s Outstanding Professional Performance Award "for his coverage of the world of music." His *Tribune* columns have appeared in newspapers across the country, including the *Washington Post* and the *Dallas Morning News.* He has also contributed to *Down Beat* and *Musical America* magazines, among others. Reich has written about the arts since 1976, when his reviews appeared in the *Chicago Daily News.*

Born in Chicago, he attended Northwestern University in Evanston, Illinois, as an Illinois State Scholar and received his degree in piano performance. He lives in a suburb of Chicago with his wife, Pam Becker, an editor at the *Tribune.*